# Extraordinary People

Derek Wilson is a historian who studied at Cambridge and has taught at home and overseas. His previous books include *The World Encompassed*, *England in the Age of Thomas More*, *The Tower* and *The World Atlas of Treasure* (also in Pan), and a biography of the Earl of Leicester entitled *Sweet Robin*. He is currently working on various projects on national and local radio.

Derek Wilson

# Extraordinary
# People

Pan Books
London and Sydney

First published 1983 by Pan Books Ltd,
Cavaye Place, London SW10 9PG
© Derek Wilson 1983
ISBN 0 330 28098 8
Printed in England by W. S. Cowell Limited,
Butter Market, Ipswich, Suffolk

Picture research by Faith Perkins

# Contents

# Introduction

The following pages exult in the glories of human individualism. They celebrate the fact that in every age and in every place there are men and women who do not, cannot, conform. They applaud eccentrics, geniuses, people of vision and unbridled enthusiasm, people who lived life to the full and 'did their own thing', oblivious of the censure or ridicule of their contemporaries, people who pushed out the frontiers of human experience and, perhaps, crossed them to enter the realm of the supernatural. If *Extraordinary People* has any moral at all it is that we should draw our inspiration from such individuals rather than from those who are the enemies of excellence, the suppressors of initiative, the crusaders who stamp the indignant cliché 'élitist' on every attempt to break the common mould.

In the many years that I have been involved with 'history' as teacher, author and broadcaster, I have been increasingly aware that what normally passes for acceptable chronicling of the past is a blow-by-blow account of the deeds of the great and famous. The more I reflect on this the more absurd it seems. If history is ever to be more than an academic catalogue of events whose significance rarely outlived their perpetrators it seems to me that we need to widen our field of study. If we look to the past for guidance, inspiration and illumination in the present, it is to the extraordinary that we should look rather than to the great and famous. After all, what is fame; what is greatness?

Fame has much to do with the accidents of history – being in the right place at the right time. Greatness is normally achieved through advancement in a chosen profession – politics, army, commerce or whatever – and the qualities that make for such advancement are the conventional qualities of which superiors approve. By contrast, extraordinary people are those who do not give a fig for what others approve or disapprove. If they achieve fame or greatness it is despite the system, not because of it. They operate outside systems and conventions. That is why many of them live and die in relative obscurity or are only recognized posthumously. Some, of course, do make their mark and earn a place in the history books but I still maintain that their importance for us lies in their extraordinariness. Let me illustrate with an obvious example. Winston Churchill was 'great' and 'famous'. As leader of the nation in the crucial years of the Second World War he is rightly revered. But, suppose one of the many plots to assassinate Adolf Hitler in 1938 or 1939 had been successful. There would then have been no war and it is very unlikely that Churchill would have attained high office. No state funeral or deep national mourning would have marked his passing nor would posterity have acknowledged his greatness. But he would still have been an extraordinary individual, possessed of those qualities that made him an angry, clear-sighted observer of the international scene during the wilderness years and a firm, determined leader throughout the 1939–45 holocaust.

For every Churchill there are many Thomas Tophams, Mary Easts and Frederick Selous – men and women whose names are unknown, or known only within a relatively small circle of people who share the same interests. Therefore in *Extraordinary People* you will find celebrities rubbing shoulders with nonentities. It is a book I have long wanted to write and that for two interrelated reasons. The first is that over the years that I have studied and written about the history of our own and other lands I have been struck by the fact that there are always men and women who stand out from the crowd, whose lives are of an altogether different order. Several of them are individuals who would never attract biographers. By collecting together over a hundred of these individuals and deliberately mixing up the celebrated and the obscure I have been able to demonstrate, I hope, that many little known men and women are worthy of our attention. My second reason for writing this 'anthology of individualism' is that in throwing together under chosen sub-headings such unlikely bed-fellows as Emmeline Pankhurst and Thomas Beecham, Howard Hughes and Simeon Stylites, Helen Keller and Lola Montez, I have been able to reflect, and, I hope, induce my readers to reflect, upon what it is that makes certain people stand out from their fellows.

Some readers may, by now, be thinking 'What exactly does he mean by "extraordinary"?' It is a question I am loath to answer because the book itself *is* the answer. By the time readers reach the last page they will, I hope, have a full understanding of just what it was that made all these remarkable people so different. However, at the outset I will try to provide a working definition. The extraordinary individual is one whose whole life is literally above or outside the ordinary; 'extraordinariness' is a state of being; a separate plane of existence. For those who inhabit that plane the restrictions and conventions that frontier the lives of the rest of us have no meaning. Such people simply do not recognize the need to behave as other men and women behave. The path they tread is not one worn smooth by a million

other feet and they follow it less from conviction than from an inevitability that comes from the depths of their personality. They do what they do because, whether it leads them to power or poverty, fame or obscurity, they can do no other. There is about them a certainty, a positiveness, a clarity of purpose. They know where they are going, what they are doing and why. Their reasons may satisfy no one else but for them they are totally convincing.

I believe that such people sound a clarion call we would all – individually and collectively – do well to heed. The tendency of modern Western society is largely, unless I take too gloomy a view, in the direction of grey egalitarianism. The quest seems to be for the lowest common denominator of our shared humanity. It is a quest that leads to the gutters and sewers of existence. Mankind's progress has always been led by the extraordinary men and women in our midst, those who reach for the stars. They are the ones who push back the frontiers and demonstrate, not what we can do with little effort, but what we can achieve with audacity, boldness and courage – a full life well lived.

But they do more than that – they link mortality and immortality. There are certain basic questions about life, death and the beyond that we must all ask sometime. We may go to the philosophers and theologians for our answers and end up sharing the disillusionment of Old Khayyam:

Myself when young did eagerly frequent
Doctor and saint and heard great argument
About it and about: But evermore
Came out by the same door as in I went.

We shall probably gain more from the vision of those of our fellows who have scanned eternity and explained their discoveries in the language of deeds and behaviour or demonstrated spiritual powers beyond human comprehension. It is the lives of extraordinary people which provide for us windows through which we glimpse those realities we call by such banal words as 'truth', 'beauty' and 'love'.

And now follow those acknowledgements which must appear to most readers to be mere convention but which anyone who has ever been involved in writing or publishing a book knows to be confessions of real indebtedness:

The writing of this book has involved wide reading and I am grateful to the staffs of many libraries for their cooperation in seeking out for me little known volumes as well as standard works. The ladies of the West Somerset Library have been particularly diligent in this regard and I am in their debt. Other collections I have used include those in the university libraries at Cambridge and Exeter and in the British Library. The titles included under the heading 'Suggestions for Further Reading' by no means comprise an exhaustive catalogue of all the works consulted during the compilation of this book. My intention in providing this bibliography was to give readers who wish to study more fully any of the subjects treated a starting point for further reading. To conclude my own very grateful acknowledgements I must thank Faith Perkins for her work on the illustrations which are such an important part of this book and Harriet Thistlethwaite, my editor, for her overall supervision and for her patience when the book took longer than envisaged to complete.

Behind every great man, it is said, there is a great woman. While in no way claiming the epithet 'great' for myself I cheerfully acknowledge the great woman behind me and everything I do, including this book. For producing the finished typescript, for frequent critical comments, and for being my constant inspiration a simple 'thank you' to my wife is far from adequate.

# Eccentrics

An eccentric is by definition someone whose behaviour is abnormal, someone who refuses to conform to the accepted conventions of his society. This, of course, immediately begs the question, 'What is normal?' Most of us, after all, have our quirks and oddities. It may be a passion for entering newspaper competitions, a compulsion for collecting beer mats, a tendency to write indignant letters to the press on every conceivable subject. Eccentricity is the assertion of our individuality. Within most of us that urge is constantly in conflict with the contrary force. It is as though in the depths of our psyche we have two locomotives head-to-head on the same track, pushing against each other, one is called 'individualism' and the other 'conformity' and in most of us it is conformity that is the more powerful. The desire to be accepted, loved, appreciated, to feel at one with our fellows, is stronger than the desire to stand out in the crowd, to be our own man, to do our own thing. Notice, for example, how people who have unusual hobbies, strong opinions, or even behavioural abnormality (such as homosexuality) tend to congregate. They form clubs, hold meetings, organize rallies, have special bars or assembly places where they can get together and discuss their common enthusiasms or problems. The important word is 'common'. They look for other people with whom they can share what in the normal run of events is regarded by relatives, friends and neighbours as an oddity. A crowd, even a small crowd, is reassuring. Probably all of us recognize this tension within ourselves between these two forces, for at the same time that most of us are going with the crowd we tend to resent any suggestion that that is what we are doing. We feel a self-conscious need to assert our individuality as when the belligerent man at the bar informs his small audience, 'Well, I say what I think.' Or the wary stranger to whom we have just been introduced announces, 'You must take me as you find me. I don't stand on ceremony.'

Any of us can, at any time, reverse this trend. We can stoke the boiler of individualism, assert our own personality. Many people have made it to the top in their chosen professions, basically by doing just that. One example is Bob Dylan, the American singer, who has gone on record as saying, 'When you feel in your gut what you are and then dynamically pursue it – don't back down and don't give up – then you're going to mystify a lot of folks.' But that self-conscious assertion of individuality is not eccentricity, at least not in the early stages. When a pop singer deliberately wears bizarre clothes to gain publicity or a society hostess makes outrageous comments about her guests in order to get herself noticed in the gossip

*Life was always full of surprises in the household of eccentric Lord Berners.*

columns, that is not eccentricity. Some years ago Mr Henson of the Rare Breeds Trust wished to draw public attention to the plight of certain domestic animals which were threatened with extinction. To do so he drove a flock of sheep down Fleet Street. It was an eccentric act, but it didn't make him an eccentric. However, if the pop star and the society hostess and the campaigner perpetuate such activities until they become a part of themselves, until they are no longer able to return to what most of us consider 'normal behaviour', then they certainly would qualify. For the most important ingredient of eccentricity is its naturalness. Eccentrics are not people who deliberately try to be odd, they simply *are* odd. When Jack Mytton spent several hours immersed in icy water simply to shoot a duck, he didn't do it to impress his neighbours. When the Reverend George Harvest threw his pocket watch into the Thames, he didn't do so to get himself noticed in the newspapers. When Charles Waterton filled his house with grotesque examples of taxidermy it wasn't in order to amuse or frighten his guests. The true eccentric is not merely indifferent to public opinion, he is scarcely conscious of it. It does not come into his calculations. Indeed he does not calculate at all. He simply does what he does, because he is who he is. And this marks the eccentric as essentially different from almost every other category we shall be considering in this book. Enthusiasts, visionaries, practical jokers, brilliant criminals, exhibitionists, recluses, are all very conscious of the world around them. Much of what they do, they do in reaction to the world in which they live. Some wish to make an impression on society, some wish to escape from society, but all are very much aware of society. The eccentric alone goes on his merry way regardless.

Is it true, as is often suggested, that there are fewer eccentrics around today than in previous ages? Probably. Eccentrics, like rare orchids, flourish best in an ideal climate. Important features of that climate seem to be wealth and social standing. The family trees of the aristocracy and landed gentry fairly bristle with eccentrics and it is not difficult to see why. A gentleman of independent means had no need to earn his own living or to seek the approval of his neighbours. He could follow his own inclinations, however strange they might be. He had been brought up with servants who did his bidding. As a child and a young man he was probably unaccustomed to having his actions questioned. Thus a man like Sir George Sitwell, finding the nineteenth century uncongenial, could elect to speak and act as though he lived in an earlier age.

The Earl of Bristol could stud the landscape with lavish houses built to whatever design he chose, because he could afford to do so, and it would not have occurred to anyone to try and stop him. Things are very different today. Even if a modern equivalent of the eccentric Earl could be found who possessed the money and the inclination to build a second Ickworth, he would have to contend with a thousand obstacles: public outrage at such an ostentatious display of wealth; constant hassle with dilatory contractors; delays occasioned by union disputes; and a deluge of red tape from planning authorities and government departments. He would probably throw up the idea and go and live in a bungalow in Brighton. Hervey, Sitwell, Lord Berners, Jack Mytton and others of that breed were by modern standards very wealthy. But even those in our selection of whom this was not true were certainly, for the most part, financially secure. William Spooner, for example, held a Fellowship at Oxford, from which he could not be ousted. It provided him with a modest but very satisfactory income and ensured him a continued place in a society where his oddities were very happily accepted. Had he been trying to hold down a job in industry today he would probably have been obliged to try to overcome his verbal and behavioural peculiarities. A psychoanalyst would doubtless have been advised for the benefit of Spooner's career and the good of the company.

People like Spooner, Harvest and George Sand may be said to have been born with their own peculiarities: their eccentricities were inherited rather than environmentally induced. Here, of course, we approach the vexed question, 'Where does eccentricity end and insanity begin?' It is a minefield into which I do not intend to venture. As Alexander Pope might have said, 'A little psychology is a dangerous thing.' One commonly held opinion is that the eccentric is essentially harmless, but this does not bear very close examination. No man is an island and though most of us may laugh at and enjoy the antics of the eccentric, he can by his very obliviousness to the feelings of others be a menace to society. For example, supposing Jack Mytton driving his gig at breakneck pace along the lane and then deliberately upsetting it had inadvertently killed his companion, he would undoubtedly have faced a murder charge and then insanity may very well have been pleaded in his defence. He could have ended his days in Bedlam. Only so long as they do not threaten society is society prepared to categorize such people benevolently as eccentrics.

## A restless soul

The bright-painted gig rattled at breakneck speed along the rutted lane. Hedges, trees and gates flashed past as the driver whipped his grey pony to still greater effort. The only passenger held on to his high-crowned hat with one hand and the seat with the other. The gig lurched violently and the poor man cried out in alarm.

'What's the matter?' the driver asked casually. 'Have you had a bad injury at some time from being upset in a gig?'

'No, thank God,' came the disjointed reply. 'I never was upset in one.'

'What!' replied the driver. 'Never upset in a gig! What a damned slow fellow you must have been all your life!'

So saying, he yanked on the rein, ran a wheel up the bank, and overturned the vehicle, sending himself and his friend sprawling in the road. This was one of Jack Mytton's more celebrated escapades. It typifies his impulsive nature and his total disregard for danger.

John Mytton of Halston, Shropshire was born in 1796. His father died before the boy was two and the lack of parental discipline goes a long way towards explaining Mytton's wild, untameable nature. Little is recorded of his childhood but he must have been appallingly spoiled by his mother

*A portrait miniature of the great sportsman and eccentric, Jack Mytton.*

and her servants, for his schoolmasters later found him quite ungovernable. He was expelled, in turn, from Westminster and Harrow, and when a private tutor was engaged he thrashed the man soundly and sent him packing. After very brief university and army careers he returned to enjoy his inheritance and become one of the most celebrated of all sporting squires. Hunting and shooting he pursued with total enthusiasm and complete disregard for his safety and health. He frequently outlasted all other riders in the hunting field and would put his horse fearlessly at 'impossible' jumps. He waded rivers in full spate in pursuit of his quarry. When duck-shooting, he was known to have waited hours in icy marshes clad only in the skimpiest of clothes. There was scarcely a bone in his body which was not broken at some time. Mytton simply refused to allow such details to restrict him. On at least one occasion he completed a day's hunting with a couple of broken ribs sustained in a fall during the morning. It seems that for some years he really did achieve the triumph of mind over matter. He never took to his bed with an illness. His iron constitution was not even assailed by a common cold.

In all areas of life Mytton refused to acknowledge the word 'impossible'. Just as he ignored the restrictions of physical limitation, so also he never allowed lack of money to inhibit him. The maintenance of his house, his stables and kennels plunged him heavily into debt. Almost all his property was mortgaged. Yet such facts never restrained his generous nature. He was famed and widely loved for his impulsive charity. Once he was in a silversmith's shop in Calais when a French soldier came in to pawn a watch, ostensibly for a needy friend. When the proprietor began haggling over the sum demanded, Mytton threw the money on the counter and, with the words 'take this to your comrade also', he returned the watch.

It was for such impulsive gestures – whether of generosity, mischievousness or foolhardiness – that Jack Mytton was chiefly remembered. For some years he kept a female brown bear. This creature was frequently the occasion of fun for Mytton and consternation for his guests. Once he donned his hunting pink and rode his bear into the drawing room at Halston, scattering the assembled company in all directions. On another occasion a dealer named Clarke brought a carriage horse for the squire's inspection. He rigged it with another horse in tandem (one behind the other), and the two men set out on a trial run. As they bowled along Mytton suddenly asked if Clarke thought the horse might make a good jumper. Scarcely pausing for an answer, 'Mad Jack' announced, 'We'll try him', and pointed the animal straight at a turnpike gate. The lead horse

*To the impulsive Mytton an idea was no sooner conceived than executed. He kept a tame brown bear and played many pranks with her. Invited dinner guests not used to their host's odd behaviour were more than a little alarmed when Mytton and bear rode into their midst.*

cleared the obstacle, and galloped away as the traces snapped. Mytton, Clarke, the other animal and the badly-damaged gig were left behind in a sprawled heap. One evening he had entertained to dinner a parson and a doctor from a nearby town. As soon as they had left, Mytton threw a smock over his clothes, loaded a brace of pistols with blank charges and road across country to waylay his guests on the road. When a dim figure appeared before them shouting, 'Stand and deliver', and firing shots in their direction, the two travellers were frightened out of their wits. They turned and fled and Mytton chased them several miles before tiring of his nocturnal sport.

The man who was at home with sporting friends and trusted servants, who enjoyed rude cameraderie and rough practical jokes, lacked the talent for a sustained, gentle married relationship. Mytton was wed twice, on each occasion to a virtuous lady of breeding. His first wife died young, having borne one daughter. In 1821 he married his second wife, Caroline, a girl of seventeen. It seems that Jack Mytton loved both of these ladies but affection could not regulate his way of life when all other forces had failed. Caroline found herself both neglected and confined by a husband whose jealousy was easily and needlessly aroused.

Eccentricity had by now begun to give way to madness – if, indeed, any dividing line between the two can be drawn – and liquor had begun to undermine his health. Mytton had always been a heavy drinker. Normally he had his first glass of port while shaving. By the time he retired to bed he had disposed of six or seven bottles. Creditors began to press more urgently. Mytton's moods became totally unpredictable, his behaviour more irresponsible. One night he set fire to his nightgown to cure a bout of hiccoughs. The prompt action of friends saved his life but the shock weakened even Mytton's iron constitution. He was forced to sell up his effects at Halston, and Caroline returned to her family. In 1831 Mytton fled to Calais to escape his creditors. Three years later he returned, only to be incarcerated in a debtors' prison. It was there that he died of *delirium tremens*. He was thirty-seven.

But such a larger-than-life character could not pass away obscurely. An impressive funeral procession conveyed his body to the family vault at Halston. According to the local newspaper:

> The number of spectators was immense, and the road along which the procession slowly moved was bedewed with the tears of thousands who wished to have a last glance.

# The scandalous life of Aurore Dupin

What might we expect of a woman whose maternal grandfather was a birdseller and whose father was descended from the King of Poland? Amandine Aurore Lucile Dupin's heredity was strangely mixed. So was her childhood. Her soldier father died when she was four, leaving her in the charge of two extremely strong-willed women, her mother, Sophie, and her aristocratic grandmother, Mme Dupin de Francueil, who agreed with each other on almost nothing, particularly the upbringing of young Aurore. Not surprisingly, two characteristics showed themselves at an early age – rebelliousness and a strong need for affection. She was sent to a Paris convent where she won the hearts of nuns and fellow pupils by her lively mischievousness. During holidays on her grandmother's estate at Nohant she loved to ride, shoot and carouse with the local peasantry. Always for these escapades she wore men's clothes, enjoying the freedom of action that this 'masquerade' gave her.

When Aurore was seventeen her grandmother died, leaving her not inconsiderable fortune to her only grandchild. Within a year the girl had married. She undoubtedly loved Casimir Dudevant – insofar, that is, as a shielded eighteen-year-

old can know her own heart – but she also needed someone to rely on, someone to protect her. Here there was a basic contradiction. The wild creature who loved roaming free in the fields and woods found herself restricted by her new role of wife and, very soon, mother. It is little wonder that she came to regard conventional marriage as a trap: 'a union in which there is neither liberty nor reciprocity is an offence against the sanctity of nature'. Within a few years the couple fell to arguments and mutal recriminations. Still more time elapsed, however, before Aurore took a lover. After ten years of marriage she and Casimir separated for a while, he to remain at Nohant, she to live in Paris.

The year was 1831. The Romantic movement was in full flood. In the literary and artistic quarter of Paris painters, musicians, poets, novelists and playwrights excitedly discussed the new, liberated ideas which were as revolutionary in their way as the political radicalism with which Europe was awash. Everything was questioned, nothing sacred – religion, traditional morality, old conventions, everything went into the melting pot. The beautiful young Aurore became the toast of these brave spirits. Once again she adopted male attire. And, to earn a living, she began to write – articles at first, then, in 1832, her first novel *Indiana*, in which she poured out all the emotion which had been locked within her by a loveless childhood and marriage. To avoid embarrassing Casimir and his relations she used a pseudonym, George Sand.

She was a prolific writer – novels poured out of her, novels extolling freedom, alive with the freshness of the countryside she loved so much,

*George Sand inspired some of Chopin's finest works.*

illuminated by masterly characterization. She now alternated between Paris and Nohant, needing the intellectual and emotional stimulus of the one and the peace and quiet of the other. In 1836 she obtained a legal separation from Casimir under the terms of which she retained Nohant. It was not as a novelist that George Sand made her mark upon her age and upon posterity. She acted as a catalyst in the creative world of Paris. Men of genius were attracted to her – Prosper Merimée, Chateaubriand, Victor Hugo, Alexandre Dumas, Franz Liszt, Eugène Delacroix, and a host of others, some still famous, others whose reputations have not survived. Some were her devoted friends; some she accepted as lovers. All of them she inspired to produce their finest work. She sensed greatness in others and longed to draw it out.

Frederic Chopin fell under her spell for nine years, during which he played and composed some of his sweetest melodies. They became lovers in 1838, when Aurore was thirty-four and Chopin twenty-eight. After the first, fiery passion of their relationship sexuality played little part in it. George had an almost maternal urge towards the slight, sensitive, young Pole, already weakened by the consumption that would kill him. Their affair ended at last, as did most of Aurore's affairs, with bitterness and misunderstanding.

It was her lot to be misunderstood. In popular gossip she was dismissed as an insatiable nymphomaniac. Society hostesses and rejected lovers enjoyed tittle-tattling about her 'scandalous' conduct. For herself, Aurore rejected the charge of promiscuity. She sought, for years, the ideal relationship, complete harmony of body, mind and spirit.

The one thing I have placed above all else is faithfulness. That I have preached, that I have practised, upon that I have insisted . . . whenever I have been untrue to faithfulness, it has always been because I seemed driven on by a sort of faith, an instinct for the ideal which has compelled me to leave the imperfect for what I thought was closer to the perfect.

With her romanticism went a revolutionary fervour. She supported with pamphlets and letters the uprising of 1848 which ushered in the Second Republic, and dubbed herself a communist. But there was very little in common between George Sand and Karl Marx. She had a romantic idea of the 'noble' peasant, believed that wealth should be shared but rejected any suggestion that this might be brought about by force.

As she entered a long and happy old age, Aurore cast off many of the outrageous ideas of her early years, becoming more conservative and more conventional. Always she wrote – novels, articles and a flood of letters to her many friends. She loved to spend time with her grandchildren, who visited her often at Nohant. It was there that she died in the summer of 1876. Many were the tributes paid to her, including these words in a letter from Flaubert to another literary giant of the age, Ivan Turgenev:

The death of our poor mother Sand has caused me infinite pain. I cried my eyes out at the funeral . . . Only those who knew her as I did can realize just how much of the feminine there was in that great man, how deep the tenderness which was so integral a part of her genius . . . She will remain one of the splendours of France.

## 'He never was bored'

Gerald Tyrwhitt-Wilson, fourteenth Baron Berners, who died in 1950, was probably the last great wealthy dilettante. He inherited considerable money and property and these absolved him from the necessity of earning a living. The cataract of events which swept Europe towards and finally over the brink of war in 1914 did not carry the young Tyrwhitt-Wilson with it. After leaving Eton around the turn of the century, he spent several years travelling on the continent and served as honorary attaché in the embassies of, first, Constantinople and then Rome. He professed no political or religious creed. He hated convention and, thanks to his secure social position, he was able to flout it. He lived for the moment and acted on impulse. Whenever he felt boredom setting in he did something outrageous. It might be inviting a horse to tea in the elegant drawing room at Faringdon House. It might be startling visitors by appearing at a window in a grotesque mask. It might be causing an explosion in the hall to bring guests rushing from their rooms in the middle of the night.

He was adept at practical jokes. For the most part they were spontaneous pranks, designed to deflate the egos of the pompous and self-important. He once booby-trapped the spectacles of one of the justices in Chancery so that as the learned judge raised them from his desk with a

*Berner's ballet 'The Triumph of Neptune' was performed by Diaghilev's company in 1927. In this photograph he appears with two of the principals.*

*Lord Berners enhanced the appearance of impressive Faringdon House with doves whose plumage was dyed all the colours of the rainbow.*

flourish, pens, ink, paper and notes crashed to the floor in full view of the crowded, solemn court. On another occasion he delivered daily an assortment of other people's visiting cards at the house where a honeymooning couple were staying, thus causing them to live in constant apprehension of having their seclusion disturbed by unwanted callers. One of his closest friends described how Lord Berners managed to gain privacy when travelling by train:

> Donning black spectacles he would, with a look of fiendish expectation, beckon in the passers by. Those isolated figures who took the risk became so perturbed by his habit of reading the papers upside down and taking his temperature every five minutes that they invariably got out at the next station.

In his own home Lord Berners surrounded himself with eccentricities. The doves which fluttered about his lawns were dyed in a variety of bright colours. He had a spinet fitted into his Rolls Royce so that he could play as he was driven through the countryside. His dogs wore diamond-studded collars. Guests invited to houseparties at Faringdon never quite knew what to expect. They might be entertained with a bonfire and fireworks and asked to make effigies of their enemies to burn. They might awake in the morning to discover that the peaceful lawns had been transformed into a fairground. Lord Berners' most permanent memorial to the bizarre and the useless was Faringdon Folly. This was a hundred-and-forty-foot tower built on a hilltop overlooking the town. Local landowners protested angrily and the council attempted to block the proposed construction. But Berners won the day, and in 1935 he held a special party to celebrate the opening of a building dedicated to complete uselessness. The folly was open to visitors but all who came were confronted at the door with a solemn warning: *Members of the public committing suicide from this tower do so at their own risk.*

Yet all this buffoonery concealed a man of varied talents and considerable accomplishments. He mastered several languages. He painted with skill and concentration. He wrote six satirical novels and a two-volume autobiography. But it was in the sphere of music that he made his most important contribution to the art world. He was friend, patron and popularist of William Walton, Diaghilev, Constant Lambert and other prominent members of the avant garde establishment. Ballet, especially, he loved. He was excited by the work of Diaghilev and his companions who broke away from the classical tradition and established a modern style. In ballet Lord Berners found a medium which expressed his own attitude to life. In 1939, when Britain was overshadowed by the appalling inevitability of another hideous war, he wrote that ballet was

> escapist art in its purest form. There is in ballet no insidious motive of edification and uplift. And although ballet companies may call themselves 'educational' their primary object is, or should be, to entertain rather than educate.
>
> It is to ballet that you may flee from the wrath to come and from the wrath that seems almost at hand. In these troublous times we may at least escape for an hour or two to Sadler's Wells and other places where there is ballet.

Lord Berners himself wrote the music for six ballets, of which the most successful, *The Triumph of Neptune*, was performed by the Diaghilev Company in 1926, Ninette de Valois and Margot Fonteyn being among the dancers. Even in these stage pieces satire was always a prominent feature. Tyrrwhit-Wilson debunked the smart set, the establishment and the lions of the art world with an outrageous sense of fun that could only upset those who deserved to be upset. He numbered most of the famous and successful among his friends and even those he lampooned loved him. The surrealist painting of Salvador Dali he caricatured in verse:

*This 1938 cartoon shows Berners with Lady Cunard and Sidney Beer, two fellow music enthusiasts.*

On the pale yellow sands
There's a pair of Clasped Hands
And an Eyeball entangled with String
And a Bicycle Seat
And a plate of Raw Meat
And a Thing that is hardly a Thing.

Frenetic gaiety sometimes masks a melancholy spirit. It may have been so with Lord Berners. In his later years he wrote no more music, played fewer pranks, withdrew increasingly into himself. He must have known that the Second World War and the social changes it heralded meant the end of the way of life he and his friends had enjoyed. He saw society slipping down the slope into egalitarianism and grey mediocrity. It was a society which did not appreciate his flamboyant colours and for which he had no love. It was a boring society and boredom was something he could not tolerate, as he clearly stated in the epitaph he wrote for himself.

Here lies Lord Berners
One of the learners.
His great love of learning
May earn him a burning.
But praise to the Lord
He never was bored!

## 'This great, confirmed, notorious, desperate sinner'

A handsome, elegant young courtier chanced to be emerging from the main entrance of Whitehall Palace when a carriage drove up and from it descended the magnificent Duchess of Cleveland, Charles II's current mistress. The young man stepped forward, threw his arms around the lady and tried to kiss her in full view of servants, guards and passers-by. The next second he was sprawling on his back in the dust, sent flying by a blow from the duchess's delicate hand. Quite unabashed, he leaped up, swept a low bow and with an impudent smile addressed an impromptu verse to the lady's retreating back.

> By heavens, 'twas bravely done,
> First to attempt the chariot of the sun,
> And then to fall, like Phaeton.

*The cynic crowns with laurel a pet monkey who is tearing up his books.*

Bold, mercurial, charming, imprudent, witty and talented – John Wilmot, second Earl of Rochester, was all these and more. Spoiled as a child by wealth, a doting mother and the absence of a father's disciplining hand, he never learned to be restricted by financial limitation, decency or the feelings of others. While still little more than a child he discovered that what money could not buy might yet be attained by charm and audacity. Rochester was a complete libertine, a drunkard, womanizer and gambler who overtaxed both body and mind and went to an early grave. Yet he was no mere pampered debauché, for he left behind him a volume of poems, plays and letters which prove him to be one of the keenest observers and the most biting satyrists of the age.

John Wilmot came at the age of seventeen to the court of King Charles II and was at once taken to the heart of the pleasure-loving monarch and his friends. He won women's favours with his good looks and graceful air. He kept his male companions amused with bawdy and personal comments about courtiers. He could produce witty and often cruel verses virtually to order, especially when his genius was lubricated with wine. One such couplet he devised was to be inscribed on the collar of one of Charles' spaniels:

> I am his majesty's dog at Kew.
> Pray tell me, sir, whose dog are you?

And he once dismissed half the human race with the words,

> Ye powers above, why did you woman make,
> Without an angel and within a snake?

A rival at court was caricatured with these lines:

> Half witty and half mad and scarce half brave,
> Half honest (which is very much a knave),
> Made up of all these halves, thou can'st not pass
> For anything entirely but an ass.

Rochester never took refuge, as many contemporary satyrists did, in anonymity and, naturally, he made enemies by the score. Cuckolded husbands, outraged churchmen, vengeful victims of his pen – all had cause to hate Lord Rochester. But as long as he enjoyed the king's protection he was safe from harm. Yet he could not restrain himself even from putting royal favour at risk. Knowing that Wilmot had run through his inheritance, Charles advised him to seek the hand of a wealthy heiress, Elizabeth Mallet. Rochester fell to the courtship with vigour. Much to his consternation, Elizabeth was not bowled over by his charms. She took refuge in that favourite stratagem of women, she would not say 'yes' and she would not say 'no'. When even the king's

*Most of Rochester's pranks were played against the background of pleasure-loving Charles II's court.*

pleading failed to move her, the earl took the law into his own hands. He abducted her as her coach was passing through Charing Cross and sped westwards. He was caught at Uxbridge, brought back to court and from there conveyed to the Tower by a very angry king. It says much for Rochester's winning ways that Charles forgave him after a few days and still more that Elizabeth eventually married him.

On another occasion, when the court was at Newmarket, king and earl went in disguise to spend the night at a nearby brothel. When Charles had set his clothing aside and was enjoying the pleasures of the house, Rochester removed all the money and valuables from the royal pockets and left the establishment. When the time came to pay the reckoning Charles found himself acutely embarrassed. The proprietress took him for a pauper and a cheat, and, of course, dismissed his claim to be king. Only when he persuaded her to wake a local goldsmith to show him a ring which he took from his finger was the truth discovered. Total confusion, and Rochester, once again, temporarily banished.

Wilmot loved disguise and masquerade and often took his play-acting to extreme lengths. He wanted to be able to study all manner of people at first hand and had no doubt of his ability to pass himself off as an innkeeper or a City merchant (both roles which he played for several weeks). Once he set himself up in London as a newly arrived German doctor, well versed in astrology and medicine. His reputation spread so rapidly that soon ladies from the court were resorting to him to have their fortunes told. They were amazed at the secrets this 'foreigner' knew about them and their friends and were quite convinced that he possessed occult powers.

All these experiences fed Rochester's cynicism, reinforcing his convictions about the silliness and gullibility of his fellow humans.

Were I (who, to my cost, already am
One of those strange, prodigious creatures, Man)
A spirit, free to choose for my own share,
What case of flesh and blood I'd please to wear,
I'd be a dog, a monkey or a bear,
Or anything but that vain animal
Who is so proud of being rational.

Yet Rochester was not totally a detached observer of the human scene. He fought with some distinction against the Dutch, and some of his more outspoken verses were devoted to political comment. In a society where flattery was the common coin Wilmot's bitter satire may have had a challenging, even at times a cleansing, effect.

His disdain of man was stretched to embrace God also, but when in 1679 he fell seriously ill, he repented of his former ways and was seldom without a clergyman at his bedside. Thus it was that the funeral elegy delivered the following year could rejoice in the conversion of 'this great, confimed, notorious, desperate sinner'. Rochester died in July 1680, at the age of thirty-three.

# The Apostle

*Something of Joseph Wolff's stubborn determination can be seen in this portrait.*

It is not easy to understand Joseph Wolff or what he thought he was trying to do. He was by turns Jew, Catholic and Anglican. He was a brilliant linguist and compulsive traveller. He was a scholar of an extremely individualistic caste of mind, a missionary and an anti-slavery campaigner. Everything he undertook, every change of opinion, every new crusade was embarked upon with boundless energy and the total conviction of the eccentric that whatever he does is self-evidently right.

He was born the son of a German Jewish rabbi, in 1795. His father ministered to the Hebrew communities in a succession of towns so that, as a child, Wolff travelled quite widely. He also came under many different influences and, having a lively, inquisitive mind, he explored eagerly every idea that came his way. At seven he elected to become a Lutheran but no one took him seriously. It was rather different when, at the age of eleven, he declared himself to have been converted to Roman Catholicism and called to be a Jesuit missionary. The relative with whom Wolff was staying at the time 'threw a poker at him, and cursed him and turned him out of the house'. For several years he simply wandered Europe as a penniless scholar picking up instruction, magpie-like, wherever it was to be found. The amazing fact is that because of his charm, his zeal and his undoubted intellectual gifts, he was accepted for courses of study in several universities and centres of learning – Prague, Vienna, Tübingen, Rome and Cambridge, to mention only the most important. By the time he was twenty-five he had mastered several languages: besides German and Hebrew he could speak and write Latin, Greek, Arabic, Syriac, Chaldean, Persian, French, Italian and English. He had studied theology and philosophy with a bewildering variety of masters. It is not surprising that his own beliefs were something of a patchwork of ideas which did not agree with any brand of Christian orthodoxy.

Wolff proved to be a real irritant at the college in Rome where he trained to become a priest. At the very first lecture he jumped up to launch a protest against the doctrine of papal infallibility and he also objected to the worship of the Virgin Mary. The other students dubbed him 'Luther'. He happily accepted the name but at the same time told his colleagues that he intended to become pope. He had even chosen his papal title – Hildebrandus I. Amazingly, it was two years before Wolff was thrown out of the papal city. He spent a short time in a monastery but that did not suit him and in 1819 he came to England. Here he experimented with various churches before becoming an Anglican.

His overmastering passion at this time was the conversion of the Jews. So ardently did he cam-

*Wolff's sketch of a senior, and very unfriendly, official in Bokhara, where he was imprisoned.*

*Though somewhat idealized, Levant coastal scenes such as this were very familiar to Wolff.*

paign that the church sent him as a missionary to the Mediterranean area in 1821. The church did not know what it had let itself in for. Wolff was quite incapable of a planned strategy. During the next five years he swept like a tornado through Egypt, Palestine, Syria, Turkey, Iraq, Iran and Cyprus. He preached in most of the major cities and was, indeed, the first Christian to do so for centuries in many places. He made few converts but he certainly made an impression on the people who met him. A clergyman sent out from England to find Wolff and bring him home had this to say about his elusive quarry:

When I should have addressed him in Syria, I heard of him in Malta; and when I supposed him gone to England, he was riding like a ruling angel in the whirlwinds of Antioch or standing unappalled among the crumbling towers of Aleppo. A man . . . to whom a floor of bricks is a feather bed and a box a bolster . . . who can conciliate a Pasha or confute a Patriarch; who travels without a guide; speaks without an interpreter; can live without food and pay without money; forgiving all the insults he meets with and forgetting all the flattery he receives . . . such a man must excite no ordinary degree of attention . . .

Wolff did not confine himself to Jews; he preached to Muslims, Zoroastrians, devil worshippers and even Christians of other churches. Naturally, he provoked opposition. He was imprisoned often. Once someone tried to poison him. An outraged nomad chief had him tied to a horse's tail and dragged across the desert. He was shipwrecked twice and robbed many times. Once he walked naked for six hundred miles having been stripped of all his possessions.

His missionary society disowned him but that could not stop him fulfilling his self-appointed role, 'Apostle of our Lord Jesus Christ for Palestine, Persia, Bokhara and Balkh'. His journeys continued almost unabated until 1838, and took him as far afield as Afghanistan and India. Among the few possessions which he took on his wanderings there were always items designed as presents for Oriental dignitaries – Bibles, of course, in a variety of languages, silver watches and, somewhat surprisingly, *Robinson Crusoe* in Arabic. In 1843 he was off again, this time as a one-man expedition to find two British officers captured by the Amir of Bokhara. It was a mission which captured the imagination of the nation. Money poured in, the P & O line offered a free passage, and a crowd gathered at Southampton to cheer him on his way. After a journey of incredible hardships he reached the realm of the cruel Amir Nasrullah. The two officers had been executed and Wolff was imprisoned. Not for the first time he came close to death. Only intense diplomatic pressure secured his release.

Wolff spent the last years of his life in comparative quiet as a vicar in Somerset. But to the end of his days he was a vigorous eccentric whose parishioners never knew what to expect of him.

# The great collector

The boundary between eccentricity and insanity is clearly marked even though it may frequently be lost sight of in the luxuriant undergrowth of odd behaviour: the madman behaves irrationally; the eccentric justifies his actions by logic, although that logic may be peculiar to himself. That is why many people whose personal lives and attitudes are bizarre in the extreme stumbled across important truths or made discoveries which were of value to subsequent ages.

Take Charles Waterton, for example. He was a nineteenth-century country squire of some means. Yet he habitually wore old, tattered clothes, foreswore alcohol and was abstemious in his eating habits, slept on the floor with a block of wood for a pillow, sometimes lurked under his dining table pretending to be a dog and littered his house with a collection of stuffed animals and 'monsters'. By any standards he was an eccentric but he also did valuable pioneer work in the fields of natural science, taxidermy and animal conservation.

Charles Waterton was born in 1782 into an ancient, staunchly-Roman Catholic, Yorkshire

family at a time when members of that religion were excluded from most important offices. He thus knew what it was to enjoy moderate wealth and influence while at the same time being, to a certain extent, an outcast. He was educated by Jesuits and nothing he learned at home or school challenged the conviction that the Watertons stood for all that was best in English tradition, a tradition largely betrayed by the Protestant establishment. It was natural, therefore, that he should devote his life to personal pursuits. During his formative years the French Revolution and the Napoleonic Wars raged but these world-transforming events seem to have affected Waterton not at all. He early developed an interest in animals and gained quite a reputation at school as a catcher of rats, foxes and rooks. It was when he went to Demerara in 1804 to manage the family estates there that his career as a collector of animal specimens really began. The serious study of natural history was still in its infancy though gentlemen of a scholarly turn of mind had begun to assemble and study collections of stuffed animals. It now became Waterton's passion to capture as many creatures as possible that were unknown to Europe's armchair experts – the wilder and more dangerous the better. It was important that the specimens should be as well-preserved as possible. Waterton's determination and impatience made him absolutely fearless. He would not shoot his prey from a safe distance because that would involve the grave risk of damaging the skin. Nor would he indulge in the elaborate, time-consuming practice of constructing traps. His method was simple: when he saw an animal he wanted he would try to grapple with it himself and despatch it with knife or gun in such a way as to do the least damage. During the several journeys he made to parts of South America and Africa he frequently put himself in dangerous situations. Once, while travelling by boat up the alligator-infested Orinoco he saw a deadly jaracara snake on the bank. He only had time for a quick shot, which wounded the reptile. Rushing in pursuit, Waterton found himself grappling with the wounded snake while clinging to an insecure branch hanging over the water. But he succeeded in getting his trophy aboard the boat. 'As soon as I had got a change of clothes,' he laconically recorded, 'I killed it and made a dissection of the head.'

On another occasion he decided he wanted to catch an alligator alive. A line was baited with rabbit and a specimen successfully hooked. Waterton then had the ten-foot monster pulled out of the water by a gang of camp servants.

I instantly . . . sprang up, jumped on his back, turning half round as I vaulted so that I gained

*How Waterton 'bagged' an alligator in South America. His only concern was to kill the animal with the least possible damage to its skin; hence the unorthodox method.*

my seat with my face in a right direction. I immediately seized his forelegs, twisted them on his back; thus they served me for a bridle.

With the alligator pinned down, Waterton's men were able to lash its jaws and legs and render it harmless. In a similar encounter with a boa constrictor Waterton sat astride the creature and eventually bound up its mouth with his braces.

Waterton never gained the approval of the scientific establishment, a fact which greatly annoyed him. He amassed a vast collection and wrote copious reports on all the flora and fauna he observed. But, thanks largely to his eccentric behaviour, he simply was not believed. He perfected a better technique for preserving his specimens. This involved soaking skins in perchloride of mercury dissolved in alcohol. Waterton would then shape the creature from the inside. As the skin dried it would harden and maintain its shape, thus rendering stuffing unnecessary and preventing the wrinkling of skin which had always been a problem for taxidermists. Waterton's technique was one which also lent itself to the creation of 'freaks' and 'monsters'. He could change the appearance of any animal during the remoulding process and created a number of oddities as hoaxes upon the scientific fraternity. Some of his other escapades were even wilder and certainly more dangerous. While on a visit to Rome he climbed the dome of

St Peter's and left his gloves on the lightning conductor surmounting the cross. In the privacy of his own estate he made some experiments in winged flight – with the inevitable results – from which he was lucky to escape without serious injury.

When he was forty-seven Waterton married a girl thirty years his junior. When she died shortly after giving birth to a son Waterton was heartbroken. His whole manner of life changed. Though he still travelled frequently to the continent his exploring and collecting journeys were over. He adopted a rigorous daily routine, sleeping on the floor, rising at 3.00 a.m. for an hour of devotional exercises, then working in his study until breakfast at 8.00 a.m. Sometimes he would sit for hours in contemplation before a portrait of St Catherine of Alexandria, who reminded him of his child-bride. Waterton spent most of his time at his house at Walton. He had a nine-foot wall thrown round the estate and forbade all shooting and trapping. The ban was difficult to enforce so he had a large number of wooden pheasants made and nailed to trees around the park in the hope that poachers would waste their shot and grow discouraged.

Waterton remained healthy and vigorous to the end of his days. He was still climbing trees at the age of eighty. He died in 1865 as a result of tripping and falling heavily while walking in the estate.

# The odd fellow

There are few men or women who by their very existence have added a word to the English language. William Spooner is one of that select band. A 'spoonerism' is a particular slip of the tongue of the kind which most of us make occasionally but to which the celebrated Warden of New College, Oxford was particularly prone. His most famous outpouring, supposedly made under the stress of chastising a delinquent student, is

You have tasted a whole worm. You have hissed my mystery lectures. You were fighting a liar in the quadrangle. You will leave by the town drain.

Unfortunately, so many legends have grown up around this singular man that it is difficult now to be sure which spoonerisms are original and which have been invented by later wits. One thing, however, is certain: the oddities of this distracted academic far exceed the catalogue of verbal errors attributed to him.

For one thing he had an extraordinary appearance: he was an albino. He had white hair, a pink face and a large head. He was small and his pale blue eyes were very short-sighted. All his life he looked something between a baby and an old man; his features changed remarkably little with age. When he sat for a scholarship at Oxford, he recalled, one of the rival candidates commented, 'I don't mind who gets the scholarship as long as that *child* does not.' And when, later, he was being considered for a fellowship he overheard a member of the interviewing board enquire, 'Isn't he rather old to be elected?'

William Spooner was born in 1844 into a family whose connections were entirely ecclesiastical and academic (two of his relatives became archbishops of Canterbury). He was sent to a grammar school because his parents could not afford to pay public school fees. By his own ability he won what wealth could not bring him – a university place. Spooner was clever, hard-working and loved learning. He was a born academic, never happier than when engrossed in the study of classical authors. He spent all his post-childhood life at New College, first as undergraduate, then fellow, dean, and finally warden, a post he held from 1903 to 1924. It is difficult to see him in any other walk of life. Within the ivory towers of academia he was safe from the harsh realities of the world. There his eccentricities were accepted. In some other vocation they might well have led to failure and ruin. He lectured well in Ancient History and

Philosophy, concerned himself closely with the welfare of undergraduates and was a popular figure.

He was absent-minded and often distracted from the world of reality. Probably his albinoism had something to do with the confusion which often overcame his speech and behaviour. Once at a dinner party, he reached for the salt-cellar and made a little pile of salt on the tablecloth. Then, he poured a few drops of claret from his glass on to it until it was a little pink pyramid. Presumably he thought he had spilled some wine, for it was quite a common procedure to pour salt on to a stain to lift it from the cloth. Somehow, he got things round the wrong way. Any kind of emotional disturbance seemed to throw him into verbal confusion. Once his wife had an accident which involved surgery upon one of her fingers.

*'Spy's' cartoon of William Spooner in 'Vanity Fair' emphasizes his short-sightedness, but it was his eccentricities of speech and behaviour that most endeared him to contemporaries. On a note asking a friend to visit him urgently he added the postscript, 'I have dealt with the matter, please do not come.'*

Explaining the operation to a friend Spooner said, 'They mended it on again afterwards, but she lost it permanently, for a time.' Usually, people could work out what Spooner *meant* to say. Talking with a member of the colonial service, he enquired, 'How far are you in Nigeria?' But sometimes they were baffled: 'My wife has been in many ways a singularly peaceful and happy but more limited than I had once hoped.' And, when writing about Tacitus, 'to forget is not equally easy with being silent'. Presiding at a college meeting to decide whether to place one or two wrought-iron gates at a particular entrance, he closed the discussion with the comment, 'My own view, for what it is worth, is that two gates are quite enough.'

What makes the real spoonerism amusing, of course, is that verbal confusion leads the speaker to say something which makes sense but is not what he intended to say. In a sermon, Spooner is reputed to have asked the rhetorical question, 'Which of us has not felt in his heart a half-warmed fish?' He once described seeing a cat fall from a window: 'It came to no harm; it popped on its little drawers.' He once gave it as his opinion that the 'weight of rages' would continue to rise. He agreed with St Paul (or intended to) that 'now we see in a dark glassly'. He explained to his wife that the distance from Spitsbergen to the North Pole was no farther than 'that from Land's End to John O'Gaunt'. With these and other examples, what lay at the root of Spooner's problem was not a transposition of sounds but a transposition of ideas. Walking with a friend in Oxford, he passed, and greeted, a lady dressed in black. A few paces farther on he explained to his companion: 'Poor soul. Very sad. Her late husband, you know, eaten by missionaries. Poor soul.' As the years went by Spooner found his reputation something of an irritating embarrassment. There were times when he may have 'performed' deliberately in order to embarrass others: 'Mr Coupland, you read the lesson very badly.' 'But, Sir, I didn't read the lesson.' 'Ah, I thought you didn't.' Or, again, 'Do come to dinner tonight to meet Casson, our new fellow.' 'But, Warden, I *am* Casson.' 'Never mind, come all the same.'

Spooner was greatly loved in Oxford, not just because he was an oddity but because, beneath his strange behaviour (and often expressed through it) there was considerable wisdom and understanding. One day in 1904 he sent for one of his undergraduates and the following conversation ensued:

'I think when you came up to Oxford you had every intention of taking Holy Orders? And I am afraid that you have quite abandoned the idea?'

*'The Spoo', as he was called by generations of undergraduates, was a fellow of New College from 1867 to 1924. In a farewell speech he explained, 'For the first quarter of my life I was too young to be a member of the college. For the last quarter I have been too old to be anything but warden. But for the remaining half I think I may claim that I did what lay in my power to serve the college.'*

'Oh rather, yes, quite, Mr Warden, quite given it up.'
'And what do you propose to do?'
'Well, I want to be a schoolmaster. I've done a little at odd times and like it awfully, so I think I'm going in for it permanently.'
'Oh yes, a schoolmaster, really. Well, Mr Woolley, I have decided that you shall be an archaeologist.'

Sir Leonard Woolley became one of the most outstanding archaeologists of the twentieth century. Many ex-undergraduates, like him, looked back with great affection to the eccentric Warden of New College.

# A breed apart

I was never under any illusions as to the hostility of the great book-hating public: a large and powerful body . . . I realized that everything I said or wrote would be misunderstood by a great many – and my heredity, coming as I do on all sides of stock that for centuries have had their own way, and have not been inured to suffer insolence passively, made it hard for me, and for my brother and sister, not to fight back.

Those words of Osbert Sitwell reveal clearly the dilemma in which the remarkable trio of Edith, Osbert and Sacheverell found themselves. They were aristocratic down to their well-manicured fingertips and, though they loathed much of what their eccentric parents stood for, they were all marked by the Sitwell dissociation from reality. Their earliest recollection of their grandparents' home was of

. . . a different world, given over to those pomps and vanities which, in their own day so overwhelming, notwithstanding leave no shadow behind them . . . Here there were major-domos, grooms of the chamber, powdered footmen wearing velvet knee-breeches on the right occasions, grooms, gamekeepers, the cool and ordered processes of the dairy, and stables full of haughty and glossy gods.

Their father lived in a world which was if anything even more remote. Sir George Reresby Sitwell, the fourth baronet, was an antiquarian and genealogist who made no secret of his preference for an earlier age and did his best to withdraw into it. He refused to install electricity at Renshaw Hall, Derbyshire, his principal residence; candles were good enough for the splendid seventeenth century, therefore they were good enough for the twentieth. Yet, like his great ancestors, he thought nothing of employing four thousand labourers to dig out a new lake and spent years planning his gardens. A guest once observed him passing along the front of the house on all fours. It transpired that he was thinking of lowering the level of the lawn by three feet and simply wanted to see how this would alter the view. On another occasion he had his herd of white cows stencilled in a blue Chinese pattern to improve the prospect from the terrace. Osbert describes well his air of permanent distraction:

My father is fond of walking, extremely rapidly, in these gardens he has made. All day long he can be found in them: and this year . . . he is there for a longer time than ever, because to him the Middle Ages are the model for all life to follow . . . he lives behind invisible barriers of pedigrees and tourneys and charters and coats-of-arms, and all around him hang its shields and banners, all round him sound its discordant trumpets and the battle-cries of armoured men – and since every medieval

*Of Osbert, Sacheverell and Edith, it was Edith who dressed and behaved with the most striking individualism.*

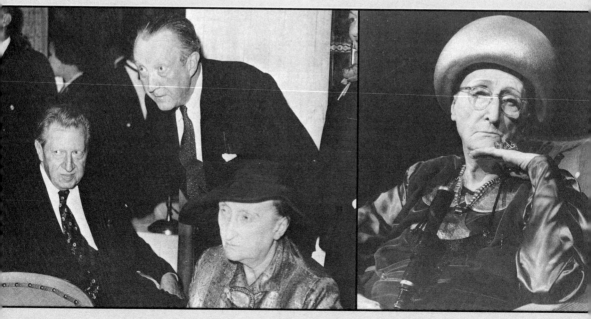

romance opens in a garden at the hour of sunrise, he has, this summer, chosen to be called every morning at five . . .

In 1914 Osbert went away to the war and found himself in the muddy, bloody chaos of the Western Front. He received a letter from his father containing the helpful advice that he must be sure to keep warm, eat plenty of plain, nourishing food at regular intervals and always take a nap in the afternoon.

Lady Ida, Sir George's wife, was beautiful, remote and vague. She was married at the age of seventeen to a man she did not understand and whom she rather feared. She was extravagant and had no concept of the value of money. She ran herself increasingly into debt, fell into the hands of money lenders, and did not dare tell her husband about it. The upshot of it all was an unsavoury court case in which Sir George allowed his wife to stand trial alongside those who had preyed upon her rather than settle her debts and allow the criminals to get away scot free.

The three Sitwell children were all born in the closing years of the last century. Edith, the eldest, felt that her parents never forgave her for not being a boy and not being beautiful. That unconscious barrier, whether real or imagined, marked her from the beginning as different. When she was four someone asked her the inevitable, infuriating, grown-up question, 'And what are you going to be when you grow up?' Without hesitation Edith replied, 'A genius.' She was a serious, sensitive, questioning child who early came to reject the snobbery and class-consciousness upon which much of her parents' world was based. Edith stayed at home to be tutored while her brothers went to boarding school. Osbert recalls that he 'liked Eton, except in the following respects: for work and games, for boys and masters'. He, too, rebelled against the establishment, even more so after his experiences in the war. For Sacheverell it was the same. The three young Sitwells looked for something new in the world, something they could associate with. They found it in the outrageous, misunderstood modern movements in painting, music and literature.

In 1916 they launched an annual poetry magazine called *Wheels*. It was a self-conscious, youthful challenge, full of the poetry of the Sitwells and their friends. They were defiant in their championing of the new spirit in art, a movement they were determined to lead in Britain. Soon after the war the great operatic singer Tetrazzini came to perform at Covent Garden. The Sitwells decided on a demonstration of friendship and brotherhood in the name of 'the young writers of England'. They would solemnly present her with a wreath of bay and myrtle. The scene was set in Tetrazzini's private suite. The young geniuses

*The Sitwells' childhood home, Renshaw Hall.*

were lined up. The press were present in force. A door was flung open. The great singer, fat and ageing, advanced into the room with graceful, theatrical gestures. Sacheverell waited to begin his speech. Tetrazzini sailed forward, tripped over a rug and fell headlong.

But the most celebrated event with which the name of Sitwell is associated is the first performance, in 1923, of *Façade*, William Walton's setting of some of Edith's poems. The critics turned up in force to see this avant-garde work by a little-known poet and musician. They were confronted by an orchestra and a closed curtain. Through this curtain a kind of megaphone protruded. The music began, and then Edith Sitwell began to recite through the megaphone in her crisp, brittle voice. As Osbert said, 'we were obliged to go about London feeling as if we had committed a murder . . . In fact, we had created a first class scandal in literature and music.'

Of course, *Façade* subsequently became one of the most popular twentieth-century works and the eccentric Sitwells, such is fashion, became part of the new establishment. By the time the Second World War came along their poetry readings were quite popular. One such reading in 1944 took place during a German rocket raid. Edith was reciting her poem *Still Falls the Rain* when the siren sounded. She went on reading. The drone of an approaching missile was heard, and gunfire. The racket grew louder. Edith paused, lifted her eyes, raised her voice and continued. The reality of Hitler's war might not have existed. She was in her much more important world of poetry and her audience was with her. She was certainly Sir George's daughter.

## The Earl Bishop

All of us have noticed, from time to time, hotels both in this country and in European capitals, which bear the name 'Bristol' and we may have wondered why this title should be so popular. The answer is that it was once an indication of a high standard of excellence. Permission to use the name was granted sparingly by one of the most remarkable travellers of the eighteenth century, Frederick Augustus Hervey, the Earl Bishop. He was a stickler for good food and accommodation. Once in Siena he was so disgusted with a dish of pasta presented to him that he flung it out of the window. Unfortunately, a Catholic procession was passing and the glutinous mess fell upon the sacred host, an indignity for which the visitor was run out of town. It was largely to guard against gastronomic disappointment that Hervey travelled with his own cooks and a cavalcade of geese, turkeys, ducks and joints of lamb and culinary tools. These would always be sent on ahead to the next hostelry so that a suitable dinner awaited the earl on his arrival.

But it was not only as traveller and gourmand that Hervey exercised an eccentric zeal. His whole life was a bewildering array of enthusiasms and he was one of the most delightful oddities spawned by the English class system. He was born in 1730, the third son of John Lord Hervey

and the grandson of the Earl of Bristol. Like many younger sons of the nobility he elected to go into the church. Since no suitable preferment was immediately forthcoming he took himself off to the continent. He had a passionate curiosity for seeing new things and, hearing that Vesuvius was active, set off to Naples. He insisted on going up to the rim of the crater and peering over the edge. It was almost the last thing he ever did: a rock spewed out of the crater and struck him on the arm. Natural phenomena fascinated him (but then, almost everything fascinated him) and by the end of his life he had spent hundreds of thousands of pounds in patronage of scientists of all kinds. Family influence eventually procured him the Irish bishopric of Clogne and, then, in 1768 the very rich bishopric of Derry.

He was a very uncharacteristic bishop. For one thing, in an age of bitter denominational rivalry, he made friends with both Roman Catholic and Nonconformist inhabitants of his diocese. Once he organized an impromptu horse race on the beach near his house in which some of his own clergy were pitted against their Nonconformist counterparts. The Anglicans, being less fit, were beaten to a man and some of them ended up on their backs on the sand. On another day he got some of his fatter clergy down to the beach for another contest. This time the prize was a vacant living. But the bishop cheated: he devised the course across a barrier of quicksands. So no one finished the race. Despite such pranks, Hervey courted the esteem of his people. He spent a great deal of his own money on improving roads and building bridges. He improved agricultural methods and prospected for coal. He received the freedom of the cities of Londonderry and Dublin, for his services to the community. But the people also loved him for his flamboyance. He designed his clothes and equipage to magnify the importance of his office and person. Eager crowds awaiting his arrival at an important meeting in Dublin were not disappointed. The bishop arrived in a procession preceded by several well-mounted parsons. He himself 'in episcopal purple, white gloves with a gold fringe round the wrists and golden tassels and diamond buckles on his knees and shoes, was drawn in an open landau by six horses caparisoned with purple ribbons'.

Despite his tireless efforts for the people of his diocese, Hervey continued to spend much time in foreign travel. After 1779 he was able to indulge his passion more enthusiastically. In that year, his father and two elder brothers having died, Frederick Augustus somewhat unexpectedly succeeded to the earldom of Bristol. He made many tours of Spain, Italy, Austria, Germany and Switzerland but as far as possible he avoided France – 'a frippery country – a skipping dancing tribe'. On these travels he collected works of art indiscriminately and planned for their exhibition in his fine houses. For building was another of the Earl Bishop's enthusiasms. He had two splendid mansions built to his own highly-individualistic design in Ireland and, in 1792, he made plans for a new residence at the family seat, Ickworth in Suffolk. The 'architectural curiosity' was of a very classical design never before seen in England. His ideas on building, as on all things, were very clear and very forcefully expressed. His daughter wrote to suggest that white bricks might enable the house to blend more easily into the English scene.

'What, Child!,' retorted the Earl Bishop, 'build my house of a brick that looks like a sick, pale, *jaundiced* red brick, that would be red brick if it could be! . . . I shall follow dear, impeccable old Palladio's rule, and as nothing ought to be without a covering in our raw damp climate, I shall cover the house, pillars and pillasters with . . . stucco . . .'

The 'nomad bishop', as he was called, never lived at Ickworth, which was still unfinished at his death. Nor did much of his splendid collection ever reach Suffolk. While he was in Milan the French invaded Italy, Hervey's works of art were confiscated and he was thrown into prison. He paid £10,000 for the privilege of having his collection back. The revolutionaries took the money – and kept the collection.

Hervey was a bundle of contradictions: a charitable and reverend minister of religion who drank like a fish, swore like a trooper and had a succession of mistresses; a generous host who was not above playing tricks on his guests such as scattering flour outside a lady's room to discover to whose bed she resorted in the small hours; a convinced Anglican who preached tolerance at a time when that virtue was out of fashion; a cosmopolitan who could insult the King of Prussia to his face; an art connoisseur who dismissed Michelangelo as 'mad'. Even his death was surrounded by bizarre circumstances. He was taken ill on the road to Albano in 1803 and died in an outhouse of a peasant who would not allow a heretic bishop into his cottage. His embalmed body was shipped back to England for burial. Because sailors are superstitious about travelling with corpses the wandering Earl Bishop made his last journey in a crate labelled 'an antique statue'.

*Hervey saw no contradiction in being a leader of the Irish Volunteers and also Bishop of Derry. Ickworth, the neoclassical mansion which he planned in such meticulous detail to be the centre of his Suffolk estates, was a house he never lived in.*

# The protester

Most of us grumble from time to time – about the boss, the government, the state of the country and so on – and grumbling is as far as it usually gets. If we feel strongly about something we might write to the papers. If we feel very strongly we might join a march and wave a placard. But it is a passing activity. For very few people can protest be said to be a way of life. There is, undoubtedly, a tiny minority of 'professional' protesters but they all devote their activities to one or two specific causes. What makes Jesse Howard unique is that much of his life has been an indiscriminate shout of protest against the world in general.

He was born in 1885 and as a young man took up melon-growing in Fulton, Missouri. He married in 1916 and had five children. He brought up his family in the God-fearing, fundamentalist, 'old-time religion' to which he had always been dedicated. It is not clear how or by what means the conviction grew upon him that he was a prophet in the Old Testament mould but by the 1950s he had certainly adopted the role of a latter-day Isaiah or Jeremiah. He was convinced that the once-great American people were sliding into moral and economic decline because of their neglect of the Scriptures. As he often remarked about his neighbours, 'they don't know a Holy Bible from a funny paper'. He went to Washington to acquaint President Eisenhower with this information. When the guards at the White House asked Howard for his credentials he brandished his Bible under their noses. They put him on a bus and sent him home. Howard was enraged by what he considered to be a kidnapping ('When you take a fella agin his will and make him go somewhere, that's kidnappin', isn't it?') and it may have been this indignity that channelled his protest into a new activity – writing graffiti.

This angry old man turned his home into a windmill and graffiti factory and spent every day creating a multitude of signs painted on boards or on the arms of simple windmills stuck up round his property. His messages were bewildering in their variety. There was, for example, a description of his wedding, in doggerel:

Jess, will you take Maude without any regrets
to love and to cherish until one of you perish
and is laid under the sod, so help you God? I

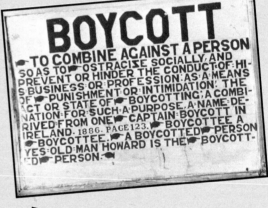

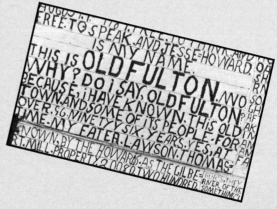

*Jesse Howard's windmill and graffiti factory at Fulton, Missouri. The billboards and the vanes on his windmills proclaim Howard's pungent messages to passers-by.*

replied in the affirmative. Maude, will you take Jess and cling to him both out and in, through thick and thin holding him to your heart until death do you part? Maude blessed his consent. Now I pronounce you Man and Wife. Go up life's rugged hill until you both reach the level. And then salute your bride you little trusty devil.

On the same board he recorded the birth of his sons and daughters, adding the comment, 'I see no future for these children.'

But most of Howard's signs are couched in denunciatory rather than whimsical vein. It is the local inhabitants that come in for the lion's share of criticism:

You want to see a gang of hoodlum police? Just drive through Fulton. Every way you turn your head you see a happy hooligan. Or a hoodlum. VOP. Worse than the East Berlin VOPS . . . There's not one decent God fearing Christian among them.

There is about Howard's graffiti a magnificent mixture of angry eloquence with a semi-literate disregard for spelling and grammatical convention:

Free thought free speech. Yes, I have been lied to! Lied on! Lied about! Talked to! Talked about! Stole from. Vandalized! Scandleized! Burglerized! The Thieves and Vandals run in gangs like a pack of wolves! On hell's eight acres . . .

It is hardly surprising that the good citizens of Fulton, Missouri do not altogether appreciate the prophet in their midst. Howard is a loner. Now that his wife is dead and his children moved away he has nothing to do but keep up his one-man campaigns. But if the neighbours find him an embarrassment others certainly do not. Visitors flock to the windmill and graffiti factory from all over America. The old man has become a tourist attraction and has been hailed as an important folk artist. His signs now sell for hundreds of dollars apiece. Kansas City Art Institute has a collection of ninety-seven Jesse Howard masterpieces and he is well represented in other galleries and museums. Examples of his work have toured Europe in exhibitions of folk art.

Visitors find Howard easy to talk to – or, rather, listen to. He is as ready to regale the world with verbal sermons as he is with printed slogans. He believes in hard work and the Bible and offers as proof of his philosophy the fact that it has kept him hale and hearty for almost a century. He could well have a point: the last I heard of Jesse Howard he was ninety-seven and still producing his graffiti. There is, apparently, no lack of sin and crime to be denounced. As long as he has breath in his body and strength in his arms Fulton's prophet will continue to denounce them.

# The distracted parson

One form of eccentricity is absent-mindedness and few men have been worse afflicted with this complaint than the Reverend George Harvest, rector of Thames Ditton, Surrey. The stories collected about this eighteenth-century cleric are legion. He was educated at Oxford and was an erudite and interesting conversationalist. He had a lively wit and a wide circle of friends. But he simply seemed incapable of holding more than one idea at a time in his mind and he could not hold even one for very long. It frequently happened, for example, that he left home in the morning with gun and dog for a few hours' sport. Passing the church he saw a large number of villagers gathering there. On going over to enquire what they were doing he was told that it was Sunday and they had come for divine service.

Among those whom Harvest counted as his friends was Dr Compton, Bishop of London. The bishop regarded him so highly that he suggested the young clergyman might like to marry his daughter. The young lady was agreeable and Harvest knew that such a match would further his career. The arrangements were made. The day was set. The guests arrived at the church. So did the bishop and the nervous bride. But there was no sign of Mr Harvest. He had gone fishing. The astonishing fact is not so much that he forgot his own wedding but that he ever came within an ace of getting married. Since he often neglected to change his clothes for weeks on end it is a wonder that any woman ever looked at him twice. Yet he did succeed in engaging the affections of another lady – even though he once arrived at her door half naked. It happened like this: wishing to pay a call upon his intended and finding himself short of time, he resolved to go on horseback and save time by changing his shirt and cravat on the way. Close to the lady's house he stopped, removed his upper garments and laid out his clean clothes on the horse's neck. But the horse grew restless and bolted. Harvest's clothes fell into the mud and when he gained control of his steed he found himself before the threshold where his blushing fiancée stood.

His friends found Harvest the easiest target in the world for practical jokes. Once he was taking a service in Oxford and was required to read some banns of marriage. Some local wit substituted the following rhyme for the well-known formula and Harvest solemnly read it out.

I publish the marriage banns between
Jack Cheshire and the Widow Gloucester,
Both of a parish that is seen

'Twixt Oxford here and Paternoster;
Who, to keep out wind and weather,
Hereafter mean to pig together.
So if you wish to put in caveat
Now is the time to let us have it.

On another occasion he was required to preach at some important service. This time some tricksters got hold of three sets of Harvest's sermon notes, jumbled them up and put them in his pocket. The poor parson clambered into the pulpit and began his sermon. He was, himself, somewhat perplexed at the thread of his own discourse but he persevered. His endurance proved greater than that of the congregation. Harvest was only persuaded to stop when the sexton drew his attention to the fact that all the pews were empty.

Despite his uncouth appearance he was a welcome guest in many fine houses because of the oddity of his behaviour and conversation. One day he rose to take his leave after dinner but instead of descending the staircase to the hall he climbed three flights to the attic where he was found by the servants some hours later stumbling around amidst piles of lumber. One evening he was invited to London to attend the theatre. The play was well under way and Harvest was ensconced in a box with his host and hostess. He put a hand in his pocket to pull out a handkerchief and, instead, brought out his striped, woollen nightcap which, as he now recalled, he had put there because he would be sleeping in town. Unfortunately, the garish headgear fell out of the box into the pit, where some of the wags had sport with it, throwing it back and forth among themselves. Harvest, totally heedless of his friends' embarrassment or the proceedings on stage, stood up and made a long speech on the importance of nightcaps and why his should be returned to him. At last it was passed up to him on a stick and the play was allowed to resume.

On another trip to the capital he was walking with a friend when he noticed a curiously-shaped pebble and picked it up. His companion chanced to ask what time it was. Harvest took his watch from his pocket, read the time, threw the watch into the river and carefully put the stone in his pocket. His lack of household management brought him to the brink of ruin. His servants took advantage of him, stole his belongings, ran up huge bills in his name and even used his house for wild parties. But his friends took pity on him. He was a frequent guest at Ember Court, the home of Mr Arthur Onslow, Speaker of the House of Commons. The Onslows were so fond of Harvest that they always kept a place for him at their table and a bed for him to sleep in. It was in fact at Ember Court, in August 1789, that the Reverend George Harvest remembered to die.

THE EXCURSION OF GEORGE HARVEST *page 52.*

*Harvest's attempt to change his clothes while actually riding to visit a lady had disastrous results.*

# Visionaries

Everybody needs dreams. Life without some kind of dream or vision or goal is quite devoid of meaning. But the visionary is the man or woman who is obsessed with a dream so vivid, so important, that all else is subjected to it. The vision may be external as in the case of Bernadette of Lourdes, literally something seen to which the visionary must testify, or it may exist only in the mind, some grandiose scheme to be brought to reality, such as Walt Disney's fantastic Disneyworld. For vision, of course, is not only to be thought of in religious terms. Robert Owen was compelled by a deep sense of social justice and a strong image of the ideal society. For a man like Mahatma Gandhi religious and humanitarian goals could not be distinguished. Much the same could be said for Albert Schweitzer whose driving force was reverence for life.

Whatever the nature of the vision one thing is perfectly clear, vision is a very uncomfortable thing to live with. It allows the woman or man who has it very little peace. The visionary is someone driven to overcome every obstacle in the realization of his dream. When Martin Luther, the great sixteenth-century reformer who wanted to change the face of Western Christendom, was brought before the emperor and ordered to recant and behave himself, his famous reply was, 'Here I stand, God help me, I can do no other.' Every visionary would if necessary echo those words. There can be no going back, a truth once glimpsed must be followed, must be carried through, must be realized as fully as possible within the world of men. A vision is of necessity something not shared by the generality of men and so the visionary inevitably exposes himself to misunderstanding, to criticism, to ridicule. For Rachel Saint to venture into the land of the Auka Indians who had murdered her brother and his companions seemed to be the height of folly even to some of her fellow missionaries. William Blake was dismissed by many as mad. To hold to the conviction that you are right and everybody else is wrong is to invite the charge of being conceited. And in a sense the charge is justifiable, for the visionary must discount the counsel of all those wiser, older, more experienced than himself, must hold to what he knows to be true, and that is a form of conceit. For the visionary there can be no counting of the cost, no careful reflection upon his reputation. If he is fortunate, he will live to see the realization of his vision as Disney lived to witness his Magic Kingdom, as the Mahdi lived to

see the overthrow of his enemies in the Sudan. But more often than not the visionary passes from this world like Schweitzer, or Mary Kingsley, with a strong sense of things still left to be accomplished, work still needing to be done. Frequently it is left to posterity to decide whether the visionary was a man ahead of his time, or simply a deluded fool. It is a question to which there may be no easy answer. Was Savonarola right or wrong? Was Yukio Mishima right or wrong? Was Robert Owen right or wrong? Everyone will give a different answer. That answer will depend upon the extent to which the person sympathizes with the vision.

Just as it is difficult for any man to take it into his head to become an eccentric, so it is impossible to cultivate vision. It is something that comes to a person whether he wills it or not. It is not to be confused with enthusiasm. For example, a person may support a political party, be convinced of its principles, seek election, become a member of parliament, even gain high government office. All that can be achieved with the application of enthusiasm. But if one has a vivid picture in mind of the ideal society and seeks with every fibre of one's being to realize that society; by touring the country making campaign speeches, writing newspaper articles and giving television interviews, one may end up founding a new political party or leading a nationwide movement for reform. One may attract thousands or millions of followers, or be dismissed as a crank, but nobody will be able to doubt one's sincerity or that one is motivated by something deeper than conviction. Sincerity and disinterestedness are the hallmarks of the visionary. They must be, because his vision may very well destroy him. For the visionary the element of sacrifice is ever present.

And it is sacrifice that endorses the vision. When we see a man suffer or die for his beliefs, we conceive not only a respect for the man but a respect for the creed he espouses. Some of us may be inspired to share that creed. For every man who seeks to live his life above the level of mere animal survival is looking for something to believe in, something greater than himself, something capable of dignifying life upon this planet with meaning and purpose. It is the visionaries in our midst who help us to see that such purpose or purposes do exist, whether we conclude that that purpose is only to be found in the spiritual realm or whether we come to realize that there are deeper possibilities within the human psyche. It is the visionary who points us onward and upward. That is why society needs visionaries. It may ridicule them, condemn them, imprison them, certify them as insane, or even martyr them, but it needs them. It is the Inquisitor in Shaw's *St Joan* who asks the question, 'Must a Christ be crucified in every age for the benefit of those who have no imagination?' The answer is probably 'yes'.

We should be wary of any society which denies the need for visionaries. Any regime which seeks to stifle the troubled conscience or silence the inconvenient voice, is claiming a monopoly of truth, and truth is always infinitely larger than any pope or monarch or cabinet or praesidium can possibly conceive. The first strategem of a repressive society when faced with an uncomfortable visionary is to categorize him, thus denying his individuality. The medieval church dubbed him a heretic. In Soviet Russia he would be called a dissident. In South Africa a communist. By thus associating his name in the common mind with a group of known undesirables, the authorities shrug off any challenge which the visionary's views might present. The next step is to put him somewhere where he can do no harm, a monastery, a rehabilitation centre, a labour camp. Then, if possible, he must be induced to see the error of his ways, the heretic must be made to recant, the political deviationist must be persuaded to confess that he has been seduced by the forces of bourgeois reactionary neo-capitalism. If all else fails there remains the stake, and its more varied modern equivalents.

But must every visionary be tolerated on the grounds that he has found his own bizarre path to some higher truth? What of the dangerous fanatic who leads thousands astray? Was not Hitler a visionary? Surely the atrocities he committed in pursuit of his goal of racial purity are in no way to be approved. The world would be a better place if Master Shikelgrüber had been strangled at birth. Would not Florence really have been better off without Savonarola (opposite)? Common sense, of course, says a hearty 'yes'. But how is common sense, which is shaped inevitably by the social and moral conventions of the age, to judge that a Wilberforce or a Shaftesbury is right, while a Robespierre or a Peter the Hermit is wrong? In fact the only judgement we can make is on the basis of results. Only in the perspective of history can a visionary be seen as a success or a failure, a champion of a lost cause, or the pioneer of a new and better way, a blessing or a curse upon his own and subsequent generations. By then, of course, it is too late; the experiment has been tried, the good has been achieved, or the harm done. But this is the dilemma we inevitably face in a compariatively free society.

## 'Give me a hat of blood'

There had never been a bonfire like it. It stood higher than the roof of the palace so recently evacuated by the Medicis and had a circumference of eighty metres. In its jumbled heap there were expensive books (and all books were expensive in the fifteenth century), paintings, jewellery, elegant clothes made from the costliest imported silks and brocades. Atop the pyre was the stuffed figure of King Carnival. As four torchbearers stepped forth to light the fire, trumpets blared, church bells pealed, and the people of Florence, crammed into the crowded piazza, cheered. This luxury-loving city whose churches, palaces and fine houses were lavishly bedecked with beautiful objects, many designed by the greatest Renaissance craftsmen, had turned its back on such 'vanities'. And this transformation had been brought about by one man: Girolamo Savonarola.

Since boyhood Girolamo had been a soul apart. Reared in a time which later ages look back on as one of the finest epochs in the history of civilization, he felt a deep revulsion for the superficiality and brutality of Italian life. Splendour and squalor were mingled in the city states of the Renaissance. Church leaders, princes, grand dukes and merchant bankers surrounded themselves with luxury, indulged every vice their wealth could command, engaged constantly in convoluted political intrigue, and periodically slaughtered each other on the battlefield. While the favoured few ate exotic foods, flavoured with Oriental spices, from golden dishes, peasants were dying from malnutrition and overwork, and

prisoners lay rotting in dungeons where they had been thrown on the whim of their enemies. All this happened in a land which was obedient to the pope, venerated the saints and worshipped in opulent splendour the God of justice and love. Few contemporaries, apparently, could discern the contradictions which riddled Renaissance Italy like woodworm in a gilded statue. Savonarola was one of that minority.

His tortured spirit turned to poetry in which he railed against a society turned upside-down:

> Gentle and beautiful of soul is he who wins most by fraud and violence,
> who scorns heaven and Christ, and ever seeks to trample on his fellows.

This angry young man might have found consolation in the arms of a woman and had the edge of his indignation blunted by the happy drudgery of family life. It was not to be. The object of his youthful ardour rejected him haughtily. He was driven in upon his inner vision, that of a wrathful, avenging God who would not much longer withhold the sword of judgement. At the age of twenty-two he fled from the world and his family, abandoned the medical career on which he was set and entered the Dominican monastery at Bologna.

Savonarola's studies and devotions reinforced his convictions about the decadence of Church and State. He experienced frequent visions, most of which portrayed in lurid and terrifying detail the coming day of judgement. This became the main theme of his preaching in the towns and villages of North Italy to which he was sent. He gradually won a reputation for eloquence and fervour, especially when he dared to inveigh against the openly corrupt court of Pope Innocent VIII. It

was in 1489 that he was summoned to Florence on the express orders of Lorenzo de Medici, the ruler of that city. Lorenzo the Magnificent, probably the most outstanding of all Renaissance princes, had a feud with the pope and thought that the support of the friar would help his cause.

Lorenzo did not realize his mistake until it was too late. Savonarola felt that he had a destiny to fulfil. So strong was this belief that he was overcome by it and fainted as he neared the city. Once installed, he unleashed his denunciations from the pulpit with unprecedented ardour. He spoke of his visions. He coupled them with biblical texts to prophesy the overthrow of the government. He called on the people to acknowledge no king but Christ. 'O Florence, then you will be rich, indeed, with spiritual as well as earthly gold. Then you will purify Rome. You will purify Italy. You will purify all lands. The wings of your greatness will spread over the whole earth.' People of every class flocked to hear him. Men and women wept openly. Such was his popularity that his enemies in high places dared not oppose him. They tried bribery, without success. The pope offered to make Savonarola a cardinal. The monk's reply was uncompromising, 'You offer me a red hat? Give me rather a hat of blood.' The reformer was closely involved in politics, and his authority grew even greater when his prophecies of forthcoming events came true. The most remarkable of these prophecies was that the French King Charles VIII would invade Italy. This event destroyed

Medici power in Florence and left Savonarola with no rival. He established a republican government. Through preaching and new laws, he maintained higher standards of personal and corporate morality. The culmination of this holiness movement was the 'burning of the vanities'. Savonarola transformed the old carnival season, celebrated every February. It was traditionally a time of gaiety, indulgence and licence. Under the new regime it became a religious festival of renunciation. In 1497 and 1498 the central celebration was a bonfire upon which citizens burned their worldly 'vanities'.

Despite this apparent success, Savonarola himself knew that there could only be one end for him – martyrdom. He was right. The forces ranged against him were too strong. As soon as those forces were able to unite they would crush him. Within weeks of the second 'burning of the vanities' his enemies in Florence obtained from the pope a bull of excommunication against the friar. He was imprisoned and tortured. But no amount of stretching on the rack could make him recant. The fickle crowd which had once packed Savonarola's church now followed the rabble rousers who clamoured for his death.

On 23 May 1498 there was another bonfire in Florence's central piazza. Sticks and faggots had been piled round a post on top of which stood a narrow platform. This in turn was surmounted by a large cross. From the arms of this cross Savonarola and two companions were hanged.

## The peasant girl who became a legend

Stripping away the layers of myth that grow up around holy people is all very well as long as you know when to stop. In some cases it is easier to find that point than in others. A clear personality emerges from autobiographical accounts or the descriptions of close friends and relatives. On them we can base judgements unclouded by later hagiography. That is not the case with Bernadette Soubirous. The veneration began too early. Throughout most of her short life Bernadette was the object of curiosity, admiration, awe and rumour.

Some basic facts can be clearly established. Bernadette was born in 1844, the eldest child of a poor couple living in a village at the foot of the Pyrenees. Her father was a miller but before long he had declined to the status of a day-labourer, then he took to thieving to support his family. They lived in one tiny room in abject poverty. Bernadette was sometimes farmed out to other homes to act as a servant. Despite their sufferings, or perhaps because of them, the Soubirous were a very close family. They were also devout, clinging to the simple faith which alone could make any sense of their wretched existence. Children grew up rapidly in such circumstances. By the time she was fourteen Bernadette already had the inner strength and resolution of the Pyrenean *paysanne*. She was used to looking after the younger children and to the responsibilities she had had to shoulder when put out to work for relatives and friends. Though not strong (she was asthmatic), Bernadette was hard-working and practical. She had a simple piety but, having received little formal education, she had found it impossible to learn her catechism and so had not yet made her first communion – which she longed to do.

One day in February 1858 Bernadette was out with her two sisters, collecting wood. They took off their clogs to cross the river Gave and, while doing so, Bernadette saw a woman in white smiling at her from a grotto on the far side. Neither of her companions shared the vision. Years later, when she had learned to write, Bernadette recorded,

> I put my hand in my pocket, and I found my rosary there. I wanted to make the sign of the cross . . . I couldn't raise my hand to my forehead . . . The vision made the sign of the cross. Then I tried a second time and I could. As soon as I made the sign of the cross, the fearful shock

I felt disappeared. I knelt down and I said my rosary in the presence of the beautiful lady. The vision fingered the beads of her own rosary, but she did not move her lips. When I finished my rosary, she signed for me to approach but I did not dare. Then she disappeared.

That was the first of several appearances during the course of the next six months. And what an incredible six months they were. First of all Bernadette was only accompanied by a few friends when she went to the grotto. Then other people in the village heard about the vision. They wanted to go as well to see if they could see 'Our Lady of Lourdes' as the vision was soon being called. Bernadette's fame spread ever wider. Soon there were over 3,000 people congregating along the banks of the Gave, some camping out overnight. Bernadette was examined by the local clergy, by the police. She was accused of being a sensation-seeker but she stuck to her story with such an obvious sincerity that her critics were disarmed. The size of her following also made it difficult for the authorities to suppress her activities. Bernadette herself changed during this period. On her visits to the grotto she went into an ecstatic trance. A doctor who was present on one occasion noted:

> For me it was supernatural to see Bernadette on her knees before the grotto, in ecstasy, holding a lighted candle and covering the flame with

*Bernadette was a simple peasant girl whose spiritual intensity made her an inspiration to millions.*

*Bernadette's visions in 1858 were very real to her, though shared by no one else.*

her two hands, without her seeming to have the least impression of her hands' contact with the flame. I examined her hands. Not the slightest trace of burns.

The peasant girl spoke with her vision (no one else ever saw or heard the apparition), which told her that she was the 'Immaculate Conception' (the doctrine of the immaculate conception of the mother of Jesus had been proclaimed by Pius IX in 1854), that a chapel was to be built close to the grotto, that Bernadette would experience suffering in this world and bliss hereafter. Bernadette began to speak with a new authority. She embraced a blind girl, who was immediately healed.

When the visions stopped, Bernadette tried to return to the simple life of home, school and work. It was impossible. A constant stream of visitors came to question her and seek her help. In 1860 she went as a boarder to the house of the nuns who ran the local school. In 1866 she asked to join the order and went as a novice to the mother house of the order of Nevers. She remained there for the remainder of her life, much of which was passed in sickness and pain. Even in the sanctuary of the convent, Sister Marie-Bernard, as she was now called, could not escape prying eyes. People were constantly calling to see her. Whenever possible she avoided these visitors. In other ways Bernadette received no special treatment at Nevers; she endured the same strict regimen as the other nuns. It may even have been that the rules were applied more harshly to her for it is known the mother superior was sceptical about Bernadette's visions and disapproved of the special attention she received.

Bernadette also had to bear official examinations. The Church had never made up its mind about her visions and up to the last weeks of her life she had to submit to detailed questions. She was increasingly reluctant to talk about her experiences. She died in 1879 at the age of thirty-five. She was beatified in 1925 and canonized in 1933. And over two million people every year still flock to her grotto at Lourdes.

*Bernadette's humble dwelling became a centre of pilgrimage.*

# King of the Magic Kingdom

In 1966, the year that Walter Elias Disney died:

240,000,000 people saw a Disney film;

100,000,000 people every week saw a Disney TV show;

800,000,000 people read a Disney book or magazine;

50,000,000 people listened to a Disney record;

80,000,000 people bought Disney licensed merchandise;

150,000,000 people read a Disney comic strip;

80,000,000 people saw a Disney educational film;

6,700,000 people visited Disneyland.

That, in crude statistical terms, is a measure of the achievement of the man who arrived in Hollywood in 1923 with forty dollars in his pocket.

Walt Disney took a primitive and undeveloped technique – animated film cartoon – and turned it into a multi-billion-dollar growth industry. He turned his basic creations to economic advantage in every possible way by licensing the production of comic strips, tee-shirts, alarm clocks, plastic mugs and a host of other manufactured goods for children. He started with nothing: he died a millionaire. But there is much more to the Disney saga than a rags-to-riches story. He was not just a very successful business tycoon. Disney had a motto which he applied to himself and which he used to drive on his employees and colleagues – 'Dream, diversify, and never miss an angle.' And for Walt Disney the dreaming always came first.

Dreams were essential to a child born into a large, poor family; there was little else to amuse the young mind. Elias Disney, the head of the household, was a man who had tried his hand at many things and failed, slipping progressively down the economic scale. Walt spent the first eight years of his life on a small Missouri farm. Then his father was forced to sell up and move to Kansas City where he organized a news round. Elias expected his sons to help him without payment. Walt was regularly hauled from bed at 3.30 a.m. and sent out delivering the heavy journals in all weathers. Elias was a hard man, mean as well as poor. His children were never given toys and the slightest transgression was punished with the strap. Walt recalled in later years how sometimes on his rounds, he would discover rich kids' discarded playthings on the verandahs and lawns of their homes, and sit down enthralled with them. Sometimes he would get home late or make a mistake and that usually meant another beating. In later life his elder brother, Roy, said of him, 'As long as I can remember, Walt has been working. He didn't play much as a boy.' But Walt Disney did play – inwardly – in his own dream world, a world that he could never express, except when he had a pencil and paper in his hand.

His obvious talent for drawing received no encouragement from his father but his meagre earnings enabled him to attend a Saturday morning art class. Disney was never able to communicate freely with people through the normal channels of social intercourse. He was never an easy man to get on with. It was his energy and vision that inspired respect in others. These characteristics can be traced to his earliest years. Deprived of a real childhood, denied many of the comforts of life, the spectacle of failure always before him in the shape of his father, Disney forced himself to succeed, to create a happy world where there was no cruelty, ugliness or hardship.

*Disney won more Oscars than any other film-maker.*

By the time he left home he had had enough of working for someone else. He was determined to be his own boss. For years this meant eking out a living on the fringes of the newspaper and commercial art worlds as a freelance cartoonist. During this period he made a few experiments with animated film cartoons. The 'short', a crudely simple piece of entertainment based on a sequence of jerky, moving drawings, had become an established part of the programme in many movie theatres. They had no sound, of course, and, like all silent films, animated cartoons might have remained museum pieces, bypassed by changing fashion and improved technology. The man who prevented this was Walt Disney. In 1923 he moved to Hollywood, determined to make his name in the film industry.

He was joined by Roy, who took care of the finances and attempted, not always successfully, to anchor Walt's soaring enthusiasm. They produced shorts and just about managed to make ends meet. They also learned the hard way about the savage competition in the movie industry: in 1927 their New York distributor poached some of the Disney artists and set up his own studio in opposition. Walt travelled to the East Coast and tried, unsuccessfully, to resolve the crisis. Refusing to be downcast, he cabled Roy before his return, 'Everything OK. Coming home.' And on the long train ride back to California he created a new cartoon character. It was Mortimer – soon to be re-christened Mickey – Mouse.

'The Mouse', as he was referred to in the studio, was an instant success, particularly when Disney, pioneering in this as in so many other fields, used sound in *Steamboat Willy*, the third Mickey Mouse adventure. Within a decade Mickey and his 'gang' – Donald Duck, Goofy, Pluto, Minnie, *et al* – were known and loved throughout the world.

Disney the businessman exploited every profit-making possibility of his cartoon characters. He worked his employees very hard – so hard that many were unable to stand the pace – but not as hard as he worked himself. When advised to exercise in order to improve his health, he took up golf. But, as his wife recorded, instead of playing like a normal person, 'He got up at four-thirty in the morning to get it out of the way before he had to be at the studio.' The problem was that he could not keep pace with his dreams.

One dream that Disney cherished for years was the 'magic kingdom'. He wanted to extend his world of illusion beyond the two-dimensional limitations of the cinema screen. He wanted to create somewhere where people could fully experience the Disney vision, could escape into the pure, happy, clean, innocent realm of idealized childhood. Even in the 1930s he played with the idea of an amusement park to end all amusement parks. No one, not even Roy, shared his enthusiasm. In 1952, using partly his own money, because his brother refused to back 'Walt's screwy idea', Disney hired technicians (immediately dubbed 'imagineers') to turn his dream into reality. He found a site. He defined the character of his kingdom. He canvassed support from financiers and fairground experts. They all told him he was crazy. The creation of Disneyland and its Florida counterpart, Disneyworld, has shown that it was not Disney who was crazy. Millions of people every year visit these incredible pleasure grounds which are now among the biggest tourist attractions in the world.

In past epochs only kings, emperors and grandees could indulge grandiose and imaginative schemes for the amusement of themselves and their privileged companions. Walt Disney is unique in the twentieth century for creating a world where everything is as he dreamed it would be, a world where he was king, a world he shared with millions.

# The vision of a new society

In 1791 this conversation took place between Mr Drinkwater, a northern industrialist, who had advertised the post of manager of a large, new cotton mill, and Robert Owen, an applicant.

DRINKWATER: You are too young.

OWEN: That was an objection made to me four or five years ago. I did not expect it would be made to me now.

DRINKWATER: How old are you?

OWEN: Twenty in May this year.

DRINKWATER: What salary do you ask?

OWEN: Three hundred a year.

DRINKWATER: What? Three hundred a year! I have had this morning I know not how many seeking the situation, and I do not think that all their earnings together would amount to what you require.

OWEN: I cannot be governed by what others ask and I cannot take less. I am now making that sum by my own business.

Robert Owen was appointed and became the youngest mill manager in Manchester, with control of 500 men. He was little more than a boy but he had already shown himself an excellent businessman. He started his working life as a pro-vincial shop assistant at the age of ten. At fourteen his already keen ambition took him to a post in a large London store. At fifteen he took a better paid job in Manchester. At eighteen he went into partnership with Ernest Owen, a mechanic producing bonnet-making machinery. After a few months he was bought out and immediately went into business on his own account as proprietor of a small spinning mill. Thus, by the time that he responded to Mr Drinkwater's advertisement, Robert Owen was already an experienced businessman with a considerable knowledge of textiles. From this point on his career continued upwards. Long before middle age Owen was a very wealthy industrialist with factories of his own and a workforce of thousands.

But what makes Robert Owen remarkable is not his rise from rags to riches but his vision of a new society and his attempts to realize that vision. The Industrial Revolution was like a coin: on one side national prosperity and the emergence of an industrial middle class, on the other urban slums, exploitation and a new kind of poverty. This was the product of unrestrained capitalism and Owen realized, long before most of his contemporaries, that the new system was not only inhuman; it was also shortsighted. The industrial class, he wrote, by seeking cheap labour and high profits,

destroy the real wealth and strength of their own country by gradually undermining the

*The New Lanark mills were a model of pay standards and living conditions to other employers.*

the fact that Owen had early forsaken Christianity; religious leaders, therefore, automatically suspected his opinions. Powerful vested interests campaigned against him when he sought to obtain a Factory Act restricting the hours and raising the minimum age of child labour. The Act, passed in 1819, was far more limited in scope than Owen had hoped but it laid an important foundation for the reforming legislation which came later and greatly improved working conditions.

By this time Owen was a public figure. Thousands flocked to New Lanark to see his 'ideal' factory system and his principles had a considerable influence throughout Europe. He now spent more time propagating his social theories and less as a working industrialist. The years after 1815 were years of mechanization and trade recessions resulting in widespread unemployment and poverty. Owen put forward the, then, revolutionary idea that society should provide work and enable all men to maintain their human dignity. This would be achieved through a system of cooperative villages, virtually self-sufficient communities having their own farmland and workshops. He worked out his scheme in great detail, even designing the cottages and schools and village plans. Such an essay in state socialism was decades ahead of its time and was dismissed by the establishment as at best ridiculous and at worst dangerous. Owen sank money into two trial villages, one in Scotland, the other in the USA (called New Harmony). Both failed within a couple of years.

morals and physical vigour of its inhabitants, for the sole end of relieving other nations of their due share of this process of pin, needle, and thread making.

Owen urged his ideas in pamphlets and public speeches and he tried to persuade leading politicans and churchmen. His first opportunity to put them into practice came when he set up a partnership to acquire New Lanark mills in Scotland. As manager he improved the housing of the workforce, installed safer machinery, stopped the practice of employing pauper children and opened a shop to provide good quality food and necessaries almost at cost. In 1816 he opened at New Lanark the first infant school in Britain. Many of his innovations were resisted by the very people Owen wanted to help. They feared change and distrusted an employer who prevented their children from earning money in the mills and introduced strict rules regulating the consumption of alcohol. But it soon became clear that he was not like other capitalists. For example, when the mill was closed for four months due to lack of materials, Owen paid the workers out of his own pocket. Opposition from other quarters was less easy to disarm. The memory of the French Revolution was still strong in many people's minds and the establishment feared radical concessions to the lower classes. Added to this was

But no setback halted the onward rush of Owen's thinking. He saw society as moving towards a more even distribution of wealth. He founded cooperative societies. He taught that labour, not capital, is the source of wealth. He helped to form what may be called the first modern trades union, the Grand National Consolidated Trades Union. Like most of Owen's schemes it had a short life but, also like much of his work, there was something prophetic about it. As the years passed, his beliefs – political, social and religious – became more extreme. Whatever he believed he held to with total conviction and propagated with total dedication. He has been called 'one of those intolerable bores who is the salt of the earth'. As a modern commentator has said:

he could never argue a case – he could only see visions and dream dreams. And he gradually lost that firm grasp of the world of fact which had made him the greatest practical social innovator of his day. He gained instead the power of prophecy, which made him the father of Socialism and of many movements; but, in a real sense, all prophets are mad.

## 'The imagination which liveth forever'

When he was four he saw God looking in at his bedroom window. At the age of eight he beheld a tree filled with angels. He was once beaten by his mother for telling her he had seen the prophet Ezekiel. Most ordinary children have a vivid imagination which fades with the coming of adolescence. But William Blake was not an ordinary child and his vision never faded.

The surface facts of Blake's life are simple and unexceptional. He was born in 1757, the son of a London tradesman. Because of his obvious artistic talent he was apprenticed to an engraver and he earned his living in that profession to the end of his days. At the age of twenty-five he married and thereafter lived with his wife, Catherine, in a succession of London lodgings. When he was not busy making engravings for booksellers, he wrote poems – which no one wanted to publish – and painted pictures – which few people could be persuaded to buy. His work was sometimes accepted for exhibition by the Royal Academy and he was a member of the Watercolour Society, but, with the exception of a few enlightened friends and patrons, his work was largely misunderstood and unappreciated. Most of his life was spent in poverty, and after his death in August 1827 he was

placed in an unmarked grave. A generation passed before Britain began to realize what an original genius she had possessed in William Blake. The artist ahead of his time, living and dying in relative obscurity, only appreciated years after his death – it is not a unique story.

But Blake's imagination *is* something unique. In both his poetry and his painting he stood alone. He was a member of no school. He modelled himself on no master. He founded no new movement in art. Blake saw visions. They were as real a part of his life as food and drink. On them, and them alone, his creative genius fed. A friend recorded finding Blake very excited one evening. 'He told me he had seen a wonderful thing – the ghost of a flea! "And did you make a drawing of him?" I inquired. "No, indeed," said he. "I wish I had, but I shall if he appears again!" He looked earnestly into a corner of the room, and then said:

Then the Lord answered Job out of the Whirlwind

"Here he is – reach me my things – I shall keep my eye on him. There he comes! his eager tongue whisking out of his mouth, a cup in his hand to hold blood, and covered with a scaly skin of gold and green." As he described him so he drew him.' Sometimes Blake and his friends would hold what amounted almost to séances. They would call up the shades of the famous dead. These spirits would manifest themselves to Blake and he would draw them. This activity was well known in the neighbourhood. An elderly lady recalled having been introduced to the artist when he was an old man and she a child. Afterwards she asked her father who it was that she had just met. 'He is a strange man,' was the reply. 'He thinks he sees spirits.'

It is not surprising that critics and fellow artists failed to appreciate the work of such an unconventional genius. One of them described an exhibition of Blake's watercolours as the work of 'an unfortunate lunatic, whose personal inoffensiveness secures him from confinement . . . a farrago of nonsense, unintelligibleness and egregious vanity, the wild effusions of a distempered brain'. Blake could not help being hurt by such attacks but his total belief in his visions and his talent insulated him against harsh criticism.

> If a man is a master of his profession, he cannot be ignorant that he is so; and if he is not employed by those who pretend to encourage art, he will employ himself, and laugh in secret at the pretences of the ignorant.

Those who knew Blake well were often as puzzled as strangers by the products of his pen and brush but they knew how amazingly and instinctively perceptive he was. As a young man, first introduced to the great masters, he had a passion for the works of Raphael, Michelangelo and Dürer at a time when those artists were largely ignored in favour of more fashionable painters (long since vanished into obscurity). Once, when introduced to a celebrated engraver, he shrank from him and confided to his father, 'I do not like the man's face: it looks as if he will live to be hanged.' Twelve years later the engraver did, indeed, go to the gallows for forging a cheque.

Blake's prophetic vision was all-embracing. Human conduct, politics, religion, morality, the spiritual spheres, the end of the world – no subject was concealed from his searching imagination. He attacked the complacency of established religion, deplored the misuse of children as sweeps' boys and factory workers, exposed arranged marriages as manifestation of

> . . . self-love that envies all, a creeping skeleton
> With lamplike eyes watching around the frozen marriage bed.

*Blake's powerful representation of the Creator shows God measuring the earth with dividers.*

He supported the French Revolution and opposed every kind of slavery. Yet Blake rarely addressed himself to purely political questions. He saw causes of social disease and not merely their symptoms. For example, if injustice and strife existed it was because 'man has closed himself up, till he sees all things thro' narrow chinks of his cavern'. The human spirit, Blake insisted, must be free.

> Men are admitted into heaven, not because they have curbed and governed their passions or have no passions, but because they have cultivated their understandings . . . Those who are cast out are all those who, having no passions of their own because no intellect, have spent their lives in curbing and governing other people's by the various arts of poverty and cruelty of all kinds.

Blake lived and died a Christian inasmuch as he believed in Jesus Christ. But his religion could be confined by no church or system of dogma. His faith was complex and unconventional. It was also vivid. A friend describing Blake's last moments on earth wrote: '. . . his countenance became fair. His eyes brightened and he burst out into singing of the things he saw in heaven.'

# The vision of non-violence

The sight of protesters sitting down outside some nuclear establishment or government office waiting to be dragged away by the police is one with which we are now very familiar. The idea behind such demonstrations is that passive civil disobedience can in its way be just as powerful a force for change as violence. Whether or not the case is proven is a matter of opinion. What is not a matter of opinion is that one man turned this belief into a philosophy and by means of it freed a whole sub-continent of colonial rule. The deceptively frail-looking little man who achieved this was Mohandas Karamchand Gandhi.

He was born in 1869 in the Indian state of Kathiawar in North-West India. He was brought up in a respectable and religious Hindu home. He was intelligent and like most clever sons of wealthy Indians he was sent to England to finish his education. He studied law and in 1891 became a barrister. His life took no extraordinary turn until two years later when he began to practise in South Africa. For the first time he came up against severe racial segregation and prejudice. It came as a profound shock to him to realize that as a coloured person there were places he could not go, railway compartments in which he could not travel, and that he was expected to carry identification documents around on him which were to be produced whenever demanded by white people. He immediately saw his role as that of helping the small Indian community to overcome injustice, but this would have to be done by peaceful means. His religion forbade all types of violence. In 1894 he founded the first Indian political party in South Africa, the National Indian Congress. Ten years later he was publishing a newspaper called *Indian Opinion*, designed to air the voice of his community, provide a peaceful medium for the expression of grievance and to rally support. Gandhi urged his supporters to express themselves solely by peaceful means. If the need came to oppose authority that opposition should be shown through *Satyagraha*, 'force born of truth and love of non-violence'. The first major opportunity to put *Satyagraha* into effect came in 1906 when the Transvaal government attempted to force every Indian to have his fingerprints taken. Two thousand men and women followed Gandhi in a protest march and the new law was dropped. *Satyagraha* was only one expression of Gandhi's philosophy. He read widely and deeply in the religious and philosophical writings of many cultures and corresponded with some of the leading thinkers of his day, such as Leo Tolstoy. His opinions were constantly evolving but by now he had become convinced that the evils he had been fighting against were inherent in the colonial system, and that exploitation would only cease when each man was free to work his own land in the traditional ways passed down by his fathers. Since Gandhi recognized no divorce between theory and practice he gave up his work as a lawyer and led a life of simplicity and poverty.

He returned to India in 1915 and spent some time travelling the country, teaching his beliefs and learning the real plight of his people. He very soon became a national figure and won the respect of many colonial officials as well as the love of the down-trodden peoples he so often represented. In 1919 his policy of *Satyagraha* experienced a considerable set-back. Gandhi called upon all Indians to resist new anti-terrorist laws which had just been passed. He asked them to set aside one day to fasting and prayer and the suspension of all business. This angered the colonial administration and Gandhi was arrested. This in turn led to mob violence and was a contributory factor to the notorious Amritsar massacre a few days later when troops opened fire on a crowd of ten thousand people. Fearing that India was not yet ready for *Satyagraha* on a large scale Gandhi suspended his campaign. Within a year he took up his work again, criticizing the colonial system in speeches and newspaper articles. Imperialism, he claimed, exploited the subject peoples in the interests of the mother country, imposing alien economic, cultural and religious practices which in their turn created tension. As a practical example of what he meant Gandhi took to wearing a simple loin cloth. The growing of cotton and the making of cotton cloth were restricted in India because the British government wished to maintain India as a major export market for the textile mills of Lancashire. The people therefore had no alternative but to buy imported cloth at whatever price the manufacturers wished to charge. Gandhi's reply was simple. Let everyone, like himself, wear as few clothes as possible. In 1922 Gandhi was arrested and sent to prison on a charge of sedition. He was released in 1924 having served only two years of a six year sentence. He immediately founded the All India Spinners Association the aim of which was to set up centres all over India which would encourage peasants to buy spinning wheels and produce their own cloth. In 1930 he organized a massed demonstration against the Salt Tax. A repressive law forbade the people to collect natural salt and thus avoid paying tax. Gandhi set out on the well-publicized march of 240 miles from Ahmedabad to the coast with a group of suppor-

announced that he was going to perform a fast unto death. All over India people joined him. The fast lasted five days before the authorities were once again obliged to change their policy.

Gandhi was not simply a nationalist figure. His opposition to British colonialism was sincere but only because that system did violence to his concept of human dignity. He opposed equally firmly elements in Indian culture which he found alien to his beliefs. For example he championed the cause of the Untouchables, the lowest stratum of Indian society, who were traditionally regarded as outcasts. His vision was humanity and in serving humanity, he refused to allow himself to be cast in any narrowly religious mould. 'All my activities,' he said, 'run into one another; they all have their rise in my insatiable love of mankind . . . I do not know any religion apart from human activity. It provides a moral basis to all other activities.' He was always prepared to assert his complete independence of current thought. For example in 1934 he resigned his membership of the Congress because he believed that it was simply using his principles and beliefs for purely political ends. The divorce was of short duration, but it made its point.

During the Second World War the Congress tried to use the international crisis to extort concessions from the British government. When this failed there was considerable unrest throughout the country. Gandhi dissociated himself from this movement. The cause he championed was far more radical. He was against all war. Fresh campaigns of *Satyagraha* were aimed at securing free speech for himself and others who wished to denounce violence as a means of settling human disputes. This led to further spells in prison for him and many of his supporters. After the war the atmosphere throughout India was tense. Independence was within the nation's grasp but the problems were still acute, particularly the hostility between Hindus and Muslims. The solution of partition and the creation of Pakistan as a separate Muslim state was something which Gandhi firmly opposed. It led, as he had foreseen, to waves of refugees crossing the new border in both directions and to considerable persecution of minorities within both the new states. Gandhi staged repeated fasts as a protest against these atrocities but feelings were running too high and Gandhi was at last to fall a victim to them. On 30 January 1948 on his way to a prayer meeting he was shot down by a Hindu fanatic. If violence seemed to have triumphed it was only for a few days, for the spirit of Gandhi has lived on and force through non-violence is a principle which has been accepted throughout the world as one method of advancing causes which people believe in.

ters. On arrival, he picked up a lump of natural salt as a symbolical defiance of the law. As he had intended, the authorities had no alternative but to arrest him. They also had to arrest over a hundred thousand other people who had followed Gandhi's example. It was for them an impossible situation. After a few months they were obliged to back down and permit the making of salt for personal use.

Until now Gandhi had avoided the political arena and had watched with interest as the Indian Congress attempted to work with the colonial authorities to achieve a measure of constitutional reform. But by 1930 these efforts had ended in deadlock. Gandhi and most other members of the Congress were now convinced that nothing short of complete independence would allow Indians the freedom and dignity they craved. In 1931 Gandhi represented the Congress at abortive talks in London. It was not that the British government was unprepared to cede considerable autonomy to the Indians; the problem was much more complex than that. The formation of an independent government had to take into account the existence of religious minorities, principally the Muslims, and the social divisions implicit in India's caste system. Over these issues both sides could not agree and Gandhi was left with only the threat of *Satyagraha* to fall back on. In 1932, while Gandhi was serving another spell in prison, the government introduced new constitutional measures with which he did not agree. He

## The Guided One

In the last quarter of the nineteenth century the European colonial powers were pushing on relentlessly, irresistibly into the heart of Africa. Sometimes the invasion was carried forward by sheer military might. Sometimes control was more subtle; protectorates were established and white officials were sent ostensibly to govern tracts of bush and jungle in the names of local rulers. However it was accomplished, the Africans were powerless to resist. Any hostility ultimately brought them face to face with the rifle, the cannon and the Gatling gun. Only one nationalist leader stemmed the tide of colonial advance and reclaimed for a time a million square miles of the continent. His name was Mohammed Ahmed ibn al-Sayyid Abdullah, better known to history as the Mahdi, the Guided One.

Mohammed Ahmed was born in 1844, the son of a Nile boat-builder in the Northern Sudan. At that time the territory was controlled by Egypt, but during the course of the next thirty years the government at Cairo came increasingly under the control of its European advisers and financiers. On orders from London, the Sudanese slave trade was suppressed and European officials were sent to Khartoum, the Sudanese capital, and other important centres to ensure that moral and economic reform was carried out. The new regulations ruined many Sudanese merchants and chiefs, for the trade in slaves and ivory was the foundation of their economy. There was growing unrest particularly among the more extreme Muslim sects, who were convinced that the government in Cairo had sold out to Christian infidels and allowed the Islamic faith to be polluted.

Mohammed Ahmed, instead of following his father's practical craft, was called to the study of religion and practised extreme asceticism. His own beliefs became increasingly rigorous and severe. In 1861 he joined the strict Sammaniyya order but even this proved too lax for the young zealot. He went off by himself to an island on the White Nile and there lived the life of a hermit. As the years passed, his holiness of life and fiery preaching attracted a growing body of disciples, whom he instructed in the strictest tenets of Islam. Meanwhile he was seeking his own destiny and in 1880 this was revealed to him. He realized that he had been called to become the Mahdi.

The term 'mahdi' means the 'divinely guided one', roughly equivalent to the Jewish messiah. Although there was little support in the Koran for a belief in a future divine messenger, many Muslims had come to look forward to the appearance of a deliverer who would rule the earth with justice and equity. Many such mahdis had appeared in the course of Islamic history, but Mohammed Ahmed was destined to be the most famous and, in political terms at least, the one who achieved the most. He did not, however, conceive his mission in political terms. His was a religious reform movement, a movement to purify the faith besmirched by the Egyptians and their Sudanese lackeys. He appointed caliphs to rule the territories about to be conquered and made his headquarters at Jabal Qadir in the Nubian mountains. At the end of 1881 an Egyptian force was sent to capture him and to destroy his army. It was repulsed with great loss of life. The same fate befell a second expedition sent against him in May 1882. Now his army went on to the offensive. Sweeping down from the hills, it overwhelmed the garrison towns of Bara and El Obeid. Another Egyptian force was speedily sent south to check the Mahdist advance. This time the leadership was assigned to an able and experienced English general, Hicks

*'Punch' celebrates a minor British victory over the Mahdists.*

Pasha. The defeat of this formidable force enormously enhanced Mohammed Ahmed's prestige. Most of Central Sudan was now in his hands. There now followed the celebrated siege of Khartoum, bravely defended by its garrison under the leadership of General Gordon. On his arrival early in 1884, Gordon offered peace to the Mahdi and proposed to appoint him Sultan of Kordofan. It was an empty offer which did not interest Mohammed Ahmed. He already controlled all the territory in question and, in any case, was not his mission to conquer the whole of the Sudan and Egypt as well? He advised Gordon to withdraw, for his quarrel was not with the white man.

The Mahdist forces now closed relentlessly on Khartoum. They established control of the White Nile, thus cutting off Gordon's lines of communication with Egypt. The siege began in September 1884 and Khartoum fell on 26 January 1885. Legend insists that the Mahdi had given specific instructions that General Gordon was not to be harmed but this order was seemingly ignored. Gordon was killed in the general massacre which ensued. On 30 January the Mahdi entered Khartoum in triumph and led prayers in the mosque.

During the next few months most of the remaining Sudanese garrisons were overrun or voluntarily surrendered. Only the most southerly Equatorial province remained outside Mahdist control. Mohammed Ahmed moved on to Omdurman and established his capital there. He organized the government of his extensive dominion along the lines of fundamentalist Islam. The Mahdist state was a strictly controlled theocracy, but Mohammed Ahmed himself did not live to see the fruition of his labours. He died suddenly on 22 June 1885, probably of typhus. In the course of time a magnificent tomb with a gilded dome was raised over his remains.

For fourteen years neither the Egyptians nor their allies were bold enough to attempt the reconquest of the Sudan. Not until the battle of Omdurman on 2 September 1898 when thousands of Mahdists were killed in a fierce and bloody conflict did Mohammed Ahmed's politico-religious state come to an end. The nationalist revolt may have collapsed in failure but Mahdism itself lived on and the movement survives to the present day under the leadership of Mohammed Ahmed's descendants.

# The man for all men

Mention a man who was outstanding as a philosopher, theologian, musician, and pastor, a man who won a Nobel peace prize and who spent the greater part of his life as a missionary among the people of West Africa and there is only one person of whom you can be speaking – Albert Schweitzer. It is interesting and perhaps heartening to learn that this future professor, prolific author, holder of many degrees, began his academic life as a dunce. He was born in 1875 into the family of a Lutheran pastor in Alsace, which was at that time part of Germany. He was an introverted dreamer of a child who infuriated his teachers. They found him quite unresponsive. Even with subjects which he enjoyed, like history and music, he had to be driven to his books and his keyboard. He was a slow beginner at both reading and writing. When he went to his boarding secondary school things were no better. He came close to being expelled for laziness. But what young Albert's teachers diagnosed as stubbornness and stupidity was in fact the irritation of a massive intellect which found nothing in tedious textbooks worthy of its attention. It needed only a spark to fire that intellect. The spark appeared when Schweitzer was only fourteen, in the shape of a new teacher, a man whose personal dedication to learning and hard work provoked an immediate response in the boy. In every department of his studies Schweitzer now surprised everybody. The dunce was soon top of the class and within a year the boy who would never practise his scales was deputizing for the local organist in the parish church.

Now that he saw the point of studying, the new Schweitzer became almost as troublesome as the old. He pursued truth in all departments of life with an unremitting passion. He became critical and argumentative, unable to allow any statement to pass without question. His passion for logic drove him to further study and at the age of eighteen he went on to Strasbourg University to read theology and philosophy. The course was a broad one but characteristically Schweitzer ignored those parts of it which did not immediately appeal to him and devoted himself with passionate intensity to what appeared to be the most important issues. Foremost among these was the life of Jesus as recorded in the Gospels. Schweitzer realized that if that life was to be properly understood the written accounts had to be stripped of the accretions of Christian belief which had, intentionally or unintentionally, influenced the Gospel writers. He laboured hard and long at this problem and years later wrote his findings in a book called *The Quest of the Historical Jesus* which is still regarded as a landmark in bibical studies. But for this son of a devoted pastor the study of the central truths of the Christian faith could never be a remote academic affair. Schweitzer devoted part of his time as a student to work among the Strasbourg poor and through all his activities he was searching for God's purpose for his life. After a process of long and careful study he reached a conclusion, 'I would consider myself justified in living till I was thirty for science and art, in order to devote myself from that time forward to the direct service of humanity. Many a time already had I tried to settle what meaning lay hidden for me in the saying of Jesus "Whosoever would save his life shall lose it, and whosoever shall lose his life for my sake and the Gospel's shall save it!". Now the answer was found.'

Schweitzer studied in Berlin and Paris before returning to Strasbourg to be awarded doctorates in both Philosophy and Theology and to take up a lecturing career in the university. He had already written many books and treatises but despite all this activity he continued his work at the piano and organ with such dedication that he became one of the major interpretative musicians of his day. He wrote a book on the life and music of J. S. Bach which is still widely regarded as the definitive work on the subject. Not only did he write the book in French, he also personally translated it into German. An outstanding academic career clearly lay before him but Schweitzer stuck to his earlier resolve. In 1905 he began the study of medicine in order to qualify himself as a mission doctor so that he could devote the rest of his life to the service of mankind. During the next six years he qualified in Medicine and Surgery, continued writing on philosophy and music, married, and formulated his plans for his future work. His wife Hélène trained as a nurse and went with Albert in 1913 to a place called Lambaréné on the banks of the Ogowe River in French Equatorial Africa. There the couple built a hospital and financed it largely from money that Albert had earned by giving organ recitals. It had to be an independent establishment because the missionary societies working in the area were not happy about Albert Schweitzer's theological views.

Schweitzer had long since accustomed himself to do with very little sleep and now this discipline stood him in good stead. His daylight hours were divided between treating the endless queue of patients who came to him with every imaginable tropical disease, and building by hand his hospital with its living quarters and storerooms. After the sun had set he worked late into the night, reading, writing and bringing his mind to bear upon a host of philosophical and ethical problems. Schweitzer came to regard what he called 'reverence for life' as the only acceptable basis for human conduct. This was set out clearly in his much-acclaimed book *Civilization and Ethics* published in 1923. In writing this book Schweitzer was able to draw largely on his own suffering. Scarcely had his work at Lambaréné begun when the First World War broke out. As German subjects living in French territory, the Schweitzers were interned and eventually brought back to a prison camp in Provence. Hélène became ill and in 1923 when Albert returned to Africa, she was unable to accompany him. It was a considerable sacrifice for both of them.

By this time Schweitzer's life and work were already becoming known to a wider public. In 1921 he had shown that he could write not only for the learned academic but also for the man in the street. In that year appeared the book called *On*

*Lambaréné hospital on the banks of the Ogowe.*

*the Edge of the Primeval Forest* in which the author described his African adventures in a robust style full of humour. This book did more than anything else to attract financial support from all over the world. With this money Schweitzer rebuilt the hospital. While continuing his general medical work Schweitzer concentrated increasingly on leprosy, one of Africa's biggest and most sickening problems. His own study of the disease and the appearance of new drugs enabled Schweitzer to experience a growing measure of success in treating leprosy. By the time of Schweitzer's death the hospital at Lambaréné had grown enormously. It could accommodate 500 patients, served by a staff of sixty doctors, nurses and orderlies. Schweitzer was loved by the local people, widely respected throughout the world. Over the years he continued writing, he paid many visits to America and Europe to lecture, give recitals and make records. Most of his income went to the work at Lambaréné. It was all important to him, and he laboured and died there in 1965 at the age of ninety.

No one could deny Schweitzer's sacrifice and tireless labour, although much of his thinking was inimical to the post-Independence world. The cast of his thought was still colonial and there was something of the remote academic in the way he spoke of the Africans as savages and expressed impatience with their customs and behaviour. He never troubled to learn the local language and always regarded himself as working *for* the Africans rather than *with* them. If this was a shortcoming it was one that he was well aware of. 'I dare say we should have fewer difficulties with our savages if we could occasionally sit round the fire with them and show ourselves to them as men, and not merely as medicine men and custodians of law and order in the hospital. But there is no time for that . . . we are so overwhelmed with work that the humanity within us cannot come out properly . . . for the present we are condemned to the trying task of carrying on the struggle with sickness and pain, and to that everything else has to give way.'

# Death wish

Vision, by definition, is unattainable in the restricted world of conflicting human desires. To pursue vision to the utmost is, therefore, to court death or, at least, to be indifferent to life. Kimitake Hirakoa always faced this reality with calm detachment.

As a child, in the 1920s and 1930s, he was driven in on himself. Though his parents were quite capable of looking after him, he was appropriated by his imperious grandmother and compelled to live with her for twelve years. The memory of that cramped Tokyo room, 'perpetually closed and stifling with odours and sickness and old age', remained vivid in Hirakoa's memory ever afterwards. It is hardly surprising that he emerged into

*Mishima in full samurai warrior uniform at a Shield Society rally.*

adolescence puny, delicate and introvert. His only escape from his claustrophobic surroundings had been in reading and writing. He wrote poetry and stories, fantastic stories revealing a vivid imagination and mature mastery of language.

Other formative experiences awaited him. His father consistently tore up his poems, vowing that no son of his would be a scribbler. Soon Japan was at war and there were nobler deeds for young men to do than scrawl verses. Hirakoa was recognized by his teachers as a remarkable literary talent but the boy's father remained unimpressed. Hirakoa's contemporaries went off to fight and die for the emperor, but Hirakoa failed his medical. It distressed him as much as it disappointed his family. Obedient to parental wishes Hirakoa studied law. The war ended in defeat, a defeat Hirakoa felt keenly.

He went to work in a government office. It could never satisfy him. He was seething with unfulfilled desire – the urge to write, the equally strong urge to die for his country, and all this was suffused with a strong homosexuality. He poured his pent-up passion on to paper. All night and every night he wrote till dawn, assuming now the pseudonym by which posterity would know him, Yukio Mishima. In 1949 he published his first novel, *Confessions of a Mask*, in which he revealed his patriotism and his fascination with beautiful young men dying for what they believed in. It was a powerful work and it was widely acclaimed by critics and public alike. It was the first of forty novels and scores of plays, short stories and essays. They poured forth from his volcanic imagination and marked Mishima as one of the finest twentieth-century Japanese writers.

Yet always the creative upsurge was kept within rigid channels as far as his personal life was concerned. Not for Mishima the Bohemian existence in which art is all and excessive indulgence needs no justification. Total commitment to traditional Japanese culture, with its strong family ties, filial obedience, and intense patriotism, was part of his vision. In 1958, despite his homosexuality, he submitted to an arranged marriage. He lived happily with his young wife and had children by her. The couple entertained lavishly in a large house which Mishima had built for his entire family to share.

In the early 1960s two important things happened. The first was that Mishima's works began to be received with less than their usual enthusiasm. The second was that the author grew increasingly disillusioned with the drift of political events in Japan. These helped to clarify his vision and to turn his energies in a different direction. He had to prove himself, had to serve his country, had to show the Japanese people that their country could still be great. His books became more and more political, extolling right-wing policies and attitudes, but Mishima no longer confined himself to literary activity. The sickly youth had already been transformed into a healthy, muscular man by a rigorous regime of regular exercise. Now he gathered around him a group of similarly motivated young idealists and formed the Shield Society, a small corps of uniformed Japanese pledged to the protection of the emperor, the upholding of traditional values and the halting of westernization. The members of the Shield Society underwent military-style training and pledged total obedience to their superiors. When the forming of the organization was announced hundreds of young men clamoured to join but Mishima established a strict screening process to ensure that only those who shared his vision would be admitted. That vision was expressed succinctly in one of the Shield Society's manuals.

> Our fundamental values, as Japanese, are threatened. The Emperor is not being given his rightful place in Japan. We have waited in vain for the armed forces to rebel . . ., Let us restore Nippon to its true state and let us die.

In 1970 Mishima decided that the time had come to match action to words. The action was planned with a ritual precision. In November he completed the fourth and final part of his major work, *The Sea of Fertility*. On the morning of the 25th he posted it to his publishers. Shortly afterwards he met with four of his Shield Society colleagues and drove to the headquarters of the Eastern Army. They were admitted to the commandant's office. They immediately seized him

*Mishima, author, patriot and political agitator.*

*Mishima with members of his military brotherhood.*

and tied him up. Using him as a hostage they ordered all the soldiers to be gathered outside. When this had been done, Mishima stepped on to the balcony and addressed the troops. He urged them to join in a *coup d'état*, to overthrow the constitution and restore unrestricted power to the emperor. His words were greeted with jeers and catcalls. The political stratagem had failed.

But Mishima was not defeated. There was one way remaining to be true to himself, true to his vision, true to his country. He stepped back into the office, stripped to a loin cloth, knelt before the captive general and plunged a dagger into his own entrails. His second-in-command stood over him with a sword. At the instant that Mishima fell forward, he brought the sword down, severing head and body. Then he too, knelt beside his dead leader and also committed ritual suicide.

The forty-five-year-old Mishima, who had been denied the right to fight for his country in the 1940s, had already left instructions that he was to be buried in uniform, a sword in his hand, so that the world might see 'that I died not as a literary man but as a warrior'.

# A twentieth-century saint

On 8 January 1956 four American missionaries were speared to death by Auca Indians on the banks of the Curary, a tributary of the Amazon. They were men whose aim was to take the Christian faith into the jungle of Ecuador, one of the last areas of this globe to be penetrated by white civilization, and to a Stone Age people who had had virtually no contact with the outside world and who were known to be hostile to strangers. One of the massacred missionaries was the thirty-two-year-old Nate Saint. Less than three years later, his sister, Rachel, went back to the Aucas. She lived and worked among them for twenty years. Rachel Saint was a woman possessed of great courage – a courage stemming from her stubbon faith.

Rachel was born in 1914 into a family of eight children of which she was the only girl. Her parents were devout Christians and Rachel was brought up in a happy atmosphere of which Bible readings and daily prayers were integral parts. Religious faith became the cornerstone of her life. She never went through a period of doubt. Nor, apparently, did her brothers; the family produced three missionaries and a minister. The Saints were not at all well off but they did have some wealthy relatives and friends. One of the friends, a Mrs Parmalee, was a childless millionairess and she decided to make Rachel her heiress. The future seemed totally secure for the young girl who, at the age of seventeen, was taken on a luxurious European tour by her benefactress. But Rachel found she had no liking for the frivolous, sophisticated life and decided to politely decline Mrs Parmalee's offer of a ready-made fortune. It was while they were returning by ship to the USA that Rachel suddenly saw, with the clarity of a vision, what it was she must do with her life. She had a vivid picture of some brown-skinned people in a green jungle and knew that she would one day go as a missionary to those people.

She studied at missionary college and eventually was sent to Peru. Meanwhile, her youngest brother, Nate, had started work as a pilot helping missionaries in southern Ecuador. It was from him that Rachel heard about the Aucas. They were a people everyone steered clear of. They had raided camps set up by oil-prospectors and other white men on the edge of the forest. They lived deep in the jungle – unknown and unknowable. The more Rachel heard, the more she was convinced that these Aucas were the people of her vision.

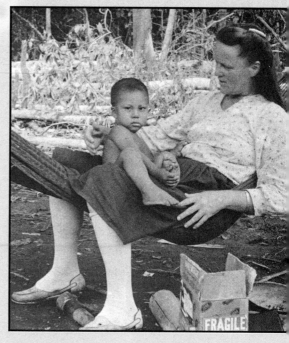

*The life expectancy of children among the Aucas in their remote forest settlements was low. Disease, malnutrition and violence all took their toll. Rachel Saint brought twentieth-century medicines and hygiene to this Stone Age people.*

Her approach to these remote and reputedly dangerous people was cautious, but immediate. She moved to a plantation on the jungle's edge called the Hacienda Ila. Among the workers were two young Auca women who had fled from the violence of their own people. Rachel got to know them, especially the one called Dayuma, and spent hours learning their language. But Nate Saint and some of his colleagues were less patient. They had a small aeroplane capable of landing on river sandbanks and jungle clearings and they resolved on a more direct approach. Rachel knew nothing of their flights over an Auca village and their gradual establishment of contact. Nate and his colleagues landed, met a group of Aucas, exchanged gifts and, as they thought, made friends. But the two sides never understood each other. They had no common language. The Indians were asking about the fate of their two runaway women. When the missionaries failed to reply they became convinced that the white men had killed Dayuma and her sister. So they killed the missionaries.

Rachel was, of course, heartbroken, but she was also angry. She knew how vital it was to break

*Rachel Saint and Dayuma, the first Auca convert, worked for twenty years among the forest hunters. Although the Aucas maintained their basic lifestyle, their traditional dwellings and foods, they could not escape some encroachments of civilization, such as metal cooking-pots and cotton dresses. Rachel worked for the abolition of violence, deadly feuds and promiscuity. Changing the Aucas' way of life while protecting them from the worst aspects of the modern world was painfully difficult.*

the language barrier as a prelude to effective missionary work. Not for one moment did she recoil in revulsion from her task of taking the Christian message to the people who had murdered her brother and her friends. She believed she was making progress in understanding the Auca. Dayuma had now become a Christian and longed to re-establish contact with her family. It was she who went back into the jungle first. She was reunited with her people and told them about the white folk, and especially her friend Rachel Saint. The Auca villagers asked to meet 'Nimu' (the nearest word in their language to 'Saint') so Dayuma went to fetch her. In October 1958 Rachel made the long foot and canoe journey to the settlement, to find that the Auca had built a special hut for her to live in.

Then began the long process of building up trust and, for Rachel, the task of persuading these people to change their way of life. Many of their customs were alien to her – deadly feuds were the constant background of life, the sick were buried alive, sexual promiscuity was the norm. Trying to change their habits was fraught with danger. One day Rachel confronted a man who was about to kill his daughter. His son had just died and, according to Auca custom, it was not fitting for a mere girl to survive her brother. Rachel took his spear from him and would certainly have been killed herself if another Auca had not come to her aid. Ironically, her protector was the man who had murdered Nate Saint.

The next twenty years were years of persistent caring, teaching and arguing. Rachel Saint introduced improved hygiene, medicines, clothes, schools, Christianity and a 'better' way of life. She came to regard the jungle as her home and the Aucas came to regard her as their 'sister'. Those were years of frequent misunderstanding and tragedy, punctuated by occasional triumph. They were also a race against time. For the Aucas were a threatened people. Encouraged by the government of Ecuador, prospectors and settlers penetrated the jungle looking for oil, gold and farmland. There was no way that the Aucas could avoid being dragged into the white man's world. For twenty years a solitary American woman working among an ever-widening circle of the little brown-skinned hunters tried to make that transition easier.

# 'One who tried to be just to all parties'

In seven brief years Mary Kingsley made herself widely loved and respected in two continents and shared with millions her vision of a common humanity from which racial intolerance was banished, a vision the world is still reaching for more than eighty years after her death.

There was nothing at all during the first thirty years of Miss Kingsley's all-too-brief life to suggest that she was in any way out of the ordinary. As the only daughter of parents of modest means she grew up a quiet, retiring child. She was not sent to school but, by shutting herself up in her father's library and devouring his books on travel and science, she gained an immense knowledge. The only tuition she ever received was a course in German. The family had little social life so that Mary was shy and awkward in company. Her constitution was not robust and she never ventured far from home. (Her first visit abroad was a week in Paris when she was twenty-six.) But her appetite for learning was voracious. Denied access to a wider world she studied avidly whatever came within her grasp. This included such unladylike subjects as chemistry, mechanics and electricity. The scope of her activities was widened when her parents moved to Cambridge in 1886. Now she found herself surrounded by libraries, and clever people and stimulating friends to talk with. Her self-confidence grew and she found that her opinions on many subjects were listened to with respect. Soon afterwards her mother fell ill and for four years Mary devoted herself to nursing her. In 1892 both her parents died. For the first time in her life Mary Kingsley was free; she had no responsibilites; she was her own mistress.

Many thirty-year-old Victorian ladies who had led sheltered lives would not have known what to do with themselves under these circumstances. Not so Miss Kingsley. She decided to travel – but not aimlessly, nor purely for pleasure. She wished to study the beliefs and customs of what were widely considered 'primitive' people.

In the 1890s the 'scramble for Africa' was in full spate. The major European powers were carving colonies out of virgin bush and jungle with no regard for ethnic or geographical boundaries. The light of Christian civilization was being shed upon the 'Dark Continent' – or, at least, that is how most Europeans regarded the political free-for-all currently in progress. Africa was drawing adventurous travellers like a giant magnet. Missionaries went to convert. Settlers and traders went to exploit the land and people. Administrators went to reconcile the rival claims of settlers, traders, missionaries and natives. When Mary Kingsley resolved to go to Africa she went with no preconceived ideas. She fitted into no category. She went with an open mind, to observe and learn.

Between 1893 and 1895 she made two journeys to West Africa, traditionally the white man's grave. She signed on as an agent with a coastal trading company and made the journeys pay for themselves by bartering cloth and tobacco for oil, rubber and ivory. She travelled through parts of the Congo, Cameroon and Nigeria, some of

*A photograph taken by Mary Kingsley showing a posed group of Gabon villagers. Wherever she went she observed local customs, took part in palavers and sampled the food.*

them regions where no white person had ever been. To the colonial authorities she might well have appeared as an unwanted responsibility, a vulnerable, unaccompanied woman. To the merchants she could have seemed an ignorant, interfering busybody. African chiefs might have regarded her as an innocent who could be easily robbed or cheated. The astonishing fact is that she seems to have earned everyone's respect. She shared the hardships of her companions, slept on the ground, ate native food, drove hard bargains – but always with a smile. She willingly clambered up mountains, waded up to her neck in swamps and bucketed down rivers in flimsy canoes. Above all, she was anxious to learn. She learned practical things, like how to stow cargo in coastal vessels and how to trap, skin and cook animals. But she also learned all she could about the peoples among whom she moved. Because she had not come to change their beliefs or ways she could show a genuine interest. With the aid of interpreters she talked with witch doctors, hunters, and the respected elders of villages where she stayed. She came to understand why the Africans worshipped their ancestors, why they believed that inanimate objects had spirits, why some of them practised polygamy and how their concept of land tenure was totally at variance with European ideas of property ownership.

As soon as she reached home she began to spread her knowledge. She wrote *Travels in West Africa*, a very popular book which related her experiences in a lively and humorous style. She lectured and wrote articles. Much of what she said was unpopular – but people paid attention. She debunked the myth of the noble missionary, explaining that often the trader had a better understanding of African peoples. She denounced the ignorance of colonial governors who did not understand local customs and the reasons for them. She defended many traditional ways as being more suitable for the Africans than imported European ideas. Above all she craved from those who made decisions in the halls of political and commercial power an understanding of both black and white in Africa. On a photograph she sent to a friend she wrote this inscription: 'The melancholy picture of one who tried to be just to all parties'.

Her activities in Britain kept her very busy but she longed to return to Africa. When the Boer War broke out she immediately sailed for Cape Town and offered her services to the authorities. She went to a hospital for Boer prisoners and it was while nursing them that she contracted enteric fever and died. She was thirty-seven. In accordance with her wishes she was buried at sea with full military honours.

# Geniuses

According to the dictionary a genius is someone who is endowed with 'native intellectual power of an exalted type', someone who possesses 'an extraordinary capacity of imaginative creation, original thought, invention, or discovery'. Genius has to do with perception and insight and not just ability. Therefore it is of a different order than talent. A man may be talented and may perfect his talent by hard work but there will always be a barrier between his highest endeavours and those works which are the product of genius. As the philosopher Arthur Koestler said, 'The principal mark of genius is not perfection but originality, the opening of new frontiers.' If this is true then it suggests that genius is something that cannot be measured. It is not possible surely to put a mark on an IQ scale and say that everybody whose intelligence places them above that mark is a genius. Geniuses are, without exception, very intelligent but that alone does not make them geniuses. There must also be the special gift, whether it be artistic perception, intuitive grasp of musical convention or an extraordinary facility for understanding and applying mathematical concepts. This selection of geniuses includes painters, poets, a philosopher, a musician, an inventor, a scientist, an actor and a jockey, and although more could be drawn from many other fields of human activity, the selection does throw light upon some of the questions most commonly asked about genius.

First of all there is the 'nature versus nurture' argument – to what extent is genius the product of heredity and to what extent is it the product of environment? There are two awkward facts which somehow have to be accommodated in any theory we may use to explain genius. One fact is that genius may occur at any time and in any place, quite unexpectedly. Jonathan Swift's father, whom he never knew, had no great literary gifts. Robert Dudley's father, with whom he had very little personal contact, was a courtier and certainly not an engineer or navigator. Swinburne did not spring from a long line of poets nor was Han van Meegeren's ancestry studded with brilliant painters. The other fact is that genius does run in some families, for example, the Bach family or the Huxleys (neither featured here) and certainly genius tends to flourish when there is a sympathetic understanding of it in the home. Thus the gifts of a Mozart, a Betty or an Archer were fostered, not to say deliberately exploited, by parents who understood the skills they were keenly fostering in their children. In the absence of genetic details we are forced to conclude, as far as our own representative selection is concerned, that some inherited their gifts and some did not, and that some owed their development, at least in part, to the encouragement they received as children.

This brings us to the problem of child prodigies. Are they 'for real' or are they, as often as not, the product of 'pushing' parents? Was William Betty really a brilliant actor or just a precocious child deliberately trained up by an ambitious father for purely mercenary ends? His career certainly petered out later on but was that because he lacked ability or because the public had grown tired of him? We do not know because gramophone records and video tape had not been invented in the eighteenth century. We cannot recreate the young Roscius's performances in order to judge them for ourselves. It is otherwise with Mozart. We know he was a musical genius of the highest order. His works exist to prove it. But suppose all Mozart's papers and scores had been destroyed, during or shortly after his lifetime, would he not now, like Betty, be reduced to a mere historical footnote, a child prodigy paraded before the courts of Europe by a Svengali-like father who created great interest for a time and then dwindled into obscurity? Particularly interesting is the case of Fred Archer because he was a man of considerable intelligence and almost no formal learning. But because his father was a man of the turf he taught his son at a very early age to ride. It was as a horseman that Archer's innate genius demonstrated itself. Dylan Thomas's poetic flair showed itself at a very early age. He was a youthful prodigy, if not exactly a child prodigy, but was it not because of his father's passion for literature that Dylan's life followed the course it did? If Mr Thomas's enthusiasm had been directed into building model railway engines or dabbling in oils, might Dylan Thomas now be remembered as a great engineer or a great painter?

Another question sometimes asked is whether the old adage 'genius will out' is really true. Of course there can be no answer to that question. Thomas Gray may have been right. There may be countless potentially great men who have lived and died in obscurity just as

Full many a flower is born to blush unseen,
And waste its sweetness on the desert air.

But we have no means of knowing whether or not that is true. On the other hand there are those who have struggled against great odds to reach the atmosphere in which their genius could breathe. Sir Robert Dudley left a country where his talents were not appreciated in order to become one of the greatest engineers and inventors of his day. Jonathan Swift fought against neglect and his own abrasive personality to find outlets for his genius. And poor Han van Meegeren dissatisfied with the poor recognition he had received adopted the painstaking craft of forgery to oblige the world to recognize in him a genius equal to Vermeer.

Must a genius be at odds with his age? No, of course not. The image of the artist starving in his garret is a romantic Victorian creation. He may be opening new frontiers but that does not mean that he has to leave his home territory behind for good and all. Most geniuses have kept at least one foot firmly in the hard world of commercial reality. Hume, Swift, Beardsley, Galileo, all worked for a living. They sought patrons and customers. They tried to sell their wares. As men of business they may not have been very successful but they did keep body and soul together. What does seem to be true is that genius often sets up inner tensions which success and recognition are powerless to resolve. The lives of Dylan Thomas and Fred Archer are vivid testimonies to this fact. An excess of natural ability does not make automatically for satisfaction and happiness any more than does an excess of wealth.

*Albert Einstein*

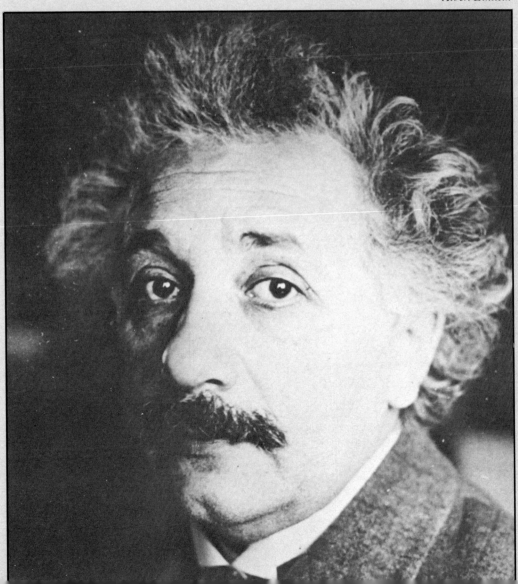

# The prodigy

*Leopold Mozart, who paraded his young prodigy around the courts of Europe, introduces him to Empress Maria Theresa.*

When we think of infant prodigies, it is the name of Mozart that probably comes most readily to our minds. The child who was composing music at the age of four and who was a brilliant virtuoso performer on the harpsichord by the time he was seven grew to be one of the greatest (and some would say *the* greatest) geniuses in the history of Western music. But what form did this genius take and how did it affect his life?

Wolfgang Amadeus Mozart was born in 1756, the youngest of seven children, five of whom died in infancy. Only he and his sister, Nannerl, survived. They were both extremely musical. This was hardly surprising for their father Leopold Mozart was a composer and teacher of repute who held an important post in the household of the Archbishop of Salzburg. Leopold was highly ambitious for his gifted son. He drove him to practise and to develop his talents as fully as possible. Even though the child loved making music this pressure necessarily imposed something of a strain upon him. In those days artists could only live by attracting wealthy patronage and there

were many gifted competitors for every musical post available in the courts of European kings, princes, nobles and church dignitaries. In 1762 Leopold began a tour of major European courts to show off his talented children. They played for the Austrian emperor in Vienna, several German princes, and went on to achieve considerable acclaim in Belgium, Paris, London and Amsterdam. Leopold also had another motive in mind, the completion of his children's musical education. Each nation had its own distinctive school of music and its own masters and father Mozart was anxious to expose Wolfgang and Nannerl to as many influences as possible. It was this that was uppermost in his mind in 1769 when he took his son on an Italian tour. This experience inevitably had a profound influence on the young man's musical development. Perhaps no single fact is more indicative of the growth of Mozart's genius than that he was able to absorb all these strands of musical tradition and weld them into a style which was solely his own.

As a child prodigy, Mozart had attracted a considerable amount of curiosity and appreciation. Promises had been offered to Leopold that when his son grew up there would be definite openings for him. However, when the time came for Mozart to seek a musical post and to begin his own career he found the situation very different. Leopold sought openings for his son in Salzburg and Vienna without success. They fared no better

*Mozart the accomplished performer – aged eight.*

in 1777–8 in Mannheim and Paris. In fact the Paris trip ended in tragedy, for Mozart's mother died on the way home. Although a permanent post eluded him, Mozart was making money from performances and from commissioned works and achieving considerable successes in both fields. He wrote works in almost every known musical form – solo keyboard, chamber orchestra, full orchestra – and in 1781 he produced his first full length opera, *Idomeneo*. It was these achievements that led to him being offered a post by the Archbishop of Salzburg. This professional appointment which Leopold had laboured hard to acquire for him did not last very long. There were faults on both sides, but Mozart's pride undoubtedly contributed to the row which led to his dismissal. Ever since he could remember Mozart had been told that he was a brilliant musician. The acclaim he had received in various European capitals reinforced this opinion. But in the Archbishop's court he was expected to knuckle under as a servant, one among many equals. It was a situation he could not accept. Mozart's arrogance

and boastfulness were to make it difficult for him to attract lasting friendships, and musical collaboration of any kind was always for him fraught with difficulties.

Mozart continued to earn his living as composer, performer and teacher. In 1782 he married Constanze Weber. Now, with marital responsibilities and a wife who loved spending money, Mozart had to work harder than ever. His output was prodigious and amazingly all of it was stamped with his genius. His quality was recognized by every discerning patron and by other leading musicians of the day. It was Haydn who described him as 'the greatest composer known to me either in person or by name, he has taste and, what is more, the most profound knowledge of composition'. But neither fame nor prolific output guaranteed financial stability. Artists in the eighteenth century were completely at the mercy of their patrons when it came to payment for works they had produced. Mozart probably fared no worse than others in this regard but he and Constanze managed to spend money faster than they earned it. In 1787 Mozart was given a minor post as a chamber musician in the emperor's court. He was now accepting eagerly any work that he could get. This included arranging the music of other composers and writing jingles for musical clocks. All the time, his own compositions were growing in intensity and maturity.

In 1787 his father died. There was now little domestic harmony in his own home. Mozart turned increasingly to the mysteries of freemasonry, both for consolation and to find some purpose in life, and freemasonry, with its exotic imagery, was one of the principal ingredients of his last great opera, *The Magic Flute*, which was first performed in 1791. By that time Mozart's health was deteriorating and at the end of the year he died. If he could have organized the more mundane aspects of life with a tenth part of the facility with which he mastered musical notation he might have lived a happier and richer man. But that is probably too much to expect of a genius.

*Beethoven owned this drawing of Mozart's funeral.*

## The 'Atheist'

'I have always considered him, both in his lifetime, and since his death, as approaching as nearly to the idea of a perfectly wise and virtuous man, as perhaps the nature of human frailty will admit.' That was the verdict of Adam Smith, the economist, on David Hume. It was not a view that went unchallenged. Dr Johnson would not stay in the same room as Hume. Such disagreements raged throughout his lifetime. In Paris he was lionized by high society, a fact which astonished the cynical Horace Walpole: 'It is incredible the homage they pay him . . . his French is almost as unintelligible as his English.' James Boswell regarded Hume as 'the greatest writer in Britain'. The Roman Catholic church banned all his books. He attracted a wide circle of devoted friends and admirers but his funeral was marred by the attentions of a hostile Edinburgh mob. The confusion was inevitable, for David Hume was the most independent British thinker of his age (on a par with the continental giants Voltaire, Rousseau and Kant), a man of soaring intellect whose mind embraced every sphere of human activity. You either agreed with Hume or disagreed; there was no middle ground.

David Hume was born in 1711, the son of a Scottish laird of modest means. His father died before he was three and his mother had some-thing of a struggle to bring up her two sons and one daughter. David was the brightest of the three. He was little addicted to the boisterous games and outdoor pursuits of other children. 'From my earliest infancy,' he once wrote, 'I found always a strong inclination to books and letters.' Before the age of twelve he was familiar with the great Greek and Latin authors and was well versed in both English and French literature. At twelve he went to Edinburgh University and afterwards was put to the study of the law. He persevered in it for a few years but his mind had already been fired by the great thinkers and writers of ancient and more recent times. The riches of speculative thought and masterly expression acted upon him like a drug. He could not escape their clutches. He longed to spend all his time absorbing truth and responding to it. After a few years he abandoned law and gave himself to the study of literature and philosophy, subjecting his mental muscles to rigorous training and discipline. He overdid it; in 1729 he suffered a nervous breakdown.

Indulging in a literary career in the eighteenth century was only possible if you were wealthy or could obtain wealthy patronage. Hume had to earn a living. He went to Bristol and took a post as clerk to a leading merchant. It was no good. Employer and employee fell out after a few months. Hume took to correcting his master's letters. The merchant did not appreciate this service. 'I have made £20,000 with my English and do not intend to have it corrected by a Scot,' he said. Hume travelled to Paris and stayed there three years as the guest of influential friends and patrons. He wrote his first major work there, *A Treatise of Human Nature*, a monumental subject for a man in his mid-twenties. Critics were not slow to point this out. They resented the arrogant and positive way in which Hume set himself against the prevailing worship of reason. Hume pointed out the shortcomings of logic and affirmed that opinions are formed much more by feeling and experience than by rational thought. On the other hand, traditional churchmen disliked what they considered Hume's tendency to atheism. In fact, the philosopher was anti-religion rather than anti-God. He objected, he said, 'to everything we commonly call religion, except the practice of morality and the assent of the understanding to the proposition that God exists'. Hume stated that because the deity is invisible and incomprehensible, worship, prayer and devotion were irrelevant. He opposed the dogmatism of the rational atheist as firmly as that of the churchman. However, he was branded as a non-believer and this lost him the chair of Moral Philosophy at Edinburgh in 1744 and the chair of Logic at the same university in 1751.

*David Hume, brought up at Ninewells in the parish of Chirnside near Berwick, the second son of Joseph Hume, who claimed descent from the baronial family of Hume. His researches and various employments took him to England, Europe and North America but it was always to Ninewells that he returned and it was here that he wrote some of his profoundest works.*

He spent the next few years writing whenever possible and sustaining himself with a variety of jobs. He was employed for a year as tutor-companion to the insane Marquis of Annandale, an unfortunate young man given to fits of violence and vomiting. He served as secretary to James Sinclair on various foreign embassies. In 1752 he was appointed keeper of the Advocates' Library in Edinburgh. At last he was able to live in a world of books and settle to serious writing. His six-volume *History of England*, which set new standards of objectivity and comprehensiveness, brought him instant fame and was soon translated into French and German. In this and other writings the breadth of his great intellect became apparent for the first time. He wrote informatively and clearly on politics, art, economics, religion, philosophy and ethics. His reputation paved the way for a triumphant three years in Paris where he was accepted in all the fashionable salons and admired for his wit and wisdom.

On his return he was offered a post as an under-secretary of state. It did not enthral him; 'I am now, from a philosopher, degenerated into a petty statesman,' he informed a friend. Hume had the intellectual's aloofness to all practical affairs. He retired to Edinburgh in 1769 and spent his remaining years writing and enjoying the company of friends. He died there in 1776. He was a controversial figure to the end. Posterity seems to have come to regard him as a cold intellectual, remote from the world of reality. That this was not the case is suggested by a story told about Mrs Adam, mother of the celebrated architect Robert Adam.

'I shall be glad to see any of your companions to dinner, but I hope you will never bring the Atheist here to disturb my peace,' she is reputed to have said to her son. Unperturbed, Robert, one day, found a way of smuggling his banned friend to the table under an assumed name. After the guests had departed, Mrs Adams commented, 'You bring very agreeable companions, but the large, jolly fellow who sat next me is the most agreeable of them all.' Robert enjoyed his moment of triumph, 'That was the atheist you were so much afraid of.' 'Well,' she replied, 'you may bring him here as much as you please, for he's the most innocent, agreeable, witty man I ever met with.'

# Napoleon's rival

In 1805 Britain was in the grip of 'Bettymania'. The threat of invasion by Napoleon's forces was real. Before the year was out stupendous battles had been fought at Austerlitz and Trafalgar. Yet the talk in taverns, coffee houses and smart salons was all about William Betty, the 'Young Roscius', a boy of fourteen. Charles James Fox, the Whig leader, was only one of the members of fashionable society who was caught up in the latest craze. 'Everybody here is mad about this boy actor,' he wrote to a friend. 'We go to town tomorrow to see him, and from what I have heard, I own I shall be disappointed if he is not a prodigy.'

A prodigy William Betty certainly was. He was born in the Irish town of Lisburn and grew up a pretty and precocious child. He enjoyed the admiration of doting adults and was always ready to perform 'party pieces' for his elders. There was nothing remarkable about that. What was remarkable and was commented on by many who saw him perform was a dramatic talent, quite amazing in one so young. It was not only that he could easily commit to memory lines of dialogue and lengthy speeches, nor that he had a natural feel for the rhythm of language. What most stirred his audiences – and frequently moved them to tears – was the emotional intensity he conveyed through word and action. His father, who was both a shrewd businessman and a spendthrift, soon realized that nature had blessed him with a gold mine. He hired William Hough, a man of considerable stage experience, to act as the boy's tutor and promoter. Together the two men planned to take British high society by storm.

The adventure began in Belfast in August 1803 with Master Betty appearing, not in a juvenile role, but as the tragic hero Osman in the popular play *Zara*. Dublin, Waterford and Cork were the next venues, where he played to packed houses in a variety of parts, including Romeo and Hamlet – demanding roles, indeed, for a twelve-year-old boy! The travelling circus now crossed the sea and Betty repeated his success in Glasgow and Edinburgh. A careful PR campaign paved the way. Hough sent 'rave' notices from the local press to theatre managers throughout Britain. He wrote letters to stage friends and acquaintants, foremost among them Richard Brinsley Sheridan. The result was that young Betty's fame went before him. Performances were sold out in advance to people eager to see the 'Young Roscius' (Roscius was a famous Roman tragic actor), the 'greatest actor since Garrick'. From Scotland Betty's southward progress became a triumph. Almost everyone who saw him was moved by his performance. The *Times* likened him to that other prodigy, Mozart. Tributes to him were written in the press and popular broadsheets.

By the time Betty reached London the town

*Opie's portrait of Betty in a dramatic role.*

was agog to see him, on or off stage. Crowds thronged Covent Garden from early morning waiting for the doors to open, and when they did open pandemonium broke loose as people rushed for the better seats. The Duchess of Devonshire wrote to describe to her son the transformation that had come over the city:

> As for politics, though every day an account of Bonaparte's coronation and Russia's decision is expected, nothing is hardly seen or talked of but this young Roscius. I saw him his first night . . . I saw him last night as Norval in *Douglas*. He is but thirteen and yet I never saw anything to compare to him. His is the inspiration of genius, with the correctness of taste belonging to experience and study alone, feeling far beyond his years, and a knowledge of the stage equal to any performer, and far more graceful. In short, he has changed the life of London. People dine at four, go to the play, and think nothing but the play.

Another critic affirmed of Betty that, 'when he became warmed into action, his soul expanded, and his fame seemed to rise to a gigantic height'. Theatregoers both male and female wept openly at his performances. His first appearance on stage brought an explosion of applause and the action of the play was frequently interrupted by clapping and shouts of approval.

The boy and his entourage were frequently the guests at dinner parties arranged in their honour. Everyone wanted to entertain them. They were presented to the King and Queen. The Prince of Wales received them and presented Master Betty with a carriage and four. Charles James Fox played host to the family over Easter. The Duke of Clarence spent time with them. Fashionable artists vied with each other to paint the boy's portrait. As for the leading actors and actresses of the day whose stars were quite eclipsed by the new planet, they either joined in the chorus of adulation or waited with sullen resentment the further turn of fortune's wheel. The rival managements of Covent Garden and Drury Lane, London's leading theatres, almost came to blows in their endeavours to sign up the Young Roscius. Eventually they agreed to divide the boy's appearances between the two stages. The playwright, Sheridan, wanted to take Betty under his wing, but the boy's father was more interested in exploiting to the full his son's present than in making provision for his future.

That fact goes some way towards explaining William Betty's subsequent fate. While the public still loved their golden boy they were turning against his father, who appeared to be (and indeed was) shamefully exploiting his son's talents. Betty senior fell out with and dismissed William Hough who immediately gave the press a jaundiced account of the prodigy cottage industry. At the same time Master Betty's success had spawned a legion of imitators. Little boys and girls were being paraded on stages up and down the land. Suddenly the whole Roscius business began to look a little ridiculous. Fashionable society felt embarrassed and abandoned Bettymania as abruptly as it had taken it up. The boy actor gave his last performance in July 1808.

Four years later he returned to the stage in an attempt to take up a legitimate adult career. Objective critics still admired his obvious talent but others, led by the *Times* newspaper, pursued him with a quite unprecedented venom. It was as though they felt they had made fools of themselves once and were determined not to do so again. The young man's frustration must have been acute and, on one occasion, drove him to attempt suicide. However, he refused to give up and made sporadic appearances until 1824, in which year he formally retired from the stage. Throughout the remainder of a long life (he died in 1874) he lived comfortably on the fortune he had amassed as a child actor but he who had known fame and adulation such as few men have known found it hard to accept oblivion. He designed for himself and his family an elaborate marble tomb at Highgate, perhaps in the hope that future generations of fans would have somewhere to lay their tributes.

## The un-Victorian

Where does genius come from? Perhaps, one day, the geneticists will be able to tell us. For the moment it remains a mystery why, from time to time, a totally undistinguished family throws up someone so different, of such heightened perception and singular gifts that only the word 'genius' will serve to describe him. Algernon Swinburne's ancestors were aristocrats but scarcely one of them had ever done a noble deed or thought a noble thought which might have justified their inherited prestige. He was born in the year Victoria came to the throne and was brought up by a doting mother and sister, his father having died. He was sensitive and shy, with a large head, a mass of vivid, red hair and incredibly striking features. He loved solitary pastimes – climbing, riding, swimming – and, above all, reading. By the time he reached adolescence, he knew by heart many passages from the great poets and playwrights, and he had already begun to write his own verses.

This delicate aesthete was, in due course, packed off to Eton to fend for himself in the violent microcosm of a Victorian public school. No one thought to enquire whether or not it would be good for him. It was simply the thing for sons of the nobility to be sent to boarding schools, to have the namby-pambyism knocked out of them, and to fit them for their role as rulers of men. In the society of boys the odd one out is either persecuted or pedestalized. Swinburne came into the latter category. So completely did he live in his own world that he was impervious to the less pleasant aspects of the system. He endured the beatings and the bullying and won great admiration from many of his colleagues for his intellectual brilliance. He took prizes in French and Italian and his companions came to accept such quirks of behaviour as his standing on his bed proclaiming heroic verse.

At Oxford he rebelled against his upbringing and, indeed, against the basic tenets of Victorian society. He threw off his high church Anglicanism in favour of agnosticism. Later he bitterly complained about the influence of Christianity:

Thou has conquered, O pale Galilean; the
 world has grown grey from thy breath;
We have drunken of things Lethean, and fed on
 the fullness of death.

Even more shattering for his family was Swinburne's rejection of monarchic government in favour of republicanism.

Calling a crowned man royal
That was no more than a king.

His outrageous views and brilliant conversation drew a crowd of undergraduate admirers and his obvious intellectual gifts were recognized by the professors. But his highly nervous disposition made it necessary to withdraw at times into rural seclusion. Sometimes he stayed in a country vicarage where his host and hostess were used to his odd behaviour, although it still caused them some headaches. Once the vicar came out of his empty church on a Sunday morning to see what had become of his parishioners. He found them on the vicarage lawn where Swinburne, clad in long red dressing-gown, was holding court. On another occasion the poet asked his friends what they thought of some of his latest verses. They were mildly critical. Swinburne's reaction was to scream at the top of his voice, run to his room, and burn the offending manuscript.

He moved to London in 1860 and embarked upon what was to be, probably, the finest phase of his life as a poet. Much of his inspiration was drawn from his involvement with Dante Gabriel Rossetti and other members of the Pre-Raphaelite Brotherhood. Swimburne shared their ideals and their interest in the antique. His poetry found an equivalent in words for their sumptuous colours, seductive lines and romantic subjects.

*Rossetti depicted Swinburne as a medieval lover in this frontispiece to an anthology.*

Heart handfast in heart as they stood, 'Look
   thither,'
Did he whisper? 'look forth from the flowers to
   the sea;
For the foam-flowers endure when the rose-
   blossoms wither
And men that love lightly may die – but we?'
And the same wind sang and the same waves
   whitened,
And for ever the garden's last petals were shed,
In the lips that had whispered, the eyes that had
   lightened,
Love was dead.

In his work he broke free entirely from earlier
conventions. He gave lyric poetry a new direction
and inspired a generation of poets to greater freedom. He did this both by his writing and his conduct. For Swinburne's output of poetry, essays
and plays was as prodigious and striking as his
personal life was bizarre. He was asexual.
Indeed, he was incapable of even very close
friendships. Most people who got to know him
very well discovered that, when intimacy reached
a certain point, they were suddenly cold-
shouldered. Swinburne found his substitute for
close physical contact in flagellation and other
sado-masochistic exercises which he indulged in
certain houses of pleasure where such esoteric
tastes were catered for – at a price. Even in these

*Swinburne sits at an upper window of The Pines,
Putney, where he lived protected from himself and his
reputation by friends.*

liberated times such behaviour would be regarded
as pretty sick. To the Victorians it was scandalous, and Swinburne's friends sought to rescue
him. It was Theodore Watts-Dunton, his lawyer,
who effected the cure. He took Swinburne to live
with him in his house, The Pines at Putney. There
he closely supervised the poet's timetable, regu-
lated the number of visitors he received and generally took off Swinburne as much pressure as
possible. Almost certainly Watts-Dunton pre-
served Swinburne's sanity but he did little for the
quality of his poetry which lost much of its original fire. In 1892 he was suggested for the post of
poet laureate but Gladstone found his political
views – and probably his personal life – unaccept-
able. It was as well. It would have been something
of a betrayal for the outrageous rebel to have
made his peace at the last with a social order he
found so alien. He was able to meet death unrepentant and happy.

From too much love of living
   From hope and fear set free,
We thank with brief thanksgiving
   Whatever gods may be
That no man lives forever,
That dead men rise up never;
That even the weariest river
   Winds somewhere safe to sea.

## 'A tormented, exaggerated man'

Nothing illustrates more clearly the isolation of the genius than the life of Dylan Thomas. It is an isolation in part inevitable and in part self-willed. Thomas himself explained it well in a letter to a friend written in 1938:

I have been in London, in penury, and in doubt: in London, because money lives and breeds there; in penury, because it doesn't; and in doubt as to whether I should continue as an outlaw or take my fate for a walk in the straight and bowler-treed paths. The conceit of outlaws is a wonderful thing; they think they can join the ranks of regularly-conducted society whenever they like. You hear young artists talk glibly about, 'God, I've a good mind to chuck this perilous, unsatisfactory, moneyless business of art and go into the City and make money.' But who wants them in the City? If you are a money-and-success-maker, you make it whatever you do. And young artists are always annoyed and indignant if they hear a City-man say, 'God, I've a good mind to chuck this safe, monotonous business of money-making and go into the wilderness and make poems.'

The pungent irony is that Thomas's isolation was in no sense alleviated by financial success. Recognition and fame came to him as to few other living poets. His work, though never easy to understand, struck a common chord for many people. The lilting rhythms of his verse were captivating. He was greatly in demand on both sides of the Atlantic for poetry readings and lectures. He was a frequent broadcaster. He did what few poets manage to do. He made money from his art. He could have made a great deal more. He found a degree of happiness and contentment in married life and yet he lived and died alone.

Dylan Thomas was born in 1914 in a semi-detached house in Swansea, the son of a disappointed schoolmaster and an over-protective mother. It was by his father that Thomas's first love of poetry was kindled. The schoolmaster had a passion for literature which he read in a sonorous Welsh tenor designed to impress his young charges. Dylan later described it: 'His reading aloud of Shakespeare seemed to me, and to nearly every other boy in the school, very grand indeed . . . it was his reading that made them, for the first time, see that there *was*, after all, *something* in Shakespeare and all this poetry.' Yet Dylan's feel for the English language, his ability to mould words like plasticine, was something essentially inborn. When he left school Dylan worked briefly on a Swansea evening paper. But all he wanted to do was to *be* a poet. He dressed as he thought poets dressed in vivid green shirts and a thick knotted tie. He drank heavily, partly no doubt because this too seemed to be part of the poetic image. His wild, unruly nature, his determination to write whatever he felt was appropriate or true, meant inevitably that his days as a reporter were numbered. He was given the sack in 1933 and lived for the remainder of his life as a freelance writer and poet.

He worked hard, writing poems, sending them in to magazines and to the BBC. He paid visits to London and began to meet members of the literary intelligentsia. He had a love affair with Pamela Hansford Johnson (who later married C. P. Snow). Many women were drawn to Dylan Thomas. There was about him an intensity, a wildness and a romantic impetuosity that was very attractive. There was also a great deal of exaggerated self-advertisement. For example, when he suffered from a bad asthmatic cough, made worse by heavy smoking, it became for him

*In this house overlooking the estuary at Laugharne, Dylan Thomas wrote some of his best work between 1949 and 1953.*

consumption. He wrote to tell Pamela that doctors had given him only four years to live. It was all part of a craving to be the ideal poet, a being who conformed to Thomas's romantic vision of what a poet really was. He conceived a profound contempt for his body – 'That creature whose sad-sack body encircles me and whose fat head wakes up on my pillow every morning' – because it did not conform to that image.

Soon he moved to London and earned a living reviewing books and writing magazine articles. He became a well-known figure around the West End pubs. When he tired of one bar he would move on to another, usually taking a considerable following with him. As the night wore on he would become maudlin and morose. The session would end with him being put to bed in his own flat or somebody else's by understanding friends. Alcohol rapidly took over Dylan Thomas's life and it played havoc with his work.

Marriage had a settling effect upon him. This came about in 1936 when he met a girl called Caitlin. They were genuinely happy and soon started a family but life was hard. For several years they had no settled home and Thomas's income was always sporadic, sometimes non-existent. During the Second World War Thomas was employed by the Ministry of Information writing the scripts for documentary films but there were still wild flashes of the old, irresponsible, pub-crawling life. Dylan's friends felt that if only he could settle down in the right atmosphere he would be able to concentrate on his poetry. In 1949 a wealthy patron bought the Thomases a house on the Welsh coast at Laugharne. It was here, overlooking the estuary, with his wife and children around him,

*Dylan, the pub wit and entertainer.*

that Dylan experienced the only moments of real contentment he was ever to know. In 1949 he was also invited to America for the first of a series of lecture and poetry-reading tours of literary clubs and university campuses. There he made money, he spoke to rapt audiences, he was lionized by the intelligentsia of the New World, and alcohol reasserted its dominion. Frequently he would arrive drunk for a poetry recital, but when he began reading the poems he was like a man transformed or as some said 'like an angel'. He declaimed in those ringing Welsh tones still familiar to us from the recordings he left behind, and his audience would fall silent, entranced. This was poetry. This was a poet. This was poetry as it should be read.

From now until the end there were two distinct parts to Dylan's life. There was the public Dylan, travelling, drinking, reciting, fornicating, clowning and frequently ill. And then there was the private Dylan, secure and cared for in the community at Laugharne where nobody was impressed by the reputation of the celebrity and where he had no need to act a part. These twin personalities could not be kept separate. Dylan's drinking and women placed strains upon his marriage towards the end. The last months of Dylan Thomas's life saw him reach new heights of fame and public recognition, with the publication of his collected poems and the broadcasting of his radio play *Under Milk Wood*. The end was inevitable, only its location was the subject of chance. By 1953 his constitution was completely undermined. Gout, a bronchial cough, gastric disorders, alcohol poisoning – they all competed for the privilege of carrying Dylan Thomas to the grave. He died in New York on 9 November 1953.

*Dylan and Caitlin – a rare moment of peace.*

# England's lost genius

The blood of two great English families – the Howards and the Dudleys – flowed in his veins. He was the most brilliant son of either house and one of the most gifted Englishmen of his time. Yet he left his native land in disgust and spent most of his life abroad where his varied talents were placed at the service of a foreign prince. Such was the life of Sir Robert Dudley, courtier, mathematician, explorer, engineer, author, physician and sportsman.

Robert grew up at the court of Elizabeth I during the stirring days when great captains like Drake, Hawkins and Cavendish were making the name of England one to be respected and feared on all the oceans of the world. He was twelve when the great fleet led by his uncle, Lord Howard of Effingham, drove the Spanish Armada to its destruction in the northern seas and his father, the Earl of Leicester, commanded the land forces ready to confront any Spaniard who dared set foot on English soil. It was natural that the lad would

be determined to copy such exploits. He had the intellectual gifts to match his enthusiasm. He was a natural mathematician and was possessed by the scientist's burning curiosity. He applied his mind to the problems of navigation and shipbuilding.

At the age of nineteen he turned theory into practice. He had inherited considerable wealth on the death of his father and his uncle, the Earl of Warwick. Now he invested much of it in a voyage to the Orinoco basin in search of El Dorado. Instead of buying or chartering ships, he designed and supervised the building of his own. In December 1594 he proudly led his little fleet out of harbour and set sail for the Spanish Main. It was an unusual expedition not only because of the youth of the commander but also because of his pioneering scholarship. It was the first to find its way across the Atlantic by means of great circle navigation – a new technique based on trigonometrical calculations. It was one of the first to compute speed with a log and line. Dudley also tried out navigational instruments which he had invented. He did not find El Dorado – no one ever did – but the taking of some Spanish prizes more than defrayed the costs of the voyage.

His reputation as a prodigy in maritime affairs was now acknowledged and, in 1596, he commanded the great warship *Nonpareil* in the ambitious and successful siege of Cadiz. For his services he was knighted. Soon after his return he married and spent some time at his great country house, Kenilworth Castle. But even in the peaceful seclusion of his Warwickshire estates his active mind could not relax. He wrote a treatise on navigation and an account of his voyage to the Caribbean. He conducted chemical experiments and perfected a concoction known later as the Earl of Warwick's Powder which apparently relieved or cured many conditions. Even when out shooting in Kenilworth's coverts and chases he was busy inventing new and better methods. It was Dudley who first trained gun dogs to retrieve fallen game.

Wealthy, successful and popular as Dudley was, there was yet a cloud over his life. He was illegitimate, or so it was widely believed. This meant that the earldoms of Leicester and Warwick had passed to his cousins, the Sidneys. Over the years, however, he gathered evidence from servants and friends of his parents which supported the view that Leicester and Lady Sheffield had, in fact, gone through a valid marriage ceremony. In 1604 he decided to try this evidence in the ecclesiastical courts. All seemed to be going well when royal officers arrived to stop proceedings and remove the case to the King's law court in London. The new king was James I and the Sidneys had won his support during the early days

*When Dudley left England he forsook Kenilworth Castle, one of the finest houses in the land.*

of the reign. When the case was recommenced there was no pretence at justice. The main issue was never tried. Dudley's witnesses were pronounced fraudulent and heavily fined. All the evidence he had collected was confiscated and held during his majesty's pleasure.

The public humiliation, the ingratitude and the unfairness were more than Sir Robert could stand. In his anger he turned his back on his whole former life and he did so with a defiant gesture which shocked the nation. Within days he left the country with a small personal entourage. It included a slim young page. The party had crossed the Channel before it was realized that the 'page' was Elizabeth Southwell, a beautiful nineteen-year-old woman and one of the queen's maids of honour. Dudley had burned his boats dramatically and finally. He never saw wife, children or homeland again.

After some wanderings he and Elizabeth settled in Florence where they enjoyed the protection and patronage of Ferdinand I, Grand Duke of Tuscany. The court of the Medici was one of the most cultured in Europe. It was a delight to Dudley to be able to debate and study with leading artists and scholars, including the great Galileo. Thus stimulated, and settled at last in a congenial atmosphere, his genius had full rein. He now poured forth a series of brilliant schemes which enhanced the reputation of Tuscany and her rulers. He designed new ships for the ducal navy, of which the greatest, the *San Giovanni Battista*, had a long, distinguished record and was acknowledged one of the finest vessels afloat. He reorganized the shipyards, enticing to Florence some of the finest English craftsmen. He planned new voyages of exploration, including

another expedition to the Orinoco. It was thanks to Dudley that the port of Livorno came into existence. The plans which he drew up and whose execution he supervised created a wide, deep harbour out of a heavily silted bay. His next major engineering project was the draining of the marshes around Pisa which became a highly fertile plain. He brought a fresh water supply to Pisa and Livorno by means of a system of aqueducts and canals. Dudley's fertile mind also turned to commercial affairs. He suggested that Livorno should be liberated from customs duties and be made a free port. The Grand Duke implemented this suggestion. As a result trade flowed into the new haven from all over the Mediterranean. Sir Robert also patented an invention for improving the manufacture of silk.

Dudley continued to experiment with navigational instruments and to write books. He produced a medical treatise called *Catholicon* and even wrote a political tract for James I advising him how to handle his troublesome parliament. Yet his greatest work was a monumental six-part study of every aspect of maritime affairs. *Dell 'Arcano del Mare* contained the finest and most beautifully executed maps and charts, the latest mathematical data for the calculation of latitude and longitude and detailed studies of shipbuilding, harbour construction, military and naval discipline.

Robert Dudley, who died in 1649, and whose titles Duke of Northumberland and Earl of Warwick were recognized by the Holy Roman Emperor and therefore were valid throughout most of Europe, must be regarded as one of the greatest Englishmen ever exiled from his native land.

# Vermeer's equal?

*A forged seventeenth-century Dutch interior in the style of Pieter de Hooch.*

*Experts found it virtually impossible to distinguish between Van Meegeren's work and genuine de Hooch paintings.*

Who decides whether a painting is or is not a great work of art? The answer is, in reality, a comparatively small coterie of dealers, academics and critics who have the reputation of being experts in that particular field. There is no appeal beyond this informal jury. There is no clearly defined standard. Genius remains a matter of opinion. Thus, the little band of experts, the high priests of public opinion, wield considerable power. They can make or destroy an artist's reputation; elevate him to fame and fortune or consign him to the garret, leaving it to posterity to rescue his name – posthumously. It was this fact which stuck in Han van Meegeren's throat, a fact he longed to expose.

He had always been at odds with the establishment. His childhood had been spent at Deventer during the last decade of the nineteenth century, in the strict, puritanical home of his schoolmaster father. It was a regime he had rebelled against and this had led him to oppose all authority. Once, when he was about twelve – a pale-faced, sickly boy – he noticed as he was passing the local police station that the key was in the door. With scarcely a second thought, he locked the door and threw away the key. Minutes later, he stood among the jeering crowd which watched the red-faced custodians of law clambering out of a window and breaking down their own door. His only regret

was that he could not add to their embarrassment by standing forward and saying 'I did it'. It was about this time that he discovered his artistic talent. Far from pleasing his father, young Henricus' ability annoyed him. He tore up the boy's drawings and ordered him to abandon such 'frivolities'.

Father van Meegeren decided that his elder son should become a priest and young Henricus an architect (where his artistic ability could be put to some practical use). He lived to see them both desert professions they had not chosen for themselves. For Henricus architectural studies at least meant escape from the claustrophobic atmosphere of home. He kicked over the traces and changed his name from Henricus to Han as a symbol of his new-found freedom. He neglected his studies in favour of painting and achieved immediate recognition. His *Interior of the St Laurens Church in Rotterdam* won him the Hague Academy's gold medal and a handsome fee. He applied to join the Academy. To qualify he had to produce two paintings; a portrait and a seventeenth-century-style interior. He failed the portraiture test. Rejection angered him. Van Meegeren's personality was the sort that feeds on every imagined insult or slight. They thought he could not paint portraits, did they? Well, he would show them. Not only was his interior scene a masterpiece; when the examiners looked at it they discovered that the artist had represented every one of them in the painting.

Van Meegeren's talent was recognized. He was offered a professorial post at the Academy. There was no question, now, of his art being unappreciated. By his mid-twenties he had proved to the academic establishment that he possessed a fresh and original genius. He was working regularly and selling his canvases. He held a very successful exhibition. As a portrait painter he was in constant demand. But he was still discontented. In 1914 he had volunteered for military service and been rejected on health grounds. He had contracted a marriage and had now grown tired of his wife and two children. However fast he made money, he spent it faster. He believed that his genius was greater than anyone had yet recognized and was determined to force the experts to appreciate him fully. Eventually, he decided how to do it; he would forge a 'Vermeer' and, when it was publicly acclaimed as a masterpiece, he would come forward as the painter.

Han devoted himself totally to the new project. He took a house and studio in the south of France. He studied the technique of the great Dutch masters. He collected antique goblets, dishes and jugs to use as props. He bought a genuine seventeenth-century picture and carefully removed the paint. He made brushes of badger hair and mixed paints using only ingredients available in the seventeenth century. He perfected a method of artificially ageing the finished painting by baking it in a kiln. But his preparation went far beyond materials and techniques. He thought himself into the mind of Vermeer; almost he became Vermeer. All this took years but at the end of it all Han van Meegeren found himself looking at a painting of *The Disciples at Emmaus* which was indistinguishable from the work of Jan Vermeer of Delft.

Now came the test. Han took the painting to a Paris dealer, telling a story to account for the sudden appearance of a hitherto unknown picture by the great Dutch master. The canvas was submitted to the experts and van Meegeren waited in a state of nervous tension. They applied all the known scientific tests and then gave their verdict: the work was not only genuine, it was Vermeer's crowning achievement. In 1938 the painting was solemnly unveiled in the Boymans Museum, Rotterdam, and Han van Meegeren was there to laugh inwardly as the intelligentsia of the art world gazed in rapture and hailed the forgery as a 'miracle'. It was the little boy outside the police station all over again. For Han still could not bring himself to confess. In any case, there seemed little point now; *The Disciples at Emmaus* had brought him a small fortune and

what he had done once he could do again. He and his wife moved to a magnificent villa in Nice where they spent money like water. When it began to run out, Han 'discovered' and sold two paintings by the great Pieter de Hooch.

The van Meegerens returned to Holland for the war and Han now confined his attention to producing more 'Vermeers'. Money poured in. He invested. He began a profitable sideline as a restorer. He worked compulsively, casting discretion to the winds. His behaviour became increasingly odd and brought his second marriage to an end in 1944. The following year he was examined about a picture which had found its way into the collection of Nazi leader Hermann Goering. Suddenly he found himself facing criminal prosecution, but not for forgery; ironically the charge was collaborating with the enemy by selling national treasures. The only way to avoid a harsh sentence was to tell the truth. Now his genius proved an embarrassment: the paintings were so good that no one would believe they were forgeries. The only way Han could convince the court was by painting another 'Vermeer' in prison under observation.

Van Meegeren was awarded a year's jail sentence and given permission to paint while in detention. Commissions poured in and while red-faced experts hastily revised their earlier judgements, proclaiming van Meegeren's work to be unworthy of comparison with the seventeenth-century master, the general public appreciated Han's genius for what it really was. Alas, he did not long enjoy his triumph; he died in 1947 at the age of fifty-eight.

# 'Fierce indignation tore his heart'

It is the almost inevitable lot of the genius to be a man apart but there are those who cultivate this separateness and foremost among them stands Jonathan Swift. Whether it was ill-treatment by other people, disappointment at not obtaining the preferment that he considered his due, or over-weening pride that lay at the heart of his distem-pered view of life is something that has been frequently discussed. What is clear is that Jonathan Swift had a genius for observing the life and manner of his times and describing them with a maliciously satirical pen. For as he frankly remarked, wherever around him he looked he did not much like what he saw.

> I have ever hated all nations, professions and communities, and all my love is towards indi-viduals . . . but principally I hate and detest that animal called man.

He might perhaps have added that the principal object of his scorn and detestation was himself. Life seems to have marked Jonathan Swift out for misfortune from the beginning. His father died before he was born and as soon as she was able his mother left her husband's home in Dublin to return to her own parents and left Jonathan also to be cared for by a nurse. He saw her occasion-ally during the ensuing years but was principally brought up by an uncle and was thus deprived of the close bonds of family affection by which all later relationships come to be judged. He grew up full of resentment for his relatives and contempt for his teachers. He scraped through his course at Trinity College Dublin with the minimum work and was obviously an extremely difficult student, frequently in trouble for not attending chapel, missing nightly roll call and using insulting behaviour towards university dignitaries. He

*Swift and Stella – a strange relationship.*

recalled later that a friend told him at the time that his mind was 'like a conjured spirit which would do mischief if I did not give it employment'.

In about 1690 Swift entered the household of Sir William Temple, a prominent statesman, recently retired. He served his patron as secre-tary and amanuensis and after some turbulent early scenes the two men eventually became close friends. At Temple's splendid house in Surrey Swift had plenty of leisure and a large library in which to browse. It was at this time that he began writing the first of what would become an immense output of books and pamphlets. Almost everything he wrote was published anonymously and though this is partly to be explained by the nature of the sharp satire he produced, it also reflects an element of self-doubt. Another attrac-tion of the Temple household was Esther Johnson, the young daughter of a senior servant in the establishment. Esther was eight years old at the time when she and Swift first met and a tender if curious relationship sprang up between them and continued until Esther's death. Swift acted as a tutor to the girl whom he always called 'Stella'. Year by year he watched her grow into a beautiful young woman with raven black hair and 'every feature of her face in perfection'. Temple died in 1699 and Swift was obliged to go cap in hand to several influential men seeking preferment. He was eventually offered some Irish parishes (he had become ordained some years before). These provided him with a basic income and enabled him to divide his time between Dublin and London. Stella now went to live with a lady friend in one of Swift's houses in Ireland. However whenever Swift was in residence they moved into lodgings nearby. Stella was devoted to him and Swift's letters and journals reveal that his feelings for her went far beyond friendship. Yet their rela-tionship was purely platonic and in order to avoid scandal Swift scarcely ever allowed himself to be alone with Stella.

Alternating between London and Ireland, Swift now led two very different lives. In London he moved in the very highest society, mixing with political leaders of the day as well as literary giants like Pope, Steele and Addison. He was welcomed everywhere for his morose and wicked wit and for the brilliance of his writings. He was particularly close to Addison who once described him as 'the greatest genius of the age'. Every aspect of social and political life was grist to Swift's satirical mill. One of his most popular jokes was played upon a certain John Partridge, a pamphleteer and self-styled astrologer. Partridge was very given to making alarming prophecies about leading figures. Swift turned the tables on him by writing, under the name of 'Isaac Bickerstaff', a prediction that the notorious almanac-maker, Partridge, would die at eleven o'clock of the night of 29 March. On 30 March Swift published a letter confirming that this had in fact taken place. Partridge was, of course, the laughing stock of the town. Swift was now widely respected and feared. Leading politicians came forward with commissions for attacks on their rivals. His contributions to the news sheets were eagerly read in London's coffee houses and salons and his influence on public opinion was considerable. In Ireland, on the other hand, he lived both quietly and frugally, a third of his income given to charity. Though he was at great pains to make all his donations anonymously and even to affect considerable surliness towards petitioners, most people knew his generosity and he was widely loved. He was loved also by women. It was not only Stella who found him attractive. A girl called Vanessa, the daughter of a Dublin merchant, came to him for lessons and fell in love with him. She pursued him everywhere, deliberately lived close by him and called upon him as often as possible. He was beset, then, by two ladies who wanted to marry him. Although strongly attached to both of them, Swift was quite devoid of passion. This strained situation continued for several years until at last Vanessa wrote to Stella demanding to know what her relationship was with Swift. Stella sent the letter on to Swift and Swift angrily confronted Vanessa with it. The distracted young woman died within a few weeks.

Swift was by no means only an aloof, contemptuous, satirical observer. This he showed most notably in 1724 in the case of Wood's half-pence. A patent had been granted to William Wood, an English tradesman, to provide copper coinage for Ireland. Wood had obtained the patent at the request of the Duchess of Kendal, George I's mistress, and the two of them were set to make a vast profit on the deal. Swift exposed all this in six letters signed 'M. B. Drapier'. Public indignation was intense and the patent had to be cancelled. Everyone knew that Swift was the real author of the letters but the government was never able to prove it.

It was in 1726 that Jonathan Swift's most famous work was published, again anonymously. This was his *Travels into Several Remote Nations of the World by Lemuel Gulliver*. Under the guise of a sequence of fantastic adventures, Swift satirized every aspect of English politics and society. For example the King of Brobdingnag, the land of the giants, questions Gulliver about the English parliament. At the end of the examination he concludes:

I observe among you some lines of an institution, which, in its original might have been tolerable, but these half-erased and the rest wholly blurred and blotted by corruptions. It does not appear, from all you have said, how any one perfection is required toward the procurement of any one station among you; much less, that men are enobled on account of their virtue; that priests are advanced for their piety or learning; soldiers for their conduct or valour; judges for their integrity; . . . or counsellors for their wisdom. . . . I cannot but conclude the bulk of your natives to be the most pernicious race of little odious vermin that nature ever suffered to crawl upon the surface of the earth.

The following year Stella died. Swift was desolate but affected unconcern. After his own death an envelope was discovered containing a lock of her hair. On the outside Swift had scribbled the words 'only a woman's hair'. After her death he never left Dublin. He had been appointed Dean of the Cathedral in 1713 and he now concentrated upon his duties there, which he fulfilled faithfully for many years. He remained active as a political writer especially on Irish affairs and was diligent in his support of local charities. Swift was a thorough-going pessimist and in the mismanagement of government in Ireland he found much to feed his pessimism. In his latter years Swift declined into insanity. He died in 1745 leaving a considerable fortune for the purpose of founding a hospital in Dublin. On his tomb in the cathedral he ordered a simple Latin legend to be inscribed. Translated it reads 'Where fierce indignation can no longer tear his heart.'

*The fearless enemy of corruption. Hibernia proclaims Swift's services to Ireland. Wood grovels at his feet.*

## 'All lines and blots'

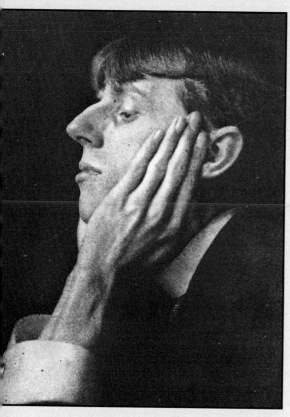

Aubrey Beardsley was twenty by the time he fully developed his unique graphic style. He was twenty-five when he died. In those few, brief years, and despite declining health, he took the art world of London and Paris by storm. He astounded artists and critics. He outraged polite society. And he left posterity ample proof of his unique genius.

Even as a child Aubrey was delicate and by the age of ten tuberculosis had been diagnosed. It may have been his physical limitations that caused him to excel in other ways or it may simply have been that his talents could not be denied expression. By the age of five he could play works by Chopin at the piano. He read avidly and had soon forsaken children's books for dramatists such as Shakespeare, Congreve and Wycherley, poets, especially Poe, Chatterton and Pope, and such 'solid' works as Carlyle's *French Revolution*. He enjoyed arranging theatrical performances for his school. He was no mere bookworm. He had a bird-like restlessness. He talked excitedly, always with expres-

sive hand gestures. Whenever there were pranks young Beardsley was usually at the centre of them. And always he was drawing – outrageous caricatures of his teachers or scenes from his favourite books and plays. Even at that early age he seems to have been attracted by the grotesque and to have had an unerring eye for the bizarre in human personality and conduct. As he passed through adolescence, Beardsley hankered after a literary or artistic career. Any career, he knew, would be brief and he was consumed with a sense of urgency.

But even sensitive souls need to face the reality of earning a living. At sixteen he became a clerk in a district surveyor's office, one of an army of anonymous, black-coated men perched on high stools, crouched over massive ledgers. In his, all too little, spare time he wrote stories for magazines and compiled a portfolio of drawings. But talent needs to be discovered. Many geniuses have gone to the grave unrecognized, their gifts lost to humanity or only acknowledged posthumously. It might have been so with Aubrey Beardsley, had it not been for a spontaneous visit to the studio of Sir Edward Burne-Jones one Sunday afternoon in July 1891. The famous artist opened his studio to the public on occasion and Beardsley had gone there with his sister to see the great man's work. By chance they met the artist himself and Beardsley diffidently showed him some of his own drawings. Burne-Jones was impressed. 'There is *no* doubt about your gift,' he said, 'one day you will most assuredly paint very great and beautiful pictures. I *seldom* or *never* advise anyone to take up art as a profession, but in your case I can do nothing else.'

*A Beardsley illustration from 'The Yellow Book'.*

It was intoxicating to receive such advice from England's most famous living painter but how could Beardsley act on it? Some months later the answer came in the form of a £500 legacy under the will of his great-aunt. It was not a large sum but it enabled him to travel to Paris, gain introductions to London's fin-de-siècle literary and artistic set – Oscar Wilde, James Whistler, W. B. Yeats and many others. Yet still he clung to the security of his City job (he was now with an insurance firm). Most lunchtimes Beardsley was to be found browsing in a London bookshop. He had an arrangement with the proprietor, Frederick Evans, who sometimes accepted drawings in exchange for books. It was Evans who showed Beardsley's work to the publisher J. M. Dent and Dent immediately commissioned the young man to illustrate a new edition of Malory's *Morte d'Arthur*. At last Beardsley felt that recognition and success were his. He gave up his job, moved more freely in the artistic *demi-monde* and was enthusiastically taken up by that world as the man of the hour.

It went to his head, perhaps inevitably. The once-shy, sensitive young man now affected languid airs, wore outrageous clothes and cultivated clever talk. He was taken up by Oscar Wilde and allowed himself to be influenced by the celebrated wit and dandy. It was not a natural alliance for Beardsley was not a sincere devotee of decadence and free thinking. Yet he fell under Wilde's spell and in the exuberance of success, recognition and discovering his own highly-distinctive style, he threw off all restraints. He devoted himself not only to the grotesque but also to the erotic and pornographic. There was about much of his work an implicit or explicit cruelty. He held nothing sacred – least of all convention. And, of course, respectable society was outraged. Beardsley affected unconcern, treating critics with amused contempt. When one art critic dubbed him 'sexless and unclean', Beardsley replied, in a letter to the paper:

> . . . As to my uncleanness I do the best for it in my morning bath, and if he has really any doubts as to my sex, he may come and see me take it.

The bubble burst when Wilde was convicted on charges of sexual immorality and sent to prison. Outraged society took its revenge on everything and everyone connected with the broken idol. Magazines and publishers no longer took Beardsley's work. A brief recovery came in 1896 with the publication of a journal called *The Savoy*, of which Beardsley was the principal artist but, by then, Beardsley's health was rapidly deteriorating and his output was decreasing. He was depressed now, not only by illness and rejection but by

With their lines and juxtaposed areas of black and white, Beardsley's unique drawings portrayed voluptuousness, decadence and cruelty.

doubt. Freed from the sophistication of Oscar Wilde's set, his mind turned to a more serious evaluation of life. He became a Roman Catholic and he bitterly regretted the decadent nature of much of his work. His last letter, written from France where he had gone on his doctor's advice, was to a publisher friend.

Jesus is our Lord and Judge
Dear Friend,
I implore you to destroy *all* copies of Lysistrata and bad drawings. Show this to Pollitt and conjure him to do the same. By all that is holy – *all* obscene drawings.
　　　　　　Aubrey Beardsley
In my death agony

Fortunately much of his work survives, leaving each of us to make up our own minds whether Aubrey Beardsley was 'the Fra Angelico of Satanism' or a genius with 'immediate access to some world outside our own . . . which creates its own skill'.

# The man who asked questions

It was not the done thing to ask questions in the universities and schools of sixteenth-century Europe. Knowledge was the carefully stored harvest of the ages. It was distributed by teachers who totally respected its authority and who instilled that respect into their students. So what happened when a student appeared who had such a commanding intellect that he could see flaws in the received wisdom of the ancients, who asked awkward questions and supplied novel answers to those questions? He ran the risk of being branded as a troublemaker, even a heretic. And in the sixteenth century the Church burned heretics.

Galileo Galilei was born at Pisa in 1564, the son of a musician, Vincenzio Galilei, who was, himself, an unorthodox figure. Vincenzio was interested in the Renaissance revival of classical forms in music and sought to enliven the existing sterile traditions with new ideas. Galileo was thus brought up in a household where academic argument was a vivid part of the fabric of life. Vincenzio recognized early his eldest son's genius. He was a boy who *observed* things and asked why they happened. Why was it, for instance, that a lamp hanging in the cathedral and moving in the swirling currents of air always took the same time to complete its swing, however short or long that

swing might be? These and a thousand other speculations already teemed in his brain before he went to the university at Pisa at the age of seventeen. He found no solutions in his medical studies. Vincenzio had decided that Galileo should be a physician, a lucrative profession for one so gifted.

In 1583 the young man attended, by chance, a course of lectures on geometry. It was the turning point of his life. In mathematics he found the science that would explain the puzzles presented by the natural world. Galileo forsook the medical school and took up philosophy and mathematics. And soon he became a thorn in the flesh to his lecturers. He would keep pointing out the apparent contradictions between what they taught and what he could observe with his own eyes. No less a figure than Aristotle had asserted that falling bodies descend with a speed directly proportionate to their size. If that was true, Galileo wanted to know, why did hailstones of varying dimensions strike the ground simultaneously? Such questioning outraged the professors while, at the same time, Galileo grew increasingly frustrated by the arguments over philosophical niceties which passed for scientific debate at Pisa.

But he learned all that anyone could teach him about mathematics and physics. He read all the books of the great Greek scholars and their later commentators. At last he was left with only nature as his tutor – nature and his own genius. Freed from the shackles of convention, Galileo pursued his studies in solitude scorning those

*Galileo's study in Florence is today kept as a museum to the great scientist.*

tower, showed that Aristotelian theories were wrong. He became interested in astronomy as a result of studying the motion of the tides which inclined him to accept the revolutionary theory of Copernicus that the earth moves round the sun and not vice versa. He obtained one of the newly-invented telescopes and by improving the measurement and manufacture of lenses produced a much more powerful instrument, the first practical astronomical telescope. This opened for him a whole new world of discovery – sunspots, the surface of the moon, the satellites of Jupiter, etc., and convinced him that Copernicus was right.

It was this that brought Galileo into conflict with the Church. He had won wide acclaim as one of the most gifted and original thinkers in Europe. In 1610 he was offered the new post of philosopher and mathematician to the grand duke of Tuscany. This meant that under the patronage of Cosimo de Medici he was able to devote more time to research and publication. Not only did he venture into new fields but he deepened his study of subjects on which he had already written. His fame, especially in Italy, extended far beyond the academic world. His conflict with traditional teaching now came into the open.

> I seem to discern the firm belief that in philosophizing one must support oneself on the opinions of some celebrated author, as if our minds ought to remain completely sterile and barren unless wedded to the reasoning of someone else . . . that is not how things are. Philosophy is written in this grand book, the universe, which . . . cannot be understood unless one first learns to comprehend the language and to read the alphabet in which it is composed. It is written in the language of mathematics, and its characters are triangles, circles and other geometric figures . . .

Galileo's enemies sought the support of the Church and because the Copernican theory seemed to contradict the Bible Galileo and his writings were examined by the Inquisition. The confrontation was long drawn out. Galileo was forbidden to write on certain subjects and, for fifteen years, he worked quietly at Florence trying to avoid conflict. Yet he lived under constant threat and, in 1633, despite the fact that he was ill and sixty-nine years of age he was ordered to Rome to stand trial. He was condemned and sentenced to imprisonment – mercifully commuted to house arrest.

On his estate near Florence the torrent of challenging new thought and discovery continued to pour from Galileo's brain, even after he went blind in 1637. That great brain never failed, it simply wore out the body which contained it on 9 January 1642.

who thought it 'better to remain in error with the herd than to stand alone in reasoning correctly'. His work usually began with observation and ended in the invention or perfection of instruments with practical application. In those early years he was fascinated by hydrostatics – the characteristics of fluids, their pressure and equilibrium. Traditional teaching had insisted that flat solids float better than those of other shapes. Again, Galileo disproved this by simple demonstration: he made some cones and showed that the only way they could be made to float was point downwards and not flat surface downwards. One result of his experiments was the hydrostatic balance. This was followed up with a pioneering treatise on the calculation of the centre of gravity of solid bodies.

Galileo went on to lecture in mathematics at Pisa and then to become professor at Padua University. His many-faceted work continued. He made calculations in trigonometry and geometry for the use of artillery commanders and produced what he called the 'geometric and military compass'. He studied the rate of acceleration of falling bodies and, in a celebrated demonstration in which he dropped a hundred pound iron ball and a one pound iron ball from the top of Pisa's leaning

## The unconquered

*Archer's last appearance at Newmarket.*

The accident of birth has a great deal to do with genius. Frederick James Archer who was born on 11 January 1857 was highly intelligent and sensitive. Had he been born into the professional or landed class he might have excelled as a businessman or barrister, an artist or churchman. As it was he was the youngest son of an innkeeper and one-time steeplechase jockey and he became the finest and most celebrated horseman of his age.

Fred's mother doted on her youngest and envisaged for him a marvellous future. She wanted him to be educated so that he could better himself but Mr Archer, the dominant and domineering head of the family, had other ideas. He was a rough, practical man with no time for book-learning. As a result, Fred's attendances at the village school were sporadic. It was something that he bitterly regretted in later life. Being virtually illiterate embarrassed him and he was very self-conscious at having to ask a friend to write his letters for him. But Fred's father had recognized in his son something which in his eyes was much more important. The boy was a natural genius in the saddle. The way he sat, his natural movement and his sympathy with the animal were

qualities which, as old William Archer well knew, some jockeys never acquired after a lifetime. He put Fred and his pony through a rigorous training, making them ride round and round the paddock, urging them on with swear words and blows until they perfected their movements. Fred was much more frightened of his father than of any injury that might befall him by falling off. At the age of eight Fred was entered for his first race, a contest with a local boy mounted on a donkey. The donkey won. Fred came home shedding tears of disappointed rage. William had already dinned into him an intensely competitive spirit. Winning was all-important to him and would remain so to the end of his days.

At the age of eleven Fred was sent as an apprentice jockey to Matt Dawson, an up-and-coming Newmarket trainer. Like every apprentice in a well-run stable Fred had to endure a hard and strict regime. The highest standards were expected and he was cursed and cuffed when they were not achieved. But Fred had more than that to put up with. He was a gangling, awkward, shy lad. The other boys teased and bullied him mercilessly. He was miserable and homesick but the hard lessons instilled by his father had been well learned. Fred stuck to his task with dogged persistence. He was fearless and could conquer the wildest horse. He rode with such sensitivity and assured mastery that the jibes of his colleagues soon gave way to respect. Dawson entered Fred Archer for his first races in 1870 and he acquitted himself well, though not outstandingly. In 1871 he was put up to ride a horse called Salvanos in the Cesarewitch. He had been chosen because he was a lightweight and because he was the only person in the stable who could manage the notoriously difficult Salvanos. He came home a

clear winner by several lengths and created a sensation. Requests for his services now began to pour in.

Success could not come fast enough, not only because Archer wanted to win but also because his parents were now desperately in need of the money he could earn. He soon showed that he was not only a brilliant rider but an intelligent one. Before a race he studied carefully not only the horse that he was to mount but also all the others who were competing with him, weighing up their strengths and weaknesses and calculating the best way to defeat them. Archer had many tricks and strategems. For example, if he was running a close race he would make sure to finish sitting well forward over the horse's neck. The theory was that he would catch the judge's eye and gain the verdict even if his horse's nose was not in fact ahead. The result was increasing success. 1874 was his first big year. He rode 147 winners and became champion jockey. He remained champion jockey for the next twelve years, a quite unprecedented feat which has never been surpassed. He now reigned as undisputed king of the course and was among the big money. Unfortunately, his father spent it faster than he could earn it. Old William Archer was trading on his son's fame, indulging himself freely and running up credit in Fred's name.

Fred also had other problems. Until 1874 he had always been able to ride at under six stone, then in a sudden burst of growth he added another two stone. From that time on he was fighting a continual battle against overweight. He took Turkish baths and imposed savagely rigorous diets. When the problem became really desperate he was restricted to castor oil and orange juice for breakfast and one sardine and a glass of champagne for lunch. In his pursuit of success, Archer was hard on his horses and his rivals as well as himself. He had a reputation for whipping on his horses with unnecessary severity and never thought twice about bumping and jostling other runners.

Season followed triumphant season. Archer was at last able to amass a considerable amount of capital. In 1882 he married his trainer's niece, Helen Dawson, and built a splendid new house to take her to.

But there was another side to the coin. Archer's dieting was imposing an increasing strain upon his constitution and his nerves. This showed in his conduct on the racecourse, which was not good at the best of times, and there were a number of unpleasant incidents when Archer became the subject of stewards' enquiries. Nothing was ever proved against him but some owners began to lose confidence in him and for the first time his popularity with the public waned.

*Was Archer 'caged' by patrons or his own reputation?*

These things weighed heavily upon him and he experienced frequent bouts of depression. Then in 1885 his wife Helen died shortly after giving birth to a daughter. Archer was prostrate with grief. For months he did not ride and could scarcely speak to anyone. With the aid of a trip to America he recovered and returned to racing. It was now the only thing he had to live for, and he threw himself into it with exaggerated frenzy. There were more winners and more disputes. Archer's reputation sometimes acted against him. If he lost a race, disgruntled owners and backers accused him of not trying. In his increasingly depressed state, he took these rebuffs very much to heart. Towards the end of the 1886 season he fell ill but ignored the symptoms and drove himself to honour his racing commitments. As a result typhoid set in and he was confined to bed. Slowly he recovered but his mental depression grew steadily worse. On 8 November he staggered from his bed, took up a revolver and shot himself. He was twenty-nine years of age. He was the unbeaten champion jockey of England. As one colleague aptly commented, 'The only man who could conquer Archer was Archer.'

# Enthusiasts

The word 'enthusiasm' comes from the Greek *enthousiasmos*, meaning literally 'possessed by a god'. So that an enthusiast, in the strict sense of the word, is someone filled with an almost divine passion, a passion which goes beyond reason, a passion which is not daunted by setbacks, not whittled away by failure, not quenched by apathy, misunderstanding, or rejection. Genuine enthusiasts are few and far between but they are the ones who get things done. They are the ones who stay to the end of the course. It was Emerson who said, 'Nothing great was ever achieved without enthusiasm.' Somebody else, I can't remember who, put it round the other way when he said 'The worst bankrupt is the person who has lost enthusiasm.' The enthusiast enriches his own life and by extension, almost inevitably, the lives of others. Certainly this is true of the men and women whose stories follow.

I suspect there is in all of us an enthusiast trying to get out. The trouble is it sometimes takes several years before we discover something worthy of our enthusiasm, some pursuit or hobby to which we are prepared to devote time, money, effort and thought without stint. It was thus for John Dodd who emerged from a Japanese prisoner-of-war camp in 1945 as a misfit, unable to settle to anything until he found the one thing that he and he alone could do supremely well. Similar in many ways is the story of Austen Henry Layard, the great archaeologist whose childhood reading had filled his head with romantic visions of the Golden Kingdoms of Ur, Babylon and Baghdad and who would not rest until he could devote a major portion of his life to digging for these kingdoms. Was it so, one wonders, with Celia Fiennes? We know virtually nothing about her earlier life and must assume that it was devoted to the conventional, unexciting pastimes of the distaff side in seventeenth-century England. Then, suddenly, she blazed forth with an enthusiasm for travel, a desire to see, note, and record her opinions on every vista that her native land had to offer.

There were those, however, who threw themselves enthusiastically into every sphere of life, transforming 'the trivial round, the common task' into a daily adventure. It was so with Julia Cameron who was always the life and soul of the party, the organizer, the one who could persuade her friends and neighbours, often against their better judgement, to take part in her latest escapade. Mel Fisher had rushed impatiently and often successfully from one business venture to another before he discovered the quest for sunken treasure which was to dominate the rest of his life.

Another aspect of enthusiasm is that it is infectious. Mortimer Wheeler took a dry-as-dust subject like archaeology and fired two generations of students with his love for what he called 'digging up people'. Then in his later years he conveyed that enthusiasm to a wide public through the medium of television. Emmeline Pankhurst caught her enthusiasm from her husband. For years she listened to him holding forth eloquently across the dining room table or from the public platform on those many issues which were close to his heart, and she came to share them too and to go on fighting for votes for women long after Dr Pankhurst's death. It was because of her enthusiasm, her willingness to espouse an apparently lost cause, to stand in public places being jeered at, to endure constant rebuffs from politicians and church leaders, and still to go on, that thousands of women were inspired to believe that perhaps

*Last night at the 'Proms'*

the world could be changed. Why is enthusiasm so infectious? Is it not because secretly all of us want to believe in the impossible? We long to reach out and touch the stars but lack the courage until someone comes along to lift our limp hands and raise them skywards. That is the only way I can explain why intelligent businessmen should have sunk good money in Mel Fisher's treasure diving syndicate, despite his many failures and near bankruptcy. I can see no other reason why a diplomat of the stamp of Stratford Canning should have obtained financial and political support for a headstrong young man like Layard, who had no archaeological experience, to go digging in Mesopotamia.

Enthusiasm cannot guarantee success but it has an uncanny way of leading to success. Layard *did* find an ancient Assyrian capital. Wheeler *did* raise millions of pounds for archaeological endeavour. Thomas Beecham *did* establish two orchestras and bring many little-known composers to the public's attention. Harry Reichenbach *did* persuade millions of cinema goers to pay good money to watch mediocre films. Bess of Hard-wick *did* leave behind her magnificent houses and an immense fortune. John Dodd *did* begin an extremely important work among ex-convicts. For none of them was the achievement of their goal easy. They faced appalling hardships and had to endure both rejection and misunderstanding, yet their stories read like fun and often riotous adventures. That is the vital point. Enthusiasm changes a pilgrimage into a crusade; transmutes a chore into a delight. The enthusiast tells us that life is meant to be fun, rather in the manner of the following piece of doggerel:

Everyone told him it couldn't be done,
But he with a chuckle replied,
That maybe it couldn't, but he for one
Wouldn't say so 'till he'd tried.
So he buckled right in with a trace of a grin
On his face. If he worried he hid it.
He started to sing as he tackled the thing
That couldn't be done, and he did it.

And the important thing is the 'grin', for at the end of the day success or failure is unimportant.

## The prisoner

*In Changi jail, John Dodd wasted to a mere six stones and had his portrait drawn by fellow-prisoner Ronald Searle.*

John Dodd had plenty of time to foster his anger and bitterness with authority. He was one of the 36,000 defenders of Singapore when the island, claimed by the high command to be impregnable, fell to the Japanese at the beginning of 1942. He was one of the 'lucky ones' who got away in the ramshackle evacuation of the following weeks. His escape took him as far as Java. There the Second World War ended for RAF corporal John Dodd. He spent six months on the run in the jungle aided by a remarkable Eurasian woman called Marquita and her daughter, who came close to paying with their lives for their help. Then he was captured, beaten and tortured. The Japanese wanted him to name local people who were helping Allied troops. Dodd told them nothing. He was shipped back to Singapore and thrown into the notorious Changi jail. The death rate and the conditions in Changi were appalling. Malnutrition, vitamin deficiency and a variety of diseases were rife. The latrine pits crawled with maggots. There was virtually no medication. Above all there was no hope; what little news filtered through to the POWs was all bad. Dodd, who had witnessed the stupidity which had allowed Singapore to fall to the enemy, could scarcely believe that the Allies could turn the tide of war. There seemed nothing for it but to endure and wait for the inevitable. Yet, unlike many others, John Dodd did not lose the will to survive. His body wasted from a strapping thirteen-and-a-half stone to less than six. He was weakened by amoebic dysentery and renal colic. He had to

have a kidney operation under primitive conditions. Release, when it came, in the autumn of 1945, was not an easy business. First of all there was the long climb back to health and physical fitness. Then there was the separation from his companions in suffering, men with whom close bonds had been formed during the appalling years in Changi. Added to this was the ordeal of being questioned by military personnel gathering information for use against Japanese war criminals, being forced to relive the agony, the indignity and the squalor. Finally, and perhaps worst of all, came the bitter-sweet experience of England, home and readjustment to a life he had left an eternity before.

Returning to his parents' house on the Isle of Wight, John found that he had virtually nothing in common with neighbours who grumbled about food rationing and grew indignant at petty local government chicanery. He was restless and purposeless. He went through a succession of cars and women. He gambled heavily. He had fits of violent temper. Amazingly, he found a girl, called Alyson, who put up with his tantrums and with her help he found Christian faith. Only then could his incredible energies be turned to some positive end.

John threw himself enthusiastically into church work and established a thriving Sunday school. Then someone suggested to him that he might try his hand at prison visiting. In 1952 he began calling at Parkhurst to talk with some of the inmates. To his surprise he found it, in a way, easy. Unlike other prison visitors, he really understood these men. He knew what they were thinking and feeling. It was satisfying work. John and Alyson were married and had children. John prospered in his job as a salesman. They bought a large house and lived comfortably, as active members of the community.

In 1959 they left all that behind, moved to a house near Winchester and began living on a fraction of the income they had previously enjoyed. John's concern for prisoners had grown and particularly his interest in the problems they experienced over rehabilitation. He had seen hundreds of habitual offenders; men who were in and out of prison like yo-yos because they could not adjust to freedom. John helped to found the Langley House Trust to establish rehabilitation centres for released ex-convicts. Over the years the Trust has grown into the largest organization of its kind in the world with more than a dozen centres throughout Britain, but the early days were hard.

John and Alyson sat down to a magnificent Christmas dinner in 1959 with the occupants of Elderfield, the first home. Just as the Christmas pudding came in one of the ex-convicts leaped across the table and grabbed John by the throat. That was the signal for a free-for-all. The room was wrecked. The police had to be called in and John had to take stock of six months of hard work and self-sacrifice. Some of the men he had tried to

help were already back in prison. Others had simply disappeared. There had been incidents locally and many examples of unpleasantness inside the hostel. The critics, and there were many who had told him that he was attempting the impossible, seemed to be vindicated.

But the Dodds and their growing contingent of fellow-workers persisted. They learned from their mistakes. They stopped thinking in terms of success and failure after a terrible incident in 1960. One of their model residents left them to get married and settle down. Three months later he battered his wife to death with a hammer. Unknown to all but his immediate family, he had suffered brain damage at birth. It was always difficult to persuade local communities to accept ex-prisoners into their midst. Often, much to John's bewilderment, it has been church people who have led this opposition. Often they have gained the support of local councils. It is, perhaps, fortunate that Dodd has maintained a healthy disregard for authority. He has stuck to his convictions and over the years more and more people have come to share them. Money has come in from public and private funds and as a result many of society's outcasts have been given a fresh start in life. For the majority rehabilitation is a reality. It takes time but John Dodd understands that – it took him fifteen years to find his niche in the world outside prison.

*After a difficult period of readjustment to civilian life, John Dodd found married happiness with Alyson and purpose in his work with prisoners. He never sought personal publicity and was surprised to be featured on a television programme.*

# The gentle tyrant

'She has a tendency to make the house shake the moment she enters.' So wrote one of her neighbours about Julia Cameron. She was a bustling enthusiast, an organizer. It was an attitude to life that she had learned as the daughter of a civil servant in India. Many admirable women were converted into bossy *memsahibs* when they became part of the colonial regimes of Africa or the Orient. They were endowed with an army of servants and twenty-four hours a day of completely free time. They indulged the conviction that they knew what was best for everyone and no one dared challenge that conviction. They justified their existence by organizing the social life of their husbands and the moral welfare of the natives.

Julia Cameron was a member of that caste. What lifted her above the ridicule and opprobrium levelled against it was talent. She was no empty-headed teacup tittle-tattler. She was a brilliant conversationalist, a gifted organizer and she

*Julia Cameron by G. F. Watts*

had a genuine interest in people. For example, while still in India she was touched by the sufferings in Ireland because of the great potato famine and collected a considerable sum for the relief of that unhappy country. Julia married Charles Cameron, a brilliant lawyer and twenty years her senior, in Calcutta and returned to England with him in 1848. Soon she was cultivating famous people like Wordsworth and Carlyle and constantly adding to her circle of friends by her conversation, her witty letters, her generosity and her sometimes outrageous conduct (such as disconcerting a fashionable West End preacher by constantly blowing kisses at him throughout the sermon).

In 1860 Charles Cameron retired to Freshwater, Isle of Wight, and it is fairly safe to see Julia's hand in the choice of this location. For Queen Victoria's favourite residence, Osborne, was only a few miles away, while Freshwater itself was the home of Alfred Lord Tennyson around whom gathered a coterie of fashionable artists and literateurs. Julia became immediately the major domo of the Freshwater community, organizing parties and diversions for the distinguished residents and visitors.

But the event which made Julia Cameron's name live on beyond her own circle and her own age was the gift of a camera. She received this from her daughter in 1863 and a large measure of her enthusiasm now went into the art of photography. And in her hands photography *was* an art. She was one of the first really talented performers in this medium. She had a passion, as she said, 'to arrest all the beauty that came before me'. She had a natural eye and tireless patience in arranging her subjects. She carefully learned the techniques of exposing and developing photographic plates. She turned the coal cellar into a dark room and the poultry house into a studio. She captured every famous person who came anywhere near her. Tennyson, who was very camera shy, she photographed several times. The artist G. F. Watts, Robert Browning, Henry Wadsworth Longfellow, Thomas Carlyle, Charles Darwin and the Crown Prince and Princess of Prussia were among the many celebrities she persuaded to sit for her. And sitting could be a real ordeal. For example, Browning was posed in a position of some discomfort and told not to move while Mrs Cameron went in search of some piece of vital equipment. And he did not move – for two hours. Only then did the forgetful Julia come back to rescue him. Even when everything went according to plan the subject had to remain motionless in every muscle for several minutes until the exposure was complete. One friend recalled being ordered to 'stand with spiky coconut branches running into my head and . . . look perfectly

hand, tousled our hair to get rid of its prim nursery look . . . we never knew what Aunt Julia was going to do next, nor did anyone else for the matter of that. All we were conscious of was that once in her clutches we were perfectly helpless. 'Stand there,' she shouted. And we stood, for hours if necessary . . .

*Julia Cameron could bully almost anyone into posing for her. Children were a speciality, but famous people such as G. F. Watts were also pressed into service. 'The Return After Three Days' (above) and 'The Whisper of the Muse' are shown here.*

natural'. She did not, however, get her way with every potential victim. When Garibaldi, the Italian nationalist, came to the Isle of Wight she rushed to him and, unable to speak Italian, threw herself at his feet in an attitude of supplication. Garibaldi, assuming that she was some poor peasant woman begging alms, brushed her aside.

But it was by no means only the great and famous that interested Julia Cameron. She was always on the lookout for photogenic subjects and when she saw one she would simply pounce and drag the surprised man or woman into her studio. Most of the local people were taken into Mrs Cameron's studio at one time or another to be composed into tableaux for sentimental portrait groups with such titles as 'Pray God, bring Father Safely Home'. Children were among her favourite subjects and could never escape her clutches. One great-niece described what it was like to be grabbed by the little old lady in dark clothes stained with photographic chemicals.

Rachel and I were pressed into the service of the camera. Our roles were no less than those of two of the angels of the Nativity and to sustain them we were scantily clad, and each had a pair of heavy swan's wings fastened to her narrow shoulders, while Aunt Julia, with ungentle

Julia Cameron won medals for her photographs in England, Germany, Austria and America, and deservedly so. The results she achieved with primitive apparatus are remarkable.

In 1875 Julia's octogenarian husband took it into his head to return to the East and lay his bones to rest on his family's plantations in Ceylon. Dutifully, his wife sold up the home at Freshwater, bade farewell to her little studio, and accompanied him. In the event it was she who died first (1879). There were some things that even Julia Cameron could not organize.

## Suffrage and suffering

In the popular imagination Emmeline Pankhurst is pictured as an iron-willed lady who courageously championed the rights of her sex, a formidable banner-waving Amazon whose oratory stirred the hearts of thousands of women, and a wily feminist who outwitted the male politicians at their own game. The truth reveals a character at once less simple and more appealing.

She was born in 1858, the daughter of a self-made and class-conscious Manchester industrialist. She was educated for a life of feminine elegance and sent to complete her training to a finishing school in Paris. When she was twenty-one, she married the eminent barrister Dr Richard Marsden Pankhurst and exchanged life with a strong-minded father for life with a strong-minded husband. Emmeline was very feminine, enjoyed fine clothes, had little love of practical housekeeping, read romantic novels and devoted most of her time to bearing and rearing four children. But she gradually became more and more involved in her husband's social and political activities. Dr Pankhurst was an ardent reformer who actively campaigned for such radical measures as the abolition of the monarchy and the House of Lords, and the nationalization of land. He believed in adult suffrage and had even drafted a bill on the subject which was laid before

Parliament. In the last quarter of the nineteenth century such opinions were considered extreme to the point of eccentricity. But in one area Pankhurst had achieved success; he had helped to draft the two Married Women's Property Acts of 1870 and 1882. In 1883 Pankhurst contested a Manchester bye-election as an Independent. Enthusiastically Emmeline threw herself into the campaign but it was doomed to failure. The episode did Dr Pankhurst's practice very little good. Hard years were ahead for the family. Emmeline's own enthusiasms and convictions grew stronger in this period of her life partly as a result of what she learned from her husband and partly because of her deep sense of injustice at the way he was treated by political opponents. When he contested a London seat in 1885, the Tories spread a deliberate libel about him and Emmeline was swift to spring to his defence. Mrs Pankhurst was becoming more and more enstranged from her father and all he represented. In 1886 they had a fierce argument and never spoke to each other again.

It was this that pitchforked her into a new phase of her life. She insisted that the family should move to London so that Dr Pankhurst should pursue his political career more easily. To earn a living she opened a shop and the family lived in the premises above. Another move took them to a

*The fact that an eminently respectable lady was prepared to undergo the indignity of prison made a great impact on public opinion.*

with Christabel and a few other supporters, Emmeline founded the Women's Social and Political Union, dedicating to winning, as their slogan succinctly put it, 'VOTES FOR WOMEN'. Emmeline was not, and never had been, a solitary campaigner. She needed someone at her side, someone from whom she could draw strength. It had been her husband, now it was her daughter. They made a formidable team. While the mother addressed meetings, wrote pamphlets, and lobbied MPs, Christabel organized more forthright activities such as interrupting political meetings, demonstrating outside government buildings, leading protest marches and, later, such publicity-catching activities as chaining herself to the railings in Downing Street.

With little support at first the Pankhursts doggedly continued with their campaign from 1903 to the outbreak of war in 1914. In 1906 they moved to London, so that they could carry on the work more effectively. Emmeline led a delegation to the Liberal Prime Minister and when it became clear that he would not support votes for women she made it her objective to unseat the Liberal government, by campaigning against them in elections, interrupting their meetings and distributing anti-Liberal pamphlets. With Christabel's activities constantly keeping the WSPU before the public, and Emmeline, the older woman with her well-dressed, respectable image, speaking ardently and cogently in defence of its aims, the movement was reaching a wide cross-section of the public.

One problem which the organizers of the movement faced was diversification. As more and more strong-minded women were attracted to the WSPU and began to be very active in its councils, a variety of ideals manifested themselves. The answer was autocracy. The Pankhursts between them ruled the WSPU with a rod of iron. British history offers few other examples of a campaign pursued for so long with such single-minded devotion. Between 1908 and 1914 Emmeline Pankhurst was sent to prison on numerous occasions. These confinements only served to strengthen her cause. The WSPU abandoned its campaign on the outbreak of war and strongly supported the war effort. In 1918 a new government gave the vote to women over thirty.

Emmeline Pankhurst lived most of the rest of her life in Canada and the United States but she returned home in 1925. Still politically active, she was adopted as a prospective candidate for an East London constituency. By now she was worn out by her exertions and in 1928 she died. As a small group of suffragettes followed her coffin through the London streets, the House of Lords was passing the bill which would give the vote to all women on equal terms with men.

fine house in Russell Square where Emmeline could organize the social side of her husband's political life. The financial strain of maintaining this establishment was enormous but Emmeline did not allow that to stand in her way. In Russell Square she could entertain all the leading radical politicians and journalists of the day. It was there that the seeds of Emmeline's future work were sown in the formation of the Women's Franchise League. Financial reality eventually caught up with the Pankhursts and forced them to retire once more to Manchester. Here the doctor spent the remainder of his days as an active campaigner on behalf of the Independent Labour Party and an upholder of the rights of under-privileged groups. He died in 1898 of a perforated ulcer.

For the next few years Mrs Pankhurst was preoccupied filling the role of breadwinner for the family. She started another shop, this time in Manchester, and also became the city's Registrar of Births and Deaths. It was largely at the prompting of her elder daughter, Christabel, that she became politically reactivated. Christabel, now in her early twenties, had become a forthright and aggressive champion of women's rights. In 1903

# A formidable woman

Elizabeth Talbot, so the legend runs, was once told that she would not die as long as she was building. Since she survived eighty-eight summers (a remarkable feat indeed in the sixteenth century) and succumbed at last to the inevitable during 'a hard frost while her builders could not work', it may be that there was some truth in the tale. She drove a hard bargain with death, as she did with every human being with whom she had any business dealings. For Bess of Hardwick, as she was commonly known, was without doubt one of the most disagreeable and scheming women of her own – or any – age. She had an overriding passion for building – both in stone and gold. Her houses and her fortune she acquired by marriage and hard dealing, as Horace Walpole explained:

> Four times the nuptial bed she warmed,
> And every time so well performed,
> That when death spoiled each husband's
>   billing,
> He left the widow every shilling.
> Fond was the dame, but not dejected;
> Five stately mansions she erected . . .

Her career as a 'hideous, dry, parched, narrow-minded . . . prudent, amassing, calcula-ting buildress' (as she was described by one of her descendants) began when she was fourteen and by no means hideous, dry and parched. She was, in fact, something of a beauty when she was married to Robert Barlow, a young neighbour who had recently inherited considerable estates in Derbyshire. As part of the marriage agreement Robert was required to settle all his estates on his bride. Within a year he was dead and Elizabeth added his fortune to the one she had inherited from her father at the age of seven. She shunned wedded bliss for another fourteen years and was content to administer her wide Midlands estates. Then the middle-aged Sir William Cavendish swam into her ken.

Cavendish was besotted with her, so much so that, instead of obliging her to move south where the bulk of his estates lay, he sold up his other property in order to buy land neighbouring his wife's. In the ten years before Cavendish's death Elizabeth bore him six children. Together they began the first of Bess's great houses – Chatsworth, completed after Sir William's death for the staggering sum of £80,000. Widowed a second time in 1557, Elizabeth once again inherited her husband's complete fortune despite the fact that Cavendish's children by former marriages had a claim upon his estate.

In 1560 the experiment was repeated. This time it was Sir William St Loe, Captain of the Guard to Queen Elizabeth, who fell under Bess of Hardwick's spell. He survived scarcely long enough to

*The initials 'E.S.' (Elizabeth Shrewsbury) still proclaim Bess's greatness at Hardwick Hall.*

architecture, a lasting monument to herself and her family, a symmetrical mansion full of windows and surmounted with the countess's monogram, 'E.S.' (Elizabeth Shrewsbury), in large stone letters at every corner. In 1584 the earl and his wife separated, he to live in peace on his estate near Sheffield, she to reside at Hardwick planning her new house and watching it grow.

But there were other plans to be made as well. Trowel and plumbline were not the only tools Bess used to build her empire. One historian described her as a 'woman of masculine understanding and conduct, proud, furious, selfish and unfeeling. She was a builder, a buyer and seller of estates, a moneylender, a farmer, and a merchant of lead, coals, and timber; when disengaged from these employments, she intrigued . . .'. She now had children, and grandchildren, and she saw them all as mere stones in the edifice of Cavendish greatness. She found the best marriages that influence and money could buy for them. She married her daughter to Charles Stuart, a member of the Scottish royal house. This union produced a granddaughter, Arabella, second in line to both the Scottish and English thrones. This child held the key to undreamed of greatness and prestige. Bess took Arabella under her wing and made her a virtual prisoner at Hardwick, while she plotted a suitable match. But this time the Countess found herself up against an equally ruthless woman. Queen Elizabeth was not prepared to have the succession decided by Bess of Hardwick. She had Arabella removed and taken into royal custody.

George Talbot died in 1590. His widow survived him for more than seventeen years, immensely rich, cantankerous and ruling her household with an iron will. And when she died her work survived. For in every respect she had built to last. From her loins sprang two ducal families (those of Devonshire and Newcastle). Hardwick Hall itself still stands and as long as it does so Bess of Hardwick will be remembered.

*Bess's house at Chatsworth – much altered in the seventeenth century.*

convey all his worldly goods to the lady who was fast becoming the richest woman in England.

Bess's final conquest (1568) was George Talbot, Earl of Shrewsbury, a leading courtier and councillor. This time she made sure of tying up her intended husband's property by marrying two of her own children to two of Talbot's as a condition of the union. The earl and his countess did not get on. Bess had at last come up against a husband whom she could not manipulate. He blocked her attempts to divert Talbot property into the hands of herself and her children and the result was the most furious rows. An observer reported, 'It appeareth by her words and deeds she doth deadly hate him and hath called him knave, beast and fool to his face . . .'. We can easily imagine the sharpness of her tongue from the tone of some of her letters. To one man who had got on the wrong side of her she wrote: 'Though you be more wretched, vile and miserable than any creature living, and for your wickedness be come more ugly in shape than the vilest toad in the world . . . yet I do no way wish your death but (only) that all the plagues and miseries that may befall any man may light upon such a caitiff as you are.'

She took refuge in her building projects. She planned and oversaw fine houses at Worksop, Bolsover and Oldcotes. But her major achievement was the new hall she created at her old home of Hardwick. It was to be the perfect house, the culmination of all she had learned about domestic

# The great lover?

Giovanni Jacopo Casanova tells us in his auto-biography that he 'turned the heads of some hundreds of women'. He gives the details of several of his amours and upon these details popular imagination has built the precarious Casanova legend. 'All the world loves a lover', we are told, and perhaps if Casanova did not exist it would be necessary to invent him. All myths have a foundation in reality and once we uncover the reality we usually find it more interesting and certainly more complex than the myth. That is certainly true of Casanova: during his long and fascinating life he played a number of other roles besides that of seducer of women – traveller, gambler, swindler, author, spy, librarian, philosopher, musician, etc, etc.

He was born in Venice in 1725, the result of an adulterous liaison between an actress and a theatre-owner. His mother neglected her family in the pursuit of her career and, his legal father having died, Giovanni was brought up by his grandmother. He grew up lonely, resentful and unloved but also very intelligent, realizing that he would have to live by his wits if he were to drag himself out of the gutter. The opportunities were certainly available in decadent Italian society for an unscrupulous and dedicated adventurer to enrich himself. A somewhat desultory education qualified him to attend the university of Padua from which he emerged with a degree in law. But the legal profession was a tedious business of dusty tomes and interminable wrangles. Casanova had discovered other talents which promised more enjoyment and quicker returns. He had charm and a plausibility of manner that easily induced women to yield up their honour but, more importantly, induced mugs to yield up their cash. One trick was to seek out a greedy merchant and sell him a formula for increasing the volume of mercury at little cost. In reality what Casanova did was to add a mixture of bismuth and lead to the sample. Its volume was certainly increased but the mercury was, of course, less pure. In Mantua Casanova came across a gullible fool who possessed a rusty old blade he had bought in the belief that it had once belonged to St Peter. Casanova immediately spun a story for the old man's benefit. Did he realize that if he had the scabbard as well, he would possess an infallible talisman for locating buried treasure? Off went Casanova to manufacture a suitably ancient looking sheath which he sold for £125. He developed a reputation as a supplier of potions and nostrums for the sick. By the law of averages some of his patients recovered.

As time went by Casanova became more and more involved with 'magic'. He studied cabalistic writings and used a hotch-potch of secret writings, incantations and mystic rites to con people out of money. Probably his most outstanding success was with Mme d'Urfé in Paris. This wealthy, ageing noblewoman was an avid student of necromancy and hoped to find in the black arts the secret of youth. More specifically she wished to be reborn – as a boy. Casanova convinced her that such a transformation lay within his power but that, of course, it would require a great deal of preparation – expensive preparation. He managed to string his victim along for six years, during which time he took thousands of pounds off her in one way or another. The proceedings became progressively more bizarre. Once Casanova and the lady solemnly bathed together and, while doing so, burned a letter to the moon. As the ashes scattered over the water the moon's reply magically appeared (having been previously written by Casanova, of course). Gulling the foolish and wealthy became Casanova's most lucrative pastime, but when that failed he could always fall back on gambling. He did not always win, but by a mixture of cheating, bluff and persistence he could usually come out on top. Once he challenged a rival to a card-playing marathon. He rose victorious from the table – after forty-two hours.

Despite all the money Casanova's various stratagems brought in, it would be wrong to think of him as avaricious. He was by nature generous and he loved to make the grand – and expensive – gesture. Most of his income went on the fine clothes, carriages and other accoutrements to sustain the image necessary for his various deceptions. It was, in turn, his deceptions and his love affairs which obliged him to be perpetually on the move. Part of him would have loved to settle down, acquire an impressive estate and play the *grand seigneur*, but the other part, the adventurer, would never permit it. His escapades were legion, even if we take many of his boasts with a pinch of salt. He was jailed for sorcery in the reputedly escape-proof doge's prison at Venice but he *did* escape, in an elaborate scramble over roofs and through windows at dead of night. In

*Amorous encounters in boudoirs and arbours were common in the fashionable European society in which Casanova moved.*

Paris, Casanova introduced the state lottery. He spent some months as an army officer until some inevitable scandal obliged him to resign. Returning to Venice in the 1770s, he was employed for many years as a government spy, a role for which his free movement at all levels of society ideally fitted him. The last thirteen years of his life he spent as librarian to the Count von Waldstein where he wrote his highly-coloured autobiography.

Giovanni Casanova is a magnificent example of the enthusiast, not because of his insatiable lust for women but because of his unremitting contest with life. He had begun his human pilgrimage with nothing – less than nothing; he was an unwanted brat. And he made the world sit up and take notice of him. His weapons were a sharp wit, a cool head and abounding energy. In taking on the rich, the gullible, the greedy and the corrupt he proved himself a jack of all trades and a master of none. No, not even a master of the boudoir. For after we have examined Casanova's accounts of his various conquests and stripped away the obvious romanticizing, what do we find? We find that in sex, as in all else, the man was an opportunist. Most of his bedfellows were prostitutes, actresses (which was much the same thing in those days) and sluts. Of the others, most were women anxious or desperate for sexual adventure – older women, jilted women, plain women and boys (for Casanova was bisexual). Such conquests required little subtlety, tenderness or even sexual prowess. His bedroom adventures must be seen as part and parcel of that larger adventure which was his contest with life. Like that contest they afforded him many triumphs but no lasting satisfaction.

# The fame maker

A man in overalls appeared on a street in a Maryland town. He carried a brick in each hand. He placed one on the sidewalk, carefully measured ten paces, then set down the other. Having done that, he picked up the first brick marked out another ten steps from the second and deposited it farther along the street. As he repeated this process over and over again an inquisitive crowd gathered. Among them was a nine-year-old boy. The man in overalls had attracted a large following by the time he reached the local theatre. Then, ignoring the bricks, he pasted up a notice advertising the Cleveland Minstrels as the playhouse's forthcoming attraction. At that moment, it began to dawn on the nine-year-old boy, whose name was Harry Reichenback, that he wanted to devote his life to what he later called 'ballyhoo'.

Ballyhoo is the art of creating fame, the art, in a word, of publicity. Its possibilities for power, influence and the accumulation of wealth fascinated him. 'Publicity,' he once wrote, 'is the nervous system of the world. Through it . . . it is possible for fifty people in a metropolis like New York to dictate the customs, trends, thoughts, fads and opinions of an entire nation of a hundred and twenty million people.' It was that belief and the audacity to act on it that made Harry Reichenback into one of the greatest publicity agents of all time and one of the creative forces in the rise of the motion picture industry.

Harry was a sickly child, so ill at times that he could neither move nor talk. Being bed-ridden he craved adventure and found it in the fantasy world of comic books. He was a dreamer. As he entered adolescence his health and strength improved. But he was still a dreamer. That was why he never lasted more than a few days in ordinary jobs. That is why he ran away to join the circus. In a short space of time he learned all the tricks used by hucksters and professional frauds for getting money out of people. Harry never had an act of his own. He was the 'spieler', the front man. It was his job to attract the crowds with an excited flow of patter in which every other word was a superlative. Over the years he worked with magicians, psychic mediums, escapologists and all manner of charlatans. At last he fetched up in the Mecca of all American dreamers – Broadway.

By now he called himself a 'publicity agent' and was prepared to work for anyone who would pay him. A bookshop had ordered a thousand copies of a print entitled *September Morn* and it could not sell them. The print, after a well known painting, depicted a nude woman standing on the edge of a forest pool. Very arty. Very un-erotic. Reich-

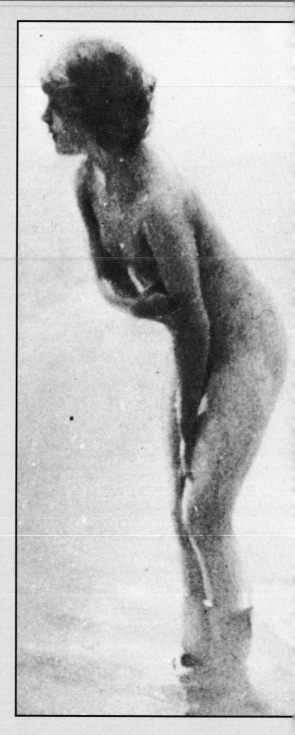

*The nude in 'September Morn',*
*Harry Reichenback opposite.*

enback went off to the city's Anti-Vice Society and complained about the disgusting picture which was corrupting New York's youth. He got the chairman to go to the shop and see for himself. When he arrived he found a gang of urchins outside the window, tittering and making vulgar jokes about *September Morn*. The guardian of public morals took the shopkeeper to court. Reichenback saw that the press was informed. The bookseller sold all his copies. And the urchins received their promised fifty cents apiece. It was Reichenback's first publicity stunt. It was nothing to the elaborate hoaxes he pulled when he joined the infant movie business.

That happened in 1913. One problem in the early days of silent pictures was to get theatre owners to show your picture as opposed to one offered by a rival. Reichenback devised many ruses to overcome this problem. Once he sent every potential exhibitor a letter.

I know you never expected to hear from me again, dear, but I couldn't help it. I am sending

you this key and in the next few days you will receive a box which it will unlock. This box holds the thing most dear to both of us . . . as ever,

Your
Natalie.

Some recipients took the letter straight to their lawyers. Others spent a guilty few days racking their brains to recall who Natalie was. One had some hard explaining to do because his wife opened the letter. When the 'box' came, it turned out to be a trade journal fastened with a padlock. On the centre pages was a large ad for Reichenback's movie, produced by National Pictures Inc. – Natalie for short.

Publicity had as much to do with the making of film stars as did talent. Once Reichenback was trying to get press attention for an up-and-coming actor called Francis Bushman. He was due to arrive at a certain hotel at 7.00 p.m. At 6.15 a glamorous blond arrived and left a box of flowers for him. She had barely left when it exploded releasing volumes of smoke and causing pandemonium. Police rushed to the scene and so did reporters. Stories about the 'assassination attempt' and the 'mysterious woman' kept Bushman on the front pages for days.

Stunt followed stunt. The first Tarzan film was publicized by letting an ape loose on Broadway. Reichenback had the animal dressed in topper and tails and delivered to the Knickerbocker Hotel. The panic he caused among the smart clientele was astounding. The police were summoned but they had no experience at dealing with wild animals and it was some hours before the creature was shut up in a safe cell. Of course, the press loved it. They wanted to know where the elegant ape had come from. It transpired that he had 'escaped' from his cage in the foyer of the theatre where *Tarzan* was about to open. The movie – a very mediocre one – was a sell-out.

Reichenback owed a great deal to masters of ballyhoo, like Barnum. But, unlike the great circus king, Reichenback was not interested in self-advertisement. He stayed in the background, using his talents to promote other people. For him the satisfaction came from making things happen. He was still the adventure-loving little boy, but he had found out how to turn his fantasy world into reality. He explained it this way: 'The difference between the things one dreamed about and reality was simply a matter of projection . . . An idea that would seem at first flush, extravagant and impossible, became by the proper projection into life a big item of commanding news value.'

Harry Reichenback died of cancer in 1932 at the age of forty-nine and the dream world of motion pictures lost one of its architects.

## The golden obsession

Would you like to be rich? Most of us if asked that question would give a fairly enthusiastic affirmative answer but few of us, if it came to it, would be prepared to pursue wealth with single-minded devotion. There are however some people who do make it their goal to become millionaires and who are prepared to sacrifice almost everything to the achievement of this objective. Some do it through business, some do it through crime, some take up treasure-hunting. There has never been a more obsessed treasure-hunter than Mel Fisher.

Melvin Fisher was born in Hobart, Indiana, in 1922. His father was a carpenter but Mel trained as an engineer, or rather he began to train as an engineer. The Second World War intervened and he left college to go into the army. Like many young men of his generation he found it difficult to settle back into civilian life after the conflict. He missed the excitement, the camaraderie, the sense of purpose. He tried a number of jobs and ended up helping his father run a chicken farm in California. His hobby at this time was fishing and it was an easy transition from that to skin diving and spear fishing. Scuba diving was a fast-growing sport in America at that time. Techniques had been perfected during the war and

enterprising businessmen had adapted naval equipment to provide the wherewithal for a new breed of underwater adventurers. Thus a modern hobby was born, a hobby which would have many branches – fishing, shell collecting, exploring coral formations and diving for sunken treasure. In the early days Mel Fisher's speciality was lobsters. He would dive down, collect them from the sea bed, and sell them to local restaurants. He also ran a diving gear shop. He wrote articles for sporting magazines. His next development was underwater photography and this in turn led to his own television show. When he was thirty Fisher married a girl of seventeen who was as mad keen on diving as he was. The future looked very bright. He was happy with his beautiful young wife. He had many successful business ventures and they were all based upon the sport which he loved. He went diving off both the east and west coasts of the United States and in other parts of the world. Some of Fisher's diving friends were now telling tales of treasure-hunting, of the quest for ancient galleons on the ocean floor and their spilled cargoes of doubloons and jewels. Fisher decided that he would try his hand at locating sunken wrecks. It was a fateful decision.

He left California for Florida. This was where the rich pickings were to be had. It was common knowledge that, in the heyday of Spain's American empire, hundreds of galleons laden with the silver, gold and emeralds of the New World had come to grief round the fringes of the storm-thrashed Caribbean. Fisher set up many unsuccessful expeditions. They were expensive; far more expensive than fishing trips. He needed a good ship, equipment for clearing sand away from

*Beside Fisher stands his son Dirk, later drowned.*

wreck sites, and for lifting heavy objects from the sea bed. This work swallowed the profits of his other businesses. He ran into debt but he could not give up. He had fallen prey to the disease called treasure fever.

In 1963 Fisher joined forces with a veteran Florida treasure-hunter called Kip Wagner. Wagner had found several coins and other artefacts in shallow water along the Florida coast emanating from an eighteenth-century wreck. Fisher now breezed in and told him that he was working too sporadically. The scale of his operation was not big enough. He offered to hire a team of professional divers, provide up-to-date equipment and locate all the wrecks on that section of the coast. Fisher's enthusiasm and dynamism startled the older man but eventually they made a deal. Fisher borrowed heavily to get together his team and all the gear he needed. They worked for a year and found nothing. It was only after Fisher had perfected a machine which could scoop great hollows out of the ocean floor by directing a powerful jet of water downwards that they had success but the success was spectacular – $1.6 million worth of gold coins. Even after paying the

expenses and giving Wagner his share there was a lot left over.

Once again Fisher could have stopped, invested his capital and lived comfortably, but already he was off on another quest, the richest Spanish galleon known to have sunk in those waters: the *Nuestra Señora de Atocha*, which sank in 1622 with nine hundred and one silver bars, two hundred and fifty thousand pieces of eight, forty-seven Troy tons of specie belonging to the king, two hundred and sixteen pounds weight of gold objects and an unspecified quantity of private treasure. It took him ten years, ten anxious, heartbreaking, backaching years. He poured into the *Atocha* expedition every penny he possessed and a great deal more besides. He borrowed money wherever he could. He built a floating treasure museum as a tourist attraction and took people out on fishing trips to gain more funds. He paid for research work to be done in Seville. He paid for divers, he paid for boats, he paid for newer and newer equipment. His search vessel moved from site to site. His divers made thousands upon thousands of dives. They found nothing. Everyone told him to give up but he knew that the *Atocha* was there and that he was destined to find her. In one tragic accident his son and daughter-in-law were killed. Still Fisher went on. At last, in 1975, his efforts were crowned with success. He discovered the *Atocha* and started salvaging her treasure. But no sooner had he done so than he found himself involved in a legal battle with the Federal Government over ownership of the wreck. More money had to be spent before Fisher established his claim to one of the richest treasures ever discovered. By that time Mel Fisher had become almost as great a legend as the *Atocha* herself.

*The converted tug 'North Wind', used in the recovery of the 'Atocha' treasure.*

# The irrepressible Tommy

I got out of bed, went downstairs to the drawing room, where I heard voices, opened the door and walked in. There I found several of the family, as well as my nurse . . . and amid profound and astonished silence I advanced to the middle of the floor and said: 'Please may I learn the piano?' The spectacles fell from my grandfather's nose as if removed by magic; the book he was reading dropped just as precipitately from my father's hands to the floor; my mother tried to scream, but surprise had deprived her of voice; and my old nurse . . . who was of immense physique and suffered from heart trouble, burst into tears and nearly fainted away.

So began one of the most remarkable musical and public careers of the last century. Thomas Beecham was born in 1879 into a family of very successful Lancashire industrialists who had made their money out of Beecham's Pills. The revelation which, he tells us, he made to the family at the age of six came after being taken to his first concert. His parents were patrons of music and his father had a passion for musical boxes. They littered the house in all shapes and sizes, some masquerading as items of furniture so that 'the visitor who hung up his hat on a certain peg of the hall rack, or who absent-mindedly abstracted the wrong umbrella from the stand would be startled at having provoked into life the cheerful strains of *William Tell* or *Fra Diavolo*. Thomas *did* learn the piano and, as the years passed, he went more frequently to concerts, recitals and operas. There was never any suggestion, how-

ever, that he should follow music as a career. His father groomed him for the family business; music was all very well as a hobby.

But Thomas was turning into a headstrong and determined young man. His career at Oxford came to an abrupt end because he took to disappearing for days at a time, dashing across to Germany or Italy for some important performance by one of the leading maestros of the day. In 1899 he fell out with his father and went to live in London. Then followed several remarkable years during which, by wholly unorthodox means, Thomas Beecham established himself as a leading conductor, a champion of modern composers, and an advocate of opera of which there was little appreciation in Britain at that time. It was by his sheer enthusiasm and flamboyant personality (as

well as his obvious musicality) that he achieved this. For example, he applied for the position of conductor with a touring opera company. He had virtually no experience and there were several applicants. They all waited in an anteroom – for hours. Then an angry little man bustled into the room, 'Is there anyone here who can play *Faust* from memory?' An auditioning singer had turned up without her music. Beecham knew the opera and said so. When the impresario later asked him what other operatic scores he knew by heart, Beecham stagged him by telling him that he was familiar with all the pieces on the tour programme. He got the job. In London and on the continent he met most of the leading musical personalities of the day. He became particularly friendly with Frederick Delius, who gave him much encouragement.

All his energy and all his money now went into music. He helped to establish the New Symphony Orchestra in 1906–7 and conducted its first concerts. In 1910 he was invited to conduct at Covent Garden and used this position to introduce the British public to little-known works by their own and continental composers. In 1916 he was knighted for his services to music. By this time he had already exhausted a fortune left him by his grandfather. In 1917 he inherited his father's estate and began to make serious inroads on that. Money poured into the National Opera Company in 1919, the Imperial League of Opera in 1927 and the London Philharmonic Orchestra in 1932. For much of his life he was in financial difficulties and plagued by accountants and Inland Revenue inspectors. On one occasion he left a rehearsal hurriedly with the explanation 'I understand there is someone to see me from the Official Receivers Office. Well, for what he is about to receive may the Lord make him truly thankful.'

'Tommy' was a great favourite with performers and audiences, not only because of his vigorous musical interpretation but also for his flashing, often cutting, wit. His most devastating remarks were reserved for other performers. Toscanini he dismissed as 'a glorified Italian bandmaster'. Beecham did not care very much for the symphonies of Vaughan Williams so the orchestra was not surprised to see him beating time at one rehearsal without enthusiasm. Suddenly the conductor noticed that the players had stopped. 'What's the matter?' he asked. 'It's finished, Sir Thomas.' He looked down at the score and beamed, 'So it is, thank God!' Once he conducted a ballet sequence at furious pace. When it was finished he leaned forward and muttered to the leader, with great satisfaction, 'We made the buggers hop that time, didn't we?' Rehearsals with Tommy were never tedious and dull. He would approach the rostrum at a slow, dignified

*Thomas Beecham's inherited fortune based on patent medicine financed a musical revival in Britain.*

pace, then throw himself into the work with arm-waving vigour, shouting his instructions above the noise and pausing to inject caustic comments into the proceedings. He might enquire of a trombonist, 'Are you producing as much sound as possible from that quaint and antique drainage system which you are applying to your face?' He might urge a zealous lady cellist, 'I wonder, madam, if you would try to take the music not quite so much *to heart*.' Instrumentalists were certainly kept up to the mark, not wishing to incur such comments as, 'We cannot expect you to be with us all the time, but perhaps you would be good enough to keep in touch now and again.' What would have passed for empty facetiousness in some men was accepted from Beecham. In a lifetime devoted to music he earned the respect and affection of other professionals and the general public. He was the most popular figure on the British musical scene for half a century and has been greatly missed since his death in 1961.

# A man of many loves

Sir Mortimer Wheeler was a man not much given to pontificating about the meaning of life but he once printed an anthology of poems that he found particularly valuable. In it the following lines by the explorer Richard Burton occur:

Do what thy manhood bids thee do, from
  None but self expect applause;
He noblest lives and noblest dies who makes
  And keeps his self-made laws.
All other life is living death, a world where
  None but phantoms dwell,
A breath, a wind, a sound, a voice, a tinkling
  Of the camel bell.

Those words will serve as well as any as a summary of Wheeler's own attitude. He followed his own inclination, did the things that he wanted to do, was passionate in every sense of the word in pursuing his enthusiasms and as a result of that passion achieved professional distinction, fame and widespread popularity. 'Rik', as he was known to his wide circle of friends, was born in 1890 in Glasgow although he grew up at Shipley, near Bradford, because his father worked as a journalist on the *Yorkshire Observer*. It was his father who imparted to Rik what was to be his first and greatest passion, archaeology. The two of them frequently went on country walks, walks which were full of interest and incident for the young child as his father pointed out landmarks, butterflies, flowers and other objects of interest. Always their most important discoveries were ancient relics. They found fragments of Roman pottery and flint implements. Rik's father would enthusiastically explain how these objects came to be made, what they were used for and what kind of life the people who created them lived. At school he gained a reputation as a fun-loving boy with an enormous capacity for hard work and no interest whatsoever in ball games. He shone academically and probably would have won a scholarship to Oxford if his family had not moved at the crucial time to take up residence in London. Instead he went to London University, studying the classics at University College. He threw himself whole-heartedly into college life and there discovered his second great love, women. He was charming, effervescent, enthusiastic and determined. Few members of the opposite sex could resist him. After many affairs he fell in love with, and married, a fellow student called Tessa. It was a quiet, almost secret, affair. Indeed, Tessa did not meet several of Rik's closest relatives until after they were married. Rik's qualities did not include a concern for other people's feelings. Scarcely had he started on his married life and his archaeological career when the First World War broke out. It gave Wheeler the opportunity to discover his third love, the Army.

He served as an artillery captain and saw his fair share of action among the mud, blood and horror of Flanders. No sane man could be said to have enjoyed the war of the trenches but there were aspects of the conflict which appealed to Wheeler enormously. He enjoyed commanding a team of men, took pleasure from working with horses and machines and was thrilled by danger. He threw himself whole-heartedly into his duties and inspired his men to do the same. For one conspicuous piece of gallantry and initiative he won the Military Cross. The citation reads, 'While making a reconnaissance he saw two enemy field guns limbered up without horses within three hundred yards of the outpost line. He returned for two six-horse teams, and under heavy fire, in full view of the enemy successfully brought back both guns to his battery position and turned them on the enemy.' The war which decimated a generation and broke the spirit of many of the men who did return, left Wheeler with a heightened sense of authority and a feeling that he had been spared to perform great tasks.

The inter-war years saw his reputation as a practical archaeologist clearly established. He worked on several sites in Wales and attracted attention particularly for his lucid and well-illustrated reports on the excavations. In 1924 he was awarded the prestigious post of Director of the National Museum of Wales, a considerable achievement by a man who was still only thirty-three. Rik now discovered the fourth love of his life, publicity. Archaeological excavation was then, as always, under-financed. Wheeler found that his personality and the romantic way in which he described work in progress attracted interest and support. It all began with his appeal for funds for excavations of the Roman fort at Caerleon. The amphitheatre where he started work was known locally as King Arthur's Round Table. By using this romantic and totally spurious association in his releases to the press, Wheeler persuaded the *Daily Mail* to provide £1000 for exclusive rights and daily reports on the work. Wheeler was often criticized as a vulgar publicist. He was quite unrepentant. His alliance with the newspapers, and later with television, served, he claimed, two ends: to win support, understanding and finance for the archaeologist and to make the general public aware of just what it was that archaeologists were doing. He believed passionately that if academics pursued their labours for the sole benefit of other members of their own little coterie, they were totally wasting their time.

In ensuing years he was active on digs both at home and in the Middle East. He was also active in other ways, pursuing a number of love affairs. Tessa knew of his infidelity but remained devoted to him and he was heartbroken by her sudden death in 1935. It was not in him to grieve long; life was too full. As well as running the London Museum, writing academic reports on his excavations and popular works aimed at introducing archaeology to the wider public, Rik worked on a

*Wheeler and his second wife, Mavis de Vere Cole.*

variety of sites throughout the country – and there were always the women. In 1939 he married Mavis de Vere Cole, ex-wife of the famous practical joker. Then within months he was in uniform again. During the Second World War he commanded a light anti-aircraft battery serving first of all at home and then in North Africa and Italy. Once again he was in his element as he indicated in a letter to a friend, 'I'm now in the crack division of the British Army! This means a seat plumb in the front row of the stalls for anything that is going . . . it's a grand and gratifying thought.' His second marriage ended in divorce in 1942 when Rik detected Mavis in an affair with another man. He was furious and obviously could not see the poetic justice in the situation. Emerging from the war as a brigadier, he returned to a hectic life of practical archaeology and a third marriage which this time ended in separation. Professional honours were poured upon him and in 1952 he was knighted for services to archaeology.

In the same year he discovered another great love, television. He was chosen as a panelist for a quiz game and became a star almost overnight. The public loved him for his wit and old-world charm and in 1954 he was named Television Personality of the Year. He entered a spry and active old age with his horizons still wide, his enthusiasms undampened, his eye for a pretty face undimmed. In 1976 the world lost one who in the full sense of the word had been a great lover.

# The compulsive traveller

If it were not for her enthusiasm we would know virtually nothing about Celia Fiennes. No portrait of her survives. She built no impressive houses, spawned no brilliant children in order to defy anonymity. She did not marry. She was just a younger daughter of a younger son of the first Viscount Saye and Sele, a mere name on one of those genealogical tables which English gentry families set so much store by: 'Celia 1662–1741'. You would have pictured her, if you pictured her at all, as a maiden aunt, living quietly in the country, adoring her garden, grumbling at her servants and devoting herself to good works.

But you would have been wrong. For Celia Fiennes was a tireless and compulsive traveller and a lady who carefully recorded in her journals everything she saw and heard as she journeyed around Britain. Even that may not sound very remarkable until we reflect on the conditions of travel in her day. For discomfort and danger the roads of Britain were worse at the end of the seventeenth century than they had been in the Middle Ages – and *then* they were atrocious. Before Celia's time only a handful of men and no women had ever set out on a descriptive tour of this country. People travelled for necessity, not pleasure. Yet Celia Fiennes meandered insatiably about the land on horseback, accompanied usually by only a couple of servants. The difficulties she encountered were many and varied.

Around Ormskirk the ways were liable to severe flooding. 'I avoided going by the famous Martin Mere that, as the proverb says, has parted many a man and his mare indeed. It being near evening and not getting a guide I was a little afraid to go that way it being very hazardous for strangers to pass by it.' Guides were important, and not always trustworthy. Approaching Darlington 'by the way I lost some of my nightclothes and little things in a bundle that the guide I hired carried'. Celia's 'bundle' contained her own bedclothes which she always took with her, simply because she could not trust to the cleanliness of the houses where she stayed. Dirt and discomfort reached their peak in Ely, 'the dirtiest place I ever saw . . . it's a perfect quagmire . . . the streets are well enough for breadth but for want of pitching it seems only a harbour to breed and nest vermin in, of which there is plenty enough, so that though my chamber was near twenty steps up I had frogs and snails and slow worms in my room . . .'. At another inn she met surly hostility: 'they had no hay nor could get none, and when my servants had got some elsewhere they were angry and would not entertain me'. Near Whitchurch Celia's party was beset by highwaymen. Danger of another kind threatened when Miss Fiennes crossed the sands of Dee: 'the sands here are so loose that the tides do move them from one place to another at every flood . . . as it brings the sands in heaps to one place so it leaves others in deep holes, which are covered with water and loose sand that would swallow up horses or carriages'. Though Celia's party was seen safe across by local guides, her horse at one point lost its footing and she found herself floundering in deep water. Add to such experiences as these all the 'normal' hazards she regularly encountered – getting lost,

*Belton House, Lincolnshire, was a very modern house when Celia Fiennes visited it.*

*Windsor Castle impressed Celia Fiennes. She described it as 'the finest palace the king has'.*

being soaked to the skin, arriving late and exhausted at destinations because she had been misled as to distance (this was before the days of reliable maps and the 'mile' differed in length from region to region) – and you will see that Celia Fiennes was a bold and adventurous lady.

The journals she left for posterity are a mine of information about life in Britain at the turn of the eighteenth century but they also reveal much about Miss Fiennes, her opinions, beliefs and prejudices. She was a great expert on the health spas where ladies and gentlemen went to take the waters and enjoy the entertainments which inevitably grew up around these centres of fashionable life. Celia never failed to test the medicinal properties of the springs. At Knaresborough she found that immersing herself in the waters was a cure for headache and gave her immunity from colds. However, she had 'little stomach' for the waters at Barnet when she observed the pool from which they issued to be full of leaves.

Frequently on her journeys Celia was put up by the nobility and gentry in their great houses. She never failed to comment on these buildings and their owners' prosperity. Her trained eye missed no significant detail. Mr Foley's mansion at Stoke Edith was still under construction but:

> What is finished is neat, good wainscote and tapestry, there is two or three damask beds and one velvet one, what they had before, so no new furniture, but the best wing, no doubt, will be finely finished and furnished.

Poverty, on the other hand, distressed her. On her first visit to Scotland she quickly retreated back over the border, appalled at the conditions she observed. The Welsh fared little better from her pen: 'at Holywell they speak Welsh, the inhabitants go barefoot and barelegged, a nasty sort of people'. Her religious opinions were very clearly formed; in this same place she 'saw abundance of the devout papists on their knees all round the well; poor people are deluded into an ignorant, blind zeal and to be pitied by us that have the advantage of knowing better and ought to be better'. She was quick to observe details about local trade, industry and agriculture. She was something of an expert on coal, iron and lead mining. At Newcastle she examined the coal carried from the pits in carts and barges and talked with the men who produced it. 'This is what the smiths used,' she wrote, 'and it cakes in the fire and makes a great heat, but it burns not up light unless you put most round coals.'

So Celia Fiennes passed on her way noting, approving, regretting, complimenting, complaining but always enthusing.

> If all persons, both ladies, but much more gentlemen, would spend some of their time in journeys to visit their native land . . . it would form [in them] such an idea of England, add much to its glory and esteem in our minds and cure the evil itch of over-valueing foreign parts . . .

# The power of dreams

'He feels himself no one in society, forgetting that a young man of twenty-one ought not to be anything in society.' So remarked a friend of the family about the restless and impatient Austin Henry Layard. The reproof was fully justified, for the young man in question had a head full of golden dreams and a disinclination to engage in the humdrum business of earning a living. Yet, bearing in mind his extraordinary childhood it could, perhaps, scarcely have been otherwise. His earliest years had been spent in Florence where his father, a connoisseur, had pointed out to him all that was most excellent in Renaissance painting and architecture. The Layards were enthusiastic hosts; poets, painters, writers, travellers and antiquarians were frequently to be found at their table, telling tales that enthralled the young boy. When left to his own devices Henry read avidly – the novels of Sir Walter Scott, Elizabethan poets and playwrights and, above all, *The Arabian Nights*. When the family returned to England and Henry was sent to boarding school it is hardly surprising that he found the conversation and interests of his contemporaries restricted and their behaviour uncivilized. At the age of sixteen he went into his uncle's law firm but this completely failed to satisfy him. His close friend Benjamin Disraeli noted in his diary about this time, 'Nature has given me an awful ambition and fiery passions', and Layard could well have said the same. However, he settled to his legal studies and passed the examinations. It was in 1839, when he was twenty-two, that Layard found his true vocation.

It had been arranged that he should go to Ceylon to work as a barrister and he eagerly prepared for the overland journey. Italy, Greece and Asia Minor, with their abundant remains of past civilizations, enthralled the travellers (Henry was travelling with a friend, Edward Mitford, who had been charged to look after him and curb his enthusiasm). They went on to the Holy Land and Layard revelled in the sites of biblical times so familiar to him from his antiquarian dabblings. Now they were close to those great centres of ancient civilization of which he had dreamed since childhood – Babylon, Nineveh, Baghdad. He wanted to travel eastwards across the desert to see for himself what remained of these once-

*Layard's detailed drawings of the bas-reliefs uncovered at Nimrud proved him to be a fine draughtsman.*

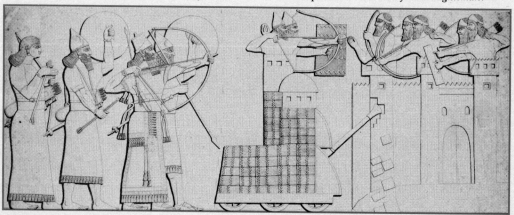

fabulous kingdoms. Mitford refused: the area in question was inhabited by warring tribes; travelling would be dangerous; in any case, they had already taken up too much time in antiquarian meanderings. The two men parted company and Layard travelled alone into Persia. Whether or not he knew it at the time, he had turned his back on the law and all the staid respectability that went with it. He ventured into unknown lands with few funds and boundless enthusiasm. He was, as he later admitted, very naive. 'I had romantic ideas about beduin hospitality and believed that if I trusted to it . . . I should incur no danger.' He adopted Arab dress, ate Arab food and lived very simply accompanied only by a servant-guide. For two years he travelled through Mesopotamia. He encountered many dangers and discomforts but nothing could diminish his delight in actually being in the land where magnificent empires had once held sway. And yet, there was so little to see. The desert had long since swallowed up the great centres of early civilization.

> These huge mounds of Assyria made a deeper impression upon me, gave rise to more serious thoughts and more earnest reflection than the temples of Baalbeck and the theatres of Ionia . . . A deep mystery hangs over Assyria, Babylonia and Chaldea . . .

That mystery he pledged himself to solve.

But the undertaking Layard had in mind would require money. Layard had almost none and he knew that his family would not subsidize his wild schemes. Fortunately he found a friend and patron in Stratford Canning, ambassador at Constantinople. Canning employed the young man in a number of unofficial diplomatic missions, then, in 1845, financed Layard's great dream, the excavation of Nineveh, capital of the Assyrian Empire. In 1846–7 Henry Layard, the young amateur archaeologist, made discoveries which took the academic world by storm. Digging into a mound at Nimrud he discovered the remains of the ninth century BC palace of Ashurnasirpal II, its walls covered with magnificent bas-reliefs. These he cut into slabs and, personally supervising the engineering work and transportation, had them conveyed to the Tigris and thence by barge and ship back to England, where they were gratefully received by the British Museum which had taken over from Canning as backer of the excavation. Layard believed he had discovered Nineveh. He had, in fact, uncovered the older and more important site of Calah or Nimrud.

Layard's work brought him immediate public acclaim. His book describing the excavation was widely read. He was made a freeman of the City of London and rector of Aberdeen University. It

was a time when there was considerable public interest in antiquity and when the leading nations of Europe were vying with each other in the establishment of public collections. Apart from anything else Layard's success was seen as a major British coup. He easily won a parliamentary seat in 1852 and was determined to make as great a reputation in politics as he had in archaeology. In this he was disappointed. Successive administrations valued his opinions on foreign policy, particularly the Eastern Question, but he was never offered a Cabinet post. Part of the problem was his avidly pro-Turkish stance which he promoted whenever possible, and his exposure of the diplomatic incompetence which precipitated the Crimean War. His fearlessness was widely appreciated and *Punch* struck out at the politicians who wanted to muzzle the Member for Aylesbury.

> Hit Layard? hit him if ye dare! avast dishonest crew,
> Humbugs, get out and make room for a better man than you!

But few political careers are built upon fearless speeches. In 1869 Layard turned his back upon the House of Commons and accepted an ambassadorial post in Madrid. In 1877 he was transferred to Constantinople and was thus able to complete his public service where he had begun it. He had made for himself three careers and was disappointed at only having reached the highest level of distinction in one of them. Yet most contemporaries would have been more than satisfied to have attained the achievements of Austin Henry Layard.

# Deceivers

Deception has been a major feature of human history every since the serpent tricked Eve into eating the forbidden fruit. Men and women have deceived each other out of love and hate, swindlers have practised deception for money, governments have perpetrated fraud on a massive scale in what they conceived to be, or claimed to be, 'the public interest'. Fortunes have been made, reputations broken, governments have fallen and states have been overthrown because of celebrated forgeries. Bearing all this in mind we might perhaps conclude that deceivers are thoroughly despicable people, universally and properly abhorred. The truth is really different, as Samuel Butler said in *Hudibras*,

> Doubtless the pleasure is as great
> Of being cheated as to cheat.

We have a sneaking admiration for the clever trickster; the man who can sell the Eiffel Tower to a gullible tourist or fool millions of readers with a bogus newspaper report gains our grudging admiration. There are several categories of deceivers and many of them are quite harmless. It is these that we want to think about in this section of the book. The men and women whose stories follow were not for the most part 'wicked' in any serious sense of the word. They did not set out to ruin other people's lives or swindle them out of their savings. Their motives, in as far as those motives can be discerned, were not vicious.

First of all we have the hoaxers and practical jokers, those who did what they did, partly at least, out of a sense of fun. Horace de Vere Cole is by many people afforded the accolade of being the greatest practical joker of all time and his antics have justifiably won him a lasting fame. His audacity at digging holes in Piccadilly and above all his organizing of the Emperor of Abyssina's visit to HMS *Dreadnought* were gigantic pieces of fun, brilliantly conceived and cleverly executed. Yet I am not sure the first prize shouldn't go to Bampfylde Moore Carew, the master of disguise who spent several years of his life bamboozling the nobility and gentry into charitably supporting him and his accomplices. The motivation of both of these men seems to have been a mixture of the love of a self-imposed challenge and the desire to deflate oversized egoes. Horace Cole admitted that he liked to see prominent people taken down a peg or two and one of the reasons why he was so popular was that everyone else likes to see prominent people taken down a peg or two, as well.

It is not a very large step to George Psalmanazar and Mary Baker. They too enjoyed hoodwinking for hoodwinking's sake. They too had the talent and stamina to sustain a role over a long period of time. Psalmanazar continued for months lecturing, writing and talking with experts about the island of Formosa and the totally fictitious society he conjured up for it. Mary's deception did not last anything like as long but while it did last she carried it off with bravura. Both of these two were poor people who elected to live by their wits. In a sense they were also victims of their own fantasies. Because society had cast them in humble roles they devised more exotic characters to portray, and for a while they managed to turn their dreams into reality. William Francis Mannix was another man acting out a dream. As a boy he had pictured himself as an ace newspaper reporter dashing around the world making sensational scoops. When he grew up he assumed the life of his boyhood hero. He *did* write sensational stories, make startling revelations, record exclusive interviews. The only difference between him and other great journalists was that most of his reports emanated from his own imagination.

When we enter the world of artistic and scientific forgery we come upon a different category of deceivers, people whose motives are more complex if indeed they can be discerned at all. What was behind the Piltdown Man hoax? What induced Charles Dawson to set it up so painstakingly over a number of years, carefully collecting fossil fragments, falsely ageing them and then planting them in the chosen site? Obviously, he wanted to demonstrate that the scientific establishment could be fooled but did he just want to prove this for his own benefit or did he mean to expose the so-called experts to public ridicule? And what are we to make of the literary frauds of William Henry Ireland and James Macpherson? There is certainly a similarity in their stories; both were disregarded young men with a sense of grievance and a desire to do something 'big' so that the world would not go on ignoring them. Both Ireland and Macpherson had learned perhaps unconsciously the first lesson of the hoaxers' craft: tell people what they want to hear. In the eighteenth century there was a growing mania for relics of the past, classical antiquities, medieval armour, ancient coins, Shakespeariana, fragments of folk literature. Amateur antiquaries collected widely and indiscriminately. When supposedly ancient manuscripts were laid before them, they snapped them up uncritically. Ireland

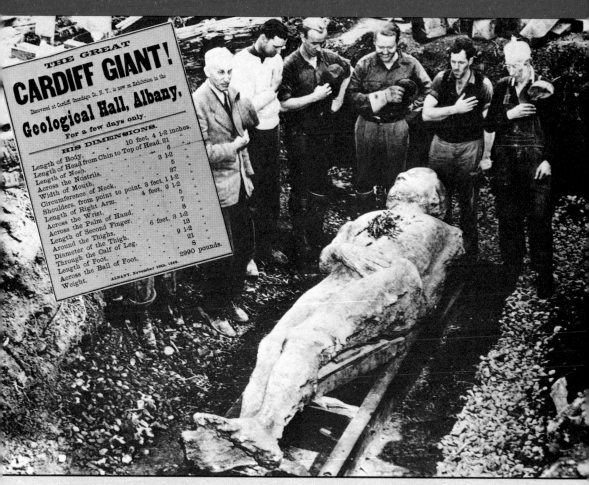

*The Cardiff Giant – a nineteenth-century American hoax. A large stone carving was exhibited for decades as a petrified giant.*

and Macpherson were aided by the fact that techniques for detecting forgeries were virtually non-existent. The same was not true two hundred years later when Elmyn de Hory was producing his fake Utrillos and Picassos. De Hory's motivation was anger, anger at an art establishment which could make or break reputations by dubbing one man a genius and ignoring another. De Hory knew that he was as good as modern masters whose works could command large sums of money and he set out to prove it by simply copying their styles.

With the next people on our list we move into a sad twilight zone, peopled by men and women who were as much the victims as the perpetrators of their own deceptions. Madame Blavatsky, the founder of the Theosophical Society, was a fake medium who was convincingly exposed before the end of her career, although that in no way inhibited her from continuing with her activities. But she was more than that. Life for her was a constant charade. She deliberately conjured up for herself an aura of mystery until in the end she became the weird person she faked for the benefit of others. And what is one to say of Burgess and McLean, the undergraduate idealists who never grew up, the little boys who were still playing at spies while their masters were in deadly earnest and who tragically involved many other people in their deception?

It is fitting that we should end this section with a mystery. For by no means all deceptions have been proven. There have been many men and women who have made extravagant claims for themselves, claims which have never been either proved or disproved. Among them none is more intriguing than the woman who called herself Anastasia.

# King of the beggars

Bampfylde Moore Carew – the name has an aristocratic ring about it and the man who bore it was of an ancient and well-to-do family. Which makes it all the more strange that he should have chosen to live for sixty years as a beggar and confidence trickster. Carew was the son of the rector of Bickleigh, a village in the Exe valley, near Tiverton in Devon. He never tired of playing pranks, nor could his father's cane beat out of him his limitless sense of fun.

But one day he went too far. He was sixteen and was out galloping over the Devon hills with some companions who, like himself, preferred the hunting field to the classroom. They put up a stag who gave them an excellent, long run. Unfortunately the beast led them through field after field of standing corn. The neighbouring farmers were furious and the lads knew that a thrashing awaited them when they returned home. So they simply did not return home. They ran off and joined a band of gypsies.

Carew immediately took to the carefree life of the open road. Gypsies in those days (the early eighteenth century) made a living from any and every kind of trickery and knavery that came to hand – begging, stealing, fortune telling and fraud. They were here today and gone tomorrow, so justice rarely caught up with them. To a high-spirited boy who loved play-acting and saw the pompous, rural squirearchy as a system to be debunked it was the ideal life. His first major coup was swindling a greedy lady of Taunton out of twenty guineas. He went to her in the guise of an oriental astrologer, complete with crystal ball, runes, cabalistic mumbo-jumbo and other paraphernalia, and told her that he could locate buried treasure by conjuring up demons. The gullible gentlewoman parted with money for Carew's 'expenses', and that was the last she saw of her 'Indian magician'.

Emboldened by this success, he extended his repertoire. He assumed a variety of disguises and studied each role with as much care as the most successful stage actors of the day. The characters he chose to play were all people who had undergone some terrible misfortune – a shipwrecked sailor, a farmer ruined when his land was flooded, a clergyman driven from his cure by religious persecution, a destitute mother deserted by her husband, and so on. His technique was simple. He would present himself at the door of the local great house and, using his knowledge of how gentry households were organized, would ensure that he got past the servants and was able to pour out his sorry tale to the master or mistress. It was not his skill as a deceiver that made Carew remark-

able; there were many beggars wandering the country who relied in whole or part upon fraud to soften the hearts and loosen the purse-strings of their victims. Carew stands apart from them by his sheer audacity. Most mendicants were driven to a life of petty crime by poverty. Carew took it up deliberately because he loved fooling people. He took quite unnecessary risks. Once he called upon a certain baronet three times in a single day. On each occasion he appeared in a different guise and each tale of woe that he told was successful.

But such escapades did not satisfy him. He had to try his skill out upon people who knew him and his family. One day he insinuated himself into the house of a Dorset landowner named Portman disguised as a rat-catcher. He was called into the parlour, where he discovered among Mr Portman's guests several old acquaintances. For an hour or more he kept the company amused with country lore and tales, both true and invented. The ladies and gentlemen laughed patronizingly and complimented themselves on having found such a 'quaint fellow' to while away a tedious afternoon. At last, Carew could stand their superiority no longer. He revealed his true identity and boasted of the ease with which he had duped them and several of their neighbours. They took it all in good part and Mr Pleydell, one of the guests, remarked, 'I have heard a great deal about you, Carew, and always hoped to meet you.' 'Oh, but we have already met,' said the beggar. 'I think not, sir,' Pleydell replied confidently. Carew smiled at his audience. 'Surely you have not forgotten the poor tattered wretch you took pity on last week. He was the sole survivor of a shipwreck near the Canaries and in a very sorry state. You were kind enough to give him a guinea and a suit of clothes, were you not?' Everyone was amused but Pleydell covered his embarrassment with a challenge. 'I'll wager another guinea you could not deceive me again.' Other gentlemen added their voices and their money to Pleydell's. They dared Carew to pit his wits against theirs and the trickster accepted the bet. He discovered when the company would be gathered again at Mr Pleydell's, and on the appropriate day there arrived at the house an elderly woman, trailing four small children. When a maid came to the door the crone set up a high pitched wail and told her story with tears and sobs. 'I am the unfortunate grandmother of these poor, helpless infants, whose dear mother and all they had, was burned at the dreadful fire at Kirton, and hope the good ladies will, for God's sake, bestow something on the poor famished infants'. The plea brought forth half a crown and some broth. Then the gentlemen came out, gave the woman some more money and told her to be on her way. The sad little entourage trailed its way across the stable yard. But half-way to the gate the 'grandmother' gave a sudden shout and a cheer and leaped into the air. Pleydell and his friends had to acknowledge themselves the losers as Carew explained how he had borrowed the children to add verisimilitude to his disguise.

Carew now became something of a celebrity in polite rural society. Noblemen and gentlemen vied with each other to be gulled by the audacious vagabond and were eager to pit their wits against his. On one occasion he was staying as the guest of a Colonel Strangeways at Melbury, Dorset. Over the dinner table his host asserted that it would be quite impossible for Carew to fool him since he had observed him very closely for many days. The following morning Strangeways went out hunting. His guest immediately slipped out of the house and sought out some nearby members of the gypsy fraternity. With their help he was soon transformed into a pitiable spectacle, with unkept beard, tattered clothes, a suppurating wound on one leg and hobbling with the aid of a crutch. He placed himself on the Colonel's route and waited. When Strangeways rode up Carew easily hoodwinked him out of half a crown. But

that was too easy a victory. The beggar now asked whether his benefactor could direct him to the house of a certain Colonel Strangeways who was famed among the mendicant brotherhood for his compassion and generosity. So it was that Carew persuaded his victim to direct him to his own home. Later, over dinner, he was able to prove his deception by producing his crutch and false beard.

By this time Bampfylde Moore Carew was famous among all the gypsies in Britain. So celebrated was he, that when Clause Patch, a 'king' among the travellers, died Carew was unanimously elected in his place. But 'royalty' did not protect him from the law. His long run of good luck ran out when he was arrested for vagrancy and convicted at Exeter quarter sessions. He was transported to Maryland and set to plantation labour. But he could not bear to lose his freedom and, even though he was encumbered by a heavy iron collar, he escaped. After staggering many miles he fell in with some Indians who gave him shelter and removed his collar. Leaving them after some days, he made his way to Pennsylvania. Since most people in that colony were Quakers, Carew now adopted the clothes, speech and behaviour of a member of that sect. Posing as a destitute brother, newly arrived from England, he had no difficulty in finding generous hospitality.

This provided him with the funds for a passage back to England. But even on board ship danger was not over. A few days out, the ship was stopped by a British man o' war whose captain needed replacements for crew members. This was a persistent hazard faced by travellers, and many men going about their lawful business found themselves pressed into naval service. No excuses were accepted by the ruthless press gangs, and many of Carew's fellow passengers were taken by force. But the master of disguise proved more than a match for rough seamen. He pricked his face all over and rubbed in salt and gunpowder. Then he went and lay down in a deserted part of the ship. When the press gang found him they fell back in horror. They could not leave the ship quickly enough – she had smallpox aboard!

Thus the King of the Beggars returned safe to Britain and to his old life. He was reunited with his wife – whom he had abducted some years before – and carried on practising deceptions until the end of his days. Offers of money and property from wealthy relatives never tempted him to a conventional, settled life. He had no need of such bribes. His own cunning earned him more than enough to live well. He was a celebrity who never lacked for hospitality and long after his death his exploits were kept alive in numerous popular biographies.

# King of the hoaxers

The man who was the greatest practical joker of all time was born plain Horace Cole but because his mother came from the ancient de Vere family, he preferred to call himself Horace de Vere Cole, *de jure* hereditary Lord Great Chamberlain of England (the office Lord Great Chamberlain had been bestowed in 1183 on Aubrey de Vere and his heirs for ever). He was born in 1881 into the well-to-do Irish family of Cole and early gained a reputation for his wild and eccentric ways. He was a creature of whim and impulse and demonstrated this most forcibly when he enlisted as a trooper in the British Army and went off to fight in the Boer War. He quickly rose to be lieutenant and then acting captain before being wounded and being sent home. The war left him with a permanently damaged shoulder and partial deafness. He went up to Cambridge where he seems to have spent more time in enjoying himself and playing practical jokes than in actually working. From then on he lived most of his life as a man-about-town in London where he mixed with the smart set and the intelligentsia and numbered among his friends people like Augustus John and Virginia Woolf. He was a patron of art in a modest way and was certainly among the first to recognize the genius of Augustus John. For a bachelor with an estate in the country and a couple of town houses, whose uncle was the Governor of the Bank of England, and whose brother-in-law was Neville Chamberlain, life could be very pleasant. There were parties and balls and trips to the races and all the events of the London season in those last years when England can still be said to have had an upper class.

But Cole was a rebel. He loved this pretentious world of which he was a part but at the same time he recognized its pretentiousness and always felt the need to take it down a peg or two; and so the long catalogue of hoaxes began. He once claimed, 'I have played and got away with more jokes than any man ever has', and he was probably right. Some were performed on the spur of the moment. Stopping in a London street to speak with an acquaintance who was a celebrated Member of Parliament he suddenly took it into his head to take out his gold watch and surreptitiously slip it into the other man's pocket. A few seconds after they had parted, Cole set off after the MP at a brisk run shouting out, 'Stop thief! Stop thief! That man's got my watch!' On another occasion he was greeted by a group of workmen who, it seems, mistook him for Ramsey Macdonald, the Labour politician. He immediately treated his audience to an impromptu lecture on the evils of socialism and then made off at a run, when the mood of the labourers became menacing. He was sent a form by the publishers of *Who's Who* and invited to fill it in as the basis for an entry. He later recalled how much fun he had had with it: 'In the space for games etc. I wrote "F— g".'

Other jokes involved much more careful preparation. Once he hailed a taxi and climbed in complete with a dummy of a partly nude woman. As the taxi cruised down Piccadilly, Cole saw the person he was looking for, a policeman. He opened the door and banged the dummy's head on the road shouting out, 'Ungrateful hussy!', hauled it in again, slammed the door, and shouted to the cabby, 'Drive like hell!' On another occasion he went to a London theatre and carefully bought a large number of stalls tickets, being very careful to specify the seats that he required. He took the tickets out into the street and began to distribute them, but only to bald-headed men. On the night of the performance, he attended with some distinguished friends who had seats in the dress circle. Just before the lights dimmed, he pointed down at the stalls. There for everyone to see, spelled out in glistening pink heads below, was a very rude word. Another scheme which demanded careful preparation was his visit to one of the leading boys schools. A preparatory letter, ostensibly from the Diocesan Bishop, explained that the date of a forthcoming Confirmation would have to be changed and that he was sending a deputy, the Bishop of Madras. Cole solemnly arrived in ecclesiastical garb and proceeded to confirm several boys. It was during his undergraduate days that with a party of friends all dressed as workmen and equipped with tents, lamps and all the necessary tools, he dug a large hole in Piccadilly, then went away leaving it there. Later, to underline the joke, he reappeared on the scene posing as an angry member of the public and complained loudly to the police. It was also while at Cambridge that he played a joke on the civic dignitaries of the town. He and his conspirators dressed up as the Sultan of Zanzibar and entourage, arrived by train, were greeted with great honour and treated to a full mayoral reception.

It was probably this that gave Cole the idea for his most celebrated hoax of all. The great *Dreadnought* hoax was a strange mixture of careful preparation and spontaneity. On 7 February 1910 Horace donned top hat and morning coat and posed as a certain Mr Cholmondeley from the Foreign Office. A number of his friends blackened their faces, dressed in turbans and robes, and richly decked themselves in jewels (the jewels alone cost Cole £500). They set off for Weymouth in a train from Paddington. Meanwhile, an accomplice sent a telegram to Admiral Sir William May, Commander of HMS *Dreadnought*, the pride of the British fleet, saying that the Emperor of Abyssinia and his suite, who were currently guests of His Majesty's government, had expressed a desire to see the ship, and were already on their way. Few detailed preparations had been made and it was only during the journey in the train that members of the company swotted up some Swahili from a grammar book borrowed from the Society for the Promotion of Christian Knowledge. They arrived in Weymouth to find the red carpet out, a ceremonial guard awaiting to receive them and the ship's band in full panoply. Many things went wrong with the conspirators' plans: Cole got muddled over the names they had all agreed upon; in the launch crossing the harbour some of the cast's whiskers began to come adrift; but the hoax was a complete success. The foreign dignitaries toured the battleship, speaking excitedly to each other in gibberish Swahili and nodding their approval to the Admiral with the oft-repeated phrase, 'Bunga-bunga!' This, as Cole explained, was high praise. As they took their leave the Emperor attempted to pin an elaborate decoration on the Admiral's chest. The embarrassed officer had to explain that he was not permitted to accept foreign orders without the consent of his superior. Returning in triumph, Cole immediately leaked the exploit to the press who gave the story front page coverage. (The group are seen in the photograph opposite.)

Cole was a lively, hearty, fun-loving man always looking for new exploits. He spent a year

*Horace's marriage to a younger woman from a different social class was something of a prank.*

in Venice working as a gondolier. He claimed to have travelled in the Sahara wandering around as a deaf-and-dumb Arab. Despite his disability he was a keen sportsman and a fine player of real tennis. Although he mellowed throughout the years, he remained always a wildly extrovert character with a roar like a lion. If anything it was the times that changed, not Cole. He lost nearly all his money in the depression of the 1920s. It was largely financial hardship which put an end to his first marriage in 1930. When he was forty-seven he fell in love with and subsequently married Mavis Wright, a ravishingly beautiful working class girl of nineteen. For a while they were very happy together but Cole's worsening financial plight obliged them to live in France, where everything was much cheaper, and after a couple of years Mavis left him. He died in cheap lodgings on 26 February 1936. His body was brought home for burial. Augustus John, his old friend, attended the funeral.

I went in hope of a miracle – or a joke. As the coffin was slowly lowered into the grave, in dreadful tension I waited for the moment for the lid to be lifted and a well-known figure to leap out with an ear-splitting yell. But my old friend disappointed me this time.

## Shakespeare revisited

*A fake portrait of Shakespeare on stage.*

Shakespeare is a mystery. Apart from the plays and poems themselves, little is known about him. Did he really write the works which bear his name? Where did he live and work for the greater part of his life? Did he exist at all? These and a host of other questions mark out the battlefield over which scholars have fought for two centuries and more. Nor is it only learned academics who have had an interest in the Shakespeare enigma. Providing 'newly discovered' plays and poems by the Bard has kept many skilled forgers in business. None of them was more prolific or audacious than William Henry Ireland.

William Ireland flourished during the closing years of the eighteenth century – the self-styled 'Age of Reason'. It was a time of scientific enquiry. No young gentleman's education was complete until he had made the Grand Tour, absorbing the wonders of ancient Rome and Greece. Clergymen and other members of the leisured classes devoted their time to minute studies of natural history. There was a positive mania for collecting 'curiosities' of all kinds. William's father, Samuel Ireland, both shared and profited from this obsession. He was a cultural jackdaw, collecting anything of historical or artis-

tic interest – a lock of Edward IV's hair, Oliver Cromwell's jacket, a portrait by Van Dyck and a variety of ancient books and manuscripts. He earned a living as a dealer in such curios from a shop in London's fashionable Norfolk Street. William, therefore, grew up surrounded by ancient relics – some genuine, some spurious – in a world of dilettante collectors, scholars and dealers.

The trouble all seems to have started because Samuel did not like his only son. The boy was lazy and a poor scholar. As such he could only be a disappointment to Ireland senior, who loved nothing more than abstruse debates with his circle of learned friends. William was a withdrawn lad who loved reading and the theatre. He was as well read in history and literature as his father but he brought to his studies the mind of the romantic dreamer not the scholar. William had a genuine affection for his father and was hurt by the near-contempt which greeted his every attempt to please.

In 1792 he was put to work as a lawyer's clerk in New Inn. He spent all his days, often alone, surrounded by boxes of ancient documents – deeds, wills, agreements and so on. Frequently he doodled to pass the time, copying ancient handwriting on odd scraps of parchment or vellum. One day, having bought a sixteenth-century book of prayers from a Thameside stall, William amused himself by writing a letter from the author to Queen Elizabeth I begging her patroness to accept the dedication of the volume. For ink he used a liquid that dried to a faded brown colour and looked genuine. Pleased with his work, he inserted the letter in the book and, that evening, asked his father's opinion of them. Samuel was delighted. He pronounced the letter genuine and complimented William on his discovery. The young man was overjoyed. At last he had found a way of winning his father's approval. And, in the end, it had been so easy.

William knew that what would excite Samuel still more would be a genuine piece of Shakespeariana. A few days later he had produced such a document – a land lease bearing the poet's signature and an old, but indecipherable, seal from another deed. But it was not enough, he realized, to forge a manuscript; he had to invent a story to go with it. So William told his father of a wealthy young gentleman of his acquaintance, a Mr H., who had inherited, with other property, a chest of documents many of which related to the Shakespeare family.

It was now that matters began to get out of hand. Samuel over-reacted. He showed the land lease to his expert friends, who were all as excited about it as he was, and he urged William to acquire more of the documents. Encouraged, and highly amused at his skill in being able to deceive the scholars, William now churned out forgeries by the score – love letters between 'Willy' Shakespeare and 'Anna' Hathaway, correspondence between the poet and his supposed patron, the Earl of Southampton, a handwritten manuscript of *King Lear*, and a variety of domestic and legal documents. Public interest was now aroused. So much so that Samuel had the collection printed and published under the title, *Miscellaneous Papers . . . of William Shakespeare*. Among the eager subscribers to this volume were James Boswell, Richard Brinsley Sheridan, Warren Hastings and several members of the aristocracy. In addition Samuel arranged an exhibition of the originals at his home and charged the public for the privilege of coming to view them.

The master forger soon announced the discovery of a hitherto-unknown Shakespeare play, *Vortigern*. This tragedy was the work of William and an actor friend, Montague Talbot, who had discovered William's secret and forced his way into partnership. As soon as the news leaked out, London's theatre managers vied with each other to stage the first production. Sheridan won the

contest and *Vortigern* had its first – and last – performance at his Drury Lane Theatre on 1 April (a suitable date 1796. The house was packed and it must have seemed to a casual observer that the Irelands and their colleagues were about to enjoy their greatest triumph. But the audience was composed of rival factions. Opposition to the *Shakespeare Papers* had been mounting in academic circles. On the day before the performance Edmund Malone, a leading literary critic, published a blistering and detailed exposé. The crowds in Drury Lane had come to enjoy a battle off the stage not on it. Whole sections of the play were lost amid aggressive applause on the one hand and shouts of derision on the other.

The bubble had, after two years, finally burst. The interesting point is that the forgeries were not very good forgeries. William had taken great care over materials but had been too lazy to master such matters as Jacobean spelling and points of historical detail.

But poor Samuel refused to accept the truth. After the *Vortigern* débâcle William confessed everything to his father – and he was not believed. If the papers were forgeries, Samuel insisted, they must have been conceived by someone far cleverer than his blockhead son. Their relationship was broken, never to be healed. William left home and never saw his father again. He lived to be sixty but, despite his obvious talents, he never achieved success in his own right and ended his days an impecunious hack. Perhaps the *Shakespeare Papers* had exhausted his genius. Perhaps the literary establishment which he had made look foolish never forgave him.

*Ireland's forgeries included letters by Shakespeare and one by Elizabeth I authorizing a performance before the court.*
*He later graduated to full-length 'Shakespearian' plays.*

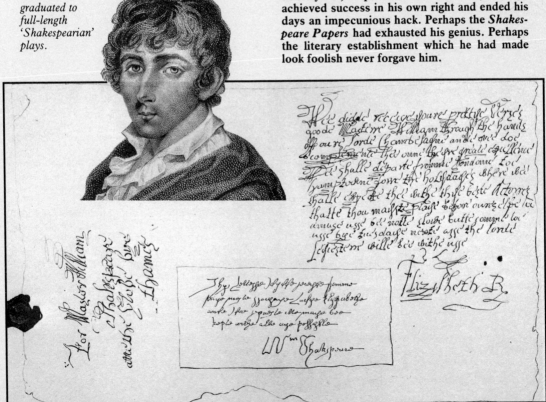

# Forging the link

The lecture hall was packed and humming with excited conversation. Then a bulky, forty-eight-year-old man, with a moustache and a bald head, rose to speak and everyone fell silent.

I was walking along a farm road close to Pilt-down Common, Fletching, when I noticed that the road had been mended with some peculiar brown flints, not usual in the district . . .

Quietly and with great scientific detail, Charles Dawson described the discovery of Piltdown Man, the most sensational discovery in the history of palaeontology. Within days, Piltdown Man was being hailed in the popular press as 'the missing link'. Ever since leading scientists had accepted the general evolutionary principles first elucidated by Darwin, principles which associated man with the family of higher primates, the hope had existed that archaeological proof would be found linking *homo sapiens* with the apes. If it was true that apes and man had, to put it crudely, a common ancestor, then it seemed reasonable to suppose that somewhere, sometime, fossil remains of this ancestor would be discovered. Now, in 1912, such remains had been discovered. More than that, they had been discovered in England and by an English amateur archaeologist. What was set before the public on that winter's day and what had been examined carefully by sci-

entists during the previous months were fragments of a fossilized skull found by Charles Dawson in a gravel pit on Piltdown Common near Lewes in Sussex. The jaw was undoubtedly that of an ape-like creature but the cranium was much more like that of a modern man and quite dissimilar to those of Java Man or Neanderthal Man and other early hominid remains. It had a large brain case and was devoid of high eyebrow ridges. Its age had been estimated at about five hundred thousand years and in honour of the man who had made this stupendous discovery, it was named *Eoanthropus dawsoni*. The scholarly world was not unanimous in accepting the authenticity of Piltdown Man but most palaeontologists, archaeologists and geologists believed that Dawson had indeed made a major breakthrough in the study of human origins. The scientific world was waiting, hoping for such a discovery; therefore it was conditioned to accept that discovery when it was made. It took forty years for Piltdown Man to be exposed for what it was – an elaborate hoax.

Charles Dawson was a passionately keen amateur scientist. He would have loved to make science his career but his father, a successful barrister, had decided that his son should follow a legal profession and accordingly Charles was articled to a firm of solicitors. He worked dutifully at the law for twenty-five years, first in London and then at Uckfield in Sussex. To all outward appearances he was a typical, successful provincial lawyer. He played a prominent part in local affairs being Clerk to the Magistrates for the Uckfield Petty Sessions, Clerk of the Urban Council and a valued member of many committees. But inside he was a resentful man who felt cheated of his true vocation. He had already made his name as an amateur scientist of considerable distinction. During many years of patient excavation in Sussex and Kent he had found and carefully catalogued many fossils, some of hitherto unknown species. He had presented considerable collections to both the British Museum and the Natural History Museum. He had been elected a Fellow of the Geological Society and also a Fellow of the Society of Antiquaries. As the years passed, he devoted less time to his professional duties and more and more to his absorbing hobby. In the academic world he was widely respected as an enthusiastic and methodical scientist. Yet not all his contributions to knowledge had been received with the acclaim which he considered was their due and Dawson was certainly aware of the jealousy sometimes shown by the professional towards the talented amateur. Dawson undoubtedly wanted to impress the scientific establishment. In 1909 he wrote to a friend that he was 'waiting for the big discovery which never seems to come'. Did he

*In this group portrait of leading scientists examining the Piltdown fossils Dawson stands second from right.*

decide to show the scientific leaders that a mere amateur could discover and identify a find so stupendous that it would make all their work appear insignificant? Or did he intend to show the world that the so-called experts were not as clever as they thought; that they could be easily fooled even by a mere amateur? We do not know. Dawson never said. Any papers he left behind have long since disappeared. Perhaps his motives and intentions were not even clear to himself as, slowly, carefully, over a long period of time, he prepared the greatest scientific hoax of the century.

The details of the fraud as pieced together much later seem to be as follows. Around about 1908 Dawson found somewhere fragments of an old semi-fossilized human skull. He stained them with iron sulphate to give them a brown colour and make them appear very much older than they were. Shortly afterwards, some workmen, on Piltdown Common, who knew of his interest in such things, showed Dawson a piece of bone they had found in their diggings. During the next few years Dawson made, as he claimed, many sporadic visits to the site though it was not until the autumn of 1911 that he 'found' more fragments of skull. Now, as he claimed, he explored the site more thoroughly and over the next few months it yielded a jaw bone, flint, implements and various animal bones. All these articles Dawson

had, in fact, carefully collected and 'aged' in the period 1908 to 1911. The jaw bone was that of a modern ape. In May 1912 Dawson visited his old friend Arthur Smith Woodward, Keeper of the Department of Geology at the British Museum, and exultantly showed him his finds. Woodward and a few others who were admitted to the secret paid several visits to Piltdown in the ensuing weeks and helped Dawson excavate the site more thoroughly. Dawson made sure that additional 'finds' were made and Woodward was quite convinced of the authenticity of Piltdown Man. It was he who later that same year announced the discovery to an astonished scientific world. Further excavations were made over the next two or three years and other pieces of evidence found at Piltdown, all of which added to the picture of a human settlement of very great antiquity. Dawson must have relished the instant fame and hugely enjoyed his private joke at the expense of the scientific establishment. But he did not have long to savour his triumph. In 1915 he fell ill and in September 1916 he died. Did death prevent him, as he had intended, from telling the truth? Did he lose his nerve? Did the outbreak of the First World War in 1914 dwarf Piltdown Man even for his inventor? These are among the many questions about the Piltdown hoaxer which remain unanswered.

## 'I met a stranger from an antique land'

If a book was written describing an encounter with little green men who had landed in a flying saucer most people would dismiss it as the work of a crank. But some would believe it. The bizarre holds a fascination for most of us which is why books and films about the Bermuda Triangle, UFOs, the Turin Shroud, the secrets of the Templars, and other 'mysteries' are sure of a good sale. There have always been plenty of people around ready to cash in on this fact. Some have been remarkably successful.

In 1703 George Psalmanazar (his real name has never been known) arrived in England. He was a dusky young man in his mid-twenties and represented himself as a native of Formosa. Most educated Englishmen had never heard of Formosa. Of those who had few could have located it on a globe. Psalmanazar's affecting history was one which readily appealed to Protestant Englishmen. He had been abducted by Jesuit missionaries and shipped to France, where torture had been applied to force him to become a Roman Catholic. He had refused, escaped the papists' clutches and wandered for some time in the direst poverty. In Germany he had had the good fortune to fall in with the Reverend William Innes, chaplain to a Scottish regiment currently serving there. In response to kindness and careful instruction, Psalmanazar had accepted the Anglican faith and been baptized. This was the story the young man told when he presented himself at

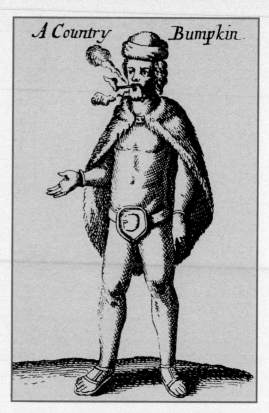

*Psalmanazar's book claimed to depict Formosan natives.*

the Bishop of London's palace and it was supported by a letter from Innes.

The bishop was delighted. He and other senior clergy started a fund for Psalmanazar's support and the 'mysterious stranger' was much in demand by fashionable society. Among those who accepted the 'Formosan' were Dr Johnson and the Archbishop of Canterbury. The scientific world was also interested – and rather more sceptical. Psalmanazar had presented Bishop Compton with a translation of the catechism into the Formosan language, a script of strangely-formed characters which was designed to be read from right to left. This was subjected to close scrutiny and Psalmanazar, himself, was questioned by travellers who had been to the Far East. He flinched from no question and was not afraid to turn the tables on his interviewers. To one man who asked for proof of his nationality, he replied, 'If you came to my country and I asked you to prove you were an Englishman, how would you do it? I might say, "You are just another Dutch merchant".' Round one certainly went to Psalmanazar; so much so that his patrons paid for him to spend six months at Oxford. The idea was that

he could teach his language to young men who could go out as missionaries. He certainly made an impression on the university where he lectured on the customs of his people and kept audiences enthralled with his tales of human sacrifice. When he was not imparting knowledge he was absorbing it – or so the lighted candle burning in his window night after night suggested. In 1704 he wrote an account of his background and his adventures in a book which quickly went to a second edition and was translated into French and German. Another book followed in 1707. Psalmanazar never seems to have been publicly exposed. What happened was that some of his statements were refuted by experts. Public scepticism grew. His patrons quietly dropped him and he gracefully retired into obscurity. Yet there were still people in the provinces ready to believe his story. Many a meal was offered and many a subscription taken up in the following years. Only after a *genuine* religious conversion in 1728 did George Psalmanazar publicly confess his deception.

The truth was that Psalmanazar was French. He studied with Franciscans and Jesuits as a child and from them learned all he knew about China, Japan and Formosa. His family fell upon hard times and he was forced to beg for a living. At first he masqueraded as a persecuted Irish Catholic. Then he moved on to the role of a Japanese convert. It was when he met Innes, who saw through his disguise, that his life radically changed. The bold Formosan scheme was the chaplain's idea. He tutored the young man and launched him on his successful English career.

It was almost exactly a century later that a young woman dressed in a turban and a tattered dress entered a Gloucestershire cottage. She was obviously exhausted. Equally obviously she spoke no English. All attempt at communication failed, though the stranger did point at herself and say, 'Caraboo'. News of Caraboo spread and people travelled long distances to see her and to try their hand at identifying her language and country of origin. She made an excellent show of being confused by English customs. She insisted on preparing her own food and she ate no meat. Only with difficulty was she persuaded to sleep in a bed. Given some cloth, she made a dress of the style worn in her country. She swam and climbed trees with agility. She demonstrated some wild, vigorous dances. At length a group of linguists, by dint of getting her to repeat her story over and over, managed to piece it together. She was a princess from the Indonesian island of Javasu who had been captured by pirates. They had sold her to another ship's captain. From him she had escaped off the English coast. She had swum ashore and begged her way from town to town until she could go no further.

Caraboo's fame spread. The fashionable from miles around came to pay court to the princess. And this was her undoing. For one of the ladies who came to see the wonder of the hour turned out to be a former landlady who recognized her as Mary Baker, a Devonshire cobbler's daughter; a servant girl whose head was always full of wild ideas above her station.

Poor Caraboo; her benefactors gave her money and put her on an emigrant ship to America. She was back a few years later trying her act in Bath. In a way she deserved to find the more exciting, glamorous life she was looking for. England was full of serving girls who dreamed of being princesses, but only Mary Baker had the ingenuity and the stamina to try to make her dream reality.

*Mary Baker alias Princess Caraboo.*

# The tall storytellers

Few careers are more open to fraud than that of the journalist. This is not to say that everyone who writes for a newspaper is dishonest, but the job does carry its own temptations. The desire for a scoop or a really sensational story sometimes leads the over-zealous reporter to embroider facts or place a false gloss upon them. Nowadays, laws and professional codes impose fairly strict limits upon newsmen, but it was not ever thus. In earlier times the unscrupulous journalist had greater opportunity for distortion and downright falsehood.

One of the worst offenders was William Mannix. In 1895 the last in a long series of insurrections against Spanish rule broke out in Cuba. It was met with ruthless opposition and stories of appalling atrocities were soon reaching the outside world. Mannix went to Havana as correspondent for a number of papers, including the *New York Times* and the *Philadelphia Press*. He ensconced himself in the café of the Hotel Mascotte and from there sent home hair-raising stories based on secret interviews with Cuban rebels – or so he claimed. There was considerable anti-Spanish feeling in the USA so Mannix had little difficulty in having his stories published and believed. At length he was deported by the colonial government. Immediately, he turned his situation to advantage. He now became an example

*Multi-millionaire Hearst did everything in lavish style. He entertained royally in his Californian mansion.*

of the suppression of truth by tyranny. He travelled widely, lecturing on his experiences to outraged audiences. He even had his case debated in Congress. In 1899 the USA took over temporary administration of Cuba to pave the way for an independent government. Then it was that the truth came out. As a result the *Philadelphia Press* found itself facing a million-dollar libel suit.

The Cuban conflict provided the troubled background for exaggerated reporting by a much more famous newsman, probably the most famous newsman of all time, and one whose success owed a great deal to deception. In 1895 William Randolph Hearst sent the artist Frederick Remington to produce pictures of Spanish atrocities for the New York *Morning Journal*. According to a well-worn story in American journalistic circles Remington found nothing worthy of his pen and could discover no evidence that Spain and the USA were drifting towards armed conflict over Cuba. He cabled New York, 'Everything is quiet. There is no trouble here. There will be no war. I wish to return.' Hearst reputedly replied, 'Please remain. You furnish the pictures. I'll furnish the war.'

Hearst, on whose career the celebrated film *Citizen Kane* was largely based, was the son of a wealthy Californian rancher and mining magnate. With his enormous family wealth he could have followed any profession (or none), but he was fascinated by the power of the press. In 1887 he took over control of his father's newspaper the *San Francisco Examiner*. Over the next forty years he built the biggest journalistic empire ever seen, with newspapers in every part of the USA. He built circulation by every conceivable gimmick – massive headlines, colour cartoons, extreme political views and sensational stories in which truth often came a very poor second to drama. The Hearst Press took a violently anti-Spanish line over Cuba, and it was partly this influence on public opinion that pushed the US government into the Spanish–American War. Remington obediently produced pictures designed to stir popular indignation. One depicted a girl stripped naked and searched by brutal soldiers. A rival newspaper, investigating the incident, discovered that the woman in question had, in fact, been examined very properly by female officers *in camera*. But by then the lurid drawing had made its point – and increased circulation.

In the mid-1920s Hearst's venom was directed against Mexico, which he suspected of harbouring Bolsheviks plotting to undermine the American government. As part of the campaign Hearst agents bought a set of forged documents from a known troublemaker. These documents, subsequently published under banner headlines, pur-

The anti-Mexican stance of the Hearst press made much use of pictures illustrating military destruction.

material supporting the proprietor's current campaign or crusade. In the mid-1930s he was sniffing out communist tendencies in the educational system. Many teachers were hounded by newspapermen for interviews, which then appeared in distorted form on the nation's breakfast tables. A little later Hearst was concerned about the crime wave and his New York *Mirror* printed a scoop interview with a condemned sexkiller. It was a fake.

The wealth and influence of William Randolph Hearst were, and remain, legendary. His magnificent house at St Simeon, California, was filled with one of the world's largest collections of antiques and works of art. He used his wealth to manipulate many public figures. Yet his own attempts to enter politics were largely thwarted. He did sit for a few years in the House of Representatives but in numerous attempts to become Mayor of New York and Governor of New York State he failed to convince the electorate to support him. Could it be that the people doubted his sincerity?

'La Capa Grande' was just one part of the magnificent Hearst residence at St Simeon, California.

ported to be records of bribes paid to a number of prominent American senators. The aggrieved parties naturally demanded an investigation during the course of which Hearst himself testified that he had always doubted the genuineness of the papers. Restitution after the misdemeanour never worried the press magnate. He was in the business of moving hearts and minds. Once the seeds of doubt, mistrust and indignity had been sown they would grow despite the cautiously-worded apologies published in subsequent editions. The anti-Mexican campaign continued. Hearst knew that one good picture was worth a thousand words. Drawings had now given way to press photographs and most readers were convinced that this ushered in an area of greater verisimilitude – the camera could not lie. When they saw a picture of dark-skinned children walking down a beach with hands upraised they believed the caption which explained that the youngsters were being driven into the water to be shot by Mexican troops. In fact they were looking at a snapshot taken in Honduras by a British tourist. It depicted nothing more sinister than a group of local boys and girls happily bathing and waving towards the camera. Equally alarming was the photograph which appeared in the New York *Mirror* one day in 1932 purporting to show angry hunger marchers storming Buckingham Palace. The truth was that the picture was an old one depicting an anxious crowd gathered to hear news of King George V's illness.

Hearst was an autocrat. His editors and journalists, if they valued their jobs, had to produce

## A talent to deceive

He had been brought up in unstinted luxury and at the age of forty he was penniless. It was 1946. He was living in a Paris still recovering from the shock of Nazi occupation. And he had only his wits and his artistic talent to rely on. That is the background to the remarkable career of Elmyn de Hory, the most prolific and successful art forger of our own or any other age.

While Europe slid slowly towards the holocaust of 1939–45 he, like other young people of his class, played with the costliest toys on wide lawns, rode his pony around rambling estates, held lavish parties, and made the annual circuit of the continent's fashionable spas. The war changed all that. The few portable treasures he managed to salvage enabled him to bribe his way out of Soviet-occupied territory. He rented a cheap room in the Rue Jacob and eked out a living selling his canvases to tourists who found the occupants of the Latin quarter 'quaint'.

It was a chance remark from one such visitor – an English lady who prided herself on her knowledge of modern art – which changed his life. Glancing at one of de Hory's sketches, she said,

'That's a Picasso, isn't it?' The stunned painter muttered a non-commital reply and soon found himself being pressed to part with the 'Picasso' drawing. Minutes later his guest had departed and de Hory was clutching £40 – a fabulous fee for a trifle he had scribbled in less than ten minutes a few weeks earlier. It took a while for the implications of that event to come home to him. Could he do it again. Could he fool the experts? The temptation to hoodwink gallery owners who had turned up their noses at genuine de Horys was too great. With trembling hands he offered three 'Picasso' nudes to a leading Paris dealer, who examined them carefully, nodded wisely and cheerfully gave de Hory the £200 he demanded.

Still de Hory had no ambition to devote himself to a life of forgery. He toured Europe selling more and more fake Picassos and, when he had accumulated several thousand pounds, he flew to America where his manners and money carried him effortlessly into high society. With friends and potential patrons in the world of film stars, financiers and industrialists, de Hory expected to gain recognition as an artist in his own right. He worked patiently to build up a collection and, at last, opened a one-man exhibition. It was a flop. The bitter irony struck de Hory hard: sophisticated collectors and self-styled experts were fools

The Bay of Nice, *signed 'Raoul Dufy'; in fact, it was painted by de Hory. This picture by de Hory shows a remarkable similarity to one by Dufy.*

*A fake Picasso 'femme'*

who would willingly be duped by a forgery with an impressive signature but had no interest in new works of obvious merit. He was faced with a choice: the garret existence of an honest artist or the luxury he craved bought at the price of turning professional forger. He did not hesitate.

It was an excellent time for the career on which de Hory now embarked. Impressionist and post-impressionist paintings were in vogue. Collections had been broken up and dispersed by the war. The market was buoyant. There was nothing remarkable about a middle-European forced to dispose of 'a few remnants salvaged from the family fortune'. De Hory toured America, hoodwinking dealers from New York to Los Angeles, New Orleans to Chicago. He graduated from Picasso to other modern masters and from pen and ink sketches to finished oils. Just as steadily his prices went up from a few hundred dollars to tens of thousands. He was fired as much by contempt for dealers as his desire for money. One of the very few dealers to unmask him was Frank Perls of Beverley Hills. One day in 1953 de Hory offered Perls a portfolio of drawings. The dealer studied them carefully, replaced them, tied the ribbons then suddenly flung the portfolio at the dapper little man sitting by the desk.

'You have two seconds to get off the block,' he shouted, 'and twenty-four hours to get out of town. If you're not gone by then I'll call the Police!)

With the world to choose from a prudent crook would have given southern California a wide berth thereafter. Not so de Hory. Two years later he was back peddling his wares on Perls' patch. Success bred confidence, especially when he frequently saw his own works pictured in glossy journals and catalogues as the proud possession of this or that gallery or wealthy collection.

The incredible adventure went on for twenty-two years. By this time de Hory had settled in Ibiza, living quietly but splendidly in a villa built specially for him. The arrest and imprisonment of some business colleagues eventually led the Spanish police to investigate. But they could not prove that de Hory had manufactured or sold forgeries on Spanish territories so he could only be charged with minor offences. He was sentenced to two months in prison. It scarcely proved to be an ordeal.

Yet to the ageing forger imprisonment signalled that it was time to retire. On his release he left Ibiza and passed into obscurity. The most energetic art swindler of all time had never been brought to trial for his deceptions. And the pictures? Most of them still grace the walls of galleries and wealthy homes and those owners who know they own frgeries by the great Elmyn de Hory have no desire to part with them. The majority remain undetected. Pablo Picasso was once sent a de Hory for authentication. He looked at it carefully. 'It could be mine,' he said, 'How much was paid for it?' '$100,000,' was the reply. 'Then it must be real,' said Picasso.

# The Highland fraud

James Macpherson started a controversy which raged for a hundred years after his death and which is still not fully resolved today. He rose from total obscurity to fame (or notoriety), wealth and a position of public service and he was buried in Westminster Abbey. And this extraordinary career was based on a fraud – or was it?

Macpherson was born into the family of a poor Highland crofter in 1736. That means that he was still a boy when the final upsurge of Jacobitism was crushed in 1745. Less than thirty miles from his home 1200 clansmen were slaughtered at Culloden. The battle was followed by a careful policy of Anglicization; Gaelic culture, customs and language were actively discouraged. As a result two things happened: the folklore and traditions of an ancient people were in real danger of being destroyed; at the same time those traditions and that folklore became romanticized by many people inside and outside Scotland. Macpherson was heavily imbued with this romantic spirit and with national pride. He was a bright lad and went, as a poor scholar, to Edinburgh University. While there he wrote a great deal of verse, much of it celebrating the deeds of ancient heroes and some of it copying antique styles. For a few years he earned a living as a tutor and this brought him into contact with some of the leading figures in Scottish society. He was resentful of his lowly station, a proud, 'touchy', ambitious young man, determined to improve his lot. Therefore, when he met two prominent scholars who were interested in Gaelic poetry he made the most of his opportunity. He read them extracts of folk poetry which he claimed to have collected. They were delighted and asked for more. Macpherson could not let his chance slip. He produced translations of extracts which, he claimed, came from a long epic poem. The writing was heroic and lyrical. It agreed in style and content with the few surviving ancient manuscripts of the old sagas.

> He fell as the moon in a storm, as the sun from the midst of his course, when clouds rise from the waste of the waves, when the blackness of the storm inwraps the rocks of Ardanmidder. I, like an ancient oak on Morven, I moulder alone in my place. The blast hath lopped my branches away; and I tremble at the wings of the north. Prince of the warriors, Oscar, my son! shall I see thee no more?

Thus, the death of Oscar, in Macpherson's 'discovered' version.

The flood gates of fame and success now opened for the young Highlander. The fragments were acclaimed in Edinburgh and London. In 1760 Macpherson bowed to the pressure of his supporters and published his translation, hinting in the introduction at the epic poem of which it was only a part. The bait was swallowed whole. Lovers of Gaelic culture clamoured for more. A group of literary and social leaders subscribed £100 to pay for Macpherson to tour the Highlands and Islands in order to collect as much original material as possible. There could be no going back now.

Over the ensuing months he collected a large amount of Gaelic verse, some in manuscript form but most transmitted orally. He then retired to Edinburgh to translate and collate it. He moved on to London, where he enjoyed the patronage of no less a person than Lord Bute, George III's favourite and first minister. In 1761 Macpherson published the first part of his eagerly-awaited collection – *Fingal, An Epic Poem in Six Books Describing the Invasion of Ireland by Swaran King of Lochlin*. It was followed, in 1763, by a second part under the name of *Temora*. Macpherson claimed that these were the work of Ossian, a legendary Gaelic hero and bard of the third century. They took the literary world by storm. They were translated into German, French and Italian. They made Macpherson a great deal of money, many admirers and some powerful enemies. Most men of letters in the capital, including Dr Johnson, denounced the books as 'palpable and impudent forgery'. Macpherson was lampooned in the press and even his admirers urged him to provide evidence and so silence the critics. The young Scot's answer was to stand on his dignity and fly into a rage whenever his honesty was called in question. This provided fresh fuel for his enemies and greatly embarrassed his friends. David Hume, the philosopher, who had been one of Macpherson's ardent supporters now declared, 'I have scarce ever known a man more perverse and unamiable.'

Had Macpherson grasped the truth of the later dictum 'no publicity is bad publicity' or was it pure conceit that caused him now to stalk fashionable society giving himself airs? Whatever the answer, the stratagem certainly worked. His friends in government offered him a post in America. Although his haughty temper soon caused him to fall out with colleagues there, he was employed on his return as a political writer. He defended government policy with a fluent and frequently vitriolic pen and was rewarded with sundry posts and sinecures from which he amassed a large fortune. He was a Member of Parliament for sixteen years but never once addressed the house. He returned to his native Scotland for the last few years of his life and died, in 1796, in his newly-constructed mansion at

Badenoch. Haughty to the end, he left £500 for the erection of a monument on his estate and requested that his body be buried in Westminster Abbey. This was done, and his remains repose close to Poets Corner.

The Ossianic poems and the controversy surrounding them lived on. In 1797 the Highland Society commissioned a thorough investigation of the Ossianic material and published its findings in 1805. The conclusion was that no such epic as Macpherson claimed to have discovered ever existed but that Macpherson had certainly collected a considerable amount of genuine Gaelic material and combined it with his own verses to create *Fingal* and *Temora*. The committee had, apparently, examined the originals used by Macpherson. Unaccountably, these papers were sub-sequently lost by the writer's family. So were other contemporary records which have a bearing on the case. Proof is, therefore, lacking and the 'Ossian file' can never be closed. As one of Macpherson's countrymen, Sir Walter Scott, wrote,

Oh what a tangled web we weave
When first we practise to deceive.

Yet, leaving aside the question of authenticity there can be no doubt about the literary importance of Macpherson's books. They made an enormous impact on the Romantic movement. Goëthe, Schiller, Byron and Coleridge were among the literary giants who admired them. And, whether it is a recommendation or not, *Fingal* was Napoleon Bonaparte's favourite book.

# The priestess of Isis

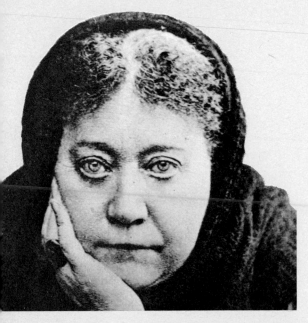

Sometimes when you look at the portrait of someone who wielded great influence it is easy to see why they did. The set of the jaw, the look in the eyes, the overall bearing – something about them commands attention and respect. But there are others . . . well, look for yourself at the face that heads this page. It is the face of a podgy old woman with bulging eyes. Whatever can thousands of people have seen in Helen Blavatsky? Perhaps it was the sheer brazenness of her eccentricity, an eccentricity, at least in part, deliberately cultivated, that compelled attention. Odd behaviour, if it is extreme enough and carried off with conviction, can bludgeon the critical faculties into insensibility. Helen Blavatsky certainly indulged in extremely odd behaviour.

She arrived in the USA in 1873, a fat, penniless, Russian emigrée of forty-one. Her language was coarse. She smoked heavily – both cigarettes, which she rolled herself, cutting the tobacco from a solid block, and also hashish. She stayed in a hostel-cum-boarding house for ladies, where she kept the other residents enthralled with stories of her past. She had been married at the age of sixteen to a septuagenarian dotard from whom she had run away. Subsequent adventures had taken her to Paris, where she was an intimate of the Empress Eugénie. She had travelled to Tibet, at that time a closed land visited by very few Westerners, and certainly not by women. In Egypt she had spent three days and nights *inside* the pyramid of Cheops. In the Sudan she had become rich by collecting and exporting ostrich feathers. Her tours had taken her to England, Syria, Palestine, Arabia, Turkey, Italy and Greece. To her wondering circle of new friends she recounted many amazing stories in her imperfect English.

The ones that sent *frissons* of pleasure up and down the spines of her genteel hearers, were the ones describing the activities of her *elementals*, spirit beings whom she could summon at will and who could speak, write, and assume material substance. But they could be mischievous, as Madam Blavatsky sometimes demonstrated. One morning, for instance, she failed to appear for breakfast. When some of the ladies went to her room they found her lying immobile with her nightdress sewn to the sheets. During the hours of darkness, she explained, her troublesome elementals had been busy with needle and thread.

The truth of Helen Blavatsky's past was very different, though in its own way just as eventful. She was born in the Ukraine of distinguished German parentage. She was a morose child, given to fantasizing, retreating into a dream world of her own, perhaps because her grotesque appearance debarred her from the company of other children. She was, indeed, married to Nikifor Blavatsky when she was only a girl, but he was forty, not seventy. She ran away from him after a few months and then lived a wandering existence, with a succession of lovers. Some of those years were spent in a travelling circus. It was probably there that she learned the illusions and conjuring tricks that were to stand her in good stead when she set up as a medium.

Very soon Helen Blavatsky had become a part of the American spiritualist scene. There was a great deal of interest in the occult at that time, and séances were very fashionable. The Russian lady soon made an impact with her powers as a medium, her mystic talk of truths learned from Indian and Tibetan 'masters' and her outlandish behaviour which, to the gullible, served to confirm her teachings. One admirer wrote of her in a letter, 'She is ignorant of all the graces and amenities of life. She is a great Russian bear.' But he continued to admire her. One man who came completely under her spell was Colonel Henry Olcott, who increasingly deserted his wife in order to follow Helen Blavatsky around. Their relationship was a long one but it was decidedly one-sided. Olcott admired Blavatsky and believed her occult rigmaroles. She used his gullibility but was at times infuriated by it and often told other people that he was a buffoon.

In 1875 she began to write her beliefs and 'astral' experiences. Olcott saw her at work and described how she obtained her inspiration: she would look into space 'with the vacant eye of the clairvoyant or seer, shorten her vision as though to look at something held invisibly in the air before her, and begin copying on her paper what she saw'. Then her fingers would fly back and forth across the paper, light flashing from the fifteen or so rings she always wore, and her mystic medallion swaying on the end of a chain which hung over her ample bosom. Even though *Isis Unveiled* was, apparently, copied down from extraterrestrial originals Madame Blavatsky was not satisfied with it. She plagued her publishers by making continuous alterations and additions at proof stage. Little wonder that, by the time she set down her pen, Helen Blavatsky had written half a million words. *Isis Unveiled – A Master key to the Mysteries of Ancient and Modern Science and Theology* was published in two large volumes, was lambasted by most of the critics, and sold out in ten days.

Blavatsky and Olcott founded the Theosophical Society for the study and dissemination of the hidden knowledge that had been imparted to them and, in 1879, they went off to India. We are now accustomed to the many cults which draw their inspiration from Eastern religion and thought. A hundred years ago such attraction was unusual; it was Western civilization which was the repository of everything that was excellent; Indian culture was dismissed as 'primitive'. The theosophists went there as devotees and were warmly received. The Colonel now spent most of his time

*Colonel Henry Olcott*

addressing meetings and making converts. Madame Blavatsky (or more strictly she should be styled Mrs Betanelly, for she had gone through a marriage ceremony with a gentleman of that name, a relationship which came to a speedy end when the husband tried to claim his conjugal rights) concentrated on establishing a central shrine for the society where she organized spirit 'manifestations' and where messages from her spiritual master or *mahatma*, Koot Hoomi, were received (usually in the form of letters which fell at her feet out of thin air). Controversy, of course, confronted the Blavatsky 'circus' everywhere but the 'high priestess of Isis' enjoyed popular adulation and a considerable degree of comfort for six years before some of her frauds were exposed and she was forced to flee India.

She travelled through Europe accompanied everywhere by a grotesque little Indian servant who was once described as 'something between a big monkey and a little fidgety devil' and who doubtless added to the aura of mystery she deliberately cultivated. That aura long outlived Helen Blavatsky, who died in England in 1891. Shortly before her demise the Society for Psychical Research published a report of their careful investigation into the activities of the theosophists. They dismissed the séances, manifestations and astral phenomena as deception, illusion and hallucination. But of Madame Blavatsky they had something rather more perceptive to say: '. . . we regard her neither as the mouthpiece of hidden seers, nor as a mere vulgar adventuress; we think that she has achieved a title to permanent remembrance as one of the most accomplished, ingenious, and interesting imposters of history'.

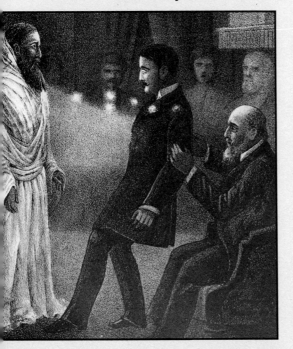

## The vanished diplomats

Guy Burgess         Donald MacLean

In early June 1951 one event monopolized press headlines throughout the world: two highly-placed British diplomats had defected to Russia. The names Burgess and MacLean had become household words. In that they had been communist sympathizers for many years, and in that they had certainly passed information to the East, they merit the title of 'deceivers'. Yet their story is no simple one of paid agents or 'moles' and whether, at the end of the day, it was they or the British government who were the more deceived is a matter for conjecture.

Guy Burgess and Donald MacLean were men of totally different temperaments and dissimilar backgrounds. They did not even know each other very well: it is only an accident of history that has coupled their names together. Burgess was an extrovert, fun-loving, openly homosexual voluptuary, brilliantly clever and witty. He always had – and always needed – a circle of friends and admirers. Wealthy parents sent him to Eton and then on to Cambridge. MacLean's father had been a prominent Liberal MP and Cabinet minister. He attended a minor public school where his talents were observed to be little above average. He, too, went on to Cambridge, arriving there in 1931, a year after Burgess. During the two years that their university careers overlapped Donald became one of Guy's many sexual conquests. He was drawn into the older man's social orbit. Both of them joined the Communist Party. There was nothing very remarkable about that: the 1930s were a time of great political ferment and many young intellectuals flirted with extreme left-wing views. By the time they went down from Cambridge both men had cancelled their party membership. But not before Burgess had paid a visit to Moscow. That was in 1934. He returned, he said, disillusioned and the pendulum of his political views now swung wildly to the opposite extreme. It puzzled even close friends who were used to his eccentric behaviour. It now seems that he was putting up an elaborate front and that MacLean, in his quieter way, was doing the same.

After Cambridge the two men's paths diverged. MacLean, an expert in languages, joined the Foreign Office, little attention apparently being paid to his erstwhile socialism. While working in Paris he met and married a lively young American woman of moderately left-wing tendencies called Melinda. MacLean should have been happy. He had a secure and interesting job and a pretty wife. But for some reason he had started drinking heavily, a fact which seems to point to some inner conflict which created stress. They returned to London at the outbreak of war and, in 1944, were posted to Washington. The drinking continued and the marriage deteriorated. The move to America seems to have induced something of an intellectual crisis in MacLean. The USA was in the grip of virulent anti-communism. The wartime alliance had given way to mutual distrust. The cold war was beginning. MacLean detested this attitude, and became more active in passing information to the Russians. He made no secret of his opinions, allowed his drinking to get out of hand and even, on at least one occasion, confided in friends that he was working for 'Uncle Joe' (his friends did not take such 'drunken ramblings' seriously). Whenever he was under the influence of alcohol, which was frequently, he became wild, violent and destructive. He was brought home by the Foreign Office who diagnosed 'overwork' and sent him to a psychiatrist. It was about this time that British security officers began to investigate Foreign Office leaks. Very slowly the field of suspects narrowed until, by mid-1951, there was only one name on their list – Donald MacLean.

Meanwhile, the flamboyant Burgess had followed a more erratic course. He did not actively seek a career immediately on leaving university.

Guy Burgess

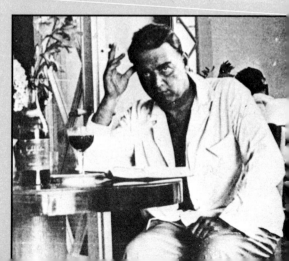

*MacLean (far right) talks with British minister Sir John Balfour in the Washington embassy.*

After a couple of years he took a job with the BBC. This coupled with a small private income enabled him to live in some style in a London flat. He threw wild parties, mostly for his homosexual friends, had a wide circle of acquaintances in Britain and Europe, and followed current events very closely. He loved intrigue and developed an unofficial contact with MI5, passing on to them information which came his way via his social contacts. It was thoroughly in keeping with his love of cloak-and-dagger theatricality that he was also sending snippets of news to Soviet agents. He was amoral and, perhaps, apolitical also. Espionage was a game for him, not a matter of deep conviction as it was for MacLean. At the outbreak of war Burgess transferred to the Foreign Office. He gained steady promotion despite his frequent breaches of discipline. He, too, was an excessive drinker and was sometimes unfit for duty. He was careless with secret documents. He was indiscreet in talking about confidential information. Like MacLean he was certainly making no attempt to convey the impression of a loyal and conscientious diplomat. Incredibly, the powers that be now decided to send this volatile character to Washington. Burgess did not like America and he made no attempt to conceal the fact. He made complaints about his colleagues. He got into trouble with the police for speeding offences and for picking up homosexuals. Within a few months he was sent home with the recommendation that he be dismissed.

Burgess had learned one thing of supreme importance in Washington and that was of the security investigation of MacLean. On his return in May 1951 he immediately contacted the man he had met only rarely since university days. They planned to escape before the net tightened. On the very day that the Foreign Secretary sanctioned MacLean's interrogation, the two men crossed the Channel and made their way to Moscow. Two years later, Mrs MacLean and her children were able to join her husband.

There both men eventually died. Life in Russia had solved no problems for them. The story of Burgess and MacLean, of Kim Philby and other communist sympathizers infiltrated into the inner sanctum of the British establishment is not the story of clear-minded Russian agents beloved of spy fiction writers. It is the chronicle of men who were compelled to seek a grand, important role, a role which they could not sustain, and whose rewards were found sadly wanting.

# The Grand Duchess?

On 17 February 1920, a young girl was rescued from the Landwehr Canal, into which she had thrown herself with the intention of committing suicide. She was then taken to the Elizabeth Hospital in the Lützowstrasse. As she would answer no questions she was transferred as a presumably mental case to the mental institution at Dalldorf, where she remained for about two years without giving any information whatsoever in regard to herself . . .

Those words from a Berlin police report dated 19 June 1925 begin one of the most mysterious accounts of disputed identity every recorded. For the woman mentioned in that report later claimed to be the Grand Duchess Anastasia, only survivor of the family of Nicholas II, Tsar of Russia.

On the night of 16–17 July 1918 the Tsar and Tsarina, their son, their four daughters, their doctor, a manservant, a lady-in-waiting and a cook were taken from their prison quarters in a house at Ekaterinburg by local Bolsheviks, acting on instructions from Moscow. They were forced into a large dimly-lit cellar and shot. Some of the bodies were attacked with rifle butts and bayonets, then loaded into a lorry and driven in the pitch darkness to a mine deep in the forest where, the following day, they were burned and their ashes scattered. A few days later White Russian troops recaptured the area and discovered fragments of bone, clothing and jewellery. The royal line was extinct. The Soviet government had removed a serious threat to its existence.

*1926 photograph of 'Anastasia' in a Berlin sanatorium.*

*Grand Duchess Anastasia is the central figure in this portrait of the Tsar's children. Did she alone survive the massacre?*

Or had it? Not according to the patient in Dalldorf asylum. When she eventually spoke about her past the mystery women told this story. When the guards at Ekaterinburg opened fire she fell to the ground screaming and immediately lost consciousness. She awoke to find herself being jolted along in a cart. She was feverish, her head was throbbing and she was spattered with blood. The journey continued for a long time, she was too ill to know how long. When she recovered she was told by one of her rescuers, Alexander Tchaikovski, that he was one of the Red Guards present at the execution, that he had seen her move as the bodies were being loaded, had taken pity on her, wrapped her in a blanket and smuggled her away in the darkness. They reached Romania where they lived by selling jewellery which Anastasia had sewn into her clothing.

In Bucharest, the story continues, 'Anastasia' and Alexander became more than friends. The young woman became pregnant, her protector married her, and she was delivered of a boy. But Alexander was gunned down in the street, presumably by a Bolshevik agent, 'Anastasia's' son was taken from her to a place of safety, and she herself left Romania as soon as she was able. She travelled to Berlin accompanied by her brother--in-law, Serge. They found rooms in a hotel, and then Serge disappeared. When he failed to return 'Anastasia' wandered out into the streets to look for him. She was exhausted, friendless, depressed and afraid. At last she reached the canal and its mist-covered waters seemed very inviting. When she later found herself in hospital, interrogated by police, she was afraid to reveal her identity and so said nothing. All that is the story told by 'Anastasia'. From that point onward we have facts to rely on.

The woman who later called herself Grand Duchess Anastasia certainly spent two years in the asylum. It must have been an ordeal for she exhibited no signs of insanity, as staff at Dalldorf later testified. Eventually, either because of something she said or because a temporary inmate thought she recognized her, part of her story came out. 'Anastasia' later wrote how much she regretted this: 'had I stayed in the asylum, I should have died long ago and so been spared all the humiliations, torments and disappointments I was afterwards exposed to'. She was visited by Russian emigrés and by distant members of the imperial family. Some hailed her as the last of the Romanov line. Others dismissed her as an impostor. Most of them believed what they wanted to believe. She was questioned incessantly about her childhood and returned only vague answers. Was this a conscious or unconscious attempt to suppress unpleasant memories or did she really not know the answers? She was released from Dalldorf into the custody of friends, one of whom engineered a meeting between 'Anastasia' and Irene, Princess of Prussia, sister of the murdered Tsarina. The encounter went badly. 'Anastasia' broke into tears and refused to speak. She later claimed that she had instantly recognized her aunt and that the shock had upset her. For her part, Irene was not sure: 'The hair, forehead and eyes are Anastasia's, but the mouth and chin are not. I cannot say that it isn't her.' To the end of her days this close relative refused to acknowledge 'Anastasia'. It was much the same when Crown Princess Cecilie of Germany, a distant cousin, was brought to meet her.

One problem was language. The imperial family had usually spoken English among themselves and Russian to the servants. While in Germany 'Anastasia' seldom used either language though it early became obvious that she easily understood them when spoken by other people. Then, in 1926, she suddenly began to write fluent English. She had very few real friends in those days. Most

*The imperial family as prisoners in Tobolsk.*

of the people she met wanted to exploit her, and that, according to her supporters, is why she was reluctant to reveal details of her past life. As time passed the press and the public generally became more interested in 'Anastasia'. Now journalists, doctors and detectives were all on the trail of people who might identify the mystery woman one way or the other. Some members of the imperial family and former acquaintances of the Romanovs supported her claims, others did not. Few of those called upon to identify the claimant could be called disinterested; as well as political considerations there was also the fact that some members of the family stood to gain financially as heirs to the Tsar's fortune if all his children were dead. From 1928 this financial consideration came to dominate all others. The leading Romanovs denounced her as an impostor. Her supporters founded a company pledged to secure her recognition and her right to monies deposited by Tsar Nicholas in various foreign banks. She was then in America. There her enemies managed to get her certified as insane and confined to an asylum. After a year friends engineered her release and smuggled her to Germany under the alias of 'Mrs Anderson'. There she spent most of the 1930s in legal battles over the Romanov inheritance.

War and its aftermath removed 'Anastasia' from the public eye. By the 1950s she had taken up residence in very humble circumstances in the Black Forest. Then it was the turn of writers and film makers to take up 'Anastasia's' 'romantic' story. None of them ever resolved the mystery which surrounded this troubled and unhappy woman. A real princess? A victim of insane delusions? An impostor who kept up her pretence for almost half a century? It is unlikely that the truth will ever be known.

# The criminal fringe

It is inevitable that some extraordinary people should use their gifts, personality and intelligence for criminal ends and it may seem undesirable to celebrate their activities alongside those of men and women whose lives were admirable or at the very least harmless. Yet what we must remember is that we are talking about *extraordinary* criminals. They were men and women of remarkable qualities and, although those qualities were diverted into undesirable courses, they nevertheless remain fascinating subjects of study in themselves.

Some members of our rogues' gallery were, one feels, scarcely aware of being criminals. They were following some higher calling, obsessed by some passion. The end was so all-embracing, so compelling, that the means scarcely entered their reckoning at all. Xavier Richier, who for years masterminded a gang which pillaged French châteaux and churches of many of their ancient treasures, genuinely believed that he was preserving these beautiful objects from neglect and deterioration at the hands of owners who were not worthy to have such magnificent objects in their possession. The Schlumpf brothers were obsessed with motor cars and with their own image as *grands seigneurs*. They belonged to a privileged élite. They were men who had the wealth, the power and the discernment to accumulate for posterity an incomparable collection of vintage machines. What did it matter that they oppressed their workforce or manœuvred company funds in the accomplishment of their grand design? And if theirs was a grand design what are we to make of the ambitions of Ivar Kreuger, the broker of nations? He became a master of every kind of commercial fraud known to man and used his funds to help European governments recover from the depredations of the First World War. The desire to play God became an obsession. In his hands the tools and materials of international finance became merely 'little bits of paper' which he could shuffle around at will. In a sense he was doing no more than successful businessmen do all the time; exploiting the intricacies of company law and international banking facilities, to capitalize commercial ventures which had no other financial support. But there is a limit to the size of the edifice which you can build on shaky foundations. Kreuger's over-ornate financial palace eventually collapsed, and great was the fall thereof. Kreuger was ultimately destroyed by the monster of his own success. The same was true of Horatio Bottomley. 'Ah what a fall was there my countrymen!' – Bottomley, the people's friend, the great tycoon, the newspaper proprietor, the Member of Parliament, self-appointed spokesman of the nation, John Bull epitomized. The rolling tumbrel of his ego crushed many victims beneath its wheels. For over thirty years he flouted the law. On numerous occasions he was taken to court, only to outwit some of the finest legal brains of the day with his specious oratory. Then, at last, he met his match and newspapers throughout the land carried the astonished headline, 'Bottomley the great is fallen'.

There are some criminals one has to admire for their sheer audacity. There is no doubt in my mind that Thomas Blood stands high in this category. He is best known to posterity for his attempt to steal the Crown Jewels from the Tower of London, an attempt which was very nearly successful, but this was only the culminating point of a bizarre and adventurous career, a career which is still wrapped in mystery. Blood was an agent, perhaps a double agent, a resourceful and cunning man, a master of disguise, a highly accomplished villain, but he also possessed largeness of spirit. He was courageous, daring and loyal to his friends. Charles II, who was no mean judge of character, took an obvious liking to Thomas Blood and this fact saved Blood's life. Audacity was also the hallmark of Arthur Orton, who after several failed careers in Australia, returned to his native land and attempted to pass himself off as an English lord. How the son of a Wapping butcher could believe that he could impersonate the scion of an ancient and noble house, it is difficult for us to understand, but believe it he did and he very nearly succeeded in his deception. In fact, it took one of the longest and most entertaining trials in British legal history to overturn Arthur Orton's ambitions. It is an interesting fact that hundreds of thousands of British people were on Orton's side. All over the country people argued about the case and there were many who believed that the impostor was, in reality, the long-lost Roger Tichborne. Even after Orton had been sent to Dartmoor, many people continued to believe in his innocence. The reason, I imagine, is that they wanted to believe it, they wanted it to be true. They wanted Orton to get away with his masquerade. Why do we have this admiration for the audacious criminal? Is it

An eminent psychologist has said:

> We are all criminals – it's a matter of degree. Crime is as human as being charitable. Of course we must have tribal laws. But crime . . . is like art and the artist has always understood the criminal.

We all admire artistry, even the artistry of crime.

Of course not all criminals are admirable people, some are quite the reverse. Although some offenders possess such extraordinary qualities that it is possible for us to consider them, in a certain sense, apart from their crimes, there are those whose transgressions are of such an appalling character that it is impossible to view them objectively as interesting phenomena in themselves. I have found no place in my catalogue for any murderer or assassin, any psychopath or mindless thug. Yet one man is included here who had a reputation so black and so richly deserved that he has achieved lasting notoriety as a prince among villains. He was responsible for many deaths, although it was the assassination of character in which he specialized. His name was Titus Oates and his specialities were rumour-mongering, perjury and slander. Oates spent a few years in prison and then was restored to a liberty he did not deserve and which he was able to preserve to the end of a totally unwholesome life. He was a survivor. So was Elizabeth Chudleigh whose matrimonial complications amused and scandalized a generation and enabled her to live to a wealthy and celebrated old age, striking proof, if any were needed, that crime can be made to pay. Perhaps the life of Ronald Biggs, train robber, escapee, and successful fugitive from justice, makes the same point.

These and the others in our list of celebrated criminals were very different people with very different motives, who committed a variety of offences. Yet one characteristic at least seems to link them all. I have detected in none of them any trace of repentance, any tinge of remorse. Whether they were successful in their defiance of the law or whether they paid the price demanded by society, they stood foursquare by their convictions and their actions. Perhaps it was an attitude they inherited from the father of all crimes, the one whom Milton pictured as hurling defiance at the Heaven from which he had been expelled:

> What though the field be lost?
> All is not lost; th' unconquerable will
> And study of revenge, immortal hate,
> And courage never to submit or yield:
> And what is else not to be overcome?

not because we can see ourselves in his place, because, secretly, we would love to conceive and execute the brilliant crime and get away with it?

# The baron of Arizona

On 2 February 1848, after years of warfare and diplomatic wrangling, the Mexican and United States governments signed the treaty of Guadalupo Hidalgo, which formally ceded New Mexico and Upper California to the USA. Among the copious small-print clauses of the treaty was one protecting Mexican landowners in the ceded territories. The federal government pledged itself to uphold all lawful Spanish and Mexican land claims. That was the *intention* of the clause. But legal documents can, in the hands of unscrupulous men, be made to serve ends which their framers never contemplated. Soon the territories were plagued by a locust horde of tricksters brandishing false claims before settlers and extorting money from them in return for freeholds they had no power to grant. One of these swindlers was Dr George M. Willing Jr. By means of an impressive appearance, a confident manner, a bundle of official-looking documents and a sixth sense which told him when to move on, Willing relieved several frontiersmen of their hard-earned cash. In 1876, however, rough justice caught up with him when he was poisoned by one of his victims.

Willing's assistant at the time was a bright young man called James Addison Reavis and he lost no time in going through his partner's belongings and removing everything that might be of use

to him. Reavis soon realized that with careful thought and planning he could exchange his 'hit-and-run' life for one of permanent wealth and luxury. It was basically a question of thinking big enough. He devoted the next seven years to working out and preparing his plan. He travelled to Mexico and Spain where he called upon government archives and land registries. He inserted forged documents into certain files and made fake entries in the record books. He read everything he could find on eighteenth-century Spanish colonial history. By these means Reavis created a fictional family and gave them documentary substance.

The story he spun was as follows: In 1742 King Philip V of Spain sent a captain of dragoons to Mexico to examine irregularities of revenue collection. The captain's name was Don Miguel de Peralta de la Cordoba and he did his work so well that in 1748 the new king, Ferdinand VI, created him a baron. To support his dignity Don Miguel was granted an estate of some 17,000 square miles of excellent farmland in New Mexico and Arizona. The Baron had only one son, Miguel de Cordoba of San Diego who had disinherited his own wife and child because of a domestic upheaval and willed all his property to his very good friend, Dr Willing. The doctor in his turn had made a grant of the baronial estates to Reavis. Sensing that a claim resting upon the contestable will of Miguel of San Diego might not be watertight, Reavis set about building a second pillar to support his ornate deception. He found a

*Reavis and the orphan girl he 'transformed' into wealthy heiress Sophia de Peralta.*

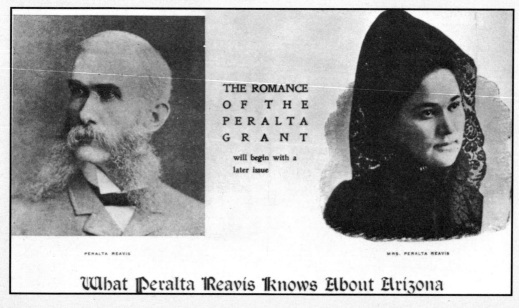

PERALTA REAVIS

THE ROMANCE
OF THE
PERALTA
GRANT

will begin with a
later issue

MRS. PERALTA REAVIS

𝔚hat 𝔓eralta 𝔯eavis 𝔎nows 𝔄bout 𝔄rizona

*Reavis (shown in a prison photograph) carved a fake map of the barony on an Arizona rock.*

pretty orphan girl named Sophia Treadway and, by forging the necessary documents, established her identity as the only surviving descendant of Don Miguel of Cordoba in the female line. As soon as Sophia was of age he married her.

By 1883 Reavis was ready to make his claim. The federal authorities were stunned but when they checked the claimant's documents they found that every one matched with an original in archives as far apart as Mexico City, San Diego and Madrid. The fact that the records showed the first baron to have lived to a hundred and sixteen was not easy to swallow but the details were there in black and white. The claim was allowed and Reavis became a very wealthy man. He collected millions in freehold and leasehold grants. Mining companies paid him handsome royalties. The proprietors of the Silver King Mine alone made

*Had Reavis's plan gone unchallenged, his twin sons would have inherited vast wealth.*

him a down payment of $25,000 for prospecting rights. The Southern Pacific Railway had to pay $50,000 to take their track across the barony. Reavis built himself a magnificent hacienda at Arizola between Tucson and Phoenix. It grew into a sizeable township. He bought impressive houses in New York, St Louis and San Francisco. He moved in the highest society, dining with senators, tycoons, and foreign dignitaries. He was one of the wealthiest men in the United States of America. For twelve years.

Patient work by a dissatisfied minor official gradually discovered inconsistencies in Reavis's carefully concocted family chronicle of Baron Miguel de Peralta de la Cordoba. The official went to study the original documents instead of relying on locally-sworn affidavits. Once doubt had been cast on a single document the higher powers were prepared to re-open their investigation. Once they had enlarged their minds to take in the enormity of Reavis's crime it was easy for them to see just how he had fooled them. Like other criminals, Reavis almost succeeded because he was able to think big. That fact probably also kept him from a severe sentence. He was jailed for less than two years, then allowed to disappear into obscurity. The government had no wish to make a big public issue of the fact that they had been duped. As for Reavis he may well have concluded that twenty months in prison was a small price to pay for having pulled off one of the major confidence tricks in American history and lived in the lap of luxury for a dozen years.

# The mysterious Blood

Here lies the man who boldly had run through
More villanies than ever England knew;
And ne'er to any friend he had was true.
Here let him then by all unpitied lie,
And let's rejoice his time was come to die.

So ran a mock epitaph in 1680. The subject was Thomas Blood, alias Allen, alias Ayliffe, a mysterious figure who died leaving many unanswered questions behind him. He was born about 1618, the son of an Irish blacksmith. During the English Civil War he served the parliamentary cause faithfully and was rewarded with considerable estates in Ireland. Exactly what services Blood performed for his masters is not clear but it is fairly certain espionage was among them. On the restoration of the monarchy in 1660 Thomas

Blood lost everything. His position and lands were taken from him. Blood continued as a political activist in plying skilfully his talent for ruthless and subtle intrigue. In 1633 he and a group of confederates attempted to kidnap the Lord Lieutenant of Ireland, the Duke of Ormonde, at Dublin Castle. The elaborate but well-planned scheme involved disguises and secret signals and split-second timing. Unfortunately for the conspirators they were betrayed and most of them were arrested. A price was put on Blood's head but he was quite undaunted by it and made an attempt to free his colleagues which very nearly succeeded. He was obviously a man of boldness, courage and audacity. He was skilled at disguise and for months escaped capture by moving around rapidly, changing his appearance frequently, and by relying on his very smooth tongue.

We next find Blood very active among such opponents of the government as the Fifth Monarchy Men and the Scottish Covenanters. This is where the mystery begins to develop, for Blood had certainly become deep in the counsels of these dissident groups. It seems certain that by this time he was being used as a government agent or fifth-columnist. But was he a double agent? Was he playing both sides against the middle? We do not know. All that is clear is that Blood showed an uncanny knack of staying with rebellious groups up until the time that they were discovered and then escaping to safety while his erstwhile colleagues were arrested. In 1667 Blood came to the assistance of an old friend, Captain Mason, who was being taken under guard to York. With only three accomplices he surprised the soldiers and, although severely wounded, succeeded in rescuing the prisoner. Again he was on the run and again he eluded capture. In 1670 he made another attempt to capture the Duke of Ormonde, this time in London. Whether it was a case of simple revenge or whether he was put up to it by Ormonde's enemies in the government is again another mystery. The Duke was dragged from his coach, hauled up on one of the attacker's horses and carried away towards Tyburn. The cry went up and Ormonde was rescued but once again the criminals escaped.

This brings us to the most amazing event in an extraordinary career. In May 1671 Thomas, or as he preferred to be called 'Colonel', Blood attempted to steal the Crown Jewels. As with all his coups this one was very carefully planned. Blood, disguised as a clergyman, made several visits to the Tower and ingratiated himself with the seventy-seven-year-old deputy keeper, Talbot Edwards, who unlocked the cupboard containing the royal insignia on more than one occasion for the delight of Blood and his friends. When they had thoroughly acquainted themselves with the security arrangements the accomplices were ready for their crime. On 9 May they entered the Tower with weapons concealed under their cloaks. They persuaded Edwards to open up the jewel cupboard and when he had done so, they threw a cloak over his head and thrust a gag into his mouth. When, despite this, he insisted on making a noise they hit him over the head and stabbed him. They took the St Edward's Crown (squashed flat so that it was more portable), the sceptre (which had to be filed in two) and the orb.Unluckily for them as they were making their get-away, the alarm was sounded. They reached Tower Wharf but there three members of the gang were caught and this time Thomas Blood was among them. Now, mark the sequel. Here was a notorious criminal, wanted for several acts of villainy, a man who had just attempted the most audacious crime imaginable. You would have thought that he would very soon be swinging at a rope's end. Not a bit of it. When he was examined

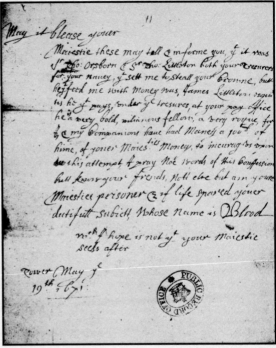

*From prison, Blood wrote to Charles II implicating leading courtiers in his attempted robbery. He was granted a free pardon.*

*Thomas Blood and his accomplices attempting the most audacious jewel theft of all time.*

in his Tower cell, he refused to speak to anyone except the king and two days later he was taken to Whitehall for this purpose. Charles spoke with him for some time and then sent him back to the Tower. On 18 July he was released; on 1 August he was pardoned. All his confiscated lands were restored and he was granted a pension of £500. Some time during the course of that summer John Evelyn the famous diarist was invited to dine with Lord Clifford, one of the king's closest advisers. He was surprised to find among the company at the table Thomas Blood. He recorded his astonishment.

> How he came to be pardoned and even received to favour, not only after this, but several other exploits almost as daring, both in Ireland and here, I could never come to understand. Some believed he became a spy of several parties, being well esteemed among the sectaries and enthusiasts and did his Majesty service that way, which none alive could do as well as he. But it was certainly . . . the only treason of this nature that was ever pardoned.

And what puzzled John Evelyn then has puzzled historians ever since.

# The most wanted man

I am not malicious really, although all through my life I think I've been determined that I will not allow people to get the better of me easily; somehow I will stage a comeback and get on top if I can.

Ronald Biggs has spent the greater part of his life preventing society getting the better of him – so far with considerable success. A childhood spent in the back streets of south London taught him toughness and self-reliance. The family was not desperately poor but if Ronald wanted pocket money, sweets or other luxuries he had to work for them – or steal them. 'Nicking' things from shops, scrumping, and generally putting one over on the adult world was second nature to young Biggs and his friends. The bomb sites and empty, condemned houses of war-torn London were their playgrounds. Stealing became habitual and it was only a matter of time before he was caught. In 1945 Biggs made the first of many appearances before the magistrates. He went through several jobs, joined the Royal Air Force, deserted, and was eventually given a dishonourable discharge for stealing. In 1949 he served his first six-month term in prison. From then on his career for several years was typical of most petty criminals – in and out of jail like a yo-yo, serving progressively longer sentences.

But Biggs was not typical. For one thing he had a high IQ, as tests made during his Borstal days showed. He read Hemingway and Steinbeck.

When he took a carpentry course in Lewes jail he achieved better results than anyone else had ever achieved. Another factor that marked him out was his refusal to be intimidated. Whatever punishments were imposed on him in prison he was always involved in whatever rackets were going – gambling schools, escape bids, cheating other prisoners out of their pay. He was restless and amoral. No principles governed his conduct. No moral values underlay his judgements. He knew no loyalty except to himself and his comrades of the hour.

So things continued until 1960. In that year he married Charmian, a girl he had fallen in love with nearly four years before. He decided to go straight, especially after the birth of their first son. With a home and family, life suddenly took on a purpose. Biggs worked as a self-employed carpenter and went into partnership with a builder friend. He and Charmian had another son. They lived in a rented semi. They had become typical respectable citizens. Then, in 1963, the opportunity arose to buy their house. They could not find the cash. That was when a friend approached Biggs offering him a share of a really big 'job'. And so an unsuccessful small-time crook found himself part of the gang that pulled off one of the most famous crimes of all time – the Great Train Robbery.

Biggs's share of the haul amounted to about £148,000, which he split into two consignments and persuaded friends to hide for him. The robbery was audacious but it had been well planned and the crooks thought they would get away with it. But too many people were involved. There were awkward loose ends. Inside three weeks

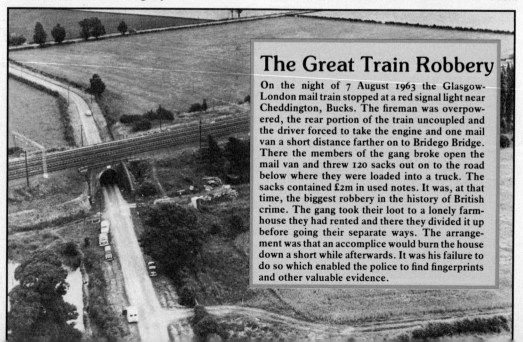

## The Great Train Robbery

On the night of 7 August 1963 the Glasgow-London mail train stopped at a red signal light near Cheddington, Bucks. The fireman was overpowered, the rear portion of the train uncoupled and the driver forced to take the engine and one mail van a short distance farther on to Bridego Bridge. There the members of the gang broke open the mail van and threw 120 sacks out on to the road below where they were loaded into a truck. The sacks contained £2m in used notes. It was, at that time, the biggest robbery in the history of British crime. The gang took their loot to a lonely farmhouse they had rented and there they divided it up before going their separate ways. The arrangement was that an accomplice would burn the house down a short while afterwards. It was his failure to do so which enabled the police to find fingerprints and other valuable evidence.

"Well, can we have it back for the Spithead Jubilee review?"

*In 1977 the exiled Biggs went aboard the destroyer HMS Danae which was visiting South America, a piece of audacity which caused much embarrassment.*

Biggs and some of the other accomplices were in prison. At the trial and conviction most of them received staggering thirty-year sentences.

Ronnie Biggs had never been one meekly to accept incarceration. Now, with a fortune waiting for him on the outside he was even less disposed to remain in jail. He had planned to escape even during the trial. That attempt was thwarted and it was a year after his arrival in Wandsworth Prison that his successful breakout came. £40,000 bought the help of a squad who parked a furniture van beside the prison. A special platform had been built on it to reach the top of the wall. Biggs's friends let down a rope ladder into the exercise yard and, in a matter of seconds, the escapee was speeding through the streets of London in a Ford Zephyr. He was hidden, smuggled across the Channel and received plastic surgery, which included work on his fingerprints. By the beginning of 1966 he was in Australia where he was soon joined by his family. Some of the robbery proceeds were smuggled to him there but much more remained in England and Biggs never enjoyed the lion's share of his ill-gotten gains. However he had enough to make a new life and for three years he settled to a domestic existence. Then the police tracked him down and he was forced to move on again. This time his destination was South America.

Throughout his travels Biggs never lacked for friends or helpers. People took to him readily, gave him shelter, gave him money, lied for him and protected him from prying authority. He had many close shaves but the closest came in 1974. Needing money, he had offered his story to the *Daily Express*. They revealed his whereabouts to Scotland Yard and, within days, Ronnie Biggs found himself handcuffed to a British policeman. There remained only the formality of extradition proceedings before Biggs was brought back to serve out his sentence. At the last moment he found a way out. His current girlfriend was pregnant. Under Brazilian law paternity is grounds for the refusal of extradition. Superintendent Slipper returned to London empty-handed. Biggs had another scare in 1981 when a pair of adventurers abducted him to the West Indies from where he could be more easily extradited to Britain. Once again a legal technicality saved Biggs at the eleventh hour.

Ronnie Biggs is safe as long as he remains in Brazil. He is not only safe; he is a celebrity. He earns money from newspaper features and books about his extraordinary life. The one thing he lacks is the freedom to live an ordinary life. Brazil may be a tropical paradise but for Biggs it is as much a prison as Wandsworth.

*Biggs' life revolves round his son Mike.*

# An aristocrat among thieves

Xavier Richier was impelled by a deep sense of injustice. Fate had endowed him with a sensitive soul, an appreciation and understanding of beauty; but she had neglected to provide him with the wealth necessary to indulge his fine – and expensive – tastes. Richier was in his late thirties. He was a doctor with a country practice at Liévin, a small coal-mining town in northern France. It was a dreary place and Richier's was a dreary life. What made matters worse was that his younger brother, Jean, enjoyed a much more sophisticated lifestyle – or so it seemed to Xavier. In fact, Jean was a small-time Paris antique dealer and interior decorator and hardly less dissatisfied with his lot than his big brother. He was more than ready for the get-rich-quick scheme which Xavier presented to him in 1959.

As often as possible Dr Richier left the little house in rue Thiers where he lived alone, squeezed into his ancient, rusting Renault Dauphine and ventured forth to pay homage to beauty. His pilgrimages took him to museums, churches, cathedrals and châteaux, where he could gaze upon medieval statues, cabinets of Sèvres porcelain, Renaissance paintings, and gilded furniture from the workshops of the finest eighteenth-century *ébénistes*. Richier cared about these things with a passionate intensity. Night after night, in his cherished isolation, he studied books and learned monographs about the skilled artists and craftsmen of the past. He developed an incredible knowledge of which any dealer or collector would have been proud. Nor was it a highly-specialized knowledge; Richier's expertise was catholic: he understood the variety of factory marks on porcelain; he could distinguish Louis XVI *fauteuils* from the most skilful forgeries; he appreciated the different brush techniques of all the old masters. On his cultural tours Dr Richier made two discoveries which both intrigued and outraged him: the security arrangements safeguarding so many great treasures were woefully inadequate and several items were suffering badly from neglect. It was but a short step to convincing himself that he had a right, nay almost a sacred duty, to relieve careless owners of the magnificent objects which they clearly did not appreciate. Out of this conviction the 'Château Gang' was formed. Over the course of six years that gang stole more than £3,000,000 worth of precious antiques, in a series of audacious raids which totally baffled the police.

The raid on the Château de Dampierre in May 1963 illustrates their sophisticated technique.

*Part of Richier's incredible magpie collection.*

The house was filled with the most exquisite treasures to which the thieves could help themselves. It was like an antiques supermarket. But the Château Gang were sophisticated and disciplined. They had a shopping list and they took only the items on it. There were twelve carved Louis XV dining chairs. The thieves removed the four previously selected by Richier. They were stamped with the mark of master craftsman Boulard. The others, which looked identical in the torchlight, were top quality nineteenth-century copies. They selected three *bonheurs du jour* (small writing desks), one bureau, a Louis XV *écritoire* and two Faïence vases.

Richier kept aloof from the other members of the group, only travelling to Paris to examine the plunder and give instructions for new sorties. He always had first pick of the proceeds. Whatever the little doctor did not want for his own collection was sold. He did not involve himself in that side of the business; it was too distressing. The Dampierre chairs, for example, had to be changed out of all recognition. The gilding was removed, the seats and backs recovered and one – too finely carved – was newly chiselled to alter the design.

The vases from Dampierre went back to Liévan in the decrepit Renault to take their places in the growing magpie collection at 6, bis rue Thiers. The objects over which Richier gloated in private were piled up around the small house with little attempt at arrangement. Many items were

## The stolen martyrs

Le Mans cathedral houses five magnificent tapestries which are more than the crowning glory of the church; they are national treasures of incalculable value. The beautiful and exquisite late medieval needlework portrays the lives of the holy martyrs of Milan. The set was given to the cathedral in 1510 by the Cardinal of Luxembourg and hung there, undisturbed, until 15 December 1962. On that day Xavier Richier walked into the deserted building after early mass, cut down the finest of the set, rolled it up and walked out with it under his arm.

All France was scandalized. The art world, the Church, and the press were appalled. Awkward questions were asked in the Chamber of Deputies about the security of the national heritage. Several police ears were very red. Commissaire Chevalier, in charge of investigating the Château Gang, was furious. He was, he felt sure, getting close to the criminals, but such audacious coups as the Le Mans theft made him look like a bungling amateur. He decided to 'lean' on one of the men he knew (but could not prove) to be connected with the syndicate. For over an hour he grilled the man but he found out nothing. At last Chevalier lost his patience. 'If they think they can steal things like that for their own amusement and make everybody look like an idiot,' he shouted, 'they'd better think again. You just pass the word around. You've got two entries on your record. I can pull you in whenever I like and next time it'll be five years.'

A week later the sacristan at Le Mans received a parcel. It was bulky and expertly wrapped. The name of the sender was clear: JACQUES DUPONT, HISTORIC MONUMENTS DEPT., THE LOUVRE. The label was Xavier Richier's angry joke; his way of cocking a snook at the art establishment. He was furious at losing the finest piece in his collection. But he had no alternative if the Château Gang was to continue.

unique and of the greatest historical and artistic importance. Such was the marriage chest made for King Henry II and Diane of Poitiers about 1563. Not all of these items were stolen by the Château Gang. Richier had been lured into larceny by his conviction that it was easy. Done Richier's way it certainly was. His technique was simplicity itself. He walked into quiet country churches, and even cathedrals, removed whatever took his fancy – carved images, altar frontals, communion plate, candlesticks – wrapped them in brown paper, and walked out.

Success made Xavier and his confederates wealthy men. The doctor increasingly ignored his practice, employing a locum to do the work while he took extensive holidays in the sunshine. It was on his return from one such excursion to North Africa that he found police waiting for him at the airport. Only dogged investigation by the country's best detectives – men who had been prepared to study their subject until they were almost as expert as Richier himself – had brought success. They now subjected Xavier to a long and detailed 'grilling' with the aid of photographs, inventories and detailed accounts of the gang's crimes. If they had thought Richier would be hard to crack they received a surprise. He boasted of his achievements, cheerfully acknowledging how he had duped his victims, laughing over the stupidity of supposed experts. One of the interrogators asked,

'And you did all this for money?'

Xavier was shocked.

'Never, never, never! Everywhere I saw artistic treasures ruined and defaced, even in the most important museums. I stole in order to care for

*Tracked down: Richier's police file photograph.*

things and restore objects which were left to rot through the carelessness and indifference of the art establishment.'

Richier's confederates went to jail but 'Mr Big' himself was given a five-year suspended sentence. He sank into obscurity. Perhaps it was the most effective sentence. He had revelled in being a celebrity, had taken every opportunity to lecture the court on the subject of aesthetic values, had never wavered in the conviction that he was one of the cleverest, most sensitive men in France.

## A notorious perjuror

Living, as it is often asserted we do, in a post-Christian age, it may be difficult for many of us to appreciate the strong fears and intense hatreds engendered by religious discord in this country as little as a hundred years ago. If we could go back still further to the late seventeenth century, we would discover that divisions between non-Conformists, Anglicans and Roman Catholics were very bitter indeed and that men's denominational loyalties were correspondingly strong. Those were the days when only membership of the Anglican church gave a man respectability and when severe laws restricted the movements and career opportunities of both dissenters and papists. It is against this background that the extraordinary career of Titus Oates must be seen.

Oates's father was a religious opportunist. He had left the established church during the course of the civil war to join the extreme Anabaptist sect. But when Anglicanism came back into fashion at the Restoration in 1660 he was quick to take up again his old allegiance and became rector of a church in Hastings. Young Titus seems to have been a wastrel and a profligate from his earliest years. With a father like Samuel Oates it could scarcely be otherwise. He managed to get himself expelled from one school and two Cambridge colleges during the course of his sporadic education. Yet somehow he managed to obtain sufficient qualifications to get himself ordained and became vicar of Bodding in Kent in 1673, doubtless concluding that being a Church of England parson

was the easiest way of earning a living without having to do very much work. It was in the following year that he made his first foray into the crime of perjury which was later to make him so notorious. In his father's parish there was a certain schoolmaster called William Parker. Titus wanted the man's job so that he could add a second income to his existing emoluments. The easiest way to achieve this was to bring false charges of scandalous behaviour against Parker. Father and son combined to bring about the teacher's downfall but they miscalculated and the indictment was quashed. Samuel Oates was evicted from his living and Titus was thrown into prison.

Oates managed to escape and obtained a berth as chaplain on a Royal Navy vessel bound for Tangier. His behaviour proved so bad that he was sacked within a few months. We next find him serving as a chaplain in the Duke of Norfolk's household. He did not last long in this post either, but it was here that the germ of an idea entered his scheming mind. The Duke was a Catholic, and in his brief stay at Arundel Oates met a number of leading Catholics. He talked with them about their grievances with the existing regime. In London he met up with Israel Tonge, a fanatical anti-Papist. Tonge was convinced that a Jesuit plot was being hatched to overthrow the government and it was his aim through pamphlets and sermons to whip up popular hatred against the Catholics in order to foil their dastardly plans. Oates was convinced that there was an easier way to achieve this goal: calumny. In 1677 Oates was received into the Roman Catholic church and eagerly set about mixing with prominent Catholics, carefully noting down names, dangerous opinions and especially contacts with foreigners. Oates was a very plausible villain, confident, self-assured, and able to lie with complete conviction. So convincing was his performance that he was offered a place at the Jesuit college in Spain. But he could not sustain a role for long. After a few months he was expelled for scandalous behaviour. He moved to another Roman Catholic college in France and the same thing happened again. However, Oates had achieved his main objective in acquiring a miscellaneous collection of information to add substance to Tonge's supposed Jesuit plot. When he returned to London the two conspirators put their heads together and concocted a story of an insidious Roman Catholic scheme to assassinate Charles II, place his brother James, a Roman Catholic sympathizer, on the throne, seize several prominent members of the government and restore England to the old religion. Thus was the celebrated 'Popish Plot' hatched. Oates and Tonge provided names and a considerable amount of detail to back up their general allegations. Oates laid his information before the Privy Council in September 1678, describing the means by which the various Catholic crimes were to be carried out, the way that English agents were to be paid and the plans that had been laid with Catholic sympathizers throughout the country to take control of government at local as well as central level. It was an exotic and elaborate fiction but it had sufficient fragments of truth embedded in it to convince those who wished to be convinced. Most members of the Council believed Oates's account of the Catholic plot. When the story leaked out into the streets of London it generated widespread popular alarm.

The scheme succeeded far better than Oates and Tonge had dared hope. Oates was provided with a troop of soldiers and ordered to tour the capital arresting those Catholics who were supposedly in the Popish Plot. The murder a few weeks later of a prominent Protestant Justice of the Peace, Sir Edmund Godfrey, was very fortuitous for Oates and Tonge. It gave their movement added support. Widespread accusations were now made against known Catholics. Parliament decreed that the existence of the Popish Plot had been proved and in November a spate of trials began. Oates was the chief witness in many of these trials and on his testimony a number of innocent men were sent to their deaths. Oates's perjury was often transparent but that was unimportant against the general background of fear and panic. When Oates deposed against one prisoner that he had seen him on two specific dates discussing treasonable designs with other members of the conspiracy, defence counsel was able to show that on one of those occasions the defendant was in another part of the country while, on the second date, Oates himself was in France. The defendant was still convicted. A grateful parliament paid Oates's expenses and the government granted him a large pension. Throughout 1679 the accusations and the trials continued. Eventually Oates overreached himself. He accused Sir George Wakeman, the queen's physician. His indictment would have involved the queen herself in the conspiracy to kill Charles II. Wakeman was acquitted. Oates was shaken. He retaliated by bringing accusations against Lord Chief Justice Scroggs who had presided over the Wakeman trial. Scroggs defended himself and completely demolished Oates in cross-examination. Even this could not undermine Oates's position. He now enjoyed considerable wealth, prestige and power.

He walked about with his guards, assigned for fear of the Papists murdering him . . . he put on an episcopal garb, silk gown and cassock, green hat, satin hatband and rose, long scarf, and was called . . . the saviour of the nation . . . three

D.ʳ Oates difcouereth ỹ Plot to ỹ King and Councell

servants were at his beck and call, and every morning two or three gentlemen waited upon him to dress him . . . .

The tide turned in 1682. More and more of Oates's victims were acquitted. Public fear of him waned and he was lampooned in cartoons and on the stage. In 1684 Oates was arrested on sedition charges, convicted and thrown into prison. It was the accession of James II in 1685 that marked the perjurer's real downfall. He was immediately put on trial for giving false information under oath. He was found guilty and sentenced to a flogging and life imprisonment. The flogging almost killed him but he recovered and after the expulsion of King James and the accession of the Protestant William III he was set at liberty in 1689. The new regime also granted him a pension. Shortly after this he took another step in his religious pilgrimage by joining the Baptist church but from this he was expelled in 1701 as 'a disorderly person and a hypocrite'. He died peacefully in his bed in 1705. It was an end that was far too good for a man who has been described as 'a most consummate cheat, blasphemer, vicious, perjured, impudent, and saucy, foul-mouthed wretch . . .'

141

# The great imposture

Arthur Orton was the youngest son of a Wapping butcher. His mother had produced eleven other children before she gave birth to Arthur in 1834. He grew into a lumbering, thick-set youth, with a slight twitch (the legacy of a childhood attack of St Vitus's Dance). In 1848 he was bound apprentice to a ship's captain and sailed on the cargo ship *Ocean* for South America. His beginnings were, thus, humble, and the rest of his life might have followed the pattern of his beginnings. But when the ship docked at Valparaiso, Arthur Orton did something which showed that he was no ordinary young man. He deserted and travelled inland. We do not know what secret dreams and ambitions Arthur had cherished in the narrow streets of Wapping and the fly-infested butcher shop but he certainly developed ideas 'above his station', as his contemporaries might have said. He was not prepared to accept the role of fat ship's boy, laughed at by the crew. He would enjoy a life of adventure. And he would gain the education afforded by travel to make up for the schooling his upbringing had denied him. He returned home after eighteen months to impress the family and the neighbours with his knowledge of Spanish and his fine clothes. Soon, however, he was off again, this time as chief steward on a ship to Tasmania.

On the far side of the world Orton made several attempts to establish his fortune. He ran a butcher's stall in Hobart market. He worked as a stock driver in various parts of New South Wales. He set up a slaughter house in Wagga Wagga. He worked in stables. He worked in a hotel. He worked in a butcher's shop. In fact Orton never kept a job long and his few attempts to start business on his own account failed, leaving him with only a pile of debts. There were even unpleasant rumours attached to his name concerning horse-stealing and a possible murder in the Outback. Arthur's ambitions to make a fortune and return home a gentleman were nowhere near fruition. Perhaps it was disappointment with the performance of Arthur Orton that had driven him to change his name to Tom Castro and assume the speech and character of a Spanish immigrant. He was soon to exchange this for a very different role.

In August 1865 the following notice appeared in some Australian newspapers:

A handsome REWARD will be given to any person who can furnish such information as will discover the fate of Roger Charles Tichborne. He sailed from the port of Rio Janeiro on 20th of April, 1854, in the ship *La Bella* and

Orton

has never been heard of since, but a report reached England to the effect that a portion of the crew and passengers of a vessel of that name was picked up by a vessel bound to Australia . . . the said Roger Charles Tichborne . . . would at the present time be thirty-two years of age, is of a delicate constitution, rather tall with very light brown hair and blue eyes. Mr Tichborne is the son of Sir James Tichborne Bart., now deceased, and is heir to all his estates . . .

The ancient family of Tichborne was among the wealthiest in England, with two fine mansions in Hampshire and extensive interests in many counties. Roger Tichborne, driven from home by family arguments and an unhappy love affair, had sailed for Valparaiso in March 1853, intent on spending some years in foreign travel. He journeyed into the interior, visited other ports along the South American coast and, eventually, sailed from Rio in the *Bella, en route* for Mexico. The ship foundered soon after leaving port. No survivors were ever traced. In the event of Roger's death the baronetcy and family fortune would devolve upon his younger brother, Alfred, who was a wastrel and an eccentric. He once spent £200,000 on a yacht, ordering the decks to be of inlaid mosaic and the doors covered with mother-of-pearl. Roger's mother wished to avoid Alfred inheriting and also had complex family reasons for persisting in the belief that her elder son was alive. She therefore spared no expense to trace him. Thus it was that news of the Tichborne inheritance reached distant Wagga Wagga. Orton now decided to return to England as the long-lost Roger. It was an incredibly audacious plan. He had only the skimpiest knowledge of the missing heir and his family, yet he was prepared to face Lady Tichborne and her suspicious relatives, and brazen it out. He contacted a lawyer in Sydney, wrote to his 'mother' and set out, complete with new wife and baby daughter. Orton's resolve was not totally unshakable. On the journey he did suggest to a pretty servant girl that the two of them might cut and run when the ship reached San Francisco. However, Arthur eventually reached his homeland and once there relentlessly pursued his fortune.

He made a striking initial success: Lady Tichborne accepted him as her son. Whether it was wishful thinking or a desire to spite her family we shall never know but her recognition gave Arthur the only encouragement he needed. Orton now presented himself to relatives, servants and friends of Roger Tichborne. Some accepted him; some denounced him as an impostor. The press turned the issue into a *cause célèbre*. The general public took sides and argued it in ale-houses and drawing-rooms throughout the land. Orton's supporters held public meetings to gain financial support (Lady Tichborne had suddenly died, thus cutting off Orton's flow of funds). The truth, eventually, had to be tried in court. The two trials which constitute 'the Tichborne Case' lasted from May 1871 to February 1874 and were avidly followed by a vast public. Witnesses were brought from Australia and South America; affidavits were sworn in remote corners of the globe; mountains of evidence were accumulated on both sides. The first case was a civil action for ejectment brought by the claimant, a test case designed to give him possession of one of the Tichborne properties which, he insisted, were being unlawfully withheld from him. This suit ultimately failed. It was followed, swiftly and

Lady Tichborne and her vanished son Roger, heir to a vast estate.

inevitably, by a criminal action against Orton for perjury. After a mammoth trial lasting one hundred and eighty-eight days, Arthur Orton was convicted and sentenced to fourteen years penal servitude. It was a harsh punishment but it must be seen in terms of the social prejudices of the time. The march for popular parliamentary representation was well under way. Its opponents had rallied in 1866 behind the slogan 'democracy is inimical to good government', but had been unable to prevent the passage of the Reform Act the following year. The aristocracy realized that they could not prevent more working class people gaining the vote but they could, through the courts, resist the social disintegration of society symbolized by a Wapping butcher who aspired to be a peer of the realm.

# Prince of darkness

In 1846 God came to live in the Somerset village of Spaxtead. Fifty-three years later, much to the consternation of his followers he died there.

The life of Henry James Prince is a proof that the more extravagant the claims a man makes the more likely he is to find people to believe him. Of course, it does help if the man himself believes those claims. Prince had a way with women. It was a gift, a trait of personality. He became aware of it when he was still a child and he traded on it for the rest of his life. He was a sickly infant, one whom female relations and friends instinctively wanted to mother. Yet there was also about him a sensuality which gave to their ministrations a quality which was not purely maternal. One of his early admirers was a spinster lady of a religious turn of mind. She and the child spent hours reading the Bible together, especially concentrating on the voluptuous love poetry of the Song of Solomon. Experiences such as this shaped the boy's whole concept of life. His family's attempt to steer him away from the religious and the erotic into a medical career was doomed to ultimate failure. He qualified at Guy's Hospital and returned to practise in his native Bath.

But the young medic who wandered the wards of the Bath General Infirmary was no ordinary doctor. His treatment was directed more to patients' souls than their bodies for he regarded illness and disease as manifestations of evil to be exorcised by bringing the sufferers to a realization of the pangs of eternal damnation. He was equally conscious of his own spiritual shortcomings. His sexual urge was strong and temptations to indulge it were many. His journal tells how guilty he felt about impure thoughts and the spiritual agonies he endured as a result: 'My horror increased to such an extent that I was on the verge of fainting and when I was able to rise my body trembled and perspired . . .' Overwork and mental strain brought on a near-fatal illness. During his recuperation he became increasingly subject to visions. The visions impelled him to seek ordination. He returned to Bath full of revivalist zeal and drove his mother to distraction by filling his room with doting women and leading them in long, noisy prayer meetings.

Soon he was off his mother's hands – away at Lampeter College learning to be a priest. He was in some ways a model student, impeccable in his personal behaviour and zealous at his books. In other ways he was a pain in the neck. He gathered around him a group of students and local people whom he led in frequent meetings for prayer and Bible study. He was outspoken in his condemna-tion of what he regarded as corruption. On one occasion Prince was a guest at a party given by the vice-principal. Suddenly, overwhelmed by the worldliness and sinfulness of the occasion, he leaped to his feet, dashed a glass of sherry out of the host's hand, treated the company to a brief homily on the evils of drink and rushed out of the room.

Though such self-righteous behaviour made Prince many enemies, it also won him adherents. The certainty of the man's beliefs, the magnetism of his personality, and the uprightness of his life combined to attract new members to the Lampeter Brethren, as his clique was called. He exercised control over the group. No one dreamed of contradicting him. A subtle, yet profound, change was coming over him. No longer did he seek, and exhort others to seek, the will of God – he assumed that the dictates of providence and his own pronouncements were identical. One of his associates said of him, 'I never knew one who was so independent of the censure and praise of his fellow-creatures, he walked straight on, without being either checked or impelled in his path by the good or bad opinions of those who knew him.'

In 1840 Prince graduated and was despatched as curate to the relative obscurity of Charlinch. He had had the foresight to marry a wealthy and elderly admirer (it was to be, he explained, a spiritual marriage – no carnal hanky-panky!). The work of God could not be done on a curate's stipend. Within two years Prince had packed the church at Charlinch with frenzied converts, and antagonized the bishop. He was sent packing. He moved to a parish in Suffolk and repeated the procedure exactly. Prince, the incarnate messiah, as he now believed himself to be, denounced the Church of England and started preaching, on his own account, on the south coast.

*High walls and solid gates guarded the 'Agapemone'.*

*Prince (third from left, front row) with some of his respectable disciples.*

It was here that he experimented with the idea of a community of the faithful. His preaching had attracted many devoted followers, some of them rich. They would do anything for their leader and give all to him. He now called them out of the world into the 'abode of love', the *Agapemone*. The basis of the community was total obedience to the *Beloved* (Prince). Sexual relations were taboo for everyone except the *Beloved* and those ladies whom he chose to favour. The experiment was satisfactory. What Prince now needed was a purpose-built *Agapemone* – larger, secluded, more expensive. With money donated by converts who continued to pour in, Prince built at Spaxtead a suitable estate for himself and his chosen faithful. It comprised a chapel, a sizeable house for the *Beloved*, segregated accommodation for the men and women, and was surrounded by a high wall.

In 1846 the new way of life began. The faithful arrived in their smart carriages and took possession of the *Agapemone*. Their rule of life was not strict. No regular pattern of services was observed. There were billiards and croquet. All shared in the work about the house and grounds. But Prince's iron will ruled all and life within his own personal harem was distinctly more comfortable than in the abodes of his disciples. His wealth was prodigious. He visited the Great Exhibition of 1851 in an open carriage recently purchased from the Queen Mother, attended by the most beautiful women.

The final consummation – some would say the final blasphemy – occurred in 1856. Prince announced it as the Great Manifestation; the Holy Ghost, in the form of the *Beloved*, would take flesh, thereby freeing flesh from sin. The disciples can have had no idea what the words meant. They certainly found out. Before the assembled fellowship in the chapel, Prince (who was forty-five) laid a sixteen-year-old virgin on a couch before the altar and had sexual intercourse with her to the accompaniment of organ music. It was more than some of the faithful could stomach. They left, taking their money with them. It seemed that the *Beloved*'s reign might be at an end. But he was too firm in his own self-belief to be overwhelmed by such a setback. For another half century life in the *Agapemone* went on virtually unchanged though Prince was assailed by criticism and law suits (from disillusioned disciples wanting their money back). Prince lived so long that none of his devotees doubted his immortality. When death came it took the *Beloved* as much by surprise as it did his followers.

Even then, the power of Prince's personality was not dissipated. His community continued until well into the twentieth century. Not until 1958 were the *Agapemone* and its contents put up for auction.

## A feudal echo

It is interesting to reflect when we wander round a stately home and admire magnificent collections of furniture, paintings, and porcelain acquired by great lords and ladies of the past who lived in ostentatious luxury that some of the methods used to acquire such wealth would nowadays be illegal. Property was acquired by marriage, by bribery, by ruthless business deals, by blackmail. Villages were destroyed. Rivers dammed and diverted. Forests cut down in order to create beautiful parkland. Houses were built without any recourse to a planning authority and the armies of workers required to maintain this magnificance were hired and sacked at will. No one could get away with that sort of thing in the twentieth century. And yet . . .

Hans Schlumpf was born in 1904 and his brother Fritz two years later. Most of their childhood was spent in Mulhouse in Alsace where their father was a textile worker. The brothers had a flair for business and in the 1920s began their own wool brokerage company. It was an excellent partnership. Hans provided the solid business brains, he stayed in the background and attended to detail. His more ebullient brother was the front man who led negotiations and pulled off remarkable deals. The Schlumpfs prospered; so much so that Fritz was able to indulge his passion for racing fast Bugattis. By 1939 the brothers had extended their activities by acquiring the large woollen textile mills at Malmerspach. Then came the Second World War, but the Schlumpfs who had built a very successful business through the depression years were not going to let a little thing like an international conflict take it all away from them. When Alsace was annexed to the Third Reich the brothers survived by outwardly conforming while, in reality, carrying on exactly as before. While speaking contemptuously of Hitler in private, they were ostentatious in their support of his regime. They held Nazi meetings in one of the rooms at the mill. The hall was so heavily decked with Nazi insignia as to appear absurd, and amidst all this ocean of red, white and black bunting there stood a diminutive bust of the Führer.

As they survived the war, so they managed to survive the peace. They were carefully examined on suspicion of collaboration with the enemy but were cleared largely on evidence given by their own workers. Now they settled to building an enormous estate and surrounding themselves with magnificence. They attempted to acquire the whole of Malmerspach. Fritz had a large painting of the countryside made with all the houses carefully depicted upon it. Those owned by the Schlumpfs were shown with windows, all other properties were windowless. Over the years the artist had to make many visits to the Schumpfs' villa to add windows to the houses in Fritz's picture. As well as being the largest landowners in the area they were the largest employers. Between them, the mill and the estate accounted for the greater part of the local workforce and the Schlumpfs expected personal loyalty from everyone in their pay. Changing patterns of employment passed Malmerspach by entirely. For example the Schlumpfs kept an impressive herd of deer. Now, it was no use having the herd if their guests could not see it and therefore be impressed by it and so, during the evenings, when important visitors were staying at the villa, the factory workers were obliged to conceal themselves in the nearby woods and shoo the deer out on to the lawns as the Schlumpfs and their guests emerged from dinner.

Union membership was strongly discouraged by the brothers. Financial incentives and perks were offered to induce workers not to join the union. Later on as union membership increased the Schlumpfs simply bought off shop stewards with cushy jobs and extra pay. In the minds of the Schlumpf brothers there was no distinction between their private and professional lives. The mill, like the estate, was their personal property and probably, if pressed, they would have said that the workers were their personal property also. Without any compunction they freely used money from the business for their own consumption and their consumption was vast. As well as their luxurious lifestyle, they had a mania for collecting. They collected statuary, mantelpieces, and mounted antlers, but above all they collected motor cars.

They had always been interested in vintage motor cars but it was in the 1940s that their collection really began, and what a collection it was.

*Vintage Bugattis formed the nucleus of the Schlumpfs' collection.*

Considerable attention was paid to quality and the Schlumpfs were always in the market for a rare vehicle but it is the sheer size of the collection which is astounding. In 1962 they owned thirty-five Bugattis (Bugattis were always Fritz's favourite) and seventy other cars. By the end of the next year the collection had more than doubled and an ever-increasing army of mechanics was required to look after it. Eventually the Schlumpfs owned four hundred and twenty-seven vehicles, almost all of them in showroom condition. All the great European makes were represented. To house this magnificent collection, the Schlumpfs bought in 1957 an abandoned factory at Mulhouse. By the mid-1960s the Schlumpfs' car museum absorbed all their time and interest. The textile business was simply the thing that paid for their grandiose hobby. Men were frequently transferred from their work to the car warehouse, much to the union's annoyance. Only a few very honoured visitors were allowed to see the collection. Automobile enthusiasts throughout the world knew about it but its exact constituents remained a mystery. Fritz and Hans were making plans to open their museum to the public and, to this end, in 1969 they bought Mulhouse's best hotel, the Hotel du Parc, in anticipation of the many wealthy guests from all over the world who would soon be flocking to the town.

But things were beginning to go wrong. The Schlumpfs' autocratic neglect of their workers resulted in a series of strikes. The relentless march of synthetic fibres undermined the business and, above all, the enormous sums of money they had syphoned off into their private enthusiasm came to the attention of the authorities. In 1976 the Schlumpfs' business went into liquidation. Less than a year later warrants were issued for the arrest of Fritz and Hans, principally on charges of misusing company assets.

The brothers fled to Switzerland while angry employees took over their precious collection. There followed a long legal battle during which the Schlumpfs tried to retain control of their motor cars but in 1981 they were sold to the local authorities for four million pounds (which went to pay off the Schlumpfs' creditors). Thus ended the private domain of the feudal barons of Malmerspach.

*Workers demonstrating appropriately.*

# The match king

The quiet, thoughtful little boy with no great interest in fun and games was the hero of the class. He had discovered a way to beat the system. Like all good ideas it was basically very simple. Young Ivar Kreuger had realized that not all boys were good at the same subjects; some shone in one, some in another. Therefore if they all wanted good marks in all subjects, the obvious answer was for them to pool their resources. He invited the other lads in the class to join him in a syndicate and most of them did so. It was the first time that Ivar Kreuger put into practice two principles which were to make him a millionaire and a man who wielded immense power: think big and take short cuts to success. The objective was everything and to achieve it one used the most effective means. Morality and legality did not figure prominently in Ivar Kreuger's scale of values.

He was born in 1880 into a well-to-do Swedish family at Kalmar whose money came from a factory producing safety matches. But Kalmar was too small a world for Ivar Kreuger and his big ideas. After taking an engineering degree at Stockholm University he set off for America with the equivalent of about £20 in his pocket, fully intending to make his fortune. During the course of the next few years he tried various business schemes, in the United States, in Central America, in England and in South Africa. By 1907 his twenty pounds had grown to ten thousand pounds. Kreuger had a brilliantly clear, incisive mind which saw through problems which were mystifying to other people, and he was single-minded. He would do anything to make money. And so he travelled the world pulling off clever deals in several continents.

In 1907 he returned home and went into partnership with Paul Toll to form the building firm of Kreuger and Toll. After some early struggles the company prospered, their most notable project being the building of the Stockholm stadium for the 1912 Olympic Games. By this time Kreuger had already returned to Kalmar and the match business. He found an industry which was destroying itself by internal competition among three or four large companies, of which the Kreuger company was one. He now convinced his father that with his considerable experience and expertise he could revolutionize the match industry. Within a few years he had amalgamated the Kreuger company with those of leading competitors. By the early 1920s he was managing director of the Swedish Match Company with a share capital of over forty million pounds. By his early forties Ivar Kreuger was thus an international businessman of the front rank operating out of a luxurious, deliberately-impressive headquarters in Stockholm. Kreuger surrounded himself with the trappings of wealth and success. They were a vitally important part of his image. He had lavish flats in Stockholm, Paris and New York, two country houses outside Stockholm and another magnificent residence on his own private island of Angsholmen which he reached in his speedboat or his yacht. He could and did buy anything he wanted, including women. Dancing girls would be brought to one of his discreet retreats to perform for him in private or to take part in orgies with a few selected friends. But much of this was window-dressing, a display put on to impress other people. For Kreuger himself his possessions and parties were a distraction. He lived for the accumulation of wealth and power. He was a man obsessed. It has been suggested that Kreuger's growing megalomania was the result of mental decay brought on by syphilis. It seems an unnecessary hypothesis to explain the phenomenon that was Ivar Kreuger.

The post-war years were years of financial crisis, for both companies and governments. Everyone needed money for economic recovery and Kreuger, who had been building his immense fortune while others had been ravaged by war, had plenty of money. He became the pawnbroker of Europe, lending governments vast sums in

*The Boardroom in the magnificent Match Palace.*

return for match monopolies. Twenty-five million pounds went to Germany, fifteen million to France, over seven million to Hungary, six and a half million to Poland and a similar sum to Rumania, four and a half million to Yugoslavia, two million to Greece and another two million to Turkey. There was scarcely a continental power which did not experience Kreuger's Midas touch. The profits were enormous. The Swedish Match Company obtained almost a worldwide monopoly. It all sounds very simple. In fact, of course, it was extremely complicated and involved Kreuger in years of Machiavellian intrigue and clever dealing. He loved it; this rubbing shoulders with kings and prime ministers, financiers and industrialists; this holding of the fate of nations in his hands. He simply could not stop. He very soon ran through the financial resources which were under his own personal control. From then on it was a case of borrowing to lend. Kreuger was a broker, organizing vast loans on international banks, loans backed ultimately by non-existent security. He had become a monumental confidence trickster whose activities were founded on bluff or, as he sometimes said, on 'little bits of paper'. For a man with Kreuger's influence and driving personality fraud was easy. For example, if he needed to raise cash against the security of one of his many companies and if that company lacked the necessary assests and profits to secure that loan, it was the simplest thing in the world for Kreuger to have one of his accountants cook the books and produce balance sheets giving the desired information. He once founded his own bank in Holland for the sole purpose of transferring funds fraudulently from one subsidiary to another. By the end of the 1920s there were over four hundred of these subsidiaries, most of them operating on non-existent capital. Secrecy and subterfuge were the watchwords of his empire. Thousands of innocent people were drawn unsuspecting into Kreuger's schemes and were ultimately ruined with him.

Kreuger's ruthlessness increased with the years. He brought his aged mother and father on to the board of his parent company. They were totally ignorant of his schemes and were personally as well as financially shattered when the crash came. He forced competitors to sell out to him at ludicrous prices. In countries where he could not obtain a match monopoly, such as Britain and Switzerland, he controlled the output of native companies by the simple expedient of owning all the factories in Europe producing up-to-date matchmaking machinery. And, of course, all the time he was swindling shareholders without remorse. He frequently floated enormous share issues in his various companies. The certificates were worth only a fraction of the price they were sold at. Company reports were seldom strictly honest and were sometimes a complete tissue of lies. For years Kreuger company stock remained vastly over-priced in exchanges throughout the world.

It seems inevitable that Kreuger's obsessive money-making must have overreached itself sooner or later. The surprising fact is that throughout the crisis years of the 1920s Kreuger managed to survive so long. Many of the countries to which he had made large loans defaulted on their debts, as inflation and depression bit deeper into their national economies. In 1930 the chickens began to come home to roost. Kreuger desperately sought new means of raising finance to make good his loss of income and more and more of his shady deals attracted the attention of international commercial lawyers. Yet all the time he kept up the façade, continued with his commercial dealings, conceived yet more grandiose schemes for takeovers and new enterprises. Like the gambler, he could not stop. The only possible way out of his difficulties was a fresh throw of the dice, playing for higher and higher stakes. Early in 1932 Kreuger was in America when the Stockholm government agreed to come to the aid of the Swedish Match Company but only on condition that its financial experts could thoroughly examine the company's books. Kreuger was requested to return home for a meeting. On the way he stopped in Paris and stayed at his flat in the Avenue Victor Emmanuel III. There, on the morning of Saturday 12 March 1932, he lay down fully-dressed on the bed and shot himself through the heart. Sooner than be deposed, the match king had decided to abdicate.

# The notorious duchess

What could an ambitious woman who had beauty, charm and wit, but no money, do in the mid-eighteenth century to improve her fortune? The answer was 'marry a wealthy husband', a course of action many such ladies adopted. But none did so with the same ruthlessness or achieved such notoriety as Elizabeth Chudleigh.

She was brought up by her mother after the death of her father, Colonel Chudleigh, when she was still in infancy. Mrs Chudleigh enjoyed the benefit of her husband's good name and ancient family but these did not pay the bills and certainly could not keep her in the style to which she wished to be accustomed. She did, however, have a strikingly beautiful daughter and on this she resolved to capitalize. She took a fashionable London residence and gambled all on introducing Elizabeth into smart society. Her first major success came when Miss Chudleigh was selected as a maid of honour by the Princess of Wales. Moving in the highest circles and always egged on by her mother, Elizabeth attracted a throng of admirers. All she had to do was select the most likely prospect. Her favour lighted upon the nineteen-year-old Duke of Hamilton and the pair became engaged. However, when the duke set off to make the Grand Tour of Europe, Elizabeth's aunt took the opportunity to forward the suit of another contender, the Hon. Augustus John Hervey, grandson of the Earl of Bristol. By intercepting Hamilton's letters and persuading Elizabeth that she was neglected by her lover, the aunt suc-

ceeded in persuading the girl to transfer her affections. The couple were married in 1744. The ceremony was, however, kept secret for the time being so that Elizabeth could continue her employment in the royal household. Hervey, who was a lieutenant in the navy, sailed off with his ship, and for the next couple of years spent long periods at sea. It was not an auspicious beginning to married life. In 1747 Elizabeth gave birth (again secretly) to a child which died soon afterwards. After that there was very little communication between husband and wife.

Elizabeth now threw herself frenziedly into social life. She became one of the leading London hostesses. Her behaviour was so lively that it verged on the scandalous – as when she attended a masked ball as Iphigenia, a figure from Greek tragedy, almost completely naked. Men were her slaves and no one could understand why she did not marry. The answer, of course, was that she risked complete ruin if her contract with Hervey became known. Augustus, for his part, constantly pestered his wife, threatening exposure. Then, Elizabeth hit on a simple stratagem. The clergyman who had married them was now dead. The only proof of the ceremony was, therefore, in the parish church register, at Lainston, where it had been performed. Elizabeth gained access to this and simply tore the page from the book. She now felt free to encourage the attentions of one of her suitors, Evelyn Pierrepoint, Duke of Kingston. However, before this liaison had gone very far, something unexpected happened: on the sudden death of his brother, then Earl of Bristol, Augustus Hervey succeeded to the title and the immense fortune which went with it. Elizabeth now reflected that her action over the marriage register had been a little rash. She hurried back to Lainston and bribed the incumbent to write in a new entry, recording her marriage to Hervey.

*The Earl of Bristol's title attracted Elizabeth.*

*Elizabeth attended the ball dressed as Iphigenia.*

Having done that she went to live with Kingston.

This situation continued for several years and suited Elizabeth well because she had complete mastery over the duke who was once described as 'a very weak man, of the greatest beauty and finest person in England'. His mistress used his money and his title to hold undisputed sway over the social life of the capital. Pierrepoint was a quiet man but he acquiesced to his house being taken over for the most lavish and exuberant parties and smiled to see Elizabeth surrounded by male admirers. In 1768 her husband, wishing to put an end to the fiction of their marriage, told Elizabeth that he wanted a divorce. She was as anxious as he to unravel their tangled marital relations but feared the scandal which might ensue over the marriage register. Instead, she brought a suit of jactitation against the earl; i.e. she charged him with falsely claiming her to be his wife. The earl, of course, did not defend himself and Elizabeth left the court as a 'spinster'. Immediately she married the Duke of Kingston in a lavish ceremony at St George's, Hanover Square, which was attended by the king and queen and many of the nobility.

In 1773 Pierrepoint fell ill and was obviously near to death. By the terms of his will he left everything to his widow on condition that she did not marry. This restriction on her prospects of acquiring even greater wealth irked Elizabeth and she tried to force her lawyer to proffer an alternative will for her husband's signature. However, the man insisted that the duke was in no state to sign and refused. When the duke died Elizabeth went into the profoundest and most elaborate mourning for a spell and then travelled to Rome where she set herself up in considerable style. One of her indulgences was a magnificent yacht upon which she was conveyed up and down the Tiber.

Meanwhile, aggrieved relatives of the late duke had ferreted out details of Elizabeth's past. They now filed an action for bigamy against her. She returned to defend herself and claimed the privilege of being tried in the House of Lords by her peers. She was found guilty but before any sentence could be carried out she fled the country. Fortunately for her, the Pierrepoint family failed in their attempt to set aside Kingston's will. Elizabeth continued to enjoy the late duke's fortune and proceeded to dissipate it. She remained restless to the end, restless and imperious and luxury-loving and grand. In an age which regarded women as the chattels of their husbands, Elizabeth Chudleigh used the institution of marriage to gain what she wanted from life.

*Her bigamy trial brought crowds to the House of Lords.*

## John Bull

What opportunities he had, but how sadly they were wasted! His gifts were brilliant. He had personal magnetism, eloquence, enthusiasm and the power to convince. He might have been a leader at the Bar, a captain of industry, a great journalist. He might have been almost anything – but for one fatal defect . . .

So ran the *Daily Mail*'s obituary on Horatio William Bottomley, one of the strangest phenomena of his age.

He was born in 1860 and, after the death of both parents (1863, 1865), was raised in the strict and cheerless atmosphere of a Victorian orphanage. He received a good elementary education often driven home with a leather strap; his wants were cared for but the institution could not impart human warmth. Perhaps it was the quest for some kind of sympathetic contact which inspired him to break into one of the girls' dormitories one night. The transgression was discovered. Bottomley was publicly disgraced before his fellows and locked up for a week on a diet of bread and water. Soon after that he ran away. The incident established something of a pattern in Horatio's life: he had a boldness in executing daring enterprises and a marked reluctance at standing up to the consequences. A sequence of menial jobs in City shops and offices followed, Bottomley usually quitting because he found the work uncongenial or beneath his dignity. To relieve his poverty he took to gambling and playing billiards for money. He settled, at length, with a legal firm and worked as a law reporter. He thus acquired a smattering of law. He had also begun attending a debating society in his spare time and discovered in himself a gift for speechmaking. By the age of twenty-one Horatio Bottomley had grown into a stocky little man, bumptious, self-important, aggressively optimistic and with the gift of the gab. From that point his rise to fame and fortune was rapid and it rested solely on his self-confidence.

He began a few local journals and newspapers. Within a few years this had developed into an impressive chain. He was elected as Liberal candidate and, thanks to his oratory, made a very creditable showing in a safe Tory seat. He was now becoming something of a popular figure and he capitalized on this in promoting his commercial concerns. His publishing empire expanded. He obtained printing works. He inveigled prominent bankers and politicians into joining the boards of his companies. In 1886 he proposed to merge several holdings into a new company, the Hansard Publishing and Printing Union. During a complex series of negotiations over a hundred thousand pounds found its way into Bottomley's pocket, in addition to his director's salary, but the HPPU only made a profit on paper. In 1891 the bottom fell out of the enterprise and Horatio found himself facing several charges of fraud and

*Oratory and jingoism served Bottomley during the First World War when he made recruiting speeches.*

conspiracy to defraud. It seemed that his meteoric career was over. But, in one of the most remarkable criminal cases on record, Bottomley completely turned the tables on his opponents. He conducted his own defence and by a blend of elequence, bluff and specious argument, he won over not only the jury but also the judge. Mr Justice Hawkins gave Bottomley his wig as a memento and urged him to become a barrister.

Now he was a public hero – the David who had slain the legal Goliath, a great financier, a man of common origins with whom Mr Average could identify. Within a decade he made himself a millionaire by stock and share manipulation. Most of his money came from cashing in on the Australian gold rush. He floated scores of mining companies, most of which were worthless. Investors lost fortunes but Bottomley prospered. And he did it in the grand style – lavish parties, racehorses, a large Sussex mansion called The Dicker, a bevy of mistresses . . . and champagne, always champagne. Of course, he frequently had to face dissatisfied clients and hostile shareholders' meetings but his eloquence and charm were equal to most situations and when they were not, he could always fall back on the dedicated band of clever or tough men he called his 'stable'. Much of the opposition was silenced in 1902 when Bottomley brought a successful libel action against one opponent. In 1906 he won the parliamentary seat of South Hackney and immediately made an impression on both the Commons and the constituency. His speeches in the House never failed to attract attention while his lavish Christmas parties and outings for the poor of Hackney ensured his continued popularity there.

Bottomley continued as a press tycoon and 1906 saw the birth of his most famous and lasting journal, the weekly *John Bull*. It was meant to be the magazine for the common man – down-to-earth, chauvinistic, fearless and lively. It was an instant success, and if people associated the name of the journal with the character of its proprietor, well, that was an added bonus. But the profits from his various enterprises simply could not keep pace with his extravagance and his gambling. In 1912 he was declared bankrupt and was obliged to resign his parliamentary seat. This time it was a lottery that saved him; he organized public sweepstakes through *John Bull* which brought him hundreds of thousands of pounds.

For Bottomley the First World War was a godsend. *John Bull* blazoned forth, week after week, its jingoistic fury: 'Germany Must Be Wiped Off The Map of Europe', 'Lock Up All Germans, Confiscate Their Property'. And the 'great patriot' himself travelled the country making emotional recruitment speeches – for which he was handsomely paid. Not content with this he

launched the War Stock Combination, and, later, the Victory Bond Club, lotteries ostensibly investing all income in government stocks and paying cash prizes to lucky subscribers.

In 1918 the great orator was once more elected as MP for South Hackney, this time as an Independent. Now his conceit knew no bounds. An article by him in a national paper declared:

I am now preparing to proceed to Westminster to run the show . . . All Britain knew that I was aching to be returned for South Hackney as the unofficial Prime Minister and the unofficial Prime Minister I am going to be . . .

There were many who knew and thousands who suspected that Horatio Bottomley was a swindler, but, considering the man's previous record of legal success, none was prepared to face him in court. None, that is, save Reuben Bigland, one-time colleague and friend. Bigland was one of those whom Bottomley had used and cast aside. He owed the man money but not only did he refuse to pay, he dismissed Bigland as a buffoon. Goaded beyond measure, Bigland, in 1921, published a series of pamphlets exposing the Victory Bond swindle and calling its instigator 'one of the greatest crooks ever born'. Bottomley had to respond with a writ for libel and this was precisely what Bigland wanted. In court Bottomley did not dare to go into the witness box to disprove the allegations against him. He was forced to drop the case. The bubble had been burst.

Within days Bottomley faced criminal proceedings for fraud. He was convicted in 1922 and sentenced to seven years' imprisonment. He survived his release in 1927 by less than six years. He died destitute but, as his last words to a close friend indicate, he was an optimist to the end. 'Goodbye and God bless you. I'll see you again tomorrow.'

# Recluses

In the next two sections we shall be considering two contrasting groups of people whom I have called 'Recluses' and 'Exhibitionists'. The latter need human society. They demand recognition and feed on applause. Recluses are those who are impelled in the opposite direction. They have a natural inclination to withdraw from human contact. At the rational level there may be many reasons for this. Gilbert White elected to spend most of his time in his garden and in the surrounding fields to discover the ways of nature. Simeon Stylites sought to escape the distractions of human society in order to devote himself more entirely to God. Howard Hughes became convinced that all his fellow men and women were germ carriers and that his continued health depended on separation from them. Men have sought solitary lives out of disillusionment, despair, disgust with their fellow men, or a quest for spirituality. Yet whatever the avowed reason for a withdrawal from the world of human affairs may be, it stems ultimately from a deep sense of rejection. The recluse feels himself cut off from a world with which he is at odds, a world which has either turned its back on him or which is not worthy of him. Fear of rejection is something we all experience. It is one of the most powerful forces in our day-to-day relationships with each other. Perhaps more than anything else in human affairs it is this fear which stifles initiative. We fail to offer someone friendship or help for fear of a rebuff. We decline to embark on a new enterprise out of concern for what the neighbours might think. We are all of us sensitive to ridicule and misunderstanding. The recluse takes this to an extreme. Either unconsciously or consciously he rejects a society with which he is not in sympathy. His withdrawal may involve physical separation from his fellows as was the case with Howard Hughes, Greta Garbo or Paul Gauguin. It may be a partial separation from society as it was for Mary East and her companion. Or it may be an inward withdrawal which results in behaviour so bizarre or idiosyncratic as to form invisible barriers between the recluse and the world at large; Nathaniel Bentley, John Elwes and General Gordon, all in their own ways erected such invisible barriers.

The life of the recluse need not necessarily be negative and unproductive. Western Christianity has a very strong monastic tradition which is matched in the Eastern church and some of the other major world faiths. The thinking behind ascetic withdrawal is partly self-centred; the religious enthusiast, be he Christian, Muslim, Hindu or whatever, is seeking to deepen his own spiritual life by prayer and meditation away from the distractions of the world. But there has always been in most strands of monastic thought the concept of service to the world; the religious thought of themselves as undergirding society with their prayers as well as providing practical help in the form of hospitality and charity. The magnificent abbeys and monasteries which at one time studded the landscape of Europe were in themselves testimonies to a spiritual world and a higher way of life. Much the same can be said about many artists who have found it necessary to withdraw either temporarily or permanently from society in order to refresh their own vision and in order to be able to enrich that society with the products of their genius.

There seems to be something of a paradox at the heart of this whole area of our study and it is this: many of those who have been most closely bound up with the world and concerned to serve it, have been those most impelled by the need to withdraw from it. General Gordon was a man who millions admired and hero-worshipped but whom nobody understood because he spent so much of his time in inward reflection, whether on military or political affairs or on such abstruse speculations as the location of the Garden of Eden. He found in himself and in spiritual reflection the answers he sought to the world's problems. Yet he died in the service of his fellow men trying to save the Sudan from barbarism and the slave trade. Gilbert White was absolutely engrossed in the world about him, in the vegetable and animal (including human) life of his little corner of southern England. Yet in order to study it and record it for posterity, it was necessary for him to lead a very solitary life. Even Simeon Stylites who spent the greater part of his life elevated on a column high above the heads of ordinary mortals devoted hours every day to preaching, showing people the need for repentance, piety and high moral standards in human affairs.

Of course such high motives cannot be discerned in all our recluses, some simply wanted to get away from the world. They were disillusioned people like Ludwig of Bavaria and Greta Garbo. They were people like Howard Huges who had never found it possible to achieve a worthwhile human relationship with anyone. There were misers and misanthropists like John Elwes, who grew obsessed with the need to make and keep money. And what are we to make of Mary East

and 'Dirty Dick' Bentley who were driven by some earlier tragedy to lead a somewhat bizarre way of life? According to Socrates man is a social animal who only finds real fulfilment and meaning in full communion with his fellows. If that is so then a recluse is a person to be pitied as one whose vision of life is distorted and who impoverishes himself by his withdrawal from society, whether that withdrawal be total or partial. Indeed pity is the usual response of society towards the hermit, the miser and the man turned in upon himself. And yet, if truth is discerned inwardly, as well as in the world around us, may there not be something the recluse can teach us? Do we not all need the stamina to puzzle out our own individual answers to life's questions and the courage to stick by those answers no matter what the world may think? If some of those whose lives are chronicled below seem to have found somewhat exaggerated answers to those questions, can we not turn this very exaggeration to our advantage? To convey a truth it is often necessary to overstate it. Looked at in that light does not the story of Mary East speak to us about fidelity, or that of Charles Gordon about duty, or that of Garbo about the value of privacy? I leave you to draw your own lessons if you wish to do so from these extraordinary recluses and I hope that like me you will be amused, mystified, amazed, but also instructed by their strange histories.

# The mask behind the mask

Howard Hughes remains what he was in his life, an enigma – unknown and probably unknowable. He spent the last twenty years of his life as a recluse and the last five as an exile. Why did one of the world's wealthiest men, who had once commanded multinational companies, directed films, loved beautiful women, set aviation records and exercised great political influence, end up a drug-dependent old man who feared the world and sheltered from it behind a phalanx of hand-picked Mormon bodyguards? Some believe that his mental instability was inherited. There is, however, another and a more convincing explanation: Howard Hughes became increasingly prey to an obsession which had its roots in a personality defect and was watered by riches. For wealth, like power (and the two went hand-in-hand in Hughes), tends to corrupt.

One ingredient which went to make up the complex character of Howard Hughes was awe – the awe he felt for his father. Howard Hughes senior was a remarkable man – enthusiastic, self-confident and talented. He went to Texas at the turn of the century, like many other hopefuls aiming to share in the oil boom. He never found oil but he did perfect a drilling bit for the extraction of oil which revolutionized the industry. This

*Broadway's tickertape welcome for Hughes in 1938.*

took place when the inventor's only son was an infant. As young Howard grew up he saw the family wealth increase as the Hughes Tool Company expanded into a multi-million-dollar concern. Hughes senior fully lived up to his income – a fine house, lavish parties – everything that he wanted he bought. Having no liking for administration, he left the day-to-day running of the business to deputies. His son held him in great admiration as a man with panache and style who had worked his way up from nothing. Then, at the age of fifty-four Howard Hughes senior died of a heart attack. His wife had been struck down with equal suddenness two years earlier. At the age of eighteen Howard Hughes was alone – and a millionaire.

The shock was profound. The early deaths of his parents instilled in young Howard an obsession with health and a fear of dying. His mother had always cosseted her only son and this had given him a totally false conception of his physical well-being. This grew into a phobia about dirt and germs. Along with this went the need to prove himself as his father's son. He could have settled to running the tool company and lived very comfortably off it but he was impelled by an unconscious desire to equal or better Hughes senior's exploits, and that meant branching out into new fields. He had many of his father's attributes – a skill amounting almost to genius in things mechanical and mathematical, restless energy, and a dislike of administration. To these he added a disastrous trait of his own – one that has destroyed many – perfectionism.

He now showed an aggressive zeal not only in business but in every other aspect of life. He became an excellent golfer. He learned to fly aeroplanes and shone as a pilot also. He set himself to marry the most sought-after girl in Houston society – and succeeded. Then he went to Hollywood to carve out a career in the exciting new world of movies. For a while he was content with the role of financial backer but in 1927, while the experts laughed, Hughes began to direct his own films. The now-legendary *Hell's Angels*, about aerial combat in the First World War, took two and a half years to make, swallowed up $3.8 million, and cost the lives of three pilots and stunt men. Because of Hughes' demands for perfection, scenes were shot over and over again until two and a half million feet of film had been used. It began life as a silent picture, but the advent of talkies in 1929 obliged Hughes to reshoot many sequences to include dialogue and sound. Skilful promotion ensured box office success (though Hughes never recouped his total investment) and the film launched the career of Jean Harlow, one of Hollywood's great sex symbols. But *Hell's Angels* did more than that: it began a genre of spectacular epic, high-entertainment films and it

*Hughes was his own test pilot.*

created the popular image of the movie mogul.

Another exciting new world presenting itself for conquest was aviation. He threw himself into this both as designer and flier with his customary enthusiasm. He twice broke the trans-America speed record and, in 1938, he led the fastest round-the-world flight. Considering his passion about health there is something contradictory about his total recklessness in the air. He insisted on test-flying his aircraft and was several times injured in crashes, once almost fatally. When the Second World War began Hughes obtained government contracts for seaplanes and reconnaissance aircraft. He never delivered: his concepts were so extreme and his specifications so precise that the war was over before operational aircraft could be produced.

For a decade after the war Hughes continued to build his empire. He acquired control of RKO Pictures and Trans World Airlines. He won and lost millions in business deals. But already he had begun to distance himself from colleagues and associates. By 1957 a new pattern of life had been established: Hughes would take over the whole floor of a hotel and live there with a few aides who catered for all his needs. The floor was sealed off, neither visitors nor staff being allowed in. He would stay for an indeterminate time, then move suddenly to another residence where the same routine would be established. From this point it was but an irrationally logical progression to Hughes' final state – spending his time in a hermetically-sealed apartment, incessantly watching old films, injecting himself with

codeine, having everything brought to him wrapped in germ-free tissues. Howard Hughes finished his life in a private asylum; not an asylum dedicated to the cure of the patient but one where his every wish, no matter how bizarre, was pandered to because he paid well.

But Hughes did not *become* a recluse in the last two decades before his death in April 1976; he had always been a recluse. He had never been able to establish simple, genuine human contact with anyone. He married twice but rarely lived in the same house with either wife. He had no children. He increasingly used intermediaries for business deals and even spoke with close colleagues by telephone. He was always secretive, given to clandestine meetings and behaving with extreme caution. His actions defy rational explanation. Yet there was one clear reason for his ultimate seclusion. Howard Hughes had, in his younger days, built up a public image – the aviator hero, the hard-headed tycoon, the film-maker with the golden touch. It was a false image but he valued it, he needed it, he owed it to the memory of his father. He knew that his bizarre behaviour would destroy that image, so he concealed it, preferring to create instead a mystery, an enigma.

*Hughes ended his life in frail isolation and left claimants to squabble over his will.*

# The man of money

The miser has always been a stock figure of fun – Shakespeare's Shylock, Molière's Harpagon, George Eliot's Silas Marner (though here the man's ludicrous obsession makes him a pitiable rather than a humorous character), and, of course, the endless stream of jokes about Scotsmen and Jews. We tend, quite irrationally, to applaud generosity and even extravagance and to condemn financial prudence. Most of us try to strike a balance between the two. Those who disdain a middle path, who are excessively profligate or tight-fisted, we rightly regard as extraordinary.

Such a man was John Elwes, the eighteenth-century miser, whose parsimony was for many years a talking point throughout Britain. John grew up a fairly normal young man of well-to-do family. He was educated at Westminster School and, like many of his contemporaries, completed his preparation for adult life with a continental tour. The trouble seems to have started when he was named the heir of his wealthy uncle, Sir Harvey Elwes. Sir Harvey had spent years redeeming his estates from the debt and decrepitude he found them in on succeeding his father. He had vowed to avoid all unnecessary expenditure and never to leave his house at Stoke-by-Nayland in Suffolk until his fortunes were restored. Thrift became a habit, then, by degrees, an obsession. He made it quite clear to his heir that he would not leave his estate to a wastrel. So, whenever John went to visit his uncle he put on an elaborate act. First, he dined at a neighbour's house to take the edge off his appetite. Then he made a brief stop at an inn to change out of his clothes into a set of patched, threadbare garments. Thus attired and mounted on an aged, hired hack he completed his journey. At Stoke Sir Harvey habitually presented his guest with the most frugal of meals then, as they sat sharing a single glass of wine before a few flickering twigs in the hearth, he would impress upon his nephew the importance of careful housekeeping. Before nightfall the two men would retire, so as to avoid the expense of candles.

You might have thought that once he came into his aged relative's money, John would have kicked over the traces and really made the most of his fortune. In fact something of Sir Harvey must have rubbed off on his nephew. He inherited an estate worth over a quarter of a million pounds – a very large sum for those days. Instead of enjoying it, his whole mind was bent on adding to it. Income poured in in the form of rents from his many farms and houses and much of his surplus cash Elwes tried to multiply by gambling, lending at interest, and speculating in various commercial enterprises. He owned much land in and around London and built Portman Place, Portman Square, part of Haymarket and many streets of houses in Marylebone. He had no head for business, kept no proper accounts and thus, not surprisingly, he lost a great deal of money. It was presumably to counteract this drain on his resources that he developed his exceptional meanness. Often, after playing cards all night and, perhaps, losing thousands of pounds, he would walk back to his own house to save the cab fare. Once he rode over from Stoke to Newmarket with a friend and there put up £7,000 for a wager. The day wore on and the friend grew very hungry. Eventually he suggested to Elwes that it was time to eat. 'Oh, you should do as I do,' said John. He pulled from his pocket an unappetizing piece of pancake and proudly announced that he had been living off this particular reserve food supply for two months. When travelling he always carried scraps of food with him so as to avoid the necessity of calling at inns. He also planned his routes with care so as to use as few turnpike roads as possible.

John Elwes resented paying professional fees and would never consult a doctor or lawyer if it could be avoided. Once, he stumbled in the dark

*Most of Elwes' money came from London property such as fashionable Portland Place.*

and bruised his legs badly. He was at the time staying with friends who insisted, despite his protests, in summoning an apothecary. The man examined him and proposed certain remedies. This was Elwes' reply: 'In my opinion my legs are not much hurt. Now, you think they are. So, I will make this agreement: I will take one leg and you shall take the other. You shall do what you please with yours. I will do nothing to mine, and I will wager your bill that my leg gets well before yours.' It is recorded that Elwes won the bet.

It goes without saying that he kept the minimum of servants, spent as little as possible on the upkeep of his houses and never possessed more than a few sticks of furniture. On his visits to London it was his custom to reside in any of his many houses which chanced to be vacant. If a new potential tenant appeared he would move at a moment's notice, attended only by an elderly woman. Friends and business acquaintances, therefore, never knew where to find him. Once, when he had been missing for several days, he was tracked down to a sparse upper room where he lay on a pallet bed, desperately ill. His servant woman was found dead in one of the attics.

He recovered his health and, in fact, lived in full command of his physical faculties until well into his seventies. This is rather surprising when we consider how consistently he abused his body. His diet was frugal. He slept badly, partly because he would not go to the expense of sheets and blankets and partly because he used to lie awake worrying about money. He was frequently soaked to the skin because his clothes were worn thin and because he would rather walk in the rain than hire a carriage. A man who died leaving an estate of £800,000 lived the greater part of his life like an inmate of the workhouse. He was courteous and well-mannered yet so intense was his obsession with money that it built a barrier between Elwes and his fellow men. He did not entertain his friends and neighbours and as he became more solitary he grew convinced that everyone who called upon him was intent upon swindling him. As a newspaper epitaph on this unfortunate man stated, he was one,

Lost in the lust of adding pelf to pelf*,
Poor to the poor – still poorer to himself.

*'Pelf' riches.

## Dirty Dick

When Dickens wrote *Great Expectations*, with its description of the appalling Miss Havisham and her crumbling mansion, where time, but not vermin and dirt, had stood still, did he know the story of Nathaniel Bentley, alias Dirty Dick, who was in many ways a male counterpart of Pip's tormentor?

Nathaniel was the son of a well-to-do London merchant and received a good, if strict, upbringing. The young man spoke several languages and travelled extensively on the continent. Having fallen out with his father, he preferred to keep as great a distance as possible between them. In 1760, on the death of his father, he came into a sizeable fortune. He was now able to enjoy life in considerable style. He had a fine carriage and wore the finest clothes, being particularly fastidious about his appearance. He was known as the 'Beau of Leadenhall Street'. He moved in fashionable society at home and abroad and was particularly popular at the French court. He was, in fact, a guest at the coronation of Louis XVI. In the course of time he contracted marriage with a well-connected and attractive young lady. Before the ceremony he invited his bride and several friends to a banquet in the chambers above his business premises in Leadenhall Street. It was while he was waiting in eager anticipation that news was brought to him of the lady's sudden death. He shut the room up just as it was and it remained undisturbed for over thirty years.

From that unhappy event can be dated the complete change which overcame his character.

His business was built around a large hardware warehouse from which he conducted a considerable import and export trade as well as retailing to individual customers. His business and social life fell into two distinct categories, work in the store obviously calling for practical clothes rather than velvet and lace. Now he devoted himself entirely to the shop. His face was no longer seen in ballrooms and clubhouses. That was very understandable. Bentley was not the first man who sought solace for a broken heart in hard work. Unfortunately it did not stop there: Bentley neglected himself and his surroundings completely. He did not wash (although he did continue to shave). He changed his clothes only when they were too tattered to hold together. It was not long before his nickname had changed from the 'Beau' to 'Dirty Dick'. His premises were widely known as the 'Dirty Warehouse' and became quite a landmark.

Who but has seen (if he can see at all)
'Twixt Aldgate's well-known pump and Leadenhall,
A curious hardware shop, in general full
Of wares from Birmingham and Pontipool!
Begrimed with dirt, behold its ample front,

*The Dirty Warehouse, a London tourist attraction.*

*When Bentley's friends explored his deserted living quarters they found incredible dirt and disorder.*

With thirty years' collected filth upon't;
See festooned cobwebs pendant o'er the door,
While boxes, bales and trunks are strewed
about the floor.

The building's front, once of gleaming white plaster, became blackened with grime over the years. His neighbours often offered to redecorate it at their own expense. There was a certain logic in Bentley's refusal. As things were, he pointed out, strangers always knew where to find him. How would they be able to locate the Dirty Warehouse if it was outwardly as smart as the adjoining premises?

Within the shop everything was confusion, dust and vermin. Customers usually had to clean their purchases carefully as soon as they got them home. You might suppose that the appalling filth in which Dirty Dick lived and worked would have had a bad effect upon trade. The reverse seems to have been the case; people travelled miles to shop at the Dirty Warehouse and to make the acquaintance of its extraordinary proprietor. For it was only his appearance which repelled; his manners were impeccable. It is recorded that he once invited a group of his best customers to have dinner with him. They must have been rather apprehensive but they accepted. When they arrived they found Bentley still in the shop. He politely excused himself and returned after a brief interval with a pound of cheese, a loaf and two

jugs of beer which he set down on the dusty counter and bade his guests fall to.

Bentley lived alone amidst all this squalor until 1804. He kept no indoor servants and no guard dogs, claiming that both would involve him in unnecessary expense. His only employee was a man set to watch the door to warn him of the approach of customers. When Bentley was, at last, obliged to leave on the expiry of his lease, friends and neighbours were able to explore the upper storeys for the first time in decades. They found a kitchen in which the spits had long since rusted solid, a range on which Bentley had cooked his simple meals in a frying pan without a handle. It was obvious that the proprietor had lived in this one room, rolling himself in a coat to sleep on the floor. In other chambers, once-elegant clocks, chairs, sideboards, carved chimney pieces, pictures and carpets lay under sheets of undisturbed dust. Beds and their mattresses had decayed leaving rooms awash with feathers. Discarded account books littered the landings.

And what of Dirty Dick himself? He took to the road, after having sold off £10,000 worth of stock at a considerable loss. He did not settle in any lodgings. Probably no landlord would have him. Walking from town to town, this solitary man eventually crossed the Scottish border and reached Haddington. There he died in 1809. Never was the incantation 'ashes to ashes and dust to dust' more appropriate.

# A woman of high resolve

There is something noble about a person who makes a resolution and sticks to it through thick and thin over many years. It matters not whether we consider that resolution wise or unwise, right or wrong, the virtue lies in the performance. Mary East was a woman of remarkable resolution.

Mary was born about 1715 and nothing is recorded of her earlier years. At the age of sixteen she fell deeply in love with a young man who returned her affection. They desperately wanted to get married but Mary's lover felt that he did not have sufficient fortune to lay before her. To make good the deficiency he took to highway robbery, much as Mary tried to dissuade him and much as she feared the outcome. She was right to be apprehensive. The young man was caught, tried and condemned to death. Because of his youth and the absence of any previous conviction, sentence was commuted to transportation for life. As far as Mary was concerned he might as well have been dead. They were parted for ever. Mary was desolate and in her grief she made an extraordinary decision. She resolved to forswear all male company. Many impressionable young women, disappointed in love, have vowed to live the rest of their lives in chaste fidelity to their lost amour. Few have maintained that vow for long. Nor was it an easy vow for an attractive young woman to hold to without entering a nunnery, of which there were hardly any at that time. Mary discovered an unusual way to carry out her decision. She joined forces with a friend who apparently had also decided that men no longer meant anything to her. They pooled their resources, which amounted to about £30, and left home together, posing as husband and wife. Mary put on man's clothes and assumed the name of James Howe.

At Epping in Essex they came upon a small public house which was to let. They took it and ran the hostelry successfully for some time. It was far from easy. Public houses were rough-and-ready establishments in those days. Drunkenness was common and licensing laws non-existent. The work itself was heavy. There were barrels to be humped about, heavy furniture to be moved and cleaned, food and drink to fetch and carry. It was hardly an occupation for two slips of girls. Yet the 'Howes' did everything themselves. They did not dare employ living-in servants for fear of their secret being discovered. As two young women, unprotected in the company of wayfarers, they were putting themselves at considerable risk. Yet, their deception worked. Customers noted that James Howe seemed a little effeminate but no one, apparently, thought any more about it.

It was a near-disaster that brought the two women their greatest piece of good fortune. One day a boisterous young squire swaggered in already the worse for drink and intent on making trouble. He picked a fight with the far-from-robust-looking innkeeper and, in the ensuing struggle, Mary badly damaged her hand, which never fully recovered. The brawl did considerable damage but someone called in the law and the offender was marched away. Mary subsequently brought an action against the man and obtained £500 damages. With this handsome windfall they moved to a better house, the White Horse in Poplar. Not only did they run this inn, they bought several others in the vicinity. They invested their profit wisely and over the years amassed a fortune of several thousand pounds. James Howe and his 'wife' were well known and respected in the area and over the years James held a variety of local offices. It was about 1764 that James's companion fell ill. She went to her brother's house in Essex and there, on the point of death, told her close relatives all about the deception that she and Mary had long practised. After the woman was dead these relatives lost no time in calling upon Mary East and demanding a half of her fortune. She paid up without demur.

Whether or not she intended to continue with her masquerade, it is impossible to say. In the event, fate decided the matter for her. Some years before, a woman had discovered her secret and over the years had practised sporadic blackmail. The sums demanded were not large and her victims had always paid up. Believing that now Mary East was on her own she would be even more vulnerable the blackmailer now tried to extort a much larger amount of money. She went to the White Horse with a couple of ruffians who posed as police officers. They accused Mary of a robbery and said they had come to take her into custody until such times as she could be tried and – most assuredly – hanged. They presumably expected her to panic and agree to any demand in order to escape public exposure. In fact, Mary turned for help to a neighbour, Mr Williams, and told him everything. With his help, the criminals were brought to justice. But Mary's secret was out and there could be no question of James Howe's continued existence.

It must have felt very strange becoming a woman again after thirty-three years. Her cumbersome skirts and petticoats must have taken a while to get used to. After selling the White Horse, she bought a house in another part of Poplar and lived there quietly until her death in 1781. She kept a modest establishment with a couple of

servants to whom she left generous legacies. The bulk of her estate went to a friend, as she had no close relatives. It is pleasant to think of this courageous and highly-successful business woman sitting in her garden during those last years recalling the many adventures of her inn-keeping days and, we may be sure, thinking often of her long lost lover to whom she remained faithful unto death.

## Closer to Heaven?

A man who lived thirty-seven years on top of a pillar has to qualify for a place among the world's most extraordinary people.

His name was Simeon and he lived in the Roman province of Cilicia in Asia Minor in the first half of the fifth century. He was the son of a shepherd and, although we know nothing about his childhood, it is obvious that, wandering alone with his father's sheep, he developed a simple but intense Christian faith. According to the legend (and there is little more than legend to go on) his spiritual pilgrimage began one day when he was thirteen and heard read in church the words of Jesus from St Matthew's Gospel, 'Happy are the pure in heart.' He was consumed with a desire to know how he might become pure in heart and so enjoy the promised happiness. Consulting a wise elder of the church, he learned that the path to holiness and purity lay through self-denial, penitence, prayer and fasting. Simeon earnestly prayed that God would give him the power to follow this ascetic path to holiness. Falling asleep, he had a vivid dream in which he saw himself digging the foundations for a house. Whenever he paused for breath a voice from Heaven urged him on until he excavated a very deep pit. Then, the voice told him he had done well; that, with such a deep foundation, he might build whatever house he desired. It was a typical start to an ascetic vocation – the call to supreme effort in the pursuit of personal salvation.

Simeon entered a monastery and practised the most extreme forms of mortification his flesh would bear. The church of this region had accepted the ancient Greek teaching of a duality of flesh and spirit. In order to free the spirit from its imprisonment in the body that body had to be denied every comfort and maintained on the minimum sustenance necessary to keep it alive. It is recorded that one of Simeon's self-inflicted punishments was to take the monastery's well rope of plaited palm leaves and bind it tight around his body so that it bit into his flesh. When, eventually, the fronds were cut away Simeon was so weakened that he collapsed and was close to death. The abbot, far from being pleased with this excess of zeal, told Simeon that he had gone too far and expelled him from the monastery. Perhaps he was annoyed about the missing well rope.

But Simeon was not discouraged. On the contrary; everything was fitting in with his vision; he was being called to dig deeper. He resolved to live the life of a hermit on the slopes of Mount Telanissae. There, during the forty days of Lent, he decided to endure a total fast. A friend left some bread and water at the door of Simeon's hut but, when he returned at the end of Lent, he found the provisions untouched and Simeon's emaciated form close to death. Gradually the hermit revived, took a little light food and was soon restored to full health. For the rest of his life Simeon spent Lent in this way. But still he had to dig his pit deeper. People were in the habit of coming to his hermitage to bring food and gaze upon the holy man. To his horror, Simeon realized he was taking comfort from his human contact. It was distracting him from prayer and contemplation. So he moved to the top of the mountain, enclosed a small space with a fence and, in the centre of it, fixed his leg by a chain to a heavy rock. Then, a neighbouring priest told him that he should not need a chain; his will should be strong enough. So Simeon removed the chain.

Still people flocked to see him – if anything in larger numbers. So began the pole-squatting. In 423 Simeon erected a twelve-foot pillar with a six-foot diameter and stood upon the top. He took

*Some ascetics whipped themselves to achieve holiness.*

little sleep and there was barely enough room for him to lie down. He lived there for four years. At the end of that time he doubled the height of the pillar. After a further three years he built another column thirty-five feet high. He lived there for ten years. At the end of that time he asked the local people to help him with another construction. The new pillar, if the ancient records are to be believed, soared sixty feet into the blue sky. Here he spent the remaining twenty years of his life. If Simeon seriously believed that such activity would attract no attention he must have been suffering from a touch of the sun (not at all unlikely under the circumstances). In fact he became a considerable tourist attraction. He seems to have become reconciled to this eventually for he adopted the custom of interrupting his devotions twice a day to preach to the crowds which came to gaze up at him. He urged them to abandon usury and swearing, to exercise strict justice and practise piety. It is recorded that many heathens were converted by Simeon's words and example. Emperors were among those who came to seek his prayers and advice. Ultimately, local church

S WILLIAMS DEL & SCULPT.

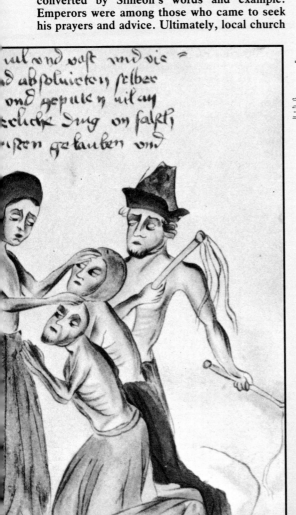

leaders became alarmed. They were convinced that Simeon was indulging in a form of spiritual pride, deliberately outdoing other Christians in self-denial and enjoying being a celebrity. The bishop ordered Simeon to descend. He immediately prepared to do so. The bishop, seeing the hermit's ready obedience and obvious humility, rescinded his order and told Simeon to continue in his sacred vocation.

Thus lived Simeon Stylites (so called after the Greek word *stylos*, 'a pillar'), until the age of sixty-nine, when still atop his column, his tough body finally released the spirit unwillingly imprisoned within it. By then he had established a 'school' of like-minded ascetics who followed his example. For almost a thousand years he was an influential figure in the Christian ascetic movement and St Simeon inspired untold numbers of hermits and monks to achieve holiness through self-denial.

## The swan-hermit

In 1864 the mountain and forest kingdom of Bavaria had a new king. Ludwig II ascended the throne that his Wittelsbach ancestors had occupied for nine hundred years. He was nineteen and darkly handsome. His subjects cheered him through the streets of Munich and looked forward to a long, successful reign. It cannot have occurred to any of them that they were watching the curtain go up on a tragedy.

Ludwig had spent a sad, solitary childhood. His father was a martinet. His mother lavished all her affection on her younger son, Otto. His French governess filled his mind with thoughts of splendour and the privileged superiority of princes. In the beautiful isolation of the Wittelsbach palaces and castles he had few playfellows and little opportunity for the rough and tumble of childhood games which might have dented his protective self-esteem. He grew up melancholy, vain and headstrong. His passions were Romantic poetry and music, the old Teutonic legends of Siegfried and the gods of Valhalla, and walks amidst the dramatic forests and chasms of the Bavarian Alps.

When he became king, suddenly and unexpectedly, on the early death of his father, the people welcomed him enthusiastically as their 'Prince Charming'. Ministers and court officials, who knew him better, were apprehensive. The young Ludwig commanded great wealth but, within his small realm, his power was limited. Little was asked of him in the day-to-day government of the country. He was expected only to play the role of impressive figurehead and grand patron, to marry and sire an heir.

His first important act and the one destined to have the greatest impact on the world was his rescuing of Richard Wagner from poverty and obscurity. The fifty-one-year-old composer had, largely through defects in his character, made many powerful enemies and virtually destroyed his own career. But Ludwig had an intense admiration for him and loved Wagner's operas, such as *Lohengrin* and *Tannhäuser*, based on old German legends. He now invited the composer to Munich where he provided him with a house and a pension and showered him with gifts. Freed from financial worry and his works frequently performed by royal command, Wagner was able to recommence work on his monumental masterpiece, *The Ring of the Nibelung*.

The results of this friendship were not so happy for Ludwig. Wagner was unpopular. His irregular personal life, his dabbling in revolutionary politics and his arrogance combined to give the impression of one who was not a suitable companion for the king. Ludwig was impatient with public censure. 'Dull people,' he wrote to his friend, 'cannot have any idea of our love. They do not know what you are, have been, and ever will be – all in all to me until my dying day; that I loved you before I ever set eyes on you.' That Ludwig was homosexual there is no doubt. That he abandoned himself to Wagner with all the unreasoning passion of a lover is beyond dispute. That there was anything improper in the relationship is extremely unlikely. Yet his feelings consumed the young king and when he learned of Wagner's affair with Cosima, wife of the conductor Hans von Bülow, he was beside himself with jealousy. Meanwhile a concerted campaign against the favourite eventually obliged a heart-broken Ludwig to request Wagner to leave the capital. The composer moved to Switzerland and eventually married Cosima. Ludwig remained a generous patron for the remaining eighteen years of Wagner's life and when the great composer died he made a secret visit, alone and at night, to pay his last respects at the graveside.

Ludwig attempted one more close human relationship. In 1867 he impulsively proposed marriage to his cousin, Sophie. Whether there was a definite attraction or whether the king was doing what he conceived to be his duty it is difficult to say. Whatever his reasons, he soon thought better of them. Weeks before the wedding day he broke off the relationship as abruptly as he had begun it. He retired to the castle of Hohenschwangau overlooking the clear waters of the Alpsee in that part of his realm known as the 'Swan Country', centre of the legend of Lohengrin, the swan-knight. He continued to perform state functions but the process of almost total withdrawal had begun.

## The sick children

Ludwig II's castles and palaces have been called his 'sick children' – the bizarre offspring of a fevered imagination. It may be that Ludwig was inspired by a desire to prove to Wagner that he, too, was a creative genius, capable of conceiving edifices as monumental and unrestrained as the composer's grand operas. His first essay in fantastic architecture was the royal apartments in his Munich Residenz. He had an artificial lake built on the third floor. It was fringed by tropical trees and plants and the colour of the water could be changed by clever lighting. On this lake he would float in a swan-shaped gondola while a hidden orchestra played favourite music. His first major building project was Neuschwanstein (above) – the swan's new castle – a fairy-tale edifice of pinnacles and towers soaring upwards from a craggy peak. By the time that Ludwig came to build Linderhof Palace he was under the influence of eighteenth-century French architecture and his new residence was a miniature version of Versailles. The decoration was exuberant, but tasteful. Yet even here the king could not resist a touch of the bizarre – his dining table was made to rise up through a trapdoor in the floor. Herrenchiemsee, on an island in the Chiem See, was also built in the French style. Thousands of workmen were employed for years to produce the architectural fantasy which had to be perfect in every detail. This untenanted splendour cost millions. The extravagance brought Ludwig to his tragic end and scandalized Bavaria's stolid politicians. Ironically the king – or his ghost – had the last laugh. His sick children soon became one of the country's principal tourist attractions. They paid for themselves many times over.

Other events reinforced his desire for seclusion. The government rejected some of his most cherished policies, such as greater privileges for the Roman Catholic church. He allowed himself to be persuaded to join with Austria in a war against Prussia which brought only humiliating defeat. He allowed himself to be manoeuvred by the great Bismarck into sanctioning the formation of a German empire headed by Prussia. The world was changing, leaving far behind Ludwig's romantic concept of kingship. And so he devoted his prime energies to a fantastic programme of building and decorating royal residences. He toured them constantly, arriving unannounced at dead of night and travelling on after a few days.

Ludwig was not yet a complete hermit. It was his brother's illness which brought about the final stage of the king's withdrawal. Popular, lively, young Otto took to his bed with a mysterious malady. His body recovered but his mind went into a rapid and complete decline. Within months he was little more than an animal and he had to be confined in one of the remote Wittelsbach mansions. To Ludwig's very real distress was added the fear that he, too, might be tarred with the brush of insanity. From that time on Ludwig regarded people with abhorrence. The obsession deepened with the passing years. Ludwig's few servants were not permitted to come close to the royal person. They were required to turn their faces away from him. He frequently dined with stone busts of Louis XIV and Marie Antoinette and held long conversations with his 'guests'. Visiting ministers had to indulge in shouted exchanges with their king through closed doors.

Ludwig's eccentricities scandalized his people. The government, however, might have tolerated them had it not been for the king's incredible extravagance. In 1886 it was decided that Ludwig II should be declared insane and confined. A commission, led by the psychiatrist Dr Bernhard von Gudden was despatched to bring him by stages from Neuschwanstein to the capital. The party reached Berg on the shores of Starnbergsee. Dr Gudden was agreeably surprised to find the king very calm, apparently resigned to his fate. On the evening of 13 June the two men set off alone for a stroll beside the lake. They did not return. Hours later fishermen discovered two bodies floating in the water bearing obvious signs of a struggle. Exactly what happened during those last moments of the swan-king's life will never be known. Did Gudden try to prevent Ludwig committing suicide? Did the king attempt to kill his captor and escape? All that can be said for certain is that Ludwig II finally found the complete seclusion he craved.

## 'I have nothing to say'

Stars are public property – such is the accepted belief. Part of the price to be paid for fame and wealth whether as a film actor or a pop musician is constant accessibility to the news media and the gossip columnist. Greta Garbo's principal claim to fame is that she refused to accept this article of faith.

She always had a penchant for believing what she wanted to believe and acting accordingly. As a child in a working class district of Stockholm she thought of herself as a boy, played games with the opposite sex and became the leader of a gang. From her earliest days, also, her life had its public and its private side. When she was not up to escapades with her friends, Greta Gustafsson retreated into an inner world, dancing contentedly in a quiet cul-de-sac or striking poses before a mirror. She was shy and found it difficult to meet strangers. She was very sensitive; other people's sorrow and anguish touched her deeply. And there was much sorrow and anguish among the poor people of Sweden during the first two decades of the century. The women struggled to bring up large families and the men drank to cover their inadequacy. For Greta the theatre became an escape from harsh reality. She went to see the play whenever she had enough money. When she had not she hung around the stage door to catch a glimpse of the actors. In 1920 her father died,

Greta left school and went to work in a department store. She was fourteen. She had long since made up her mind to become a film star. She visited the nearby studios whenever she could and pestered friends and acquaintances there to get her a screen test. In 1921 persistence was

*Garbo with John Gilbert in 'Queen Christina'. She had much in common with the Swedish queen.*

*Garbo starred with Gilbert again in 'Love'.*

rewarded when she was given a bit part in a historical film. This was followed by a bigger role in a
slapstick comedy the following year. Nothing
could deter her now. She won a scholarship to the
Swedish dramatic academy and while still there
was cast in another important film role. It was
then that she changed her name. 'Garbo' sounded
so much more suitable for a film actress than
Gustafsson. She was just eighteen.

Her director, Mauritz Stiller, knew that he had
found a star – not a great actress, but a woman
who through the medium of film was capable of
capturing the hearts of millions. She was beautiful, she moved gracefully and she accepted direction. 'She is as nervous as a fish,' he once said of
her, 'and she can't think. I don't believe a real
thought has ever entered her head. I have to break
her down . . . but when she is broken down, what
a performance she gives.' Stiller took his protégé
to Hollywood in 1925 and the MGM promotion
machine swung into action. In the next three
years Garbo starred in ten films and established
the style which was to become her hallmark –
cool, detached but stunningly beautiful. Nor was
this a pose for, as she matured, the public and
private aspects of her character developed
equally. She could put on a magnificent performance but as soon as she left the set she retired
into herself, resenting intrusion. In more senses
than one she felt herself to be a foreigner in a
strange land. Interviewers found her infuriating
and the feeling was mutual. 'What business is it of
yours?' she retorted when one of them asked
about her childhood. 'Some people were born in
red brick houses, others in plain white board
ones. What is the difference? I will not have it
pointed out that I was born in this house or that;
that my mother was this, or my father was that. I
don't want the world to talk about my mother and
father.' And so to the rapidly growing legend was
added a new ingredient – Garbo the mysterious,
the enigma. It was true, but it was also good for
the box office. Garbo, unlike other idols of the
silent screen, made the transition to talking films
with great ease. With one exception – she could
not laugh. She could go through the physical
motions but the sound would not come and had to
be dubbed. There is something significant about
that, as there is about the fact that she never
formed a close emotional attachment with anyone.

Throughout the 1930s she was the queen of
Hollywood. She made twenty-four films. She had
an enormous following of admirers throughout
the world. In 1936 she received Sweden's highest
award for the arts. Then, in 1941, she stopped.
After that date she never appeared in a film or on
the stage. She gave no interviews. She retired into
herself. The public Garbo came to an end. The
private Garbo took over. Many reasons have
been suggested as to why she should become a
recluse but, since she has never deigned to
explain herself, it must be guesswork. Certainly
she had earned and saved enough money to make
further work unnecessary. She had reached the
point in her career when she could choose her
own pictures and she may well have decided that
no script she was offered suited her. She was tired
of the Hollywood promotion machine. She had
seen it make and break other actors and actresses. She was no longer young and could not face
the prospect of being eclipsed by newer, fresher
faces. Again, she had seen that happen. The film
industry would not discard Garbo; Garbo would
discard the film industry.

Yet all that does not fully explain the total seclusion into which she now withdrew – the dark
glasses and wide-brimmed hats which hid her
face; the apartment in an unfashionable quarter
of New York with an anonymous 'G' beside the
bellpush; the aliases she assumed when travelling; her utter refusal to be interviewed; her shun-
ning of parties; her complete lack of involvement
in political or social events. Most of her time is
now divided between New York and Switzerland.
She lives by a strict daily routine and is usually in
bed by 9.30. Is she a lonely or a solitary person,
self-contained and self-sufficient, or just self-
denying? The world will never know, unless
Garbo tells the world – which seems unlikely. We,
like her, must live with the legend.

# Communing with nature

Gilbert White saw more of life than most men. Yet he rarely left his own village. He was born in the vicarage at Selborne, Hampshire, in 1720. He died in a house across the street seventy-three years later. Apart from his time at school and university he rarely left the environs of Selborne. Yet in the seclusion of his garden and the neighbouring fields Gilbert White made discoveries which have fascinated, delighted and informed the world ever since.

White was scholarly and retiring by nature. For example, he never sat for a portrait. He became a fellow of his college – Oriel, Oxford – and might well have settled to a life of academic obscurity. But he had little liking for the politics and bickering of college life. After failing in an election for the provostship of Oriel, White settled finally for Selborne. He had always loved the straggling village beneath its beach-clad scarp and, having taken holy orders in 1749, he became curate at Selborne two years later. He held two other appointments during his long ministry – at Newton Valence and Faringdon. The first village was a mile from Selborne; the other, two miles. Here he passed the greater part of his days in bachelor seclusion (he appears never to have had any romantic attachments) with a modest retinue of servants.

And he observed. He observed people and animals and birds and reptiles and insects and plants and the changing seasons. He filled notebooks with the results of his research. He wrote letters to friends and learned journals. During a long life ideally suited to creative output, he wrote only one book. But that one book has never been out of print since. It has become a classic not only of natural history but also of English literature. It has assured continuing fame for an obscure English village and its retiring parson. Pilgrims still flock to White's seventeenth-century dwelling, 'The Wakes', now turned into a museum, to explore the house and grounds where *The Natural History and Antiquities of Selborne in the County of Southampton* was born.

In an age when Captain Cook, Abel Tasman and others were exploring the unknown recesses of the globe, Gilbert White was discovering the unknown in such familiar places as his own lawn.

When earth worms lie out a' nights on turf, though they extend their bodies a great way, they do not quite leave their holes, but keep the ends of their tails fixed therein, so that on the least alarm they can retire with precipitation under the earth. Whatever food falls within their reach when thus extended they seem to be content with, such as blades of grass, straws, fallen leaves, the ends of which they often draw into their holes. Even in copulation their hinder parts never quit their holes; so that no two, except they lie within reach of each others bodies, can have any commerce of that kind; but as every individual is an hermaphrodite, there is no difficulty in meeting with a mate.

What hours of patient, nocturnal observation must have gone into such a passage. It is little wonder that White made so many discoveries which were quite new to the world of science (such as the sex life of earthworms).

Years of training enabled White to note with great precision the habits of animals and birds. He recorded, for example, that wrynecks 'walk a little as well as hop, and thrust their bills into the turf, in quest . . . of ants, which are their food. While they hold their bills in the grass, they draw out their prey with their tongues.' Fascination at the antics of furred or feathered creatures held him motionless on his garden seat or at his window for long periods of time.

A nightjar this evening showed off in a very unusual and entertaining manner, by hawking round and round the circumference of my great spreading oak, for twenty times following, keeping mostly close to the grass, but occasionally glancing up amidst the boughs of the tree. This amusing bird was then in pursuit of a brood of some particular insect belonging to the oak, of which there are several sorts; and exhibited on occasion a command of wing superior, I think, to that of the swallow itself. Nightjars have attachment to oaks, no doubt on

*Born at Selbourne Vicarage, White rarely left the village.*

individual appear safe from the ravages of birds of prey and other dangers.'

*The Natural History of Selborne* does not confine its attention to the brute creation. White recorded just as carefully and just as dispassionately the activities of his fellow human beings. It was said of him not that he was an unfriendly man but that he was a difficult man to get to know. We can readily appreciate this when we read his paragraphs on the incidence of frostbite among farm labourers and his descriptions of various epidemics. Thanks to White's diligence in observing and recording everything of interest his book provides us with many insights into rural social conditions in the eighteenth century. For example, we know that village women could earn 'three halfpence' (just less than a modern halfpenny) a bushel picking hops and that on a good day one could pick twenty-four bushels. Some women also gathered acorns, which they sold at a shilling (5p) a bushel. The frugal housewife, White informs us, made her own substitute candles by soaking rushes in bacon fat which she first heated in a deep pan to separate out the salt.

White's book tells us little about the performance of his religious duties, nothing about his political opinions, and next to nothing about his emotional reaction to the harshness of nature as manifested either in human or animal society. Indeed, the one creature that this great naturalist never put under the microscope was himself. Even the title page of the first edition of *The Natural History of Selborne* does not bear his name. In death, as in life, Gilbert White was retiring and unassuming. The headstone he ordered to mark his grave bears the simplest of inscriptions: G.W. 26th JUNE 1793.

account of food: for the next evening we saw one again several times among the boughs of the same tree.

For White natural science was not just a matter of observing and noting; nature posed puzzles which had to be solved. Frequently his mind would tease some problem for days on end as he paced the Hampshire lanes or sat in his study. Servants and neighbours familiar with his moods knew better than to interrupt his train of thought with domestic queries or civil greetings. The curate of Selborne pondered long on the migratory habits of various species of birds and the construction of the nests of fieldmice. A phenomenon which even a countryman might see but not reflect upon would occupy White's mind for hours. For example, in the middle of one severe winter he noticed that many species of birds congregated together more than usual. This puzzled him. With food in short supply, should they not, rather, have scattered in search of it? At last, he concluded: 'Perhaps approximation may dispel some degree of cold; and a crowd may make each

*The ancient Yew described in one of White's books.*

# Warrior of God

A great military commander, a popular hero and a philanthropist who spent much of his spare time in work among the poor. How can we designate such a man as a recluse? The answer is that throughout all his years of public service Charles George Gordon remained his own man, a man who kept his own counsels, a man whom even his closest friends never claimed really to know. He was brusque, self-willed, extremely modest and almost morbidly retiring. He had little patience with those who could not accept truths which were to him self-evident. When military superiors and governments failed to back him he generally acted on his own initiative. It was for this reason that he became not only a hero but also a martyr.

He was born in 1833 into a military family and there was never any question of the career that he would follow. He went to Woolwich Royal Military Academy, obtained a commission in the Royal Engineers and was sent almost immediately to serve in the Crimean War. Here he showed himself to be absolutely fearless both in the face of the foe and of superior officers. He was always at his best in charge of small scout parties seeking to discover the movements of the enemy. On such forays he had to use his own initiative and there was no possibility of interference from above.

His next appointment, and the one which made his name, was in China. Gordon volunteered for the posting after several months in a boring job at Chatham because it offered the certainty of action. The British government was committed to supporting the decrepit imperial regime against the T'ai P'ing rebels. Gordon was appointed to take charge of the 'Ever-Victorious Army'. This euphemistically-named rabble was a force of some three to four thousand men, mostly Chinese peasants and the scourings of Shanghai, got together by some European adventurers to help protect the important centre of Shanghai. By means of iron will, severe discipline and personal example, Gordon welded these irregulars into a formidable fighting force. His simple-minded, direct, bold approach earned him the respect of Chinese and Europeans alike. He was hard on inefficiency and merciless against insubordination. The only mutiny Gordon was ever called upon to deal with was settled very quickly – Gordon shot the ringleader on the spot. He personally led his troops into battle, often wielding no more ferocious weapon than a short cane. He completely turned the tide of the war against the T'ai P'ing rebels. His Ever-Victorious Army went on to the offensive, attacked and overran several enemy outposts and encircled the city of Soo-chow, the rebels' main stronghold. Soo-chow fell after a long assault and many rebels were killed and wounded. When he returned home in 1865 he found himself a popular hero, known everywhere as 'Chinese' Gordon, and if he had accepted the grateful recognition not only of the imperial gov-

*Gordon's Gravesend house resembled a mission station.*

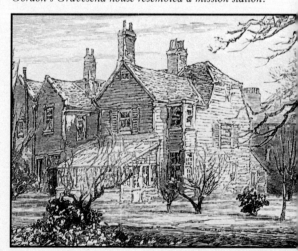

ernment but also of the leading merchant houses of Shanghai, he could have ended his tour of duty a wealthy man. As it was, he disdained money and marks of esteem and even tore up a diary of his Chinese campaign for fear that he should become a legend.

He spent the next six years at Gravesend where he worked quietly, refusing requests to give speeches and talks about his Chinese exploits. All his spare time he devoted to philanthropic and evangelistic work among the poor people of the area. He wrote his own religious tracts and had them printed and distributed. He lived frugally so that he could devote as much money as possible to teaching, feeding and clothing the street urchins of Gravesend. It was largely in order to help suppress the slave trade that in 1873 Gordon accepted the post of Governor of Equatoria Province of the Sudan which was at that time under Egyptian control. He made two stipulations before taking the post, one, that he would be allowed a completely free hand, two, that the suggested salary be cut from ten thousand pounds to two thousand pounds. In the heart of Africa Gordon repeated his Chinese tactics. Once again he won the admiration and willing suport of native and European subordinates. Once again he put heart into a dispirited band of troops. Once again by bold and resolute campaigning he destroyed the power of local chiefs and slavers. He was soon appointed Governor General of the whole Sudan where once again he inspired both friend and foe to have a very deep respect for the Khedive's representative. On one occasion when he was leading his army against a band of rebels he had in his usual impetuous way gone far ahead of his troops. With only a handful of companions he rode straight into the rebels' encampment and instructed their leader to disband his three thousand strong army. Overwhelmed by Gordon's sheer personality and bravery, the rebel chief did as he was bidden. After this spell of duty Gordon vascillated between his desire for continued military command and the equally strong desire to lead a retired, contemplative life. He spent a year in the Holy Land visiting important biblical sites and making copious notes on everything he saw. He accepted a post as Secretary to the Viceroy of India only to resign it almost immediately on realizing that the life of politics and high society was not for him.

In 1883 news reached England that a large part of the Sudan had fallen to a nationalist leader called the Mahdi. There was considerable need to relieve the Turkish garrisons which Gordon had done so much to establish. It was a difficult operation and by common consent there was only one man who could achieve it. Gordon was sent to Khartoum with instructions to evacuate the

"TOO LATE!"

*Telegram, Thursday Morning, Feb. 5,—"Khartoum taken by the Mahdi. General Gordon's fate uncertain."*

*News of Gordon's death aroused indignation.*

Sudan. Gordon went reluctantly. He did not believe in the abandonment of the Sudan to Muslims and slave traders. He did not like the orders that were given to him and he soon became extremely aggravated about the lack of support he received from Cairo and London. At home the government reposed little trust in Gordon, a man they could not understand and a man who could not be trusted to obey orders. Gordon's repeated demands for reinforcements were ignored. Meanwhile, several thousand Turkish and European residents were safely evacuated from the Sudan but at last the Mahdi's forces obtained control of the Nile and gradually encircled Khartoum. In the face of impending disaster Gordon's iron nerve put heart into his garrison. They fought on courageously and thanks to Gordon's brilliant tactics the final Mahdist siege was held off for many months, but in January 1885 the final onslaught began and Gordon fell at the head of his troops on 26 January. A relief force reached Khartoum three days later. Tennyson expressed the feelings of the nation when he later wrote, 'This earth has borne no simpler, nobler man.' Simple and noble Gordon certainly was but other adjectives also spring to mind – enigmatic, withdrawn, unknown, unknowable.

## 'Here lies a drunken dog'

'Here lies a drunken dog' – that was the epitaph George Morland suggested for himself and it reflects the self-loathing that overcame him towards the end of his life. There was an element of truth in the assessment but it certainly does not do justice to the career of the unhappy genius who was among the greatest artists of his age.

The root of his problems, which led him to withdraw increasingly from the world, was his determination to paint what he wanted, for whom he wanted. Ironically, this pursuit of artistic freedom led to his being exploited by a medley of unprincipled harpies. Morland came from a line of talented painters and engravers and his gifts soon became obvious. He was apprenticed to his father, who shut him up for hours on end to produce drawings and small works in oils. This restriction irked George and he soon found a way of outwitting his parent. He lowered some of his canvases out of the window on a piece of string and obtained payment direct. Morland's was a fresh and natural genius. He delighted in depicting life as he saw it – farmyard animals, ostlers, fishermen, simple men and women – these were his most frequent subjects. Fashionable society, on the other hand, wanted portraits and romantic landscapes, which were of little interest to the artist. He found a ready market for his homely pictures among middle-class patrons who could afford his very modest prices. Soon after his apprenticeship ended well-meaning friends prevailed upon him to go to Margate to paint portraits of the fashionable ladies and gentlemen who

*Morland loved to depict simple people and common scenes such as this country inn.*

resorted there in the summer. The plan was not a success. Morland received many commissions but so distasteful did he find the company of the idle rich that he left most of his canvases unfinished. About the same time, George Romney, the accomplished portraitist, then at the height of his fame and powers, offered to take Morland into his studio. The young man refused. It is quite clear that, had he been prepared to make the compromises demanded by the market, George Morland could have made a successful and profitable career for himself. Instead he shunned the society of wealthy patrons and leading artists and went his own way.

He set up by himself in the house of an art dealer who had no difficulty whatsoever in selling Morland's works. Thus began Morland's disastrous relationship with the parasites of the art world. His agent kept him in money and drink in return for a constant stream of paintings which he sold for sums far in excess of those he paid to Morland. As a result the artist was always either in funds or broke. When he had money he bought fine clothes and horses. He was lavish in his hospitality towards the crowd of 'ostlers, post-boys, horse jockeys, money-lenders, pawnbrokers, punks and pugilists' who eagerly gathered round the spendthrift. In his studio he was prolific. He seldom left it without an artist's pad and pencil in his hands. Even when he was drunk he had an incredible knack of noticing and committing to memory interesting details of the scene around him. Once a friend found him almost insensible in a low tavern surrounded by companions who were enthusiastically spending his money. He took the painter home and next day berated him for keeping bad company. Morland took his pad from his pocket and quickly sketched the interior of the tap room, accurate to the last detail. 'Where am I to find a true picture of humble life if not in such a place as that?' he asked.

At last, the parasitic crew of dealers and hangers-on reduced Morland to constant penury. Just as he had once spurned fashionable society, so he now fled from his chosen companions. He set up his studio secretly in another part of town, accompanied by a solitary crony employed to hawk his wares. This was the first of many moves forced upon him by drunkenness and debt. He squandered his income on spirits, borrowed indiscriminately and promised pictures which he failed to supply. When his creditors pressed too heavily he had to make another 'moonlight flit'. One patron played on Morland's fear of the bailiffs. He called on the artist about an unfinished picture, having first stationed a couple of his servants in the street, and while chatting, he casually mentioned the two strange men skulking outside. Morland anxiously peered out and

became convinced that the watchers had been sent by angry creditors. This was the signal for the customer to throw a couple of gold coins on the table and ask for his picture. Morland set to work feverishly and, in less than six hours, produced one of his best landscapes. On another occasion, the painter's secretive behaviour convinced the authorities that he was forging banknotes and his lodgings were thoroughly searched by police. It is to the credit of the directors of the Bank of England that, on discovering their mistake, they sent the artist £40.

While George Morland's paintings graced the homes of hundreds of proud owners, and were freely copied and engraved, the artist himself sank deeper into debt. He lived alone now, his sole companion the bottle, his only visitors importunate dealers and patrons intent on extracting his last ounce of talent. He was married but had deserted his wife after a few years. Brief spells in debtors' prison undermined his health. An attack of palsy robbed him of the use of his left hand. Although no longer able to hold his palette, he went on painting until the end. That end came in October 1804 in a London sponging-house (a place of confinement for debtors). George Morland died at the age of forty-one. He had painted over four thousand pictures, many of them masterpieces. Today a single canvas would fetch more than Morland gained for his total output.

He was a man who pursued his own path, sought his own companions and despised social convention. So contemptuous was he of all that men value that, when he was told that he was the heir to a baronetcy, he refused to assert his claim on the grounds that it was better to be a fine painter than a fine gentleman. The path he trod was lonely and uncomfortable, but it was the path of his own choosing.

# PAUL GAUGUIN

## The search for paradise

*Gauguin's Tahitian pictures strive for an idealized simplicity of form and colour.*

The life of Paul Gauguin was a world-denying pilgrimage. He left behind respectable bourgeois life and a good income and deserted a loving wife and family, in order to live with other painters in creative community. He quarrelled with fellow artists and fell out with friends and patrons. He withdrew to a tropical island in search of the simple life. He died alone.

He was born in Paris in 1848 into a respectable family and the only departure from a conventional upbringing was a four-year stay with his mother in Peru. This gave him a love of travel and he spent six years in the merchant navy. But in 1871 he settled down as a Paris stockbroker. Two years later he was happily married to an attractive Danish girl, called Mette, and during the next decade the couple had five children. It was about 1871 that he began to paint and shortly afterwards that he started to collect pictures by the Impressionists. From that point his career might well have moved towards a predictable, conventional ending – wealthy financier, talented amateur artist,

influential collector and patron of contemporary art. Then, about 1875, he met Camille Pissarro, one of the leading Impressionists, who convinced him that he had great talent and drew him into the exciting world of 'real' artists. Gauguin began to exhibit and became increasingly absorbed in his painting. In 1883, without warning and certainly without informing Mette, he gave up his job to devote himself to art. The family moved to Rouen, where Paul hoped he would be able to sell his pictures. He failed and was soon in a perilous financial position. He and Mette decided to go to Denmark where she could earn money giving French lessons. It was not a wise decision. Mette's parents did not approve of the son-in-law who had irresponsibly plunged their daughter into penury. After a few months Gauguin returned to France. Effectively it was the end of his marriage.

He went to live at Pont-Aven, in Brittany, a favourite haunt of artists. 'I love Brittany,' he wrote. 'I find there the savage, the primitive. But even the life of Breton fishermen and agricultural labourers was not primitive enough for him. He recalled the simple and, as he saw it, happy existence of tropical communities that he had encountered on his earlier travels. In 1887 he went, with a fellow artist, to Martinique. There they lived in a hut, lived on fruit and fish, painted the natives and the local scenery, and thought they had found paradise. Five months and several attacks of dysentery later, the golden vision had faded.

Back at Pont-Aven, Gauguin became friendly with another artist, Emile Bernard, who had begun to break away from pure Impressionism. Gauguin shared his ideals and the two men worked closely for some years until they fell out over Gauguin's apparent claim to be the initator of the new style. In 1888 he went to live at Arles with Vincent Van Gogh. It was an attempt to start another artistic community. The experiment was a disaster which ended in near tragedy. The two men disagreed about art. Their temperaments clashed – and Van Gogh was on the edge of insanity. Disagreement turned to argument and argument to fighting. On Christmas Eve Van Gogh attacked his companion with a razor. Foiled in this murderous attempt, he cut off his own ear. Gauguin left for Paris.

There followed two more attempts to find harmony and ideal working conditions with other artists first at Pont-Aven and, then, at Le Pouldu, on the Breton coast. Neither satisfied him for long. He still dreamed of his tropical paradise, where life was cheap, filled with vivid colour, and natives leading lives of noble savagery. In 1891 he sailed to Tahiti. Here he 'went native', taking a Tahitian wife and living and eating with her people. It scandalized the French colonial community and did his health no good. He became seriously ill and had to be sent home after two years. April 1894 found him back in Brittany living with a Javanese mistress, who soon deserted him and took everything of value she could lay her hands on.

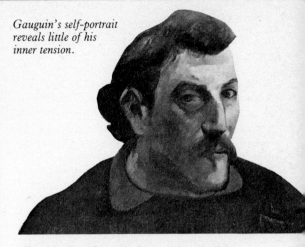

*Gauguin's self-portrait reveals little of his inner tension.*

By this time Gauguin had achieved slight recognition and when two patrons offered to support him he resolved to return to Tahiti. He sailed in May 1895 but he was a sick man. He had contracted syphilis. His legs came up in open sores which gave him long bouts of unremitting pain. He suffered attacks of depression. He ran further and further into debt and, in 1901, moved to the Marquesas Islands to live more cheaply and also to seek the ideal, simple society of his dreams. It did not exist on the Marquesas. He soon found himself involved in disputes between the natives and the colonial officials. In March 1903 he was sentenced to a prison term for libelling a policeman. He died a few weeks later. His quest for an earthly paradise failed but his quest for recognition succeeded at the very end of his life. As a friend explained in a letter in 1902, 'You are now that unheard-of-legendary artist, who from the furthest South Seas sends his disturbing, inimitable works, the definitive works of a great man who has, as it were, disappeared from the world.' That world was not slow to acknowledge the genius of Gauguin – after his death.

# Exhibitionists

I am an enormously talented man. After all, it is no use pretending that I am not, and I was bound to succeed.

Those words, spoken by Noel Coward, are really what this section is all about. They are the words of a man who was totally self-confident. Self-confidence and success, as Noel Coward said, frequently go together. A man or woman who believes in himself or herself can usually persuade other people to believe. Self-confidence is a philosopher's stone capable of turning the dreariest and most unremarkable man into a person everyone notices and of transforming failure into success. 'Think you can, think you can't,' said Henry Ford, 'either way you'll be right.' Another thing that self-confidence can do is make up for lack of talent. Earlier this century there lived in New York a lady by the name of Florence Foster Jenkins. She was rich and she was the proud possessor of a fine colluratura soprano voice – or so she believed. In fact, what really happened when she opened her mouth to perform one of the most demanding operatic arias such as the Queen of the Night's aria from the *Magic Flute* or the 'Bell Song' from *Lachme* was that the most appalling succession of screeches, swoops and off-key notes poured forth. Yet, once a year, Mrs Florence Foster Jenkins hired the Carnegie Hall to give music-loving Americans a rich treat. And the fans flocked in. Every recital was a sell-out. Seats were booked months in advance. Fashionable society paid good money to come and hear Florence Foster Jenkins ruin the classics.

Self-confidence is an enormous asset. Some people are born with it, some acquire it. Its extreme form is exhibitionism and this, I think, cannot be deliberately cultivated. The exhibitionist is someone who not only believes in himself, he also has an inner compulsion to prove himself, to force society to take notice of him. He needs applause, acclaim, recognition. His ego feeds upon it. The most obvious profession for the exhibitionists is in one of the performing arts. So it is not surprising to find that some of the people on my list are people of the stage. There is P. T. Barnum, king of the humbugs, the greatest showman on earth. A man who dealt superlatives with the rapid dexterity of a cardsharp dealing aces. There was Harry Houdini, still unsurpassed as a master of mystery, who excelled as an illusionist, escapologist and prestidigitateur. In

1912, Houdini was told by a doctor that if he did not restrict his activities, his overtaxed body could not survive more than another year. Houdini laughed. 'You don't know me,' he said. He went on performing ever more startling and dangerous escapes and lived for another fourteen years. Financially speaking and professionally speaking he did not have to do that. He could have quit the stage. He could have modified his act in order to shut out those features of it which made great physical demands upon him, but he did not do so. He could not do so; he had to go on getting better and better, always attempting the impossible and usually achieving it. The same compulsion drove Vaslav Nijinsky, that sad and totally dedicated genius of the dance who performed prodigies of physical dexterity and stamina and, in an all-too-brief career, created a number of unforgettable roles. Going back over three hundred years we find the figure of Will Kemp, contemporary of Shakespeare and one of the great clowns of the English stage, perhaps the first of a long tradition of funny men with a large repertoire including mime, dance, juggling, quips and conundrums, jokes, ad libbing – in all 'a fellow of infinite jest'.

With people like Barnum and Kemp it is impossible to decide where natural boisterousness ends and calculated self-advertisement begins. Much the same can be said of people like Salvador Dali and Marie Louise Ramée. They constantly felt the need to draw attention to themselves. They knew that they had to keep themselves in the limelight in order to sell more pictures or more books. It is a hard reality of life that every commercially-minded artist has to learn that talented workmanship does not sell itself. The painter, writer, musician, sculptor, if he wishes to be sure of success, must go out into the highways and byways and parade himself as well as his works before the world.

There are also in our list those who have paraded themselves upon a different stage – a political platform. There was George Gordon, the self-styled leader of men, and Grigoriy Rasputin, the self-styled shaper of destinies. They could never be content with relative obscurity. They had to be to the fore, moulding history, bending parliaments and rulers to their will. Their stories afford proof of the power of self-confidence to convince others. Lord George Gordon set himself at the head of a fanatical London mob which rampaged through the streets, shouting 'No popery!', leaving a trail of havoc behind. Rasputin also had a large following but he only needed to influence two people, the Czar and Czarina, to achieve the power he craved. It is not, to be sure, the people who make the most noise who always notch up the greatest achievements, but at least the world knows about the achievements they do notch up.

*Mrs Gertrude Schilling stunned fashionable society with her bizarre outfits. Her Ascot hats were famous.*

# King of the Humbugs

'There's a sucker born every minute' – that was the principle upon which Phineas T. Barnum built his astonishing show-business career. According to the self-styled King of the Humbugs, it was not only easy to deceive the public, the public enjoyed being deceived. He therefore gratified their wish on an international scale, not once, but thousands upon thousands of times.

Even as a boy in Connecticut young Phineas knew what people wanted to see and would pay to see. He dressed the family pets up in bizarre costumes and charged the neighbourhood kids 'a penny a peep'. From then on his career as a showman never looked back. In 1835 he bought an elderly Negro slave woman and put her on display in a fairground booth. There was nothing at all remarkable about the lady. It was Barnum's billboards which drew the crowds: 'See Joice Heth, George Washington's Nurse, An Incredible 160 Years of Age'. The old woman was primed to answer questions about her supposed charge who had died in 1799. She was, of course, tutored by her owner. But Barnum's ambition went far beyond cramped touring sideshows. In 1841 he bought with borrowed capital a large, impressive New York building and made it the setting for his Great American Museum. Here he displayed every kind of freak and curiosity that could be bought, found or invented. There were fat men, dwarves, 'giants', performing dogs, bearded ladies, albino animals, and 'mermaids', as well as jugglers, tightrope walkers and other performers. Whenever he felt public interest was flagging Barnum arranged stunts to keep his name before New Yorkers. Once he harnessed a bear to a cart and drove it down Fifth Avenue. On another occasion he staged a fierce controversy in the newspapers. He wrote under an assumed name to the *New York Tribune* complaining of 'Mr Barnum's outrageous frauds'. In the next issue he replied to the imaginary criticism in ringing tones: 'Let the people see for themselves the Feejee Mermaid, the Man-Faced Baboon of Java, the Great Fire-Eating Turk, the Man with One Head and Two Bodies, and the other wonders brought to our fair city from the farthest corners of the earth, and let them judge . . .' The people did see for themselves, in ever-increasing numbers. Within two years Barnum had repaid all his borrowed capital and was on the way to becoming a wealthy man.

It was at this stage that he retained the services of Charles Stratton, a well-mannered, good looking young man who stood no higher than a table top. There was nothing unique about him; dwarves were commonplace in circuses and shows. It was Barnum's training, exploitation and publicity that catapulted Stratton into international fame. General Tom Thumb, as the great impresario called him, was transformed into a perfect southern gentleman in microcosm. His speech, his manners, his dress matched in miniature those of the leaders of American society. The United States loved him. His tours, expertly publicized and stage-managed by Barnum, were a triumph. They were followed by visits to the Old World. The King of Humbugs was determined to have his protégé paraded before the crowned heads of Europe. When repeated requests to present Tom Thumb to Queen Victoria were

## 'The biggest elephant in the world'

THE LARGEST ELEPHANT IN THE WORLD, AS COMPARED WITH THE SKELETON OF THE EXTINCT MASTODON

HIS EARS ARE AS LARGE AS FOLDING PARLOR DOORS

JUMBO THE ELEPHANT GIANT, TRUNK REACHES

Barnum's greatest single coup was the acquisition of Jumbo, the most famous elephant of all time. Not only was Jumbo a major attraction but the furore surrounding his purchase gave The Greatest Show on Earth months of international publicity. Jumbo was a massive African bush elephant as big as a horse-drawn bus and the major attraction at the London Zoo. It irked Barnum that the biggest animal in captivity was not a part of his collection and he cabled his British agent OBTAIN JUMBO STOP COST IMMATERIAL. The zoo authorities were not deaf to the American's offer. Jumbo was growing vicious and was a considerable liability. But once the deal became known there was a public outcry. How dare the zoo sell Jumbo! He was a British institution! A fund was launched to keep the elephant in London (though it never reached the £100,000 claimed in Barnum's publicity). The showman revelled in the controversy and used it to maximum effect. His subsequent publicity boasted of how P. T. Barnum had resisted the 'Whole British Nation' in order to bring Jumbo to America. So great was the attraction of 'The Giant African Elephant' that Barnum recouped his investment many times over. When, eventually, Jumbo became too dangerous and had to be put down, Barnum simply had him stuffed – and the show went on.

resisted, Barnum let it be known that he was off to Paris where the French royal family was anxious to make his acquaintance. That did the trick. Not only did the English sovereign receive Barnum and Stratton, she instructed her coach builder to make a miniature open carriage for the dwarf. Tom Thumb thereafter had himself driven everywhere in the canary-coloured equipage, drawn by Shetland ponies with dwarf coachman and footman in striking blue livery.

Everything Barnum did had to be lavish, larger than life, an expression of his personality. It was so with the house he built for himself in Connecticut. In England he had been impressed by the Prince of Wales's ebullient extravaganza, the Brighton Pavilion. Barnum decided to build in the same pseudo-Oriental style. But his house, Iranistan, was to be bigger and more ornate, one of the wonders of the world. He was by now recognized as the greatest living showman. Rare animals and human oddities from every continent were offered to him in a constant stream and his exhibitions became increasingly varied, far outstripping those of his rivals. Then, suddenly, the giant bubble burst.

Iranistan was burned to the ground. Then the Great American Museum. Barnum lost money on the stock market. Within months the king was a pauper. It was in adversity that his greatness really showed. He found backers and built the New American Museum, bigger and better than its predecessor. That, too, went up in flames in 1868. Undaunted, Barnum began another venture – his most famous. With Dan Costello and W. C. Coup he opened a circus and menagerie, called, with characteristic modesty, The Greatest Show on Earth. Barnum did his best to live up to the name. As well as hundreds of individual acts he staged spectacular entertainments such as the 'Stupendous Historical Spectacular Classic Drama of Nero or the Destruction of Rome' which involved 1200 people and 380 horses. The Greatest Show on Earth, which went on tour to many countries, may have contained exhibits which hoodwinked the public but it certainly gave them value for money. They did not begrudge Phineas Barnum his fortune, even when he told them in one of his many autobiographical works – *How I Made Millions* – the tricks he had played on his patrons.

To the very end of his life he was involved in his show and the planning of new attractions. When he died, on 7 April 1891, his last words were, 'How much did we take today?'

## 'That unique, flamboyant lady'

For some people fame is a cross, for others a crown. Marie Louise de la Ramée definitely came into the latter category. She was a nineteenth-century authoress of romantic novels. She could have chosen, as most writers do, a life of relative anonymity. It is one of the advantages of the profession that it is possible for an author's name to be a household word and yet for him to be able to walk the length of Oxford Street unrecognized. That is an advantage not shared by actors of stage, screen and politics. But it is always open to the writer to parade himself before the public gaze and transform himself into a 'celebrity'. And that was precisely what Mlle de la Ramée did.

Despite her name she was English, the daughter of a French language teacher who settled in Suffolk. She grew up in the quiet town of Bury St Edmunds, far from the public glare. It was her father who filled her head with romantic notions. There was a certain element of mystery about him. He claimed to be a personal representative

of Louis Napoleon, the future emperor, and was certainly often away from home. When he was at home he did all he could to widen the vision of his only child. He took her to the Crystal Palace in 1851 to see the Great Exhibition, with its exhibits from every corner of the globe. He took her to London again the following year to witness the funeral of the Duke of Wellington. And all the time he told her stories – stories of intrigue and derring-do, stories of an adventurous élite who were privileged to be involved in great events. It was all a far remove from sleepy, unadventurous East Anglia. Yet Marie Louise loved the countryside also and the animals and the birds about which her mother was so knowledgeable. When she was not out in the lanes and fields around her home and when her father was away, her chief delight was writing, making up her own exciting and romantic tales and also writing a full-length history of England.

When she was eighteen the family moved to London. Louise immediately set about trying to get some of her stories published. She was fortunate enough to fall in with the historical novelist William Harrison Ainsworth and through him succeeded in having some of her work published in *Bentley's Miscellany*, a popular weekly. Writing under the pen-name Ouida, she soon built up a following and, in 1863, ventured a full-length novel. It was the first of a flood. Over the next quarter of a century she wrote forty-five novels. Their titles tell us a great deal about the sort of books they were – *Under Two Flags, Held in Bondage, Two Little Wooden Shoes*, etc. Her heroes were brave, handsome soldiers and her tales were as strong on action as they were weak on detailed research. Yet there was a freshness and liveliness about them and they certainly lacked the 'improving' tone of much popular Victorian literature. Many of them were about the worlds of high society and foreign courts of which she knew nothing.

Yet she longed to be part of those worlds and the money her success brought her enabled her to court the great and famous. She thrust herself into London high life and did all she could to get herself noticed. She adopted a brusque, almost rude manner, she dressed outrageously, she kept a whole pack of assorted dogs. But it was her imagined amours that made her the talk of the town. Whenever Marie Louise took a fancy to a man she simply fabricated a grand passion. She made elaborate public gestures of affection, which usually only succeeded in embarrassing everyone concerned and she 'leaked' information about their supposed relationship. In 1871, for example, it was the Italian opera singer Mario who attracted her attention. One night at Covent Garden, in full view of the audience, she tossed

OUIDA.

" O fie ! 'tis an unweeded garden."—*Hamlet*, Act I., Scene 2.

she turned her back on the world, her eccentricities now forming a barrier whereas once they had attracted intrigued admirers. She died in Lucca in 1908.

We are familiar in our own century with celebrities who have become victims of their own publicity machine. Ouida falls into the same category. She lived for public notice and acclaim. When they deserted her she turned in upon herself like a flower folding its petals when the sun goes down. Her work was ephemeral. It had its day. That day passed and she was unwilling to cultivate a new style or experiment with different subjects. Yet there were many among the literary *cognoscenti* who recognized in Marie Louise de la Ramée a talent above the norm. Some compared her to Honoré de Balzac and it was Max Beerbohm who wrote of her as 'that unique, flamboyant lady, one of the miracles of modern literature'.

*Ouida's English admirers erected a memorial in her home town of Bury St Edmunds*

him a huge bouquet, within which were small gifts and a love poem, in Italian.

In that same year – perhaps as a result of the open rebuff she soon received from Mario – she moved to the Continent and, after various travels, settled in Florence. Now Italian society was treated to her bizarre behaviour. Members of the ancient nobility and prominent courtiers found themselves named as the English lady's lovers. She entertained lavishly and was much in demand because of her eccentric behaviour. She now developed a passion for white. Everything had to be white – her hats, her dresses, her parasols, her carriages, her horses, even her dogs, whose number by this time had grown to quite an army.

Sadly, she overdid it. During the good years her extravagance kept pace with her considerable income. But eventually her popularity began to wane. Throughout the 1880s she was dogged by financial difficulties. Eventually she was forced to leave her fine Florentine villa in favour of much more modest accommodation in Lucca. There

## 'What a fanatic'

Many people feel about Salvador Dali that his exhibitionism and deliberately bizarre behaviour were affected in adult life in order to draw attention to himself and his paintings. The truth is that he was a very odd child before he grew into an even odder man. His greatest desire was always to do the opposite of what was expected of him. His behaviour was grotesque, aggressive, even violent. He once pushed a young friend off a bridge and then spent the afternoon eating cherries in a rocking chair, sitting outside the room where the injured boy was being tended. He intentionally inflicted pain on himself as well as others in order to enjoy the stimulating sensation. From his early years he showed enormous artistic talent and subjected everything else to it. If the weather was too hot for painting he would fill a tub with cold water, sit in it and work with his canvasses there. He much preferred to be alone producing or thinking about his next painting, and he deliberately shunned company. His head was bursting with ideas, ideas which were totally original and drew nothing from any school of art. But his originality did not stop with his painting. It flowed over into the rest of his life. Indeed Dali has never acknowledged any divorce between art and life. Whenever a new sensation presented itself, he experienced it. Sometimes at breakfast he would pour hot milk and coffee down his chest because he liked the feeling.

As soon as he was old enough Dali attended art school in Madrid but he found the lessons restricting, the disciplines they imposed unnecessary and the subjects he was expected to treat bearing no relationship to his vision. The teachers soon despaired of being able to show him anything. His wild originality soon won him a following among the other students at the academy. It was always he who took a lead in the excited and intense discussions in the bistros and student rooms of the city. His ideas, whatever the subject, always had to be more extreme than anybody else's. He even spent a month in prison as a suspected revolutionary. Formal instruction came to have no meaning for him whatsoever. Once his class was told to paint a statue of the Virgin. Dali painted a pair of scales. His reasoning was simple. 'You see a virgin as a virgin,' he said, 'I see a pair of scales.' Dali became obsessed by dreams, particularly after reading Sigmund Freud's book *The Interpretation of Dreams*. He believed that it was vital to capture the visions of the unconscious mind. He developed the habit of setting up his easel at the foot of his bed with the latest unfinished painting upon it, so that in his sleep further developments would occur to him and he could begin committing them to canvas immediately he awoke. This obsession with the dream world, a world in which literally anything can happen but yet a world which takes its images from reality, linked Dali

*Dali never allowed himself to remain long out of the limelight.*

with the emerging Surrealist movement in Paris. But even here among like-minded artists Dali soon became convinced that he had left his peers far behind. 'I am,' he said, 'the only true Surrealist painter.' In 1928 and 1929 Dali collaborated in the production of two surrealist films, *Un Chien Andalou* and *L'Age d'Or*. Both pieces were successions of bizarre images, some violent, some blasphemous; a woman's eye is sliced by a razor in close-up, bishops in liturgical vestments are seen swimming in the sea, a blind man is savagely beaten, and so on. The films provoked outraged comment, riots and in one case a smashed up cinema. In Paris the film was seized by the police.

If the public misunderstood or ignored his work, Dali made quite sure that they did not ignore him. His extraordinary behaviour secured almost constant publicity. His face with its thick eyebrows and half moustache became well-known. He wore the most bizarre clothes; sometimes he appeared flamboyantly over-dressed in vivid floor-length capes with shirts and jackets of clashing colours. Sometimes he wore the briefest of shorts with his shirt deliberately torn and his body soaked in a vile smelling home made perfume whose main ingredients were fish glue and goat manure. At the opening of an exhibition in London in 1936 Dali gave a lecture clad in a diving suit to which were attached plasticine hands, a radiator cap and a dagger. While he spoke (quite inaudibly because of the diving helmet) he held two wolfhounds on a leash. Frequently on public appearances he carried a crutch, a symbol which also appeared in many of his paintings. Dali found another way of attracting attention in inventing surrealist objects. He made a telephone shaped like a lobster. He tried to interest Paris shop owners in transparent mannikins whose bodies were filled with water and goldfish. He devised shoes with springs in them to increase the pleasure of walking, and artificial fingernails made of mirrors. When Dali became famous, fashionable collectors commissioned some of his works for their houses. For one he made a sofa in the shape of a woman's lips and a white grand piano which rose from the middle of a pond and had jets of water spouting from its keyboard.

It is not possible to say that as Dali's fame grew, his stunts became increasingly bizarre for they had always been bizarre, but certainly he expressed himself before an ever-widening public in whatever ways came to hand. He wrote an autobiography, books and articles on philosophy, poems, works of artistic criticism. He gave interviews to newspapers and television programmes and always behaved with complete unpredictability. On the only occasion that he met his idol, the aged Siegmund Freud, the psychologist, after the interview, summed up Dali in three words, 'What

*In 1959 Dali's latest gimmick was 'Ovociped', a spherical, foot-propelled plastic shell.*

a fanatic.' By the end of the 1930s Dali's fame had so far increased that he was much in demand for publicity stunts. A New York store invited him to dress one of its large windows. He did so in a way that was both violent and erotic. He created a large canopied bed in the form of a buffalo with a bloody pigeon in its mouth. The legs of the bed were formed by the four feet of the buffalo and it was draped with black sheets upon which rested a mannikin covered in dust and cobwebs with her head lying in a brazier of red coals. Dali now stood alone. The Surrealist movement had disowned him partly because of his right-wing political sympathies. During the Second World War he spent most of his time in America where his flare for weird money-making stunts was fully exploited.

There were periods of his life when Dali seriously doubted his own sanity, a doubt shared by some of his friends and a large section of the public. Yet there is little doubt that the antics of this incredible Spaniard have done a great deal to publicize not only himself but modern movements in art, and that many people have been drawn through his works to an understanding of the Surrealist movement and other twentieth-century schools of painting.

## Beast 666

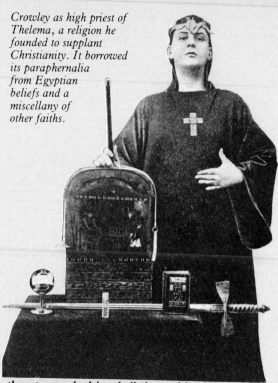

*Crowley as high priest of Thelema, a religion he founded to supplant Christianity. It borrowed its paraphernalia from Egyptian beliefs and a miscellany of other faiths.*

Is a man the product of heredity or environment? It is a question philosophers and psychologists have argued over for years. It becomes very pertinent when we consider the appalling history of Aleister Crowley. He was born the son of a wealthy brewer who was a member of the extreme fundamentalist sect known as the Closed Brethren, because of their refusal to have any dealings with Christians of other denominations. Crowley once claimed in court that his childhood years were

> . . . years of abominable torture. I once wanted to find out what a church was like and I sneaked secretly into a church at the danger of incurring the severest penalty because among the Plymouth Brethren even the idea of entering a church might have incurred damnation.

Crowley was sent to boarding school where he encountered an atmosphere totally different from that of his home. He went up to Cambridge in 1896 and found himself in the company of relaxed, fun-loving young men, many of them wealthy, and in a university where, of course, independent thought was encouraged. All these contradictory influences may well have combined to create in Crowley what was, to say the least, a disoriented personality. Yet, I do not believe that they are sufficient in themselves to explain the cruelty and bizarre self-advertisement which marked the greater part of Crowley's life.

Even as a child he rebelled against conventional, 'decent' behaviour. Once at school he took a cat, poisoned it, gassed it, stabbed it, cut its

*Crowley's first marriage ended in divorce, and his wife was driven to ill-health and alcoholism.*

throat, smashed its skull, burned it, drowned it and dropped it from a window. It was, he claimed, not done out of vindictiveness but to discover whether the animal really had nine lives. 'I was genuinely sorry for the animal; I simply forced myself to carry out the experiment in the interests of pure science.' Perhaps if, on coming down from Cambridge, he had been obliged to earn his living and settle to the humdrum routine of domestic life, these oddities would have disappeared. Unfortunately, he came into a considerable fortune and was able to indulge every whim. Crowley was determined to be noticed, to make his mark on the world. The 1890s were a time when the smart set of London-based artists, playwrights and poets including Oscar Wilde and Aubrey Beardsley were kicking over the traces against Victorian morality. Crowley was imbued with the same spirit. In books and poems which he published privately he lampooned the Queen, made fun of the establishment, extolled sexual freedom and demonstrated an interest in the occult.

Crowley established himself in society with a flat in London, where he chose to be known as Count Svareff and a Scottish estate where he posed as the Laird of Boleskine. He always dressed and behaved in public in a manner calculated to draw the maximum attention. He attended parties in full Highland costume and once appeared at the Café Royal in evening dress and a metal codpiece in the shape of a butterfly. When not at home he was usually off on some publicity-catching exploit. He carried out various daring solo climbing exploits and expeditions in the Sahara, the Himalayas, Central America and China. These were as much to annoy the exploring and climbing establishment as to notch up personal achievements. In word and action Crowley challenged every known convention and belief. His growing notoriety fascinated people. He never lacked publishers for his books or journalists ready to cover his latest escapades.

It was inevitable that, on the outbreak of the First World War, Crowley should declare himself pro-German. He spent most of the war years in America where his publicity-seeking continued unabated. He drew crowds of reporters to a ceremony at the base of the Statue of Liberty where he solemnly proclaimed Irish independence. Tiring now of more athletic pursuits, Crowley resolved, in his own bizarre way, to conquer the arts. He set up a studio, became a painter and advertised for models: 'WANTED – Dwarfs, Hunchbacks, Tattooed Women, Harrison Fisher Girls, Freaks of all Sorts, Coloured Women only if exceptionally ugly or deformed . . .' His pictures display a wild imagination and more than a little talent, but they all contain a mocking, sadistic element.

By 1920 Crowley had become the victim of his own bizarre imaginings. Convinced that the war

*Paintings in Crowley's Sicilian villa extolled violence and mocked conventional religion.*

*Crowley's female disciples were branded with the 'mark of the beast' in token of their complete submission to him.*

marked the final collapse of Christian civilization, he started his own religion, the centre of which became his villa in Sicily, which he called The Abbey of Thelema. Here he practised his own version of black magic. He took the title of Beast 666 and presided over animal sacrifices, sexual orgies and drug-induced ritual acts. The motto of Crowley and his initiates was, 'Love is the law, love under will.' There was a scandal in 1922 when Raoul Loveday, a member of the community, died at the abbey, some said as a result of drinking the blood of a sacrificed cat. Loveday's widow later exposed the activities of Crowley in a book. She described the interior of the villa decorated with obscene wall paintings, the altar where sacrifices were made and ceremonies led by Crowley in coloured robes and a 'scarlet woman' carrying a jewelled snake.

In 1934 Crowley sued the authoress for libel, claiming that he was not a devotee of black magic. It was a sensational trial to which the press gave full publicity. It came to an abrupt end when the jury decided they had heard enough and found for the defendant. In his summing up the judge said, 'I have for thirty years engaged in the administration of the law in one capacity or another. I thought that I knew every conceivable form of wickedness . . . Yet never have I heard such dreadful, horrible, blasphemous, abominable stuff as that which has been produced by [this] man . . .'

Aleister Crowley probably regarded that as a compliment. The remaining fourteen years of his life witnessed no turning aside from his odd beliefs and behaviour. Not until his last moments did he appear to entertain any doubt. He died confessing, 'I am perplexed.'

# HARRY HOUDINI

## In pursuit of the spectacular

There have been great illusionists, escapologists, mind readers, fake mediums, card sharpers, experts at legerdemain; but there has only been one Houdini, a man who combined all these skills and carried them to the highest level of accomplishment. For thirty years he thrilled and mystified audiences with performances that were skilful and daring and spectacular. When he died in 1926 he took many of his secrets with him.

He was born Ehrich Weiss, the son of a Hungarian Jewish rabbi who had recently emigrated to the United States. From his earliest years Ehrich was interested in magic and showmanship. For him the highlights of his life were when the circus came to town. Then he would attend the performances as often as he could, watching the conjurors and asking them to teach him their tricks. Back home he practised what he had learned and also tried to perfect illusions of his own. Yet it was not only magic that appealed to

him. At the age of seven he had developed a remarkable feat of his own: suspended upside down from a rope he would pick pins from the floor with his eyelashes. Locks also fascinated him and his parents early discovered that no sweets or other goodies could be shut away from young Ehrich. At the age of twelve, with his odd collection of talents and enthusiasms, he left home to seek his fortune in the big wide world. He wandered for some time, earning money in a variety of jobs but also by impromptu roadside performances of card tricks and escaping from ropes and handcuffs. When he was sixteen he went into partnership with a friend. They started a double act under the name the Houdini Brothers (the name came from Roberts-Houdin, a celebrated French magician). It was not long before the partnership had been dissolved and Houdini was performing by himself. He was nineteen when, at one performance, he accidentally spilled a little acid over the edge of the stage. It landed on the dress of a young woman whose mother raised her voice in shrill protest. Two days later Houdini called at the girl's house with a replacement dress. She slipped out of the house to walk down the road with him. Within hours they were married. Harry and Bessy were to be blissfully happy for the rest of their lives together. Bessy became his stage assistant as well as his wife and she was the only other person ever admitted to Houdini's secrets. They toured small halls, appeared in circuses and performed in fairground booths.

Always Harry was reading, studying, experimenting, doing everything he could think of to improve his act and make it still more spectacular. He also took every opportunity to obtain publicity. Once in Chicago he persuaded the police to handcuff him, shut him up naked in a cell and put his clothes in another locked cell. Within minutes he walked into the office fully dressed. Many local newspapers covered the story and Houdini found himself that little bit more famous. Another publicity stunt he frequently employed was to offer a hundred dollars reward to anybody who could handcuff him or present him with a safe which he could not open.

But it was by his perfection of extremely dangerous feats of escapology that Houdini really captured the public imagination. One stunt was to allow himself to be put in a straitjacket, bound hand and foot, and suspended several feet in the air on a crane. In full view of his audience he would then wriggle free. Probably his most spectacular feat, and one which he performed with several variations, was that of being bound, placed in a chest and lowered into a tank full of water from which he usually emerged within two minutes. The nearest Houdini came to explaining the secrets of his escapological art was his

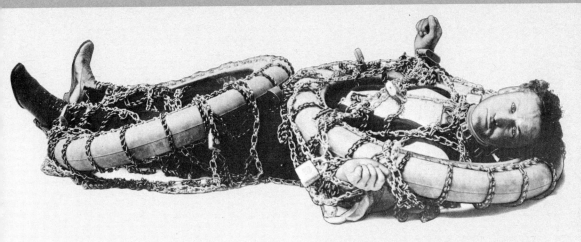

description of the two types of control he needed to exercise: spiritual and physical.

> My chief task has been to conquer fear. When I am stripped and manacled, nailed securely within a weighted packing case and thrown into the sea, or when I am buried alive under six feet of earth, it is necessary to preserve absolute

*Houdini died at the age of fifty-two. He had achieved an astonishing degree of control over mind and body.*

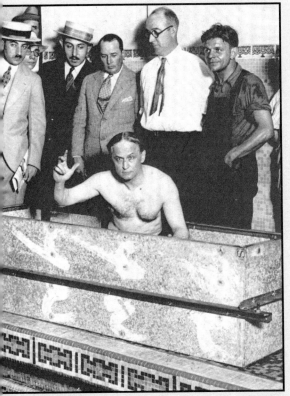

> serenity of spirit . . . My second secret has been equally vigorous self-training, to enable me to do remarkable things with my body, to make not one muscle or a group of muscles, but *every* muscle, a responsive worker . . .

Houdini came to be known as 'the greatest of American showmen, not excepting Barnum'. It was a tribute he earned by constant hard work and practice. Friends often noticed how at dinner parties he would frequently take a pack of cards from his pocket and go through a whole routine of tricks while maintaining a perfectly normal conversation. Sometimes he would remove his shoes and socks and untie knots in a piece of string with his toes.

During his last years Houdini added another dimension to his performance: the exposure of fake spiritualist mediums. He had studied so-called psychic activity for many years, knew how most charlatans' tricks were performed and had, himself, held many fake séances. It was because he knew how to levitate tables, conjure up manifestations and produce spirit voices out of empty air that he was angry to see people using these devices to extort money from, or play on the emotions of, their victims. From now on he spent part of his act revealing the secrets of psychic tricks. He challenged clairvoyants to come on stage and refute him. He attended the séances of popular mediums and showed them up in front of their own clients.

The end came suddenly, while Houdini was at the height of his fame. One day he was talking with a group of students and telling them that sudden blows could be rendered ineffective if the muscles were tensed in advance. Without warning one of the young men pummelled Houdini's abdomen with his fists. Although Houdini did not realize it at the time, the attack had ruptured his appendix. A few days later he was rushed to hospital where he died at the age of fifty-two.

# The rabble rouser

There are some people who have to be the centre of attraction who need to be looked up to, to be followed, to be admired. For such people the cause they espouse is of secondary importance. All that matters is that there should *be* a cause, some opportunity for them to display their powers, often self-imagined powers, of leadership. Such a man was Lord George Gordon.

He was born in 1761 a younger son of the Third Duke of Gordon. When still little more than a boy he was given a royal naval commission. He served on the American station, passed his lieutenant's examination, and expected then to be given a command. This was in the days before the Napoleonic Wars when promotion was slower than would later be the case. In the 1770s an officer really had to prove himself capable of independent command and it seems that Gordon failed to furnish this proof. But he was determined to be a leader of men. It was something which he believed his aristocratic upbringing and his personal talents fitted him for. He resigned his commission and returned to civilian life.

The navy having proved unworthy of him, Gordon now decided to become active in the political sphere. With little chance of succeeding to his father's title and obtaining a seat in the House of Lords, it was necessary for him to win a place in the House of Commons. He decided to sit for Inverness-shire and set about winning over the electors. In those days, when only wealthy landowners had the right to vote, parliamentary seats usually went to those men who could lay out the most money in bribes and entertainment. Gordon had plenty of money and an equal amount of high spirits. He was a personable young man of twenty-two who knew the constituency and the electors. He now set about winning them with a number of extravagant balls and the company of attractive Highland lassies whom he brought to his house by yacht. He also took every opportunity of speaking Gaelic and this impressed local people. He became so popular that his rival, General Fraser, bought for him an alternative seat and Gordon took his place in the Commons in 1774. In the House he expressed his views forcibly on several issued but found it difficult to get anybody to take him seriously. One of the matters which attracted his attention was Catholic emancipation. In 1778 there was a move to repeal a ninety-year-old statute which had imposed severe restrictions on Roman Catholics and particularly prevented them from holding high office. Despite Gordon's opposition the Repeal Act was passed.

Having failed to carry his point in Parliament Gordon looked elsewhere for support. There was considerable ill-feeling against the Act among the people and Gordon now organized this discontent into the Protestant Association. A petition was got up and thousands of signatures were added to it. On 2 June 1779 Gordon addressed a large rally of supporters in St George's Fields and then marched at their head to the House of Commons. Thousands of people crowded into the building or filled the square outside as Gordon presented the petition. The Commons discussed it at great length and then adjourned their debate. Meanwhile Gordon kept his supporters informed of what was going on in the chamber. At the end of the day the crowd dispersed but feelings were now running very high and the authorities failed to take adequate measures to contain the situation. On 6 June, when the Commons debate was resumed, Westminster was thronged by a large angry mob. The members were frightened, passed a resolution ordering the mob to disperse and then hastily adjourned their proceedings. When Gordon appeared before his supporters he was cheered enthusiastically. He spurred them on with more stirring words. At last, he felt, he had found his destiny. Lord George Gordon had proved he was a leader of men. He would force Parliament and government to remain true to their Protestant heritage. When he got into his carriage to drive home enthusiastic supporters removed the horse and pulled Gordon in triumph through the streets shouting out the slogan which he had taught them as a rallying cry, 'No popery!' After this the mob got completely out of hand. They went on a rampage of killing, burning, looting and raping. What began as an attack on Roman Catholic churches and the property and persons of known Catholics, degenerated into an orgy of unrestrained violence and looting. Shops, beerhouses, and distilleries were broken into. The prisons were opened. Several attacks were made on the Bank of England. Gunsmiths took their stock to the Tower for safekeeping and the drawbridge was raised. Martial law was declared and there were hundreds of deaths in clashes with rioters and troops. Soon the streets were littered with bodies. Including those who were executed for their part in the Gordon Riots, the total death toll of those few days was probably more than eight hundred and fifty people.

For his part in the riots Gordon was arrested and taken to the Tower with an enormous military escort, comprising a company of infantry, a regiment of dragoons, a detachment of horse guards and three ranks of militiamen. He was confined for eight months before being brought to trial. Among those who visited him in the Tower was John Wesley, who remarked that he was 'agreeably surprised to find he did not complain of any

*Incited by Gordon, the London mob burned King's Bench Prison and neighbouring houses.*

person or thing and cannot but hope his confinement will take a right turn and prove a lasting blessing to him'. It was widely expected that his trial in February 1781 would lead to his conviction on a charge of treason but some very clever pleading by his counsel secured his release.

From this time onwards Gordon took up a variety of odd schemes. He simply could not bear to be out of the limelight. In 1784 he involved himself in a political quarrel affecting the Dutch and Imperial governments during the course of which he accompanied the Dutch ambassador on a visit to the English court, dressed in a Dutch uniform with a Highland broadsword. Later that year he was in trouble for addressing a meeting of sailors. This nearly led to another riot. Various financial schemes afoot brought him into contact with the Jewish community and, perhaps in part to further those schemes, he himself became a Jew in 1786. The next year he was brought to court again on two charges of libel. When these were sustained he fled to Amsterdam but was sent home by the Dutch government and in January 1788 submitted

to be sentenced to five years in Newgate. The notorious Newgate gaol was a place where hundreds of prisoners died of typhus and other diseases and where conditions were appallingly squalid, but for wealthy prisoners life there could be very tolerable. So it proved for Gordon, he had a pleasant suite of rooms where he amused himself with books and music and spent several hours a day practising the bagpipes. He regularly had guests to dinner and kept a number of servants. Once a fortnight he gave a ball and all the *haut-monde* of London were invited to his parties. He ostentatiously performed all his religious observances as a good Jew and remained an object of curiosity and interest throughout his time in Newgate. The authorities might shut George Gordon in prison but they were not allowed to ignore him. At the end of his sentence he was unable to find the securities for good behaviour which were a condition of his release and so he remained in Newgate where he eventually succumbed to jail fever and died on 1 November 1793.

# The unhappy Samson

It was an unhappy home life that drove Thomas Topham to exhibit his amazing talents. He was a simple London lad brought up to follow his father's trade of carpenter. He was a genial, gentle soul, not above average height, but he was prodigiously strong. He delighted in outdoor exercise – wrestling, bare-knuckles boxing, cudgelling and so on. It was this coupled with wielding tools and carrying heavy baulks of timber that accounted for his muscular frame. He worked up a few tricks, such as rolling up pewter plates and lifting grown men off the ground with one hand. But these were only performed for the amusement of his friends and he might, like most of us, have lived and died in happy obscurity if his wife had not led him a merry dance.

Topham had married a pretty young coquette and her flirtatious behaviour drove him to distraction. Being a thrifty fellow he had saved enough money to buy a public house, the Red Lion near Moorfield. He was only twenty-four and seemed set for a settled and comfortable career. But his wife spoiled all that. Her 'carrying on' with customers threw Topham into fits of jealous rage. No one wanted to be goaded into a fight with the man commonly known as 'the second Samson' and so custom began to dwindle. Topham was forced to augment his income in other ways and the easiest way of doing it was by giving exhibitions of his uncommon powers.

His first demonstration took place on Moorfield. Bracing his legs against a low wall, he grasped a rope attached to the harness of a young and fiery horse on the other side. Then he took the strain while others whipped the horse and urged it on. Topham completely restrained the beast and won several pounds in wagers with the amazed onlookers. Unfortunately, someone bet him he could not repeat the trick with two horses. In accepting the challenge, Topham was pulled off-balance and sustained leg injuries which left him with a permanent limp. Despite that mishap, his fame spread rapidly and Topham soon found that he could give regular performances and charge people a shilling a time. Among his normal feats were the following: He put a half-hundredweight weight on one end of a six-foot table; then, placing the two legs at the opposite end upon his knees he raised the heavier end above his head by means of a leather strap attached to it. He raised 'Mr Chambers, vicar of All Saints' with one hand. Mr Chambers, it appears, weighed twenty-seven stone. He bent iron bars. He stretched his body between two chairs and permitted four people with a total weight of fifty-six stone to sit upon his chest. His greatest single accomplishment was recorded in 1741. As part of the public celebrations for a great naval victory, Topham announced that he would lift three hogsheads of water. A special frame was set up for this demonstration and Topham lifted the three large barrels weighing 1,836 pounds by means of a chain hung round his neck.

Topham's strength did not reside solely in his limbs and torso; even his smaller muscles were well trained. He could roll up pewter plates like sheets of paper and crush tankards with one hand. He could break clay pipes simply by placing them in the crook of his arm or leg and flexing his muscles. He could break a two-inch rope. Topham sometimes varied his act by singing but one hearer observed that 'the voice, more terrible than sweet, seemed scarcely human'.

Topham performed all over the country and everywhere he went he drew large crowds. He was soon able to recover his finances and exchange the Red Lion for a better hostelry, the Duke's Head in Islington. From there he transferred to the Bell and Dragon, Shoreditch. But he continued to give public shows in London and the provinces. He was happiest when away from home and his wife's blatant infidelities. There are few recorded examples of Topham using his powers in anger. Most men had more sense than to upset him. But the ostler at Virgin's Inn, Derby, did manage to offend him, whereupon he took an iron spit from beside the fire and wrapped it round the fellow's neck like a scarf. Once, at Hackney, where he had gone to watch a race, several spectators were annoyed by a man with a horse and cart who obscured their view. Topham simply walked across, placed his hands upon the tail board and pulled the vehicle out of the way. A sailor on a ship in the Thames made a remark that Topham found offensive, whereupon the strong man picked up a coconut, held it near the man's ear and broke it open with his hands. 'Next time, my friend, it'll be your head,' he remarked quietly.

He did not always escape injury when performing his feats. Once he challenged someone to yoke a team of three horses and try to tear him away from a stake which he clasped between his legs. During the contest the driver jerked the horses suddenly to one side and broke Topham's thigh. On another occasion he pulled down some builders' scaffolding for a joke. Unfortunately, part of the wall came with it and once again Topham was badly injured. Many pranks are recorded which this Samson performed, like the time he saw a watchman sleeping in his box, picked up the box and lowered it over the wall of a nearby cemetery without waking the occupant.

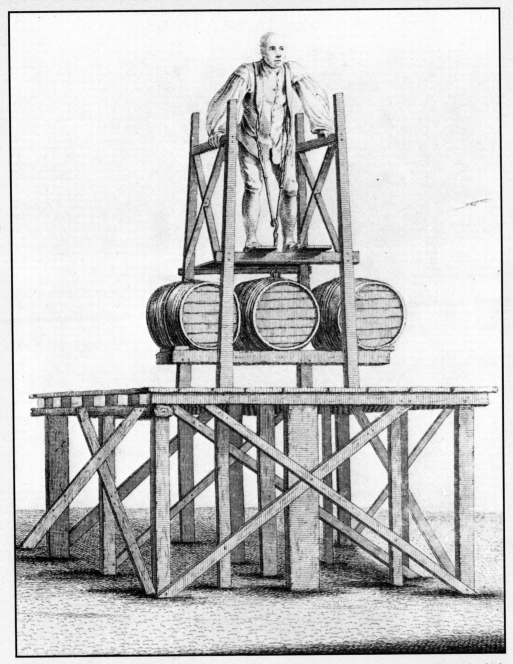

*It is difficult to decide at this distance of time what was the source of Topham's prodigious strength which enabled him to lift 1,836 pounds of water.*

For all Topham's patience, his wife refused to mend her ways. She took a perverse delight in being the only person who dared offend the mighty Samson. At last, goaded beyond endur-ance by his wife's faithlessness and taunts, he took a knife to her and then stabbed himself. He died of his wounds on 10 August 1749. He was less than forty years of age at the time.

193

# Only a poor poet

Most exhibitionists have something worthwhile to exhibit, some gift or talent, some idea which they wish to present before the world, and which makes some mark, however small, upon their age. It was not so with William McGonagall. The 'Scottish bard', as he liked to call himself, was totally devoid of poetic talent. Everyone who ever heard him recite his works or read his printed verses was painfully aware of this fact. The only person who was not, was McGonagall himself. Had not the muse descended to him with the imperious command 'Write! Write! Write!'? How could he do otherwise than devote his life to poetry?

William was born in 1825, the son of Irish parents who had settled in Scotland. His father was a skilled handloom worker but there were few opportunities for him to pursue his trade at a time when the clanking textile mills were dominating more and more of the market. Thus the McGonagalls were poor. William, the youngest son, had an elementary education but seems to have spent more of his school days playing truant than actually sitting in class and learning. However, he obviously acquired a considerable love of literature and particularly the drama. As a young man we find him occasionally working at his father's trade but more often employed as a factory labourer. Yet what marked him as different from his fellows was his ability to memorize poems and Shakespearian speeches, which he would then recite to his workmates or, for the price of a drink, in the pub at night.

Young William was stage-struck and worked for some years with the local repertory company moving scenery, looking after props and occasionally being given a walk-on part. He was convinced that he was a potentially great dramatic actor and he managed to persuade Mr Giles, proprietor of the Lindsay Street Quarry Theatre, to allow him to put on a performance of *Macbeth* with himself in the title role. The cautious Giles demanded a pound for the privilege and McGonagall raised this sum by having a whip-round among his workmates. On the night, the great play (which surely must have been abbreviated) was performed three times. Each house was a sell-out; McGonagall's friends and neighbours and a large section of the Dundee public turned up to watch the local boy declaiming the great role in stentorian tones. Before McGonagall had completed his marathon performance his voice had long since run out and by the end of the evening he could scarcely be heard beyond the first few rows. However the audience enjoyed itself and McGonagall was inspired to go on to even greater triumphs. His next appearance, again in the role of Macbeth, was at the Theatre Royal. This was a very different kettle of fish. He was now appearing with professional actors, who wasted very little time in putting the bumptious upstart in his place. The climax came in the fight scene where Macbeth is killed by Macduff. Reluctant to bring his performance to an end McGonagall simply refused to die. To quote the words of an early report, 'Macduff eventually brought the sublime tragedy . . . to a close in a rather undignified way by taking the feet from under the principal character.'

His marriage in 1846 and the starting of a family seem to have brought about no significant change in McGonagall's way of life. He continued as a humble mill worker, earning extra pennies from his recitations and performances and still waiting for his great 'break'. The business cards that he had printed were inscribed '*William McGonagall, poet and tragedian*'. It was in the summer of 1877 that the full realization of his vocation burst upon him, forcing him to give up everything else and devote the remainder of his life to poetry.

While lonely and sad in my room, I sat thinking about the thousands of people who were away by rail and steam boat, perhaps to the land of Burns, or poor ill-treated Tannahill, or to gaze upon the Trossachs in Rob Roy's country . . . well, while pondering so, I seemed to feel as it were a strange kind of feeling stealing over me, and remained so for about five minutes. A flame, as Lord Byron has said, seemed to kindle up my entire frame, along with a strange desire to write poetry; and I felt so happy, so happy that I was inclined to dance . . .

Throughout the remaining twenty-four years of McGonagall's life a torrent of verse poured from him; bad verse, excruciatingly bad verse, devoid of all metre and scansion, never dignified by any flash of poetic insight, seldom rising above the utterly banal. The poverty of his verses was in stark contrast to the magnificent subjects which usually inspired them. For, above all things, McGonagall was moved by epic events, stirring spectacles and outstanding catastrophes. Here is an extract from his long poem in celebration of the opening of the Tay railway bridge:

*The Tay Bridge disaster inspired a McGonagall poem.*

> Beautiful Railway Bridge of the Silvery Tay!
> And prosperity to Messrs Bouche and Grothe,
> The famous engineers of the present day,
> Who have succeeded in erecting the Railway
> Bridge of the Silvery Tay
> Which stands unequalled to be seen
> Nearby Dundee and the Magdalen Green.

The opening of University College Dundee inspired McGonagall to exhort his readers:

> I hope the ladies and gentlemen of Dundee will
>     try and learn knowledge
> At home in Dundee in their nice little College,
> Because knowledge is sweeter than honey or
>     jam,
> Therefore let them try and gain knowledge as
>     quick as they can.

McGonagall wrote collections of his verse which he pedalled round the streets of Dundee. He wrote introducing himself to several notable figures, especially Queen Victoria, and on one occasion walked all the way from Dundee to Balmoral through appalling weather in the hope of being able to meet the Queen and recite some of his verses to her. He got no further than the main gate. Rejection, ridicule and poverty were his constant companions yet by his dogged perseverence he did achieve a certain amount of celebrity. Sometimes he would be invited to businessmen's functions to recite his appalling verses so that well-dined businessmen could snigger at the sight of this comically tragic figure reciting his immortal lines so passionately.

In 1887 McGonagall decided to give the United States of America a cultural treat. New York impressed him.

> . . . then there's the elevated railroads about
>     five storeys high,

> Which the inhabitants can hear night and day
>     passing by;
> Of such a mass of people there daily do throng –
> No less than five and 10,000 daily pass along;
> And all along the city you can get for five cents –
> And, believe me, among the passengers there's
>     few discontent.

But McGonagall did not impress New York. Within a few weeks he sailed home again having earned not a penny. Undaunted, McGonagall continued on his poetic way, chronicling uniquely the great events of the closing years of the century.

In 1889 some public performances he was giving were stopped by the authorities. They were causing a breach of the peace. Local lads, well stocked up with drink, flocked to the hall every evening to pelt the poet with rotten vegetables. McGonagall protested at this loss of livelihood – in verse, of course.

> Fellow citizens of Bonnie Dundee,
> Are ye aware how the magistrates have treated
>     me?
> Nay, do not stare or make a fuss
> When I tell ye they have boycotted me from
>     appearing in Royal Circus,
> Which in my opinion is a great shame,
> And a dishonour to the city's name . . .

McGonagall died in 1902 and was buried in a pauper's grave, thus apparently succumbing at last to the obscurity he had fought so long to escape. Yet, William McGonagall has achieved an immortal name. In recent years his works have been republished and he is now revered and loved as the worst poet in the English language.

## 'Mad jigs and merry jests'

Upstaging is one of the worst crimes that an actor can commit. It is what happens when one person on the stage performs various tricks to attract notice to himself and away from those other players who are supposed to be the focus of attention at that particular part of the action. Upstaging is by no means a recent invention. When Hamlet is rehearsing his actors for his play within a play, he gives them these instructions:

> And let those that play your clowns speak no more than is set down for them, for there be of them that will themselves laugh, to set on some quantity of barren spectators, to laugh too, though in the meantime some necessary question of the play be then to be considered; that's villainous and shows a most pitiful ambition in the fool that uses it.

Shakespeare was talking there about the fools or clowns who were a popular feature of most plays in the sixteenth and seventeenth centuries, even very serious tragedies, and it is almost certain that he had one particular clown in mind, Will Kemp, for there appears to have been little love lost between the two men. Just as today, theatre-going audiences in Shakespeare's time had their favourite actors. Many would go to see a play not so much for the play itself but because their popular idol was in it and Will Kemp was undoubtedly a great box office draw. We know it because references to him appear in many plays and documents of the time. In a very obscure comedy of 1598 for example, the following words appear:

> Clowns have been thrust into plays by head and shoulders ever since Kemp could make a scurvy face . . . why, if thou can'st but draw thy mouth awry, lay thy leg over thy staff, saw a piece of cheese asunder with thy dagger, lap up drink on the earth, I warrant thee they'll laugh mightily.

Kemp was a by-word for all that was best in the comic art both on stage and off stage. He was, we are told, a man who spent his life 'in mad jigs and merry jests'. Certainly he was a man greatly given to self-advertisement, much to the despair of Shakespeare and other playwrights. Richard Brome complained in one of his plays:

> In the days of Tarlton and Kemp
> Before the stage was purged from barbarism
> And brought to the perfection it now shines
> with
> Then fools and jesters spent their wits because
> The poets were wise enough to save their own
> For profitabler uses.

Kemp first appears in the 1580s as a member of the Earl of Leicester's household. He served as both court clown and also as a member of Leicester's company of players. In 1585 he accompanied the Earl on a visit to the Netherlands where he received payments for such antics as 'leaping into a ditch before your Excellency and the Prince Elector as you went a-walking at Amersfoort'. He was a juggler, tumbler and dancer and performed at banquets, as well as in the plays that Leicester put on for his guests. Later he joined the Lord Chamberlain's company which was the company

*The Globe Theatre, Southwark, scene of many Kemp triumphs.*

*Kemp's London to Norwich dance added the phrase '9-day wonder' to the language.*

to which Shakespeare also belonged. Many of the clowns' roles in Shakespeare's plays were first written for Kemp. But it seems that Kemp simply could not resist improvising, which was why he and the playwright fell out. Kemp undoubtedly preferred other writers who gave him more latitude, as indicated by such stage directions as 'Enter forester, speak anything, and exit'. Playwrights who took themselves more seriously (and undoubtedly Shakespeare was in this category) argued that the clown had his moment of glory during intervals between scenes and acts when he was allotted space to perform his 'jigs'. These were songs and dances with words often made up on the spur of the moment and quite obviously Kemp was a past master at this form of entertainment. Several of Kemp's jigs were published and we have the names of them but, alas, no more details than that. There was for example 'a pleasant new jig of the Brome man' and 'Kemp's new jig betwixt a soldier and a miser and Sym the clown'.

Kemp's most famous exploit was his dance from London to Norwich. This was both a publicity stunt and also a money-making gimmick. Kemp announced his intention of dancing between the two cities and took several wagers on his ability to do so. He set out on the first Monday in Lent in 1599 and travelled through Romford,

Chelmsford, Sudbury, Bury St Edmunds, Rockland and Burford Bridge to Norwich. It took him twenty-three days, although he seems to have spent only nine of those days actually dancing along the road. The remainder of the time he was detained either by bad weather or fatigue. Crowds turned up to watch him on the way as, proceeded by his drummer, he performed a series of skilful Morris dances. Often he would get members of the audience to join in. Of a girl who took his fancy in Chelmsford he says, 'I was soon won to fit her with bells; besides she would have the old fashion, with napkin on her arms, and to our jumps we fell.' Of course the cap was passed round during the performance. When he arrived at Norwich the mayor came out of the city gates to greet him, to welcome him to a feast and to present him with a reward of £5 and a life pension of 40 shillings. Back in London, the prestigious Merchant Adventurers conferred on the clown the freedom of their company. So great was Kemp's success that he decided to repeat his dance on the Continent. He spent about two years dancing in France, Italy and Germany. He returned in 1602 and joined the Earl of Worcester's players. And that, sadly, is the last we hear of him. He died soon after this but he was long remembered and has rightfully taken his place in the roll of great comic actors.

## A blaze of glory

In five brief years Vaslav Nijinsky carried the art of ballet to a new pinnacle of fiery brilliance; then collapsed, a spent force, and declined into insanity. His career has all the tragic marks of genius which have almost become clichés – intensity, public misunderstanding, difficulties in personal relationships, ultimate rejection and self-doubt.

He was born in 1888 into a dancing family. Thomas and Eleanora Nijinsky were well known in Russia and toured together for several years until Thomas went off with another woman, leaving his wife to bring up three children single-handed. Life was hard. It became harder when Vaslav's younger brother fell from a window and sustained serious brain damage. Now there were the costs of his care in an institution to be met. Vaslav and his sister both became dancers but it was Vaslav who, at the age of ten, attracted the attention of experts at the Imperial Ballet School in St Petersburg. The lad was immensely strong

for his age, and very acrobatic, yet he was possessed of a grace remarkable in one of such tender years. These facts did not endear him to his colleagues who were jealous of him and mocked him for his 'funny' face. Already very introverted, Nijinsky withdrew even more into himself during his time in St Petersburg. In 1907 he joined a touring ballet company and began giving lessons. The combined incomes enabled him to look after his mother, brother and sister – just.

It was in 1908 that one of those rare meetings occurred out of which true art is born. Nijinsky was introduced to Serge Diaghilev, wealthy businessman and impresario, who had been commissioned to form a new ballet company. Diaghilev realized the great talent that lay in the little dancer. He also fell in love with him, for Diaghilev was a homosexual. In his diary Nijinsky wrote that he submitted to the older man's advances with reluctance but the reality of their stormy and ultimately tragic relationship was more complex. Diaghilev's gift lay in recognizing genius. He brought together in his new *Ballet Russe* an incredible group of talented people – dancers like Nijinsky and Pavlova, the choreographers Fokine, Massine and Ballanchine, composers such as Stravinsky, Ravel and Prokofiev, and artists of the stamp of Picasso, Matisse and Derain. The result was something startling, new, electrifying.

Nijinsky's debut came in Paris in 1909. It marked not merely the start of a sensational season for the *Ballet Russe* but the beginning in Western Europe of a new awareness of ballet. He was the undisputed star. At last the introverted, sensitive boy had found in himself something he could give to the world – an ability to interpret character through the medium of dance.

> In each part . . . he had the chance to give a complete and separate impersonation. He was so different in each part that he was almost unrecognizable. Where the essential Nijinsky existed was a constant mystery. His face, his skin, even his height seemed to change in each ballet.

So wrote his wife in later years and in those words we come close to the tragedy that was Nijinsky. Every interpretative artist has the problem of knowing where his own personality ends and the role he is playing begins. For Nijinsky this problem reached a level of acuteness that was, ultimately, unbearable. He created characters that were almost total and he lost himself. For discerning audiences every performance was a revelation, a feast. But there were those who could not follow the *Ballet Russe* into its fantasy world, who were left on the threshold feeling puzzled, cheated, outraged. Adulation was always mixed with

Weeks later the old Russia was trampled in the dust beneath the marching feet of the Bolsheviks.

With appalling suddenness Vaslav Nijinsky had lost almost everything. He and Romola lived in Switzerland. Now, denied an outlet for his talent, Nijinsky turned in on himself once more. He became depressive and schizophrenic. Once he pushed his wife and child downstairs. On another occasion he paraded through the streets wearing a large gold cross and calling on passers-by to repent of their sins. But, increasingly, he lapsed into silence. He lived thus for thirty years nursed by the patient, devoted Romola. Diaghilev died in 1929 and the *Ballet Russe* died with him. By then Nijinsky was, in reality, already dead, although his body refused to free his tortured soul until 1950.

*Bakst's costume for Nijinsky's controversial interpretation of 'L'Après-Midi d'un Faune' (inset). Having given the world so much, the great dancer ended his days a broken, lonely man.*

hostile criticism. A climax came in 1912 with the performance of *L'Après-Midi d'un Faune*, choreographed by Nijinsky himself. In his portrayal of the languid, lustful, mythical demigod the dancer indulged an explicit eroticism that went too far for some critics, who labelled the performance obscene and even clamoured for the police to close the theatre. That was as nothing compared to the reaction which greeted Stravinsky's *Rite of Spring* a year later.

People whistled, insulted the performers and the composer, shouted, laughed . . . One beautifully dressed lady in an orchestra box stood up and slapped the face of a young man who was hissing in the next box . . . Another society lady spat in the face of one of the demonstrators . . .

That same year Nijinsky sailed to South America to fulfil some engagements. Also aboard was Romola de Pulszky, a new member of the company. Despite the fact the two young people had no common language they had a whirlwind romance and were married in Buenos Aires. When Diaghilev heard the news he was beside himself with jealousy and anger. He dismissed Nijinsky. A peace was eventually patched up between the two men but the relationship which had sparked so many scintillating performances was over. In 1917 Nijinsky left the *Ballet Russe*.

## 'Our friend'

Grigoriy Efimovich Rasputin was born into an unremarkable peasant family in an unremarkable village in western Siberia. He grew up an unpleasant lad and an even more unpleasant young man. He was a hardened vodka drinker and womanizer by the age of fifteen. He was frequently drunk, kept riotous company, was forever brawling and terrorizing quiet village folk and, on at least one occasion, was dragged before the authorities as a thief. In other words he was a mindless thug, a vandal, a hooligan. Yet, within a few years, he became the most influential man in Russia. He was a show-off, an exhibitionist driven by a frantic desire to be noticed. He had a talent for total enthusiasm and would fling himself wholeheartedly into whatever escapade came to hand. If he had any self-doubt he seems to have suppressed it. Whether drinking, seducing a woman, fighting or setting out on an orgy of destruction, he was always looking for the complete experience. He did nothing by half measures. And one result was that other people were fascinated by him. Most women found him irresistible and many men felt a grudging admiration for him.

It was while he was running away from one of his crimes that the great change occurred. He took refuge in the monastery of Verkhoturye. There the influence of holy men and mystics wrought an incredible transformation. Rasputin's enormous energies were turned in other directions. He still craved attention, still exercised a galvanizing influence over people, still indulged his sexual appetite (though for many years he gave up drink), but now he clothed all his words

*A cartoon of Rasputin's decadence and power.*

and actions in the sombre garb of religious mysticism. In 1893 he left home to take up the life of a wandering pilgrim and prophet. At once, disciples – mostly women – gathered around him. They were attracted by his ostentatious devotion, his simple, moving preaching, his strange force of will, his magnetic eyes – and his remarkable gifts. For it was soon being noised abroad that Rasputin was a healer and clairvoyant. Stories like the following were common; a lady called on Rasputin to pray for her niece who lay dying in a distant town:

> He took my hand. His face changed and he looked like a corpse, yellow, waxy and dreadfully still. He rolled his eyes till the whites alone were visible. He took my hand roughly and said in a dull voice, 'She won't die, she won't die.' Then he let my hand go and the blood flowed back into his cheeks again.

The niece recovered. That is not the only recorded instance of apparent long-distance healing attributed to Rasputin but direct faith cures were more frequent, according to his followers. The self-appointed holy man had a considerable talent for relaxing those who came to him for help. When he took their hands, looked into their eyes and spoke in his deep, rought voice they experienced a semi-hypnotic tranquillity. Much of the relief he obviously brought to sufferers can probably be attributed to his ability to remove tension. But that does not explain all the manifestations of his powers.

Rasputin's methods of dealing with spiritual afflictions were more open to question. He would convince young women that the way to overcome sexual temptation was to share his bed. Once there he would either arouse them to a frenzy of unfulfilled desire in order to 'drive the devil from them' or, more often, make love to them, telling them that intercourse with a holy man was no sin.

incapable of reform and inadequate to resist mounting pressure. The Czarina Alexandra, like all the other women who fell under Rasputin's spell, was religious, gullible and insecure. She needed a guide, comforter and friend, someone above politics, someone who could be the mouthpiece of God and who would show her and Nicholas what to do. She had often relied upon spiritual counsellors and now she chose Rasputin as her confidant. Like most of his disciples, Alexandra was convinced because she wished to be convinced. The holy man was first called upon to heal Alexis, the Czar's infant son who was suffering from haemophilia. He certainly seems to have brought the child some relief but, more important, he gave the Czarina peace of mind by prophesying that Alexis would not die of the disease and would recover completely from it at the age of twenty. Nicholas was never completely under the spell of 'our friend', as Alexandra referred to Rasputin, but he accepted and protected him because of the effect he had on the Czarina. 'Better one Rasputin than ten fits of hysterics a day', as he once remarked.

As the political situation in Russia worsened, the imperial couple relied more and more on Rasputin, who revelled in his power: 'The Czar thinks I am Christ incarnate. The Czar and Czarina bow down to me, kneel to me, kiss my hand.' He made conspicuous displays of his wealth – a fine house opulently furnished, a handsome carriage, a new church for his village – all were designed to draw attention to Rasputin, the erstwhile peasant, now intimate of the Czar.

Inevitably, he made enemies. Men of the court and the government resented Rasputin's political influence and particularly his urging of the Czar to pursue autocratic, unyielding policies. People who loved the Romanovs could not understand how they could be duped by a licentious charlatan whose life was an open scandal. In 1914 Rasputin was stabbed by an ex-prostitute. The wound was serious. While he was recuperating Russia drifted into war. Rasputin sent letters and telegrams urging the Czar not to become involved and later claimed that had he been in the capital Russia would not have declared war. He sensed that the conflict meant the end of imperial rule. He even prophesied his own imminent death.

This occurred on the night of 16–17 December 1916. A group of officers loyal to the Czar and appalled by his increasing unpopularity shot the favourite at a private supper party. Rasputin's death came too late to save the dynasty. In fact, it demonstrated more clearly than anything else could have done that the imperial family was vulnerable. As one contemporary remarked of the shot that killed Rasputin, 'You will see this is the first shot of a revolution.'

*Rasputin surrounded by his many women admirers and (left) the Czarina, most significant of all.*

Rasputin was ambitious to be accepted at the highest levels of society and he took every opportunity to attract the attention of the wealthy, famous and influential. He was taken up by church leaders, society hostesses and great families who had access to the imperial court and they became just as devoted to him as the peasants among whom he had previously moved.

Wealthy patronage meant a changed lifestyle. Rasputin always wore peasant dress – he wished to cultivate the image of being a man of the people – but his boots were now of top quality leather, his tunic of the finest cloth and his shirts of silk. This strange mixture of simplicity and sophistication ran through every aspect of his life: he used fine perfume but refused to learn polite table manners; he was virtually illiterate but conversed well in smart company. So he came, by degrees, to St Petersburg and the palace of Czar Nicholas II. The last of the Romanovs was a weak ruler, bewildered by the violent changes sweeping his empire, who headed a creaking administration,

# Adventurers

This section is about men and women who made life into an adventure. It was Georges Simenon, the French novelist, who once said in an interview: 'I don't believe in heroes, heroic deeds are chance. The hero is the person who has the courage to make a good thing of his whole life.' I am sure he was right. Any of us might at any time be called upon to perform a brave deed; to jump into the river to rescue a drowning child, to go to the aid of someone being mugged in the street. The chance, when it comes, will come suddenly, unexpectedly, and we shall not know until it comes whether or not we will rise to the occasion, whether we will emerge from the encounter a hero or a coward, but, as Simenon says, the real hero is the man or woman who makes something of his life or, as I prefer to put it, the one who makes life an adventure.

In my selection I have included what we might call 'conventional' adventurers, people who have gone out to do great deeds, to battle with the elements. Frederick Selous, the great game hunter and explorer of the latter part of the nineteenth century, was a man who tired of the restrictions of conventional British society, who wanted to get away to a land where he could pit himself against nature. He lived for many years in Africa and travelled extensively in other lands to see strange sights, to hunt wild animals, quite deliberately to encounter danger. He risked death many times and at the end risked it again, not for the selfish pleasure of adding one more thrill to a large collection, but serving his country in a time of war when he was already an old man and might quite reasonably have left the fighting to a younger generation. William Henry Shakespear was a near contemporary of Selous and he too died in the First World War. He too had sought adventure in foreign parts. Most of his exciting life was led in Arabia and it was there that he died fighting against pro-Turkish forces. Ernest Shackleton's desire for adventure took him on repeated visits to the Antarctic. There he endured blizzards, extreme temperatures and crushing ice floes to explore the last unknown continent. When Shackleton, Shakespear and Selous died the heyday of empire was already past.

There is a temptation to think of it also as the heyday of adventure, the last age when there were unexplored tracts of bush and jungle to traverse, when man could set out with a gun and a few 'faithful native bearers' and prove his worth. It is sometimes said that with the passing of that epoch the age of adventure came to an end. Nowadays, it is claimed, political considerations, the expense of travel and the fact that most parts of the world have now been thoroughly explored have reduced almost to zero the opportunities for finding adventure. That theory does not hold water. If that kind of adventure is the kind you seek you can find it. Francis Chichester found it on many occasions in his life. He made one of the first solo flights to Australia, took part in many daring long distance trips in flimsy aircraft and ocean-going yachts. He crowned his accomplishments by making the first single-handed circumnavigation of the globe. Every year produces a crop of people performing some daring exploit or other – attempting a new mountain peak, travelling thousands of miles by balloon, or crossing the oceans in fragile craft.

But the real adventure is within. It was so for Chichester, for Shackleton and the others already mentioned. For no great mountain peak, tract of ocean, or stretch of country can be conquered unless another conquest has first taken place. I am speaking of the inner conquest, the overcoming of fear, the establishing of a vital personal discipline, the tedious application to detail that alone makes success possible. There are those for whom this inner adventure has taken on a special significance. For instance people who have had to overcome some handicap simply in order to live what many of us would regard as a 'normal' life and yet who have gone on to live far above the normal, to exceed the achievements of those of us who have all our faculties. James Holman and John Metcalf were both blind, yet the one travelled the world and the other built hundreds of miles of road and became one of England's pioneer highway engineers. Helen Keller was blind too, she was also deaf. Yet she found a way of communicating with the outside world, travelling freely in that world, of bringing inspiration to millions of her fellow men and women, of achieving high academic standards, of writing books and making speeches. If anyone 'made a good thing' of her whole life it was Helen Keller. Another person cast in the same mould was Douglas Bader, an ebullient, active man suddenly bereft, through an accident, of both his legs and yet a man who continued to be ebulliently active, who made a name for himself as a fighter pilot in the Second World War and who was active to the end of his days in bringing hope and inspiration to other handicapped people. There are other heroes and heroines, other adventurers who do

not lead such spectacular lives, people like Joni Eareckson who as an outdoor, fun-loving American teenager one day dived into a pool, struck her head on the bottom and found herself paralysed from the neck down. It was not possible for her to win her way back to normality or a semblance of normality; she would be totally incapacitated for life. Yet the day came when she was able to say, 'I wouldn't change my life for anything.' The adventure she had made for herself was in finding a faith which gave her life meaning and in travelling the world to take that faith to others through public appearances and television programmes.

It is, I suppose, indicative of the dual standards of an earlier age that while one meaning of the word adventurer is simply 'one who seeks adventure', the only definition of an adventuress is 'a woman who lives by her wits'. In bygone ages it was unheard of for a woman to go out into the world and live an unconventional life, unprotected by a male companion. It was taken for granted that any woman who did this was a woman of ill repute. This makes even more remarkable the achievements of those few ladies who did defy convention, who went out to make life an adventure. It is significant that many of those who did so had to disguise themselves as men. Loreta Velazquez lived as a soldier and a spy in mid-nineteenth-century America and there have been other examples of women who ran away to join their lovers in the army or navy and served every whit as faithfully as their male counterparts. One such woman was Mary Ann Talbot who fought against Napoleon. But there was no masquerade about Lola Montez, or at least, no pseudo-male masquerade. Madame Montez used her femininity to the utmost. Born a simple Irish girl, she assumed a Spanish identity, danced her way through Europe and into the hearts of many men, including the king of Bavaria. Hers was a varied and wildly extravagant life in which she gave no quarter to convention. She lived fully, she 'did her own thing' and, like all the other people we shall be considering in this section, she made life an adventure.

# Blind Jack of Knaresborough

Few men have packed more achievement and adventure into a long life than John Metcalf. In his ninety-three years he was musician, sportsman, pioneer roadbuilder and bridgebuilder, horse dealer, gambler and daredevil. He enjoyed life to the full and brightened the existence of everyone he met. Yet for most of his ninety-three years John Metcalf was blind.

He was born into a poor family in 1717 and he lost his sight as the result of an attack of smallpox at the age of six. Immediately, his unconquerable spirit displayed itself. He was determined to enjoy all a boy's normal games and pranks with his friends. He climbed trees and scrumped apples. He could find his way unaided around his home town. He was an excellent horseman and swimmer. He learned to play the violin and was much in demand at local dances. He was utterly reckless. Perhaps because his lack of sight made him less aware of danger, he was prepared to go where none of his friends dared venture, whether on land or water, on horseback or foot. He raced and hunted, coursed and attended cock fights. He was unable to resist a wager and, judging horseflesh or bantams by touch, was more often

right than wrong. There were, of course, gamblers who tried to get the better of him. Once he was persuaded to enter a cross-country race marked by posts. His opponents believed that he would never be able to find his way around the course and that the purse was as good as theirs. Metcalf foiled them by placing a friend with a bell at each turning point and by setting such a furious pace that he came home a clear winner.

Vitality is always attractive and Metcalf was also tall and good looking. Ladies were drawn irresistibly to him and more than one child in the Knaresborough area soon bore a striking resemblance to Blind Jack. In 1739 he won the affections of Dorothy Benson, a publican's daughter. Dorothy was unfortunately engaged to another. This did not deter Metcalf. On the night before the wedding he and Dorothy eloped. By the time the girl's disappearance had been noted the runaways were married.

His next escapade was to go to war. In 1745 the second Jacobite rebellion broke out and the government needed to levy troops urgently to fight in Scotland. Metcalf volunteered to recruit soldiers and enlisted himself as a musician. He was present at a number of clashes, including Culloden, and was fortunate to escape from one battle at Falkirk. He played at a ball given by the commander-in-chief, 'Butcher' Cumberland, in Aberdeen and received two guineas for his services.

Back in civilian life Metcalf turned to a variety of ways of earning money. He bought and sold cotton and worsted articles. He dealt in contraband brandy and tea. He established himself as a horse dealer. He sold timber and hay and could rapidly calculate the volume of any load by measuring with his arms and then doing the necessary sums in his head. This involved an enormous amount of travelling much of which Metcalf did on foot. His stamina was prodigious. Often he would walk for twenty-four hours or longer without stopping to sleep. In this way he became very familiar with several of the northern roads. His skill as entrepreneur is scarcely less astonishing. He knew, by a special system of marking, every item he bought and sold and the price he had paid. In 1754 he started the first stage-coach service between Knaresborough and York and drove the vehicle himself – twice a week in summer and once in winter.

But it is as a pioneer roadbuilder that Metcalf has chiefly gone down in history. No one knew the northern highways better than he. He was familiar with their twists and turns, their ruts and potholes. He knew which sections were rocky, which boggy, which liable to disintegrate in bad weather. The second half of the eighteenth century was the great era of the turnpike trusts, small

*Metcalfe built 180 miles of new turnpike roads in mid-18th century Britain.*

companies which built sections of road and charged tolls for their use. In 1765 Metcalf was employed by one of them to build three miles of road between Minskip and Fearnsby, North Yorkshire. The work was completed to a high standard and well within the contract time. In middle-age Metcalf was launched on a new career and one which would make him famous. Over the next twenty-seven years he built over 180 miles of road, several bridges, culverts and retaining walls. Although he employed hundreds of labourers, Blind Jack did all the surveying and planning himself. He was a familiar figure to travellers in Yorkshire and Derbyshire – a tall man equipped only with a stout stick, scrambling up and down hillsides, testing the nature of the soil with his fingers, preparing complicated estimates in his head. One such traveller records an encounter with the roadbuilder.

He was alone, as usual, and . . . I made some enquiries respecting the new road. It was really astonishing to hear with what accuracy he described its course and the nature of the different soils through which it was conducted.

Metcalf had no special training and, in any case, engineering was then in its infancy. Yet he accomplished some remarkable feats of construction. He built a new road over Pule and Standish Common near Manchester despite opposition and ridicule from people who said it could not be done. The ground was very boggy and the trustees insisted that the only way to build their road would be by the costly process of excavating down to bedrock. Metcalf persuaded them to let him try a different method and promised that he would do the work again at his own cost if he failed. He did not fail. He made the road wide (fourteen yards), laid a foundation of ling and heather tied in bundles and built his stonework up on this mattress. He gave the road a convex surface so that water would be carried to the side where drains were laid to convey it well away from the highway. When it was finished this was the driest stretch of the entire road.

Blind Jack of Knaresborough paved the way for such master roadbuilders as Telford and Macadam. But, more important than that, he showed how the human spirit can triumph over disability.

## 'What's in a name?'

If you were born with the name William Shakespear, even though you did not spell the name with an 'e' on the end, you might well feel that you had something to live up to. William Henry Shakespear, who was born in 1878, into a family which could only trace tenuous links with the bard, certainly felt the need to do something significant with his life.

He had no great literary talent but he was very clever, with a particular penchant for languages, very energetic, and developed a keen interest in the lands and peoples of Asia. With these attributes he became a virtually independent adventurer in the upright, clean-cut, 'decent' romantic Victorian tradition. His brief, exciting story reads like something out of the *Boy's Own Paper*.

He was brought up in India where his father was a member of the civil service during the heyday of the Raj. At school young William set himself high standards and achieved distinction both in the classroom and on the games field. He decided at an early age that he would be a soldier. He went through Sandhurst and returned to India where his zeal and ability soon made an impression. He excelled as a horseman and also mastered native languages with great ease. Shakespear thirsted for daring military exploits but the first campaign he was called upon to wage was against rats. He was appointed assistant district officer in Bombay in 1901, at a time when there was an outbreak of bubonic plague. To help combat the epidemic Shakespear and his colleagues launched all-out war on the city's rat population and in a week had killed tens of thousands of the rodents. In this and other matters he proved himself a bustling and efficient administrator and attracted the attention of his superiors. He even found time amidst his many duties to add Arabic to his list of languages. When, in 1904, he was appointed consul at the Persian port of Bandar Abbas and deputy resident in Persia, he was the youngest officer ever to be appointed to these posts.

In 1907 Shakespear set out on his first solo adventure. He had received delivery of one of the first motor cars to be seen in the Middle East and he now made the mammoth journey from the Persian Gulf to England. The trip took him and his eight-horsepower Rover across deserts, over snowy mountain passes and by rocky tyre-punishing roads through Persia, Turkey, Greece, the Adriatic coast, Italy, Switzerland and France, to the Channel. It was a most remarkable achievement for both man and machine. It was also a triumphant progress: at every town and village *en route* crowds turned out to cheer the intrepid young Englishman, who acknowledged their greetings with a half-embarrassed wave of the hand.

But Shakespear's most important contribution to human affairs emerged later when he became involved with the leading personalities and politics of Arabia. He was posted to Kuwait and took every opportunity of making excursions into the desert to meet the nomadic tribesmen for whom he quickly developed a profound admiration. Shakespear soon became a familiar figure in the encampments of Southern Arabia, with his protective topee, his retinue of servants, his saluki hunting dogs and his favourite hawk perched on his wrist. But there were serious political undercurrents to Shakespear's wanderings. The nomadic peoples were proudly independent but were coming under relentless pressure from the Turks who wished to make their rule a reality throughout the entire Arab world. The British government had no stake in the area, but the discovery of oil in the Gulf, the growing tension in Europe, and the ambiguity of Turkey's stance in international affairs, made Arabia a potentially important region. It was, therefore, the task of British representatives to discover all they could about the complex rivalries which were the realities of desert politics. Unfortunately, as T. E. Lawrence was also to discover, it was impossible for the man on the spot to remain neutral. Shakespear's sympathies were all with the local people.

I am convinced that the present Turkish methods in Arabia, if persisted in, will end in disaster – Turkey has not the power to coerce Arabia and should matters . . . come to a head the probable result will be a combination of all Arab tribes, the expulsion of Turkish troops and officials . . . and the establishment of an independent Arabia . . . I cannot avoid the conclusion that the Turkish Government is riding for a very bad fall . . .

In 1913 he set out on a journey of exploration and map-making across the Arabian peninsula. It was a hard and hazardous progress on which he encountered snakes and sandstorms, tribal rivalries and servants who deserted, sickness, and desert chiefs who robbed him of all he possessed. Yet the expedition had its more enjoyable moments, as recorded in Shakespear's enthusiastic prose:

> The Agheyl did not wait for baggage to arrive but rushed off direct to Bin Shaalan's deputy, a semi-negro called Amar. He was very pleasant and hospitable, largely due I think to Muhammad Al-Ruwaf having preceded me by some minutes. Fed with dates and ghi, coffee and tea until evening, then a terrific dinner of a whole sheep and rice. Young Sultan, son of Nawaf bin Nuri bin Shaalan, a ripping little chap of ten years took special charge of me, and was not a bit scared, but chatted away like blazes.

Shakespear's account of the little-known land and peoples of Arabia was of vital importance to his home government as Britain drifted closer to world war.

1914 found Shakespear trying to bring about a treaty between Britain and a league of Arab tribes. The whole area was about to burst into civil war and Shakespear's reports became increasingly frantic as the weeks passed without a positive reaction from London. Yet, at the same time, he could not suppress his excitement at the prospect of battle. In December he put his affairs in order 'in case I should get snuffed out in the desert'. In January 1915 he wrote from an Arab encampment:

> Bin Saud has some 6000 of his men here in tents and thousands of badawin all around and in a couple of days we should make a move for a biggish battle . . . there is never any knowing what these badawin will do; they are quite capable of being firm friends up to the battle and then suddenly changing their minds and going over to the other side in the middle of it. Bin Saud wants me to clear out but I want to see the show . . .

See the show he certainly did. He watched fascinated from a gun emplacement as the magnificent mounted warriors clashed and the air was filled with the sound of thundering hooves, screamed war cries and the rattle of gunfire. He saw bin Saud driven from the field after a long and bloody affray. He saw his friends turn and flee. He saw a wave of pro-Turkish cavalry bear down upon his own position. And he stayed. At last he stood, a solitary figure, firing his revolver into the ranks of the Bedouin horsemen galloping towards him, their swords flashing in the sunlight. It was a heroic end; the sort of end any reader of the *Boy's Own Paper* would have readily recognized and approved.

*Shakespear made many friends among the desert princes.*

# The lion of the north

The battle of Breitenfeld in 1631, came at a critical stage in the Thirty Years War, that mammoth politico-religious conflict which took over a million military and civilian lives and which exhausted the great powers of Germany, France, Spain and Austria which contended it. Armies had tramped inconclusively, back and forth for thirteen years. And then – like a meteor blazing out of the northern sky – King Gustavus Adolphus of Sweden and his superb Baltic troops swept across Europe with unprecedented speed and mobility. At Breitenfeld he defeated, by superior tactics, the veteran Count Tilly and left 12,000 enemy dead upon the field. Breitenfeld was a turning point in military history, for it established the superiority of well-trained musketry and artillery over massed infantry. The Swedish king drove on to cross the River Lech, where Tilly tried, unsuccessfully, to halt him. When Gustavus heard that his adversary lay wounded he

sent his own doctor, to tend the count's injuries. Onward marched 'the lion of the north' to capture Munich. Half of Europe already lay in his hands and he was now arbiter of national destinies. The conflict, it seemed, was about to end with a victory for the Protestant north. One more pitched battle remained to be fought. The Emperor's army made its stand at Lützen, near Leipzig. It was a desperate clash fought through obscuring swathes of mist. Once again, the Catholic foe was routed. But Gustavus became separated from the centre of the battle and was cut down leading a cavalry charge when the field was already won. It was all over. The great adventure was done. The comet was swallowed up in darkness. Sweden turned her back on the continental conflict and the Thirty Years War dragged on till 1648.

But the king who died at Lützen some three weeks before his thirty-eighth birthday was much more than the most brilliant tactician of his age. He inherited the troubled throne of Sweden in 1611 when he was only sixteen and his first task was to hold it. There was a strong rival claimant and there were three powerful forces – the nobil-

*Gustavus' brilliant tactics won the Battle of Lutzen, but the King was killed.*

ity, the Church and the parliament (the *riksdag*) – to be balanced. He achieved this by a combination of shrewdness, wisdom and charm far beyond his tender years. His first major act of statecraft was to appoint as his chancellor and principal adviser the man who had led the nobility against his father – Count Abel Oxenstierna. The count was an excellent diplomat and administrator and quickly established a *rapport* with the new king. Gustavus took over a kingdom at war with Poland and Denmark and weakened internally by maladministration. He and his chancellor swiftly concluded peace with Sweden's enemies and set about the enormous task of reform.

Gustavus was incredibly multi-talented. He was a fine musician, a brilliant horseman and a gifted orator. He mastered nine languages and was an accomplished mathematician. Intellectually he was in the front rank, with a mind capable of ploughing deep in many fields of study. He could lay down detailed instruction for the rigging and trim of new ships for his navy. He made a close study of education, founded the grammar school system and enhanced the prestige of Uppsala University, to put it on a par with its leading European rivals. He attracted foreign capital for the development of Sweden's nascent mining industry. His interest in religion was sincere, for he was a devout and theologically-educated Lutheran.

Yet his more spectacular accomplishments were in the military domain. He saw clearly that artillery was the key to successful warfare. The problem was mobility. The siege cannon currently in use were heavy pieces which often got left behind when an army was moving rapidly or crossing difficult terrain. Gustavus studied the problem closely, spending days at a time in gun foundries, devising a weapon that was powerful without being heavy. He experimented with many combinations of materials, including a bronze barrel sheathed in leather, before coming up with his 'regiment gun', a light all-metal cannon which revolutionized the art of war. At Breitenfeld he was able to bring forty-two light guns and twelve heavy cannon to bear upon Tilly's army. He had no difficulty keeping the smaller field pieces with him on his swift southwards dash. Gustavus also brought an independent mind to bear upon army administration. The crack troops of the day were hired mercenaries. They were efficient but suffered from the disadvantage of being more dependent on their own commanders than their paymasters. Gustavus placed greater reliance on conscripted soldiers, trained and disciplined in accordance with orders laid down by himself. On the battlefield Gustavus divided his army into small, manoeuvrable units of pikemen and musketeers and moved his cavalry and artillery swiftly

and easily whenever crisis points arose. The Swedish armies of his time were among the first to be accompanied by trained medical staff. The king took expert advice whenever he could find it. Even when his armies were on the move they were accompanied by technicians and scientists who could observe the problems at first hand and help him to reach solutions. A well-equipped army presupposes a reliable armaments industry. Thanks to Gustavus's personal supervision Sweden's war machine was well stocked from factories supplied with the most up-to-date machinery.

All these reforms were carried out in the early years of the reign. Thanks to them Gustavus was able, after a period of retrenchment, to go on to the offensive. He re-opened the war with Poland and asserted his country's total independence. He checked Russian expansion around the Baltic. All this had been achieved before Gustavus ventured into the wider field of European warfare and diplomacy, to startle the world with his brilliance, to win his country a place in the councils of the great and to die in the full flower of his success.

## The pioneer

Frederick Courtenay Selous, DSO, was, in the words of his biographer, 'a type of Englishman of which we are justly proud. His very independence of character and impatience of restraint when once he knew a thing was right was perhaps his greatest asset. He knew what he wanted to do and did it.' He led a full and exciting life and he died for his country. As President Theodore Roosevelt observed, 'Who could wish a better life or a better death, or desire to leave a more honourable heritage to his family and his nation?'

Fred Selous was born in the closing hours of 1851 into the family of a London stockbroker of Huguenot descent. It was a talented and accomplished household and the young boy was encouraged to develop his own interests. Fred's two overmastering passions (he had them from his earliest years and no one has ever been able to explain why) were Africa and the study of nature. At Rugby school he was always to the fore as a sportsman and prankster. He was full of life and fun. Yet beneath the surface there was a seriousness, a melancholy, a dedication to a destiny as yet not consciously realized. It became obvious that he was one of those rare creatures who is at one with nature. His sympathy with birds and animals was remarkable. Like them, his senses of sight, smell and hearing were developed to a high degree. But young men have to earn a living and his parents steered him towards a career in medicine. He began training for that profession in Germany, but without enthusiasm, as he wrote frankly to his mother: 'I do not want particularly to be a doctor, but I shall go in for that as I can't see anything else that I should like better, except sheep-farming or something of that sort in one of the colonies . . .' The British empire was at its height and there were large red-shaded areas of the globe where young men of spirit could find adventure, and escape the restraints of 'civilized' society. Selous was one such young man. Within months he had given up any pretence to a medical career. In a letter to his sister he explained that all he wanted to do was spend his time shooting and fishing and acquiring a collection of natural history specimens. 'But first I must make a little money, but how? Not by scribbling away on a three-legged stool in a dingy office in London. I am becoming more and more convinced every day that I should never be able to stand that . . .' At last he was able to convince his family. At the age of nineteen he arrived in South Africa with £400 and a couple of guns.

He spent almost all of the next quarter of a century in Africa. Most of those years were passed deep in the interior accompanied by a handful of native trackers and servants. He journeyed over much of southern, central and eastern Africa, visiting many areas where no white men had trod. But unlike most pioneer explorers, Selous travelled not to make maps of remote regions or to make Christians of 'savages'. He went for

*Mount Kenya and the game of the East African plain were familiar to Selous.*

sport, and excitement. He found plenty of both. On more than one occasion when hunting dangerous animals his career nearly came to a very abrupt end. Buffalo, the most unpredictable of Africa's wild creatures, gave him many close shaves. Once an angry bull attacked suddenly. Selous spurred his horse on,

> but it was too late, for even as he sprang forward the old bull caught him full in the flank, pitching him, with me on his back, into the air like a dog . . . The buffalo . . . stopped dead, now stood with his head lowered within a few feet of me. I had fallen in a sitting position, and facing my unpleasant-looking adversary . . . The old brute, after glaring at me a few seconds with his sinister, bloodshot eyes, finally made up his mind and, with a grunt, rushed at me. I threw my body out flat along the ground to one side, and just avoided the upward thrust of his horn, receiving, however, a severe blow on the left shoulder, nearly dislocating my right arm with the force with which my elbow was driven against the ground.

Brushes with lion and elephant caused him many broken bones. After 1880 he carried a scar on his cheek sustained by careering into a dead tree. Not infrequently, his overtaxed body fell a prey to disease.

Selous sustained this way of life by selling skins, trophies and ivory. Financially, it was a precarious existence, but he loved it – the open-air, wrangling with African chiefs over hunting rights, observing the habits of magnificent animals, riding furiously after fleet-footed creatures, acquiring ever-greater skill with the gun. He wrote four books about his experiences and numerous articles for sporting and gentlemen's magazines. His exploits were followed with enthusiasm by an eager public. He became a special hero to schoolboys, for whom he wrote up his own childhood exploits in the *Boy's Own Paper*. He attracted the admiration and friendship of many famous contemporaries, including Theodore Roosevelt, for whom he organized a hunting expedition to East Africa.

But the 'dark continent' could not contain all Selous' restless ambition. He would travel anywhere to add significant items to his natural history collection. He climbed mountain peaks in Bosnia to acquire the eggs of the nutcracker. He hunted chamois in Transylvania, reindeer in Norway and wolf in Alaska (where at the age of fifty-five he travelled by canoe down the Yukon). He scrambled over Iceland's precipitous cliffs in search of seabirds' eggs. He pursued seals and otters on the Isle of Mull and wild goats in Turkey. Wherever he went his companions were astounded by his agility, hardiness and youth.

With the years his fair hair and beard turned white but in all other respects he appeared not to age at all.

In the wild, noble animals are seldom allowed to sink into senile decline; they are killed by younger members of the tribe or take themselves away into a lonely place to die with solitary dignity. It was inconceivable that a man of nature like Frederick Selous should survive the failure of his powers, to endure a lingering old age. In 1914, in his sixty-fourth year, he volunteered for army service. One of the campaigns of the First World War was being fought in East Africa and he believed his experience of the country could be of value. It took months of letter-writing and pestering influential friends to persuade the War Office to bend the rules, but in May 1915 he arrived at Mombasa. For twenty-one months he took part in gruelling bush warfare, never being outpaced or outdistanced by younger soldiers. On 6 January 1917 he was killed leading his company in an attack on a much larger German force. He was buried in a simple grave in the heart of the country he loved so much.

## Out of the darkness and the silence

*Anne Sullivan, Helen's companion for almost fifty years, taught her to 'hear' by feeling lip vibrations.*

Helen Keller once asked a friend who had spent an hour walking in the woods what she had seen. The reply stunned her. 'Nothing much.' For Helen, herself, such an outing would have been crammed with delightful sensations.

> I feel the delicate symmetry of a leaf. I pass my hands lovingly about the smooth skin of a silver birch, or the rough, shaggy bark of a pine. In spring I touch the branches of trees hopefully in search of a bud . . . Occasionally, if I am very fortunate, I place my hand gently on a small tree and feel the happy quiver of a bird in full song.

Helen Keller had to rely completely on her sense of touch, for she was deaf and blind. Such affliction might well have forced her to retreat into herself and shun what little, frustrating contact she did have with the world about her. The amazing fact is that Helen Keller packed a very long life with more experiences than falls to the lot of the average person in full possession of all faculties. She travelled the world extensively. She took a university degree. She wrote books. She made speeches. She campaigned tirelessly, not only for the handicapped but for any cause she believed in. She met many of the leading personalities of her day. And she was an inspiration to millions of people.

Helen Keller was under two years of age when, in 1882, she was stricken with a disease that robbed her of the ability to see and hear. Her distraught parents tried everything they knew to communicate with her, without success. In the small Alabama town where they lived no one understood such things. Eventually they made contact in Boston with Anne Sullivan, an expert in hand language. Miss Sullivan came to stay as Helen's teacher and thus began a remarkable relationship which was to last for almost fifty years. Miss Sullivan had to teach her tiny charge almost everything from simple table manners to the names of flowers. Using a simple alphabet spelled out with her fingers on the palm of Helen's hand, she enabled her to build up a large vocabulary. She taught Helen to read Braille and to experience the subtle delights of texture and movement through her sensitive fingers. Helen learned to understand what people were saying by lightly touching their lips. She mastered speech herself, though, as she freely admitted, her voice was not a pleasant sound. All this and more she owed to her devoted teacher, her 'other self', as she called her. But it was what Helen Keller did with the skills she was taught that stamped her as a remarkable woman.

Helen learned at an incredible rate. She acquired a fine mastery of language. She decided that she wanted to go to school and so, with the aid of Miss Sullivan and sympathetic teachers, she completed a full course of study, living in most respects just like the other pupils. In 1900, at

*Helen was seldom out of the headlines.*

## "If I Could See, I Would Marry First of All." —Helen Keller

Miss Helen Keller, blind and deaf college woman and writer, knows exactly what she would do if she could see. Thinking of her as a graduate of two colleges, a writer and a lover of art, one could conceive of her, if suddenly blessed with vision, revolutionizing education, painting pictures or writing sonatas. But she aspires to none of these things.

When she was asked this question during an interview given the Minneapolis Journal she promptly answered: "I would get married," and the little laugh that accompanied her reply was almost a girlish giggle.

*Helen became a great public attraction.*

the age of twenty, she qualified for entry to Harvard University. By now she was very well known; letters poured in from other sufferers and there were appeals for help from organizations for the disabled. Helen dealt with all these enquiries and, after completing her degree course, devoted much of her time to writing and speaking and visiting blind and deaf people. Writing was her greatest gift. She learned to type and was able to express herself with clarity and feeling. She wrote books and articles on many subjects – votes for women, disarmament, political issues of the day, and also about the more intimate things of life.

> I love to sit on a fallen tree so long that the shy wood things forget it may be imprudent to step on my toes, and the dimpling cascade throws water spray in my face. With body still and observant, I hear myriad sounds that I understand – leaf sounds, grass sounds, and twigs creaking faintly when birds alight on them, and grass swaying when insects' wings brush it . . .

She took an enormous delight in everything around her and it was that delight above all that she communicated to others. She once wrote, 'I thank God for my handicaps for through them I have found myself, my work, and my God.'

Having obtained her degree it seemed to Helen that there was little she could not do. Her companion was hard put to it to keep up with her. She visited soldiers injured in the First World War (and, later, in the Second World War). She rode horses and tandem bicycles. She insisted on being taken up in one of the early aeroplanes. She sought out famous people – George Bernard Shaw, Charlie Chaplin, several US presidents, Winston Churchill, Pandit Nehru and a host of others. Most of them felt as honoured to meet Helen Keller as she did to meet them. She lobbied Congress to get through important legislation affecting the disabled. She was particularly fond of children and would spend hours with them in schools and homes, answering truthfully their most searching questions.

When Anne Sullivan (later Mrs Macy) died, in 1936, her place was taken by Polly Thomson and Helen's work continued unabated until Polly, too, died in 1959. Helen Keller's mind remained alive and vital to the end of her long life and so much of her inner strength and vitality she communicated to others. She also communicated faith. Once when she was asked what she thought she had achieved in life, she replied:

> I believe that all through these dark and silent years God has been using my life for a purpose I do not know, but one day I shall understand and then I will be satisfied.

Happy, indeed, the mortal who can echo such a sentiment.

*Sir Winston and Lady Churchill were among many great and famous people Helen met.*

# Confederate counterfeit

There was a trace of her fiery Castilian ancestry in the blood of Loreta Janeta Velazquez. She was very strong-willed, fearless and defiant. She grew up in Havana and secretly married an American soldier. That was in 1856. When the American Civil War broke out Loreta, who clearly wore the trousers in her household, persuaded her husband to enlist in the Confederate army. Not content with that, she decided, to go to war herself. To disguise her shape she had a framework of thin wire made which covered her torso and went under her shirt. Thus equipped she signed up under the name of Lieutenant Harry T. Buford and joined her husband at his camp near New Orleans. Shortly after this, however, the poor man was killed by a gun which exploded during a training session.

Lieutenant Buford was present at the first battle of Bull Run when a Union army was repulsed after many hours of fierce conflict. Some 5,000 dead and wounded were left on the field but Loreta was apparently unmoved. Any feminine tenderness and sensitivity she may have possessed had been set aside with her petticoats. She later wrote:

It was a sight never to be forgotten – one of those magnificent spectacles that cannot be imagined, and that no description, no matter how eloquent, can do justice to. I would not have missed it for the wealth of the world, and was more than repaid for all that I had undergone, and all the risks to my person and my womanly reputation that I incurred, in being not only a spectator, but an actor, in such a sublime, living drama.

And lust for battle was a stronger emotion than devotion to the humdrum duties of a soldier's life. When she discovered that there was little immediate prospect of further action, Loreta decided to give up, for the time being at least, the role of lieutenant and become a spy. She believed she could carry off a daring escapade which would provide valuable information. This would 'give me the excitement I craved and demonstrate my abilities and disposition to serve the Confederacy'. She obtained a dress, bonnet and shawl from a Negro washerwoman. She paid another black servant to row her across the Potomac at dead of night and thus entered Unionist territory. The next few days were pretty uncomfortable and hazardous – sleeping in hay ricks by night, begging food from farmhouses, inventing plausible stories to explain how a lady of social standing found herself wandering the country in borrowed clothes and unattended. There was nothing about these experiences to gratify her romantic dreams about the glories of war. Yet she loved her vagrant life. 'My enjoyment,' she explained, 'I can only attribute to my insatiable love for adventure; to the same overmastering desire to do difficult, dangerous and exciting things, and to accomplish hazardous enterprises, that had induced me to assume the dress of the other sex and to feature as a soldier on the battlefield.'

She made her way to Washington where, more suitably attired, she stayed in one of the leading hotels. There she posed as an unfortunate but loyal Unionist, widowed by the war. She attracted considerable sympathy and before long she was

Loreta Velazquez
in her disguise as
Lieutenant Buford
and as herself.

*A romantic representation of the sort of scene Loreta Velazquez would have relished.*

able to make the acquaintance of a number of Yankee politicians and generals. Loreta lost no time in probing for information. By asking innocent-sounding questions of all her new friends and by never appearing too inquisitive with any of them she built up a picture of forthcoming Unionist troop movements. Her enemies, she discovered, were preparing for a massive on-slaught in Kentucky and that combined land and waterborne forces would soon be converging on New Orleans. By engaging in this freelance espionage Loreta was, of course, courting danger. There were many Confederate agents operating in Washington both officially and un-officially and the government, very concerned at the leakage of information, had tightened the law and stiffened the penalties for spying. If Loreta had been caught and convicted she would certainly have been shot. Returning southwards, she passed on what she had learned to the Confeder-ate leaders and then resumed her military life.

But fighting amidst the crash of cannon and the whine of bullets was one thing, digging trenches in frost-hardened ground was quite another. The winter campaign of 1861–2 was hard and dispirit-ing for the rebels. The northerners were advan-cing in strength. Loreta herself was among the defenders of Fort Donelson which endured a bloody, four-day siege before finally surrender-

ing. She escaped, but soon afterwards she was wounded and this led to the discovery of her sex by one of the doctors. Her situation was now very hazardous. She was arrested on suspicion of being a Unionist spy and only with difficulty extri-cated herself. The result was that her freelance activities came to an end and she received instructions from Confederate headquarters to return to enemy territory in the guise of a Union-ist widow and try to gain access to the prisoner-of-war camps to tell the inmates about local troops' displacements and encourage them to escape. This was but the first official mission she undertook during the war. In the guise of a war widow or servant Loreta gained admission to many houses and hotels where she was able to pick up information useful to the southern cause.

The end of the Civil War certainly did not put an end to her adventures. She was far too restless a spirit to return to quiet domesticity. She travelled widely in Europe and tried her hand at mining in California. Whatever she had in mind to do, she did. In an age when convention demanded that only men could engage in dangerous, hazardous exploits, Loreta Janeta Velazquez simply ignored the convention. As her biographer says, 'She lived her life; she did not dream it, think it, hope for it, or regret her inability to experience it. She had the gift of actualizing her ambitions.'

# 'The thing is to get sport out of trying'

Francis Chichester spent the formative years of his life at odds with the world. He was brought up in the forbidding atmosphere of a strict Edwardian vicarage. From there he went to an equally strict prep school and an even stricter public school. The fundamental educational principle upon which his father and his teachers seemed to be agreed was the necessity to break a child's will. Francis, although short-sighted and not strong, although sensitive and withdrawn, was not the sort of youngster whose will is easily broken. He therefore spent the first seventeen years of his life with a smouldering volcano of rebellion inside him, which occasionally erupted in acts of open defiance. When formal education had done with him young Francis emerged into the world equipped for nothing and with very little idea of what he wanted out of life. His ambitions could be summed up in two phrases, to seek adventure and to get away from home. His father decided that his good-for-nothing son should be put to a farming career where a sturdy outdoor life would 'make a man of him'. Francis was apprenticed to a north-country farmer. The experiment came to an abrupt and catastrophic end after a few months. Having delivered milk churns to the local station one morning in the horse and cart, Francis decided on the way home to have a race with someone from a neighbouring farm. They were almost at the end of the course when one of the cart's wheels struck a stone and flew off. Francis and the empty churns were catapulted into the air. The terrified horse lumbered on, smashed through two five-barred gates, and ended up in the farmer's garden. Francis narrowly escaped a thrashing and left the same day. After this fiasco father and son hit upon a scheme which appealed to them both. Francis would be shipped to New Zealand and apprenticed to a sheep farmer.

On the far side of the world he tried his hand at several things, farming, mining, prospecting, selling books door-to-door and eventually estate agency. This last career proved very profitable. He went into partnership with a friend called Geoffrey Goodwin and from small beginnings they built up an extraordinarily successful business. Within a few years they were themselves speculating in land and property on quite a large scale. It was Goodwin who suggested that they might diversify into something which was at that time becoming all the rage, aviation. They bought some small aeroplanes, they both learned to fly, and they went into business. The idea was simply to provide joy rides for people who would pay for the novel thrill of being airborne, but Chichester was captivated by the exhilarating experience of flying and wanted to so something much more ambitious. He returned to England in 1929, bought a Gypsy Moth, spent a few weeks in practice hops around Britain and the Continent, and

then announced that he was going to fly back to Australia.

Up till that time the solo flight from London to Sydney had only ever been achieved once and that by a pilot with considerably more experience than Francis Chichester. His departure in the small hours of 19 December was necessarily covered in secrecy. He still owed money on the aeroplane. He flew for twenty-six hours out of the first forty and had less than three hours' sleep. It was hardly surprising that he had to make a forced landing at Tripoli and he was lucky to escape with only a broken propeller. While he was waiting for his plane to be repaired he had the dubious honour of representing Britain at the funeral of some Frenchmen. The local authorities were quite convinced that Chichester was the appropriate man to attend on behalf of his country for the men to be buried were also aviators who had been killed attempting to fly from France to Indo-China. Small wonder that he felt very nervous when he set off again on the next leg of his mammoth journey. Over the desert he flew, and then onward via Baghdad, Karachi, Calcutta, to Singapore and Java where he nearly crashed into the sea. Flying south from Darwin with the greater part of his journey over, Chichester lost himself and came down somewhere in the middle of the Australian desert with his petrol tanks dangerously low and miles from any human assistance. If he could not get out his chances of survival were zero. He set off again the next morning and reached human habitation with just enough petrol left in his tank for another nineteen miles flying. He reached Sydney to find that he was famous. The sky was alive with little planes coming to lead him into the airport. The newspapers were full of his exploit.

Chichester shipped his plane to New Zealand and settled back into the old life but business was not brisk and he found plenty of time for flying. He chalked up a number of 'firsts'. He flew from New Zealand to Australia by means of island hopping and he flew from Australia to Japan. It was on this trip that he almost killed himself by flying into telephone wires. His plane was a write-off and Chichester himself had to have extensive surgery. The outbreak of the Second World War found him back in Britain. He joined the RAF expecting to be allowed to fly on combat missions but the authorities rejected him for flying duties because of his poor eyesight. This was terribly frustrating for him and it was only by dint of persistent pestering that he was able to induce his superiors to make use of his undoubted talent. He was employed teaching navigation and low-level flying to younger pilots.

After the war Francis established a successful business and then looked around for something else to replace flying. He had to have something to give him the thrill of adventure and the excitement of pitting himself against the elements. He took up sailing and spent many years perfecting his skills and enjoying ocean racing. In 1958 Francis discovered that he had cancer of the lungs. The doctors told him it was very serious. They reckoned without Francis Chichester, the rebel. He had always resisted authority, always fought against hostile forces, now he fought against the disease. After two years of pain, of medication and convalescence, his lungs were declared clear. But the doctors told him he would have to take care of himself. Those words acted only as a spur, urging him to greater efforts. Life was short and he was determined to cram as much excitement and adventure into it as possible. Twice he sailed single-handed across the Atlantic.

It was in 1963 that Francis Chichester made his plan for what he intended to be his crowning exploit, a solo circumnavigation of the globe. He had a special boat, *Gypsy Moth IV*, built. She was exhaustively tested and carefully equipped down to the last detail. On 27 August 1966 he set off. As he sped southwards in his magnificent craft, all the old exhilaration came back. He rediscovered the excitement of that long journey in his first Gypsy Moth. He reached Sydney in 105 days to a rapturous reception. After a quick refit he went on again to face the perilous passage round the Horn. When he reached home again on 28 May it was to find a whole nation waiting for him. They were hailing a frail-looking old mariner who had proved that the spirit of adventure was still very much alive.

Francis Chichester had five more years left to him and they were active years with a lot more sailing and racing in them but eventually the cancer returned, this time in his spine. He died on 26 August 1972. He once said, 'Life is dull without a challenge. If your try fails what does that matter – all life is a failure in the end, the thing is to get sport out of trying.'

*Chichester knighted at Greenwich.*

# A strong-minded woman

'Really strong-minded women are not women of words, but of deeds; not of resolutions, but of actions.' So wrote the lady who will always be known by the name she invented for herself – Lola Montez. She certainly proved herself to be strong-minded. There was no adventure she would not attempt, no convention she would not flout. And, because like attracts like, her unconventional behaviour brought her into contact with odd people and strange events. Scarcely a day seems to have passed without incident for this enchanting, infuriating creature. For example, when she was in Berlin watching the flower of Prussian militarism parading with glitter and precision before the King and the Tsar, her horse bolted straight across the parade ground. When a

policeman grabbed the bridle to bring her mount under control he received a cut across the hand with Señora Montez's crop. The Prussians did not appreciate Lola and she did not much care for them. The next day she left what she called 'the city of pigs' with 'a high head and a snapping of my fan'.

This spirited Spanish creature, as she liked to present herself, was born in Limerick barracks as Marie Gilbert, daughter of a serving British officer. Ensign Gilbert moved to India with his regiment (and his family) and there succumbed to cholera. Marie's mother soon re-married and the pretty, precocious child soon learned that she could twist her stepfather around her little finger. The lesson was not lost on her. She went through life persuading men to do her bidding. She had a rag-bag of an education in England and France and emerged a vivacious and beautiful woman. At the age of eighteen she eloped with an infantry lieutenant named James. 'Runaway marriages are like runaway horses,' Lola Montez sagely commented in later years, 'they usually end in a smash.' She certainly had experience of both. Separation and divorce followed, then a number of affairs. By 1843 she found herself in London and alone. There was one conventional way for an attractive woman in her situation to earn a living. But Marie was not conventional. She decided to become a ballet dancer. And she decided to become Spanish. She took the name of Lola Montez and the identity of a poor widow, whose brave, aristocrat husband had recently been shot by revolutionaries. A fluttering of her eyelashes at an impresario and at some gentlemen of the press and she was assured of an engagement and some rave reviews. She made her debut at Her Majesty's Theatre where she danced in the intervals of the opera. Considering that she had virtually no training, all went very well. Her beauty, her dazzling costume and her sheer bravura brought wild applause and a shower of bouquets – until someone, a discarded lover, shouted out, 'Egad! That's not Lola Montez. It's Betsy James, an Irish girl. We've been swindled!' The newspapers were full of the scandal the next day. But strong-minded Lola stuck to her guns, writing letters to the press vowing that she was in very truth a native of Seville, who had never before set foot in London and who had now been the subject of a vile calumny. Lola certainly knew the value of publicity. What might have been a storm in a teacup became a long-running *cause célèbre*. When she performed at the Theatre Royal a month later it was to a packed house and rapturous applause.

She now embarked on a continental tour employing her personal charms and publicity rather than her limited talent. Where she could mesmer-

*Lola's performance aroused mixed press reactions.
A cartoonist prophesied a flop for her in New York but in puritanical Boston a triumph was forecast.
Publicity was crucial in establishing her career.*

ize leading members of society she was a success. Elsewhere she flopped. But people found it difficult to ignore Lola. Barred from a banquet in Bonn where several members of European royal houses were present, she burst into the hall in the middle of the speeches, jumped on a table and performed a spirited dance. At that time she was living as the mistress of Franz Liszt, the composer. It was a liaison that only lasted a few months. She moved on to Paris where two men fought a duel over her. By now Lola can have had no doubt about her complete power over men. She returned to Germany, determined, as she said, 'to look for a prince'. In Munich she met King Ludwig I of Bavaria and bewitched him totally. He was sixty; she was twenty-eight. The court, of course, did not approve. One member described the situation thus: 'she could converse with charm among friends; manage mettlesome horses; sing in thrilling fashion; and recite amorous poems in Spanish. The King, an admirer of feminine beauty, yielded to her magic. It was as if she had given him a love philtre. For he forgot himself; he forgot the world; and he even forgot his royal dignity.' Ludwig set his young mistress up in great luxury. Had she been content to ingratiate herself with Bavarian society, to entertain and be entertained, she might have enjoyed her privileged position to the end of the reign. But she seemed unable to control her behaviour. She boxed the ears of the chief of police. She ordered her attendants to debag another notable. She encouraged her bulldog to bite anyone of whom she did not approve. And as for her riding-whip – it was not only her servants who went in fear of that.

The high point of her power was reached at the end of 1847 with the dismissal of several cabinet ministers. The issue was certain anti-Jesuit legislation which the king, encouraged by Lola, wished to see enacted and which the strongly-Catholic government tried to block. At the same time Señora Montez was raised to the peerage as Countess of Landsfeld. This was more than the good Catholic people of Bavaria could stand. Mobs rampaged through the streets of Munich. The palace was besieged. The Countess was virtually a prisoner in her own house. Flight was the only safe course.

She returned to London, where much to everyone's surprise she soon married a twenty-year-old officer. This union with a 'notorious' woman cost the poor young man his commission. It was not all he lost. Lola was not ready for the restrictions of married life. She continued to travel, continued to welcome male attentions. When her second husband died in 1856, he died alone.

Lola, meanwhile, had turned from dancing to lecturing. She appeared in Australia and then the USA where she was much in demand as an entertaining speaker on a variety of subjects – fashion, gallantry, love, beauty, marriage and Roman Catholicism. In her way, she was an expert on all these matters. Then, in 1859, came another dramatic change in the course of her life – repentance and conversion. Montez the Magnificent became Montez the Magdalene. She devoted herself to preaching and charitable works among the poor of New York, and especially the prostitutes. It was her last role. A sudden illness brought her to an early death in 1861.

# The sky is no limit

If any life proves the truth of the Shakespearian maxim, 'There's nothing either good or bad but thinking makes it so', it is the life of Douglas Bader. He was a man of iron will and cheerful courage who refused to be daunted by mere facts.

As a boy he loved all sports and outdoor pursuits and showed little aptitude for study. He enjoyed pranks and frequently earned strokes of the cane from his schoolteachers – until they realized the utter futility of this form of punishment on a boy who had an 'uncommonly thick hide'. Young Douglas was undoubtedly spoiled. He had never seen much of his father, who died of wounds sustained in the First World War. His stepfather was a mild country parson who was unable to exercise any control over the Bader children for whom he suddenly became responsible. So Douglas developed the habit of doing what seemed to be a good idea on the spur of the moment and not weighing up the consequences. As is usual with such active people, life had a tendency to play his tune. Yet, when necessary, he was capable of sustained effort to achieve some desired end. Having decided that he wanted to gain a scholarship to the RAF flying school at Cranwell he worked desperately hard to improve his maths, a subject he did not like and had never bothered about before. In September 1928 he rode triumphantly into Cranwell on his recently-acquired motorbike. One of the most remarkable careers in the whole history of aviation had begun.

Flying school was great fun. Lessons and discipline were irksome but nothing could restrain his spirits. He was often in trouble for roaring around the countryside on his noisy vehicle or returning late after a spree. Only the threat of expulsion made him sober up. For flying was now in his blood. In 1930 he passed out of Cranwell. His report rated his aviating ability as 'above average' and his personality as 'plucky, capable, headstrong'. He was assigned to a squadron of light aircraft at Kenley and soon proved his ability. By the summer of 1931 he was the aerobatics star of the station and was selected to give a display at the Hendon Air Show. He was a popular hero and, tragically, he allowed it to go to his head. Later that year he accepted a dare from another airman, attempted some low-level rolls and smashed his plane hard into the ground. He was pulled from the wreckage and rushed to hospital where he nearly died from shock and loss of blood. Instant surgery was vital: Bader's right leg had to be amputated. He recovered, but worse was in store. Gangrene had set in to the left leg.

The doctors strongly doubted whether the airman could survive a second operation but it had to be done. For several days, it was touch and go but gradually Douglas Bader recovered – if recovered is the right word for an active flyer and athlete who suddenly finds that both legs end at the knee.

Everyone assumed that Douglas Bader's flying days were over, that if the RAF kept him at all it would only be in a desk job. But everyone did not include Bader himself. Characteristically, he simply refused to recognize the problem. It became, instead, a challenge which he knew he would overcome when the time came. Just as he overcame the difficulty of driving. Within weeks of his injury he was behind the wheel of a car. Using his right peg-leg for brake and accelerator and a crutch for the clutch he devised a method of driving that was eccentric but practical.

At last his new artificial legs were fitted. Getting used to them was slow and painful work but he persevered and eventually mastered it. Everyone admired his courage and when he eventually suggested that he could fly he was allowed to prove his point. But official rules take no note of courage. The Air Force authorities decided Bader was unfit to fly. He quit and took a civilian job. He did not like it but he stuck it because he had recently married and had a wife to support. When war broke out in 1939 he could stand inactivity no longer. He pestered the authorities, pointing out that they were in no position to reject the services of a man who was an experienced pilot. Sheer persistence won the day. By the beginning of 1940 he was back in the Air Force. By the time the Battle of Britain began he was commanding a squadron of Hurricanes. And command he did. He had always been a natural rebel but over the years he had learned to distinguish between rules that matter and rules that do not. He was a stickler for discipline in important issues but refused to tolerate red tape and 'bullshit'. His men admired and respected him. As one of them said, 'Legs or no legs, I've never seen such a goddamn mobile fireball as that guy.' When the Battle of Britain was over Bader's group had accounted for 152 enemy aircraft and lost 30 pilots. Bader himself collected the DSO and the DFC. Soon he was promoted to wing commander with control of three squadrons of Spitfires.

As the war continued Britain went on to the offensive. It was in a mission over France that Bader was shot down. As his Spitfire went into a spin he prepared to bail out. His right leg caught inside the cockpit. He was trapped. At last the force of the slipstream broke his leg harness and dragged him clear. In a hospital at St Omer the Germans refitted his missing leg, recovered from the Spitfire's wreckage. And as soon as he was whole again, Bader escaped by climbing down a rope of knotted sheets. He was recaptured within days but failure did not deter him. He was constantly planning and trying escape bids, as much to annoy his captors as anything else. At last he ended up in Colditz Castle, supposedly escape-proof, and there he sat out the remainder of the war. It was fitting that he should lead the fly-past in the victory celebrations of 1945.

The coming of peace did not mean for Douglas Bader that there were no more trophies to be won. For many years he was tireless in his work for the disabled and he thankfully returned to sport, winning many cups and medals for golf. In both activities he demonstrated what most of his life had proved, that physical disability only exists if the mind acknowledges it.

*Losing his legs did not stop Bader flying. He won the DSO and DFC.*

# The magnificent failure

. . . he might have become a great general, a great headmaster, a great politician. He could not have led an ordinary life. His energy, his combative temperament, his vision of something unknown, would have pushed him to the forefront, in whatever sphere he entered. He could not rest on his achievements. The mere fact of being alive was to him an invitation to action . . .

Thus wrote the biographer of Ernest Shackleton, a man who became a hero, not through dazzling success, but through courageous failure.

He was born in 1874 into the large, happy family of an Irish doctor who subsequently moved to South London. He was a sensitive lad with a keen appreciation of poetry and literature, but in no sense was he 'bookish'. He longed for action and decided at an early age that he wished to go to sea. At sixteen he signed on in the merchant marine as ship's boy. By the age of twenty-seven he had reached the rank of third officer on the liner *Carisbrooke Castle*. His promotion was steady and would, to most seamen, have appeared satisfactory. But not to Shackleton. He needed some new challenge, some fresh, exciting, romantic adventure.

At the turn of the century a new continent was gripping the popular imagination. Twenty years before it had been Africa but the 'dark continent' was dark no longer; most of its secrets had already been revealed. Antarctica was the new *terra incognita*. A Royal Navy expedition under the leadership of Commander Robert Falcon Scott was being planned and Shackleton applied for a place. He obtained a commission in the Royal Naval Reserve and proudly sailed on the *Discovery* in 1901. The ship anchored in McMurdo Sound and preparations were made for a small party to strike southward by sledge. The aim was simply to travel as far as they could but uppermost in everyone's mind was the Pole. Shackleton was thrilled to be chosen as a member of the overland expedition.

Scott, Edward Wilson and Shackleton reached latitude 82° 15′ before being forced to turn back. They all had scurvy but Shackleton's condition was particularly serious, though he insisted on driving himself hard. In the exhausting, glaring desert of snow Shackleton comforted himself by reading, or reciting to himself snatches of Browning, Swinburne and Tennyson. He was all in by the time the explorers reached the *Discovery* and Scott decided to send him home on the relief ship.

Now, a new challenge obsessed him: to reach the Pole as leader of his own expedition. As he made his plans he found himself in competition not only with foreign explorers but also with Scott. It was a false situation: none of the leading contenders would admit there was a race on; they were interested, they said, in scientific discovery; but the title of 'first man to the South Pole' was one that they all coveted. Shackleton's preparations for what came to be called the *Nimrod* expedition (after the name of Shackleton's ship) of 1906–9 were thorough. He read everything available on polar exploration and this, coupled with his own experiences, enabled him to fit out a less expensive but more efficient expedition. Shackleton and his men got closer to the Pole than anyone before them. Battling on despite blizzard, altitude, extreme cold and hunger, they

*Shackleton's base camp on the 1906 Antarctic expedition.*

*Bearded heroes return in 1909. Shackleton (second from left) with some of his companions.*

reached 88° 23′S, 366 miles farther than their predecessors. Another party located the magnetic pole. Shackleton returned a hero. Crowds cheered him through the streets of London. He spoke to a packed Albert Hall. Publication of his book, *The Heart of the Antarctic*, in seven languages brought him modest wealth. He lectured all over Britain and on the Continent. And he received a knighthood.

But soon he became restless. Fame was fickle and could not sustain him. He needed a new expedition – but what? The South Pole had been reached in 1911–12 by Amundsen and, tragically too late, by Scott, whose attempt had won him an immortal name. Shackleton decided on a crossing of the Antarctic via the South Pole. He set out in March 1914 but early the following year his ship the *Endurance* was trapped amidst ice floes in the Weddell Sea. For ten months she drifted before being finally crushed in October 1915. Now Shackleton's only concern was to get his men home safely. They drifted on the floes with whatever they had been able to rescue from the *Endurance* and were at last able to launch their boats in April 1916. They reached Elephant Island. Shackleton left the bulk of the expedition there and with five men made an appalling 800-mile journey by boat to South Georgia. The island, with its peaks and glaciers, then had to be crossed in order to reach the whaling station at Stromness. Shackleton now made three attempts to reach Elephant Island, first from the Falklands,

then from Chile. They were all defeated by pack ice. At last, on the fourth attempt (30 August 1916), Shackleton got through to his marooned men. The cable he sent his wife from Punta Arenas reveals his relief and the anxiety he felt over his reception at home, where the Admiralty, having a war to think of, were annoyed by Shackleton's appeals for help:

> My darling, I have done it. Damn the Admiralty. I wonder who is responsible for their attitude to me. Not a life lost and we have been through hell. Soon will I be home and then I will rest . . .

His homecoming in the spring of 1917 was different to the one he had experienced nine years before. Everyone was thinking of the war and had little concern to spare for a man whose expedition had come close to total disaster. Shackleton was anxious to play his part in the war effort and was sent as an army major to North Russia.

The war over, there could be no question of Ernest Shackleton settling to a humdrum existence. In September 1921 he set off in the *Quest* for yet another Antarctic expedition. He died of a heart attack brought on by strain and overwork at the expedition's camp on South Georgia in January 1922. And there this complicated Irishman was buried. Later a headstone was erected bearing a quotation from his beloved Browning, 'I hold that a man should strive to the uttermost for his life's set prize.'

# 'A desire for locomotion'

If we read in our newspapers that an English traveller had been found wandering in Russia and had been arrested by the authorities, then deported, we would not be unduly surprised. The Soviet leadership is highly sensitive about foreigners seeing things they should not see. In 1844, however, there was less need for such caution. Yet, in that year the Tsarist government expelled James Holman from their territory and it cannot have been out of fear concerning secret military installations that he might see, for the traveller was blind.

James Holman went totally blind at the age of twenty-five. Before that he served for several years in the navy during the Napoleonic Wars and reached the rank of lieutenant. We do not know what disease brought on his affliction. All that is recorded is that he was invalided out of the service in 1810. The sudden inactivity proved quite

intolerable. His first inclination was to study and he spent a year or so at Edinburgh University, attending lectures and learning – what was to prove invaluable later – how to commit detailed information to memory. But what his previous life had given him and what he now missed was travel – the sights, sounds and smells of foreign parts. Now that he could no longer see, the desire to visit other lands was even stronger. His awareness of his surroundings through his other senses had become heightened but they were being starved of information. Friends and family insisted that he should stay within the safe confines of the familiar where he was less likely to come to harm. The wide world was full of dangers for a blind man. For five or six years he allowed himself to be persuaded, then boredom drove him to a sudden decision. He rode alone to Dover, shipped across to Calais and for the next three years wandered through France, Italy, Switzerland, Germany, Austria and the Netherlands. He travelled by public coach. He stayed at inns. He spoke no foreign language. Yet he found that his affliction was a passport which took him wherever he wanted to go. People were kind and went out of their way to guide him, whether it was to the top of the dome of St Peters or to the brink of smoking Vesuvius.

By the time he returned he had already conceived his next mammoth journey; he would travel round the world. Within months he had set off. But the voyage almost ended in disaster before it had begun. Holman obtained a passage in a schooner bound for the Baltic. As the ship cleared the Thames estuary he turned in for the night. He was rudely awaked by a shuddering crash. The schooner had collided in the dark with a coastal freighter. All was confusion on deck. Feeling his way over a debris of broken spars and torn rigging, Holman reached the afterdeck and discovered that there was no one at the helm of the ship. He grabbed the wheel to hold it steady. The captain, seeing him only hazily in the gloom, began yelling orders at him. Holman, trained sailor that he was, complied, and gradually brought the schooner away from the other vessel and steered course for Gravesend. There is no record of what the captain said when he realized that the safety of his passengers and ship had been in the hands of a blind man.

Holman made his way to St Petersburg aided by letters of introduction and the fame that preceded him by virtue of the English newspapers. His enthusiasm was more avid than that of the most ardent unhandicapped traveller. From field to waterfront, from saloon to factory, from orphanage to imperial ball, he savoured them all, unwilling to miss a scent or sound. He was, himself, the object of considerable curiosity. People wanted

*Siberian life was experienced by Holman but never seen.*

to know his future plans and many tried to dissuade him from proceeding into Siberia. 'It was kindly meant,' Holman observes, 'but my determination was inflexible.' He did, however, manage to acquire letters of introduction to hundreds of local officials which proved valuable in his three-thousand-mile journey across the wastes of Siberia. All these letters had to be 'filed' within Holman's mind and set in order so that he could produce them as appropriate. The journey over appalling roads was made in an unsprung carriage, though Holman preferred to spend several hours a day on foot, attached to the vehicle by a strong cord. He reached Irkutsk, close to the Mongolian border, but here it was that Russian hospitality ran out. The Tsar, suspicious of this Englishman's activities, refused permission for him to proceed to the Pacific coast, and sent an escort to bring him back to Moscow. The tedious journey was, thus, made in reverse at brakeneck speed. He was conveyed into Poland and there left to fend for himself. Without the necessary documents or currency the journey home was not an easy one but Holman managed it and immediately wrote an account of his experiences which was an instant success.

He was determined not to be cheated of his trip around the world and in 1827 took ship in a naval vessel bound for West Africa. He transferred to a Dutch ship sailing to Brazil, where he spent months in the interior exploring the agricultural and mining activities of the people. Then, by grasping every opportunity that came his way, he travelled in a variety of vessels across the Atlantic, around the coast of Africa, over the Indian Ocean to Ceylon (which he crossed on foot and where he tried his hand at elephant hunting), out to Australia (where he rode up into the hill country of New South Wales) and New Zealand and thence round the Cape and back to England. He reached home in 1832 and, once again, wrote an account of his travels. For some years after this he settled at Windsor, being much in demand as a speaker and a dinner guest. Then, in his late fifties, he set forth again on a more modest voyage which took him via Portugal and Spain to the Balkans and the Levant. He died in London in 1857 while still engaged in preparing the description of this journey for the press. He once wrote that the loss of his sight had resulted in his developing 'a desire for locomotion'. There is no doubt that he gratified that desire to the full.

# Body, mind and spirit

'When you're dead you're dead!' That is one theory advanced by many people when confronted by the ultimate mystery of life, but it is only a theory, as incapable of proof as any other theory, and for every person who disclaims any belief in an afterlife there are many who hold to positive convictions about the spiritual world, and undoubtedly very many more who feel that 'there must be something there somewhere'. Over the centuries there have been countless men and women whose experiences seem to suggest the existence of spheres and forces beyond the physical universe and yet permeating that universe. They are a living proof of Hamlet's assertion 'There are more things in heaven and earth than are dreamed of in your philosophy'. An American housewife, Betty Malz, described how on a summer's morning in 1955, while in hospital suffering from a burst appendix, she died.

> Suddenly I was standing in the direct rays of a radiant yellow light . . . I saw powerful direct shafts of light coming from the earth, directly to the 'throne room' where the great light source originates. I realized that these shafts were prayers ascending from the earth to the centre of all creative power and merging with that great light. One prayer . . . was a wish, a desire, a plea [that] I had not died. It drew me back – down the hill, to the hospital room and back to the bed.

Others have had similar experiences. Devotees of many great religions draw comfort from their belief in a spiritual realm to which the soul passes after death. Spiritualists practise contact with the departed and though many mediums have been detected as frauds there are others, such as Daniel Home, who seem on good evidence to have had access to non-physical forces which manifested themselves in remarkable ways.

If we allow that Daniel Home did perform the extraordinary feats that are recorded of him, that Nostradamus did really foresee the future when he made his prophecies, that there was a real power unleashed in what Franz Mesmer called 'animal magnetism', that something which she called the 'power of prayer' brought Betty Malz back from death to life, is it necessary to believe in a spiritual realm? Some scientists prefer to regard such phenomena as examples of 'extraordinary human resources', or to use modern technical jargon 'psi'. It is only a few years since Uri Geller was mystifying audiences with his demonstrations of psychokinesis, and scientists are still exploring this unusual human attribute. In 1982 a *Guardian* reporter attending the centenary conference of the Society for Psychical Research described his own experiences:

> On two separate evenings, at two different metal-bending parties, my fork and my spoon became very hot, and . . . a rush of energy through me to them softened them so that I bent them in a way that I certainly couldn't normally, and have never done before.

Scientists in many countries are seriously studying this and other phenomena. Both the Russians and the Chinese, for example, are said to be very interested in ESP (extra sensory perception) which embraces everything which we would once have explained in terms of a sixth sense – thought transference, 'seeing' things at a distance, etc. Should we put extra-medical healing in the same category? It is a function widely practised both by those like Oral Roberts, who have strong religious convictions and claim that the power they exercise comes from God, and others, such as Harry Edwards, who ascribe the healing force to the spirits of human beings who have passed over to the other side. As far as science is concerned there is no answer, and that means that you and I cannot rely on unaided reason when we seek satisfactory solutions to the fundamental questions about human existence – 'Why are we here?', 'What will happen to us when we die?', 'Is there a world beyond that of which we are conscious with our five senses?'

That is why I think it is right to conclude this anthology with a consideration of the lives of some of the men and women who have grappled with these questions. Arthur Guirdham and Ada Stewart stand as examples of people who claim to have proved to their own satisfaction the theory of reincarnation. Both believe themselves to have experienced earlier existences. Reincarnation is a theory that Hinduism and other eastern religions have turned into an article of faith. For those who espouse it reincarnation must remain precisely that – an article of faith. Most claims to prior existence based on hypnotic reversion have been dismissed by scientific observers. Such experiences they suggest are more indicative of the

*This Hong Kong fire walker seems impervious to physical pain.*

power of human imagination and mental capacity than of any continued existence of human personality outside the body. As one writer reminds us, 'We are each of us tenants of a vast universe within ourselves, a dynamic, ever-restless kaleidoscope of images, ideas, dreams, emotions, the complexity and extent of which we have scarcely as yet even begun to grasp.'*

The same must remain true of any other conviction held by individuals or groups of individuals about the ultimate realities. Reason alone provides no ground for these convictions. They are held by faith and a man or woman arrives at faith by a very personal mixture of reason and experience. Yet, reason can be informed by the writings and lives of those who have wrestled with, and in some cases died for, the great truths of human existence. It may be that, in studying the lives of extraordinary people who have found their way to a set of convictions to live by and die for – people like Swedenborg, Anne Askew, Abelard and Bonhoeffer – we can find some illumination for our own path.

* I. Wilson, *Mind Out of Time*, p. 253.

# More lives than one?

Have we been here before? It is a question which we sometimes ask ourselves on those rare occasions when we try to grapple with the meaning of life and death. Where does the soul go after the body has died? Does it take up residence in another newly-conceived human being? Is life really just an endless cycle of repeated existences as the reincarnationists claim? Considerable interest has been shown in recent years in a phenomenon that is sometimes called hypnotic regression. Some subjects placed under hypnosis have, it is claimed, been able to recall in great detail earlier lives. For example a Swansea swimming instructor relived the rough and violent experiences of a gunner on an eighteenth-century man-o'-war, and a young Liverpool woman vividly recalled being burned to death as a witch in the sixteenth century. Such claims have been subjected to close scientific scrutiny and as yet no very clear conclusions have emerged. As with other areas of study which extend into the unknown, regression psychology has attracted charlatans and sensation-seekers. But there are quite clearly people who from the depths of their unconscious produce detailed experiences which are hard to explain in terms of our imperfect knowledge about the human mind.

Of all the claims of past life experiences which have so far been made none is more extreme or more extraordinary than that made by Dr Arthur Guirdham, a psychiatrist who identified a previous existence not only for himself but for a whole group of people living in and around the West Country city of Bath. In 1962 Dr Guirdham, an eminent and highly respected man in his profession, began treating a young woman who was suffering from nightmares and blackouts. It appeared that both sleeping and waking she received vivid impressions of life among the Cathars (or Albigensians) of thirteenth-century France. The Cathars were a group of medieval heretics who for some years exercised considerable power and influence in Languedoc, before being persecuted into oblivion by the Church. Guirdham's patient vividly recalled her own love affair with a man called Roger, an affair which

*A bas-relief depicting the fall of the Cathar stronghold of Toulouse.*

*Avignon, a Cathar centre.*

ended when her lover was thrown into prison and she herself was led out to the stake. Guirdham carefully noted all the evidence provided by the woman and had it checked by professional historians who pronounced it to be remarkably accurate, particularly in matters of obscure detail. But the affair did not end there. Guirdham and his patient recognized an increasing affinity with each other (Guirdham was at this time in his sixties) and the doctor eventually became convinced that he was a reincarnation of 'Roger', or to be more specific, Roger-Isarn de Fanjeaux, a Cathar leader who died in 1243.

Coincidence piled upon coincidence in 1968. Then, Guirdham, currently convalescing after an illness, had a chance encounter with a middle-aged spinster who suddenly asked him, apropos of nothing in particular, whether the words 'Raymond' and 'Albigensian' had any particular meaning for him. Of course, they did, for in the context of the Cathar movement Raymond could only be the Count of Toulouse whose protection the heretics enjoyed for many years. When Guirdham questioned closely his new acquaintance, a Miss Mills, he discovered that she too had had vivid dreams and visions of a thirteenth-century existence. Miss Mills claimed in her earlier life to have been burned at the stake but she, apparently, was able to offer tangible 'proof'. She showed Guirdham an extraordinary birth mark which consisted of a long diagonal line of what looked like blisters. They corresponded to the marks made on her thirteenth-century other self when a Catholic zealot had struck her across her back with a blazing torch.

Nor did the revelations end there. In ensuing years Guirdham discovered the area around Bath to be virtually alive with ex-Cathars. Some notebooks of a recently deceased Mrs Butler

showed her to have been Hélis de Mazerolles, Roger's sister. Mrs Butler's mother was apparently the reincarnation of Bruna de la Rocque d'Olmes, the wife of a Cathar soldier. Miss Mills's elderly father had back in the thirteenth century been Bertrand Marty, a Cathar bishop, and another friend of Miss Mills had been Pons Narbona, a sergeant-at-arms.

Guirdham wrote a number of books telling the story of the Cathar movement and relating that story to the remarkable chronicle of himself and his friends. Scientific observers soon came forward to examine Guirdham's claims. Such historical details as could be verified certainly appeared to be accurate and some of them were so obscure as to be little known outside a comparatively small group of specialist scholars. On the other hand, Guirdham was never prepared to allow other members of his ex-Cathar group to be examined. Some had, indeed, already died but of those remaining Guirdham claimed that they would be distressed by critically probing questions. He was also unable or unwilling to produce written material from any other members of the group, tape recorded conversations or sworn written statements. Guirdham was, himself, a man of science so it is rather remarkable that he should have neglected to produce the evidence necessary to sustain a convincing case. On the other hand, he appears to have been perfectly sincere in the accounts of his experiences which he wrote and there is no evidence to suggest that he was the perpetrator of an elaborate hoax. It seems therefore that a verdict of 'not-proven' must be passed on the Guirdham narrative. One interesting piece of information remains to be recorded: one of the Cathar heresies was a belief in reincarnation.

# Long live the king

Is there a point where imagination ends and something else begins? That is the question that arises when considering the extraordinary case and claims of Ada Stewart. She is a very imaginative lady, she has made a reputation for herself as an excellent playwright and produced work for stage and television. She was born Ada Kay. From childhood she experienced very vivid daydreams. Scenes would flash upon her inner eye – scenes about other times and other places. Were they the result of stories told her by her schoolmaster father, or was there some other reason for them? Ada also developed a strong and irrational desire to visit Scotland, a desire of which her parents took no notice.

Along came the Second World War and Ada joined up. Before long she was posted – to Scotland. Immediately the daydreams increased in frequency and vividness. They came upon her suddenly, unexpectedly, unbidden. Ada was so worried that she went to see an army psychiatrist. That produced two results: immediate discharge and a near breakdown. Gradually life settled down. Writing success came and, in 1957, she married an architect by the name of Peter Stewart. Thus she acquired a surname which was to have a very special significance for her. The couple lived and worked in London, successful, busy, fairly well off. It was in 1959, when she had to go to Glasgow for professional reasons, that the old obsession reasserted itself. Scotland seemed to claim her. She spent more and more time in Edinburgh and both her marriage and her work suffered.

The visions returned. Her life became like two strips of film laid one on top of another. She would be looking down a street and suddenly see it as the muddy, rutted lane it must have been centuries before. People in sixteenth-century costume would appear in her room and engage her in conversation. Her clothes seemed to change; she would be wearing heavy woollens and a gold chain. Most terrifying image of all was that of a battlefield strewn with mangled bodies. The encroachments of this 'other world' became so severe that they interfered with her work. She failed to complete commissions. Her income dwindled and she was soon living in extreme poverty. Worse than this, though, was the disintegration of her personality. She withdrew into herself and exhibited many of the symptoms of depressive mental illness. In 1966 she tried to take her own life. By now she had stopped trying to resist the strange compulsions that came over her. She took to wearing a black sweater and black tights and was known by friends and neighbours as a bit of an eccentric.

The crisis – or perhaps it was the solution of the problem – came one night in August 1967. She

*James III and his son, later James IV, with whom Ada Stewart identified herself.*

was staying with friends at Jedburgh close to the border. She had planned, the next day, to visit the scene of the battle of Flodden, where, in 1513, the Scottish King James IV had fallen at the head of his army during a particularly bloody conflict with the English. On this particular night Ada Stewart lay down to sleep. And immediately she found herself in the midst of the battle of Flodden. Groups of mounted soldiers were careering back and forth hacking at men on foot armed with pikes. She felt a blow on her head and seemed to fall to the ground. Then she was looking up at a ring of enemy troops with raised weapons.

> My left arm I raised to cover my head, to ward off the blows. All the hate of the world was concentrated on me at that moment, *and nobody was stopping it.*

She let out a scream and her friends came running into the room to find out what had happened.

Ada Stewart's understanding of what had happened – what indeed had been happening for years – was that she had been taken over by the personality of James IV of Scotland, that she in fact *was* the sixteenth-century king. From then on she openly wore clothes closely modelled on the costume of the period, including a gilt chain such as James Stewart (the spelling was not changed to 'Stuart' until a couple of generations later) had possessed. Her flat was decorated with furniture and pictures which were either of the sixteenth century or referred to it.

Naturally Ada Stewart's case has proved of interest to both psychiatric and historical experts and she has always cooperated in *bona fide* experiments. Scholars who specialize in sixteenth-century Scottish affairs have been impressed not only with her understanding of the period but her perception of the attitudes and personality of James IV. Whatever mental crises she may have been through in the past, she is now quite calm and rational. No one has ever detected any suggestion of fraud about Ada Stewart. She really believes that what she claims is true. In 1970 she wrote a book entitled *Falcon – the Autobiography of His Grace James IV King of Scots* and, in 1978, a perfectly lucid account of her experiences, *Died 1513 – Born 1929.*

So, is Ada Stewart living proof of reincarnation, or an example of multiple-personality, or some psychological state as yet imperfectly understood? Her detailed descriptions of the sixteenth-century Scottish court certainly tally with all that we know. But there is a great deal that we do not know and, thus, some of Ada Stewart's assertions cannot be checked. Whatever the truth of the matter, one fact emerges quite clearly: there are complexities of the human mind that we have not yet begun to probe.

# A man with a mission

Harry Edwards was always one of those people who emanated authority. His origins were ordinary enough. He was born in 1893 in London. His father was in the printing trade and Harry went into the same line of business when he left school at the age of fourteen. By that time he was already interested in politics and became an enthusiastic Liberal campaigner. He found when still a young man that he had the ability to stand on a platform and make people listen to him. He once confronted a hostile and unruly crowd in an election meeting by walking briskly on to the platform and fixing them with a keen gaze. This won him a few moments' silence and he launched into his address,

> A little while ago there was a great disaster and many people lost their lives. The *Titanic* was sunk and this country mourned.

He now had their undivided attention and he plunged straight on,

> Do you realize there is a *Titanic* disaster every day, every week, with regard to deaths from consumption? In the New Insurance Act, we are going to stop this death role . . .

It was not an oratorical trick. It was personal magnetism.

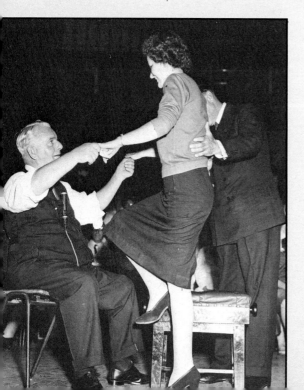

In the First World War he saw service in India. He soon became the spokesman for his comrades, the editor of the battalion newspaper and something of a barrack-room lawyer. On more than one occasion he found himself in trouble for speaking out too boldly. But he was conscientious and was commissioned before the end of the war. In India his political and humanitarian interests led him to become involved with many of the local people. He did a considerable amount of work beyond the line of duty, providing food and medicines to the needy peasants. After the war there was a return to political activity and a number of attempts to gain election to Parliament. These were unsuccessful, as for many years was his new business venture. Edwards set up a small stationer's and printer's business but like so many other enterprises in the inter-war years it failed as a result of the general economic depression. Slowly in the thirties Edwards pulled himself back from the verge of bankruptcy but those were difficult years and the dashing of his political hopes left him without a mission in life, or to be more accurate it left him not knowing what his mission was. For he felt convinced that he had not been given his peculiar gifts for nothing.

It was in 1934 that he first attended a Spiritualist church. He went, he later said, in order to expose the trickery of the clairvoyant who was leading the meeting but he came away not only having failed to detect any fraud but also convinced that there was something in the message which he had heard. He attended more and more séances and soon his psychic friends began to tell him that they were convinced that he possessed important psychic gifts which he should seek to develop. After a while he found himself going into trances at séances and speaking in strange voices. His mentors explained that these were his 'spirit controls' who were speaking through him. The same thing happened when Edwards addressed church meetings. He found himself, as he says, giving long and moving speeches which he had certainly not prepared in advance. One evening at a séance another member of the group mentioned a friend who was in hospital suffering from tuberculosis and pleurisy and suddenly Edwards had a clear picture of the patient in his bed and felt it right to concentrate all his energies on him. On that same evening the consumptive's condition began to improve. Within a week he was taken off the danger list and by the end of the year he had been restored to full health. Such experiences increased in number and Edwards, who had by now started his own group, began to get a reputation as a healer. He set aside Tuesday evenings to receive people seeking help and people flocked to his little house, people with a variety of ailments and diseases, people who had received little or no help from doctors. Soon Edwards had to devote another evening a week to this work, and then another. His methods were simple. He would talk with the patients, perhaps lay hands upon them and ask his spirit guides for their assistance. If he received a message from his guides he would tell the sufferer, in that quite authoritative tone of his, that the disease or ailment was under control.

Edwards also spent quiet hours by himself seeking the guidance of the spirit world for specific patients. His explanation of this activity and the undoubted healings which resulted from it was simple. There were among those who had passed over to the spirit world people who had deep understanding of and power over human diseases. Edwards simply consulted these people and sought to be a channel of their influence. Among the spirit guides whom he particularly turned to were the medical pioneers Louis Pasteur and Lord Lister.

In the early days of Edwards's healing ministry he was in the habit of using many techniques suggested by other spiritualists, such as making passes over the patient, asking the patient to link his thoughts with the healer's, and seeking a trance-like state for himself. As the years went by, he discarded all these and became much more simple and natural in his approach. He often found that as he spoke with a patient and sought, as he explains it, to associate his spirit mind with the patient's spirit mind, that he could see events in the sufferer's early history which had contributed to his present condition. This knowledge, which he insists could not possibly have come to him by any other means, was of great benefit in enabling him to deal with the patient's complaint. Similarly he experienced spirit transference; that is, while concentrating on a distant patient he suddenly found himself in spirit at that person's bedside watching the cure take place. At one time Edwards used to request distant patients to concentrate on their cure at a specific time when he too would be working on their particular case. He discarded this practice in 1944 when his house was destroyed by a German rocket raid. Edward was not harmed but his schedule was totally disrupted. He soon discovered that this had no effect whatsoever upon his distant patients who continued to improve. Edwards and his supporters cite many instances of healing over the years, some have been instantaneous, some gradual, some only partial. In other examples Edwards claims that spiritual healing has paved the way for medical attention. There have been instances of patients admitted to hospital for surgery who have been prevented by severe complications from going into the operating theatre. Healing given by Edwards has eased their situation and made surgery possible. Edwards possessed many

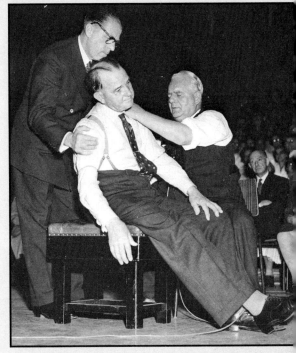

letters from grateful former sufferers. Letters such as the following:

Seven years ago I was taken ill with rheumatoid arthritis in my hands and feet. My doctor tried all he knew. It got no better but was taking firmer hold, so he sent me to Bradford Infirmary, where every treatment they had was tried and I was told nothing more could be done. By this time it was in my knees, shoulders, back and head, as well as the hands and feet, and I could only walk with the aid of a stick and had to be taken to bed and undressed, because I could not lift my arms. Then, two years ago, I wrote to Mr Harry Edwards for absent healing, and very slowly but surely I got moving my arms and head, and was able to attend myself. But my knees and back did not get any better until Mr Edwards gave me spiritual healing in the Belgrave Hall, Leeds, on July 12. The spiritual power that was used on me that night made a new woman of me. My knees and back were loosened, and where I could not lift my legs to climb one step, on Sunday September 7, I climbed the forty steps into Yeadon Town Hall unaided, also I left my stick on the platform at Leeds and have never used it since.

The scientific or religious specialist must interpret such evidence as he will. The historian can only record it.

## The mountain-mover

When he was seven Willie contracted Perthes' disease, a virtually incurable affliction which withered his right leg until it was two and a quarter inches shorter than its fellow. When all manner of treatment had failed Willie was given a cumbersome brace to wear and his parents were told that he would be a cripple for the rest of his life. One day when he was ten Willie went to a religious meeting. The large hall was packed with thousands of people who had come to hear the celebrated evangelist and faith healer, Oral Roberts. After the service the small boy forced his way through the crowd to an empty side room and there he waited patiently, expectantly. By chance, Oral Roberts came past and noticed him. He asked Willie why he was there. 'I'm waiting on Oral Roberts,' the boy said. 'I'm supposed to be healed today.' The preacher laid his hands on Willie's head and said a short prayer. The lad said 'thank you' and went home. There, he took off his brace and walked normally for the first time in over three years. 'I couldn't go to school on Monday morning,' he patiently explained to the press, 'because I didn't have any shoes that would fit me. The built-up shoe was useless because both legs were now the same length.' That story, well-attested, and reported in *Look* magazine, is one of thousands of similar incidents which have occurred during Oral Roberts' ministry over the last thirty-five years.

He was brought up as a poor Pentecostal minister's son with all the disadvantages that that entails. But Oral had other problems: he was shy, he stammered, and in his teens he developed tuberculosis. He lay in bed growing weaker and weaker. The doctors could do nothing for him. He did not expect to live and he had no faith in an afterlife, for he had long since rejected his parents' belief in a God who could inflict the kind of misery and suffering he had always experienced. One day his elder brother came to visit him. He was no more religious than Oral but he had come to take the patient to a nearby town where a faith healer was holding a series of meetings. With other sufferers, Oral was taken on to the stage for the 'laying on of hands'. The next moment, he records, 'I was racing back and forth on the platform shouting at the top of my voice, "I am healed! I am healed".' Not only did the doctors confirm that all trace of the disease had vanished, but Oral Roberts never stammered again. After that experience Oral knew that he had to devote his life to telling other people about God.

Roberts was ordained as a Pentecostal minister (he later joined the Methodist Church) but it was a few years before he felt called to offer physical healing to people. The conviction grew on him that Jesus had cured people and Jesus had told his followers to duplicate his ministry. Oral Roberts took him at his word and exercised faith. He hired a hall, for which he did not have the money to pay, announced a healing service, and prayed that God would bring enough people along. It was make or break for his ministry. To be on the safe side he made tentative enquiries about a job in a local store. He needed two things to be sure that he had taken the right course: enough money to

*Roberts laid hands on a sufferer before 10,000 people.*

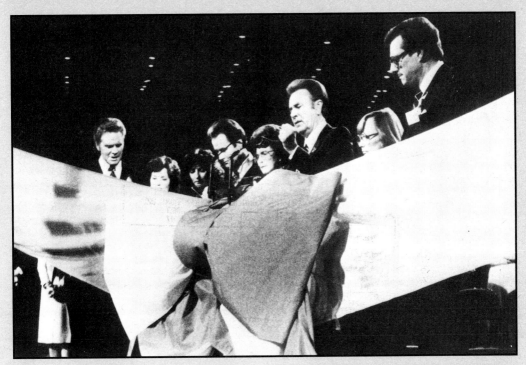

*Roberts sees no conflict between religion and medicine. Here he leads followers in prayer behind a red and white bow symbolizing the union of prayer and medicine.*

cover expenses, and evidence that people really were healed. The hall cost $160. The collection at the service amounted to $163.03. Of the many people who came forward for Roberts to touch them and pray for them several were instantly healed.

Since that day in 1947 Oral Roberts has travelled the world. His supporters claim that during those years thousands of people have been miraculously healed or have had their sufferings considerably eased – not, they claim, *by* Oral Roberts but by God working *through* Oral Roberts. The preacher himself points out that there have also been thousands of failures. When asked why some people are cured and others are not he replies 'I don't know'. He insists that his gift is in no way an alternative to medical science, 'It's just that when doctors can't, God can.'

Of course, for every believer there are scores of sceptics and opponents. Over the years Roberts has encountered a great deal of hostility. SCRIPTURE SHARK MAKES HOLY HYSTERIA A LUCRATIVE GIMMICK – so read one headline typical of the adverse comment in some sections of the press. He has been accused of 'faking' cures. Hecklers have disrupted his meetings. Mob violence forced him to cut short a campaign in Australia. He stirred the anger of segregationists in the deep South because he refused to exclude black people from his meetings.

As Roberts' reputation grew, so did the demands on his time, and so did his organization. By 1955 he was employing 150 people to deal with correspondence, bookings, travel arrangements, literature and a host of other administrative details. In that year he started a TV show. Immediately, the nationwide response necessitated a fourfold staff increase. Now his organization is housed in a large office block in Tulsa. Some criticize what they see as 'turning religion into big business'. Roberts' supporters respond that Christians don't have to be amateurish. Bigger and more ambitious television programmes followed, and were immensely successful. Famous show business personalities were pleased to appear with the by now equally-famous preacher.

But what he proposed in 1961 took even his closest friends by surprise. He wanted to build a university. He had no money for the project and there was an abundance of people who told him it could not be done. To the man who had watched the lame walk and the blind see there was no such word as 'impossible'. In 1965 Oral Roberts University accepted its first students. As far as the founder was concerned it was just another example of the power of faith.

# The prophet

On 20 June 1792 Louis XVI of France and his wife Marie Antoinette escaped by coach from Paris where they had been confined by the leaders of the French Revolution. They went in disguise. The Queen, dressed in white, posed as a noblewoman. Louis, in a simple grey costume, was supposed to be an attendant. By nightfall they reached the small, unremarkable town of Varenne. There they were halted by revolutionary troops. The next day they were taken back to the capital. The following year they went to the guillotine. A French poet described the flight to Varenne in colourful words which may be translated: 'By night will come into Varenne through the forest two married persons by a circuitous route – Herne, the white stone, and the monk in grey, the elected Capet [the name of the ancient royal house of France]. The result will be tempest, fire, blood and beheading.' The images are striking – the heartless, stone-cold queen in white; the diffident, retiring 'monkish' king in grey. The details are accurate. The interesting point is that the poem was written two hundred and thirty seven years before the events it describes.

The writer was Michel de Nostredame, known to history as Nostradamus. He was born on 14 December 1503 at St Remy-en-Crau, a bustling little town sited in a craggy river valley in Provence. His family was Jewish and though they had long since embraced the Christian faith they were still part of a minority community viewed with a certain amount of suspicion. Michel followed his grandfather's profession of physician, preparation for which involved not merely the study of anatomy and herbal remedies but also alchemy, philosophy and astrology. In addition Nostradamus almost certainly explored the Hebrew

*Louis XVI, arrested at Varennes.*

Cabala, a body of esoteric learning – part Old Testament prophecy, part science and part magic – taught in secret by mystics. In an age when education was the preserve of a tiny minority and any man who could boast 'book learning' was held in awe by his fellows, there was little real distinction between 'acceptable' and 'forbidden' knowledge. Religion, science and magic had large overlapping areas. Understanding of the universe and the forces undergirding it gave men power, or so it was generally believed in a superstitious era.

As a diligent and skilful doctor, Nostradamus travelled widely, treating men and women of every rank. He was frequently to be found in humble, plague-infested cottages and was equally at home in palaces, selling to princes of church and state his own special pomade (compounded of lapis lazuli, coral and gold leaf) which 'rejuvenates the person who uses it'. Wealth and reputation were his by the time he was thirty and for a while he settled at Agen to bring up a family. Yet all his science could not ward off personal tragedy. In 1534 his wife and his two young sons were killed by the plague. Nostradamus returned to his lonely wandering.

It was about then that he discovered, or at least first revealed, his 'prophetic' gift. It was a kind of second sight and it seems to have grown in intensity with the passage of time. It appears that Nostradamus had no power over it and that it often impelled him to eccentric action. Once, on a dusty Italian road, he suddenly fell on his knees before a complete stranger, a young monk of peasant origins who found it very strange to be addressed by this quaint doctor as 'your holiness'. Almost fifty years later that monk became Pope Sixtus V.

Many such stories are told about Nostradamus, some of them apocryphal tales which have inevitably attached themselves to the legend. One incident which was certainly being related during Nostradamus's lifetime indicates the powers he was widely believed to possess. A gentleman, wishing to test the 'prophet', pointed out two pigs in his farmyard, one white, one black, and asked Nostradamus to foretell their future. The doctor replied that the gentleman would eat the black pig, but that a wolf would take the other. In order to foil this prognostication the master of the house immediately ordered his cook to prepare the white pig for supper. His orders were carried out but when the beast had been spitted in preparation for roasting, a pet wolf-cub, kept by some members of the household, got into the kitchen and set upon the carcase with relish. The cook was horrified and, in attempting to keep the accident secret, immediately killed the black pig which was subsequently served up for the gentleman and his guest. As the pork was carved, the host told Nostradamus how he had outwitted him. The doctor asked the cook to produce the black pig and it was then that the truth came out. On another occasion a local maiden on her way to her first secret tryst with a lover passed Nostradamus, who greeted her with the words, 'Good day, little girl.' Returning, an hour later, she once more met the doctor who smiled as she walked by and said politely, 'Good day, young woman.'

But it is Michel de Nostredame's long-range prophecies that have intrigued generations of students. For many years he recorded his visions of future events and it was not until 1555, when he had once again married and settled at Salon, near Dijon, that he had them published. He explains that he was reluctant to set forth the things he knew 'not only of the present time, but also for the greater part of the future' because he knew that many of them (such as the overthrow of the monarchy) would be unpopular. He made hundreds of predictions, all in poetic form, some couched in deliberately obscure language. But the veil covering some predictions was very flimsy.

> The young lion shall overcome the old,
> In warlike field in single fight.
> In a cage of gold he will pierce his eyes,
> Two wounds one, then die a cruel death.

Three years after Nostradamus wrote those words, the French King Henry II was jousting against Montgomery, one of his courtiers. His assailant's splintered shaft penetrated the king's gilded vizor, piercing his eye and gashing his neck. Henry died in agony ten days later. And Montgomery?

> He who in fight on martial field
> Shall carry off the prize from a greater man than he
> Shall be surprised by six men by night
> Suddenly, naked and without armour.

Montgomery fled to England and stayed there fifteen years. He may well have hoped that the queen had forgotten him but soon after his return she sent six guards to arrest him in the middle of the night.

Nostradamus apparently prophesied many events in French history, including the overthrow of the monarchy which he correctly dated to 1792. The celebrated doctor did not confine his attentions to his own country. After the death of the king of Britain, he predicted, the 'destroyer' would 'make popular speeches and take over the government from his son'. James I was the first King of Britain, after the union of the Scottish and English crowns. It was the reign of his son, Charles I, which was brought to an abrupt end by

*A stone carving of Nostradamus.*

Cromwell and his associates. Nostradamus foretold that the English would kill their king. After that, 'The great empire will be held by England. It will be all-powerful for more than three hundred years.' The prophet suggested that a great conflict would engulf Europe. A leader would arise in Germany and subdue the neighbouring nations. His name? 'Hister'.

Many of Nostradamus's prophecies defy interpretation. Others, inevitably, have been 'stretched' by those wishing to prove the sixteenth-century doctor's prescience. But there is no need to make the forecasts appear more impressive than they are. It is enough that four and a half centuries ago a man lived who claimed prophetic gifts and committed himself to setting down a wide range of predictions. Some of them, as even sceptics are obliged to admit, have come remarkably close to actual events. And Nostradamus has not finished with us yet. He predicted, with great precision, the end of the world – in the year 1999 and seven months.

## The wizard

They would have burned him in the Middle Ages. Today he would be subjected to exhaustive scientific tests under laboratory conditions. In his own age – the second half of the last century – he was a widely-travelled celebrity who performed before the 'quality' of many lands, exciting wonder, scepticism and denunciation. For Daniel Dunglas Home was the most remarkable exponent in the western world of paranormal powers.

He was born near Edinburgh in 1833 and by the time he was four he had begun to 'see' distant events of which he could not possibly have had any normal knowledge. The family showed little surprise, for Daniel's mother was a clairvoyant and came from a Highland clan which had produced many seers. The infant was not under the immediate influence of his mother, however, because when he was a year old his upbringing was taken over by an aunt. Mr and Mrs Home, who soon emigrated to America, apparently could not afford to feed and clothe an eighth child. Home was nine before he was reunited with his parents in Connecticut when his aunt moved there also. Because he was both talented and delicate he became a spoiled and precocious child. He was often called upon to recite or play the piano when 'company' called and he delighted in an audience.

His gift of second sight did not weaken over the years but when he was seventeen other, much more alarming, phenomena began to manifest themselves. Furniture moved. Strange knocking sounds were heard. Daniel's aunt was terrified. Sundry ministers of religion were called in. Apart from diagnosing diabolical powers at work, they could do nothing. Within months Daniel Home was turned out into the street to fend for himself. For some years he wandered, staying with a succession of friends. Wherever he went the psychic manifestations went also and people flocked to him for demonstrations. Ever a willing performer, Home soon developed a repertoire and gave séances whenever called upon to do so. Much that Home's audiences saw was similar to the stock in trade of spiritualist mediums: the guests would sit around a table; Home would go into a trance; rappings and spirit voices would be heard, the table would tilt and rise from the floor, objects would move. Yet in some ways Home was different from other practitioners. Whereas they usually demanded darkened rooms, only performed on their own premises and used such props as special cabinets and stages, Home went to other people's houses, held his séances in rooms he had never seen before and usually insisted that all lights were kept full on. Again, unlike many mediums, Home did not appeal to the bereaved by offering to contact their departed loved ones. Many people refused to believe in Home's powers but no one ever detected anything fraudulent in his activities. As one investigator wrote:

> . . . Mr D. D. Home frequently urged us to hold his hands and feet. During these occurrences the room was well lighted, the lamp was frequently placed on and under the table, and every possible opportunity was afforded us for the closest inspection, and we admit this one

emphatic declaration: *We know that we were not imposed upon nor deceived.*

It was in 1852 that Home added levitation to his repertoire. An early account of this phenomenon reads as follows:

> I had hold of his hand at the time, and I felt his feet – they were lifted a foot from the floor! Again, and again, he was taken from the floor; and the third time he was carried to the lofty ceiling of the apartment, with which his hand and head came in gentle contact.

Between 1855 and 1864 he travelled Europe. It was a triumphal tour; Home performed at the courts of Russia, Prussia, Holland and France; he was received in audience by the Pope; fashionable hostesses vied with each other to have him at their tables; he married a god-daughter of the Tsar (his wife died after four years). But not everyone appreciated the celebrated medium. In Florence an attempt was made on his life. He was expelled from Rome as a sorcerer. Among those who publicly denounced him were Charles Dickens and Robert Browning. The latter lampooned him in the character of 'Mr Sludge' in a poem called *The Medium*. His reputation took a severe knock in 1868. Mrs Lyon, a wealthy widow, settled £60,000 on Home in order as she said to render him independent of the world (for although Home was well looked after by friends and admirers it had never been his custom to charge for séances and he had no regular income). Unfortunately, the lady subsequently repented of her generosity and attempted to recover her money by claiming in the Court of Chancery that it had been obtained by 'spiritual influence'. After one of the most hilarious cases in British legal history during which rival mediums denounced one another from the witness box, judgement was given for the plaintiff.

Home's enemies were triumphant. They, like his supporters, were motivated largely by prejudice. No reputable scientist would have anything to do with Home: to be seen to be taking paranormal activity seriously would be to invite ridicule. But, in 1871, William Crookes, a respected physicist and chemist, put his reputation on the line by carrying out a series of experiments and observations on Home and publishing his findings. He witnessed, he said, 'points of light darting about and settling on the heads of different persons', a spirit hand 'grasping my own with the firm pressure of an old friend', levitation, Home taking a red-hot coal in his hand and remaining unharmed, and several other manifestations. He subjected them to close scrutiny and concluded that they were proofs of a new power 'connected with the human organization, which for convenience may be called the Psychic

*Home staggered London gentlemen by levitating.*

Force'. There was a howl of protest from the scientific community and Crookes came close to professional extinction but none of his detractors was prepared to take up his challenge of disproving his theory by scientific means.

As for Home, he never proffered any reason for the manifestations which attended him. He joined no spiritualist church. In fact, he died an orthodox Roman Catholic. When asked, as he often was, what all the noises and appearances meant he always replied, 'I don't know.'

## 'I have been called to a holy office'

In February 1772, John Wesley, the founder of Methodism, received a letter:

> Sir, I have been informed in the world of spirits that you have a strong desire to converse with me. I shall be happy to see you if you will favour me with a visit. I am, Sir, your humble servant,
> Emmanuel Swedenborg.

Wesley was taken aback. Not only was he surprised to receive the letter; he also *did* have a strong desire to meet Swedenborg, though he had told no one about it. He replied that he would unfortunately be out of town on a preaching tour for six weeks but would be delighted to call on his return. He received a note from the philosopher explaining that unfortunately he (Swedenborg) would be entering the world of spirits on 29 March and that, therefore, he and Wesley would not meet in this world. And on 29 March 1772 Emmanuel Swedenborg peacefully passed away. Thus came to an end the life of a most remarkable scientist, philosopher and theologian. That much is beyond dispute. The question that is less easy to answer is, 'What else was he?'

Emmanuel Swedenborg was born in Stockholm in 1688. He early showed himself to have a remarkable intellect and was, in due course, sent to Uppsala University. After that, he spent several years in travel to meet and study with the great philosophers and scientists of Europe and also to master several European languages. He had a passion for knowledge and a seemingly limitless capacity for absorbing it. His studies bore early fruit in a number of extraordinary inventions. Many of them never went beyond the planning stage but they were worked out in detail. He described some of them thus: 'the plan of a ship which can go with its men under the surface of the sea, and do great damage to the enemy's fleet'; 'a device to enable an untrained person to play music'; 'a method of calculating longitude by means of the moon'; 'a water clock'; 'a plan for constructing sluices in places where there is no fall of water, by means of which entire ships, with their cargoes, may be raised to any height required within an hour or two'. In 1718 he published the first book on algebra in Swedish. It was but the first of a torrent of books which poured from his pen during the course of a long life. As well as these activities Swedenborg lectured (despite a stutter), edited a magazine, and acquired some skill as a musician. In 1716 he was appointed assessor extraordinary to the Royal College of Mines, a post he held for thirty years, during which time he greatly improved the methods used for extracting metals in Sweden. This remarkable young man was rapidly making a name for himself inside and outside his own country. He moved in the highest social circles, was ennobled in 1719 and later became a member of the Diet, the Swedish parliament. But not before he had moved on to triumph in other fields of scholarship. He probed deeper into philosophy and then added anatomy and physiology to the subjects he had mastered.

It was not until he was well into his fifties that he embarked upon another area of study. He described how it happened in a letter to a friend.

*One of Swedenborg's many inventions was a machine for raising minerals.*

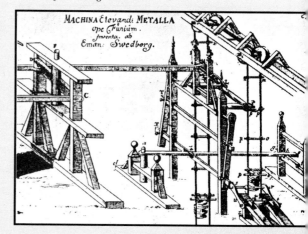

*Swedenborg's house.*

I have been called to a holy office by the Lord Himself, who most mercifully appeared before me . . . in the year 1743; when he opened my sight into the spiritual world, and enabled me to converse with spirits and angels, in which state I have continued up to the present day. From that time I began to print and publish the various secrets that were seen by me or revealed to me about heaven and hell, the state of man after death, the true worship of God . . .

He gave up his other studies, resigned his official post and concentrated on developing his religious insights. By his own confession he lived and died a Christian, though the beliefs he expressed in his many works were certainly unorthodox. He founded no new sect or religion (the New Jerusalem Church was established by disciples after his death). He did not preach. He was neither a mystic nor a medium in the accepted sense of those words. But there is no denying that he possessed insights or powers which he claimed came from the spirits.

One evening in 1759 he was dining with friends in Göteborg. Suddenly he became very distressed and left the table. When someone asked what was troubling him he told them that a terrible fire had just broken out in Stockholm (some 300 miles away). During the course of the evening he described vividly the course and extent of the blaze. Then at eight o'clock he relaxed. 'Thank God,' he said. 'The fire is extinguished the third door from my house.' Every detail of Swedenborg's description was later confirmed. Prophecy also came within his list of accomplishments. He told the Bishop of Skara that he would be smitten with an illness in a few months because God was displeased with his avarice and injustice. It came about as Swedenborg had foretold and people noticed that, after his recovery, the bishop was a changed man. Before long people were bringing their problems to Swedenborg and asking for help and information from the spirit world. The philosopher never 'performed' in public nor indulged other people's idle curiosity but he was always willing – free of charge – to consult the spirits in cases of need. In 1760 Mme de Marteville was being pursued for a debt which she felt convinced her late husband had settled. She asked Swedenborg's help and he went away and consulted M. de Marteville's spirit. When he returned he drew the lady's attention to a hidden drawer in her husband's bureau where several papers were found including the missing receipt.

Swedenborg always claimed to have brought a purely scientific approach to the study of the afterlife and his descriptions of the spirit world (to which people go from many planets in the universe), of heaven, hell and judgement were explained in careful detail devoid of pseudo-religious mumbo-jumbo. That does not mean that he was right. It does mean that it is difficult for anyone to challenge his teachings who has not a mind as broad and deep as that possessed by Emmanuel Swedenborg himself.

# The fair gospeller

Anne Askew was the daughter of an English Midlands squire who had extensive lands in Nottinghamshire and Lincolnshire. She grew up in the substantial family house at South Kelsey on the Wolds near Caistor. This was in the third and fourth decades of the sixteenth century when young Henry VIII occupied the distant throne at Westminster. On the surface those were mainly peaceful years but underneath disturbing new ideas were at work, ideas critical of the Church and centuries of Catholic dogma. They came from Germany and Holland and they struck a common chord with adherents of the old English heresy men called Lollardy. They infected the ports, the capital, the larger towns, the universities of Oxford and Cambridge, and gradually they seeped into the countryside. In her adolescence Anne Askew became a convert to the new Protestantism, perhaps as a result of forbidden books and exciting ideas brought back from Cambridge by her brother, Francis. Anne was not typical of young ladies of her class in that she had been taught to read and write. Her father, who divided his time between his estates and the royal court, was an enlightened man who did not believe that girls only needed to know how to cook, sew and order servants.

It was about 1536 that the new movement – the Reformation – burst through the surface of English society. It was encouraged by the king, largely for his own ends. Throughout the land men and women watched with amazement as the old abbeys were torn down, nuns and monks were pensioned off, and an English translation of the Bible was set up in every parish church. Families and villages were divided as Catholicism and Protestantism fought for the soul of the nation. Anne's loyalty was quite clear; she had found a personal faith in Christ through her reading of the Scriptures which required no mediating priesthood, no sacrifice of the mass. She wanted all men to share her faith and that included the majority who could not read the Bible for themselves. She started going into the local church to open the Great Bible, chained to one of the pillars, and read aloud to the peasants and simple tradespeople who gathered round. This activity, called 'gospelling' by sneering opponents, angered the clergy, many of whom were themselves illiterate, but they were powerless to take action against the squire's daughter.

In 1540 Anne was married. It was, as was the custom, an arranged match and her husband was not of her choosing. Indeed, Thomas Kyme had intended to marry the eldest Askew girl and it was only after Martha's sudden death that Anne was substituted as his bride. It was not a propitious start to wedded life, but there were other ill omens. Thomas, though wealthy, was an uneducated boor. He believed that a wife's place was in the kitchen and the bed. His home was at Friskney, deep in the flat fenland, so different to the hills and woodlands where Anne had been brought up. And he was a Catholic. There could be no harmony in the Kyme household. Anne refused to stop her gospelling. This roused the hostility of the local priests and brought ridicule upon Thomas as a man who could not control an unruly wife. In 1543 Anne fled the persecution of her irate husband and returned home. She applied to the church courts for a divorce and when this failed she went to London to take it up in the Court of Chancery.

But it was not just her own problems which drew this spirited woman to the capital. For it was there that the battle between truth and falsehood was mostly hotly joined. Rival preachers ranted against each other from City pulpits. Little groups of men and women met in secret to study forbidden books. In London Anne could learn from great teachers and she could encourage the brethren, some of whom were close to the king. Within weeks of her arrival Anne was a popular and well known figure among the Protestants, admired for her zeal, knowledge and outspokenness. When her enemies had Anne arrested and examined for heresy, she was not the least abashed. At her trial in Sadler's Hall she gave the onlookers great entertainment by pouring scorn on her examiner:

EXAMINER: Do you believe the sacrament hanging over the altar is the very body of Christ?
ANNE:   Can you tell me why Stephen was stoned to death?
EXAMINER: That has nothing to do . . .
ANNE:  Then neither will I answer your vain question.
EXAMINER: Did you say, 'God dwells not in temples made with hands'?
ANNE:  Read the book of Acts, chapters seven and seventeen, and see what Stephen and Paul said.
EXAMINER: And how do you interpret what is written there?
ANNE:  Oh, I will not cast my pearls before swine: acorns be good enough.

We can almost hear the laughter in the gallery.

In fact it was no laughing matter. The king was ill and prematurely aged, and advocates of the old religion and the new were desperately striving to control royal policy. They were prepared to use anyone to gain an advantage in their game of power politics. Anne returned to Lincolnshire after her brush with authority but by then court Catholics had discovered a link between her and Queen Catherine Parr. Messengers were sent to bring 'the fair gospeller' back to London. Once again she was put on trial.

> They said to me there that I was a heretic and condemned by the law, if I would stand in mine opinion. I answered that I was no heretic, neither deserved I death by the law of God. But as concerning [my] faith . . . I would not deny it because I knew it true.

Anne Askew was sentenced to be burned. But her enemies wanted more from her; they wanted to implicate the queen in her heresy. Anne was taken to the Tower of London and tortured to make her say what the Catholic leaders wanted. When the Lieutenant of the Tower refused to rack her, because it was against the law to treat women thus, the Lord Chancellor turned the wheel himself. Anne told her enemies nothing.

When the day of her execution came, she was so weakened by her ill-treatment that she had to be carried to the stake in a chair. She died as she had lived – bravely and never once wavering in her faith. The prayer which she wrote in prison and smuggled out to friends had been answered:

> O Lord, I have more enemies now than there be hairs on my head. Yet, Lord, let them never overcome me with vain words, but fight thou, Lord, in my stead, for on thee cast I my care.

KATHARINE PARRE

*Catherine Parr, last wife of Henry VII.*

*Anne Askew, trapped in a plot against the Queen, was burned at Smithfield.*

## Monster, magician, or medical marvel?

Exactly what was it that Franz Anton Mesmer discovered? He called it 'animal magnetism' but how should we describe it – hypnotism, auto-suggestion, faith healing? Whatever it was, it was a unique contribution to medical science and it astounded Mesmer's contemporaries.

It clearly had its roots in his personality. Even as a child (he was born in 1734) Franz Mesmer exercised a quiet but irresistible forcefulness. He was very serious, and when he spoke his voice compelled attention. He was a clever lad with an intense and inquisitive mind. He would wander for hours in the forest near his home at Iznang or along the shore of Lake Constance, observing trees, plants, flowers, birds, animals and pondering on why they behaved as they did. He studied at the local monastic school and then at Dillengen University, which was run by Jesuits. In both institutions he had opportunities to study and to practise the contemplative life and he even toyed with the possibility of taking holy orders. Rejecting that idea, he studied law for a while before discovering that his real bent lay in the field of medicine. He enrolled at the university of Vienna and in 1766 he emerged as a qualified doctor. For some years he practised his craft in a conventional way but he was impatient with much that passed for medical practice. Traditionalism and a degree of superstition ruled. Nervous and mental disorders, for example, were not understood at all

and were commonly ascribed to demonic intervention. It was this area of disease that particularly interested Mesmer. He believed he had found the clue to its understanding in ideas suggested by Isaac Newton that there are 'forces' or 'spirits' active within all living organisms which are meant to be in harmony with the rhythms of nature, such as the ebb and flow of the tides. When that harmony is disturbed the result is illness. It was this force that Mesmer called 'animal magnetism'. He believed that it was connected with magnetism proper, a phenomenon currently being explored by scientists.

It was 1774 before Mesmer ventured to put his theory into practice. He had a patient called Francisca Oesterlin, a lady in her late twenties who suffered from a complex of nervous disorders resulting in fits, depression, pain, vomiting and feverishness. He applied all the conventional remedies such as blood-letting, raising blisters, etc. which addressed themselves only to the physical aspects of the complaint and not its root causes – without success. So Mesmer changed his treatment. In an attempt to restore a correct flow of animal magnetism, he attached iron magnets to her feet and chest. The results were, he reported, dramatic:

> Suddenly she felt a burning sensation spreading from her feet through all her joints like a glowing coal, with severe pains at the hips, and likewise from both sides of the breast to the crown of the head.

The patient experienced convulsions and copious sweating but when these had passed she felt much better. Repetition of the treatment effected a complete cure. It appears that Miss Oesterlin made a total recovery, for she lived to marry and bear three strapping children. How are we to explain this? Quite clearly the magnets were not the secret. Mesmer himself in other cases demonstrated that anything could be substituted for the iron bars – cloth, paper, glass, stone (his explanation for this was that all substances possessed animal magnetism). It is interesting that the sensation of heat is one that subjects of faith healing often experience. We do not know what Mesmer said to his patient, whether he touched her, how he looked at her, but these were obviously important. Later on Mesmer dispensed with magnets altogether and passed 'animal magnetism' direct from his own body to the bodies of sufferers.

Wealthy patients now flocked to Mesmer's clinic and the variety of complaints successfully treated by means of the new technique was astounding – paralysis, deafness, muscular contraction, ulcers. Once he was among the guests at a salon recital given by a talented singer.

*Patients sitting round 'Mesmer's Tub', gripping iron bars protruding from a vat of acid.*

. . . in the middle of an aria her voice began to get hoarse and she complained of neck pains that prevented her singing any more. Mesmer . . . pointed with his forefinger about an inch from the right side of her neck towards the throat. Soon the pain went away and she was able to sing again with a clear voice.

Mesmer used the same simple technique to even more dramatic effect with a very weak man suffering from stomach ulcers. Immediately the patient fell to the ground, coughing up prurient matter. After a few days he was restored to full health. A friend once wrote of Mesmer, 'His marvellous skill in treating the sick by his penetrating gaze or merely by his raised hand inspired feelings of awe in the beholder.'

*Mesmer's methods attracted much hostile comment. Here he is shown in league with the devil.*

Mesmer travelled all over Europe practising and demonstrating his skill. His methods changed with the passage of time. He soothed patients with his compelling voice to persuade them to relax and put themselves completely in his hands. He made gestures with his hands, telling sufferers that they would experience certain feelings as a result. Of course, he was not always successful and there was no lack of enemies eager to discredit him by pouncing on every failure. Medical men and clergy were his principal opponents. They spread rumours that Mesmer was at best a charlatan and at worst a dabbler in black magic. But Mesmer had more supporters than detractors. He published his findings and discussed his technique freely with medical men. Many of them employed his methods with success. If his activities did not lead to the establishment of a new branch of medical science, the French Revolution is partly to blame. The chaos into which that catastrophe plunged Europe for a quarter of a century carried away many of Mesmer's supporters and created a climate unfavourable to new ideas.

Franz Mesmer died in 1815 and it was not until the present century that serious study of hypnotherapy and psychosomatic illness was revived. Pioneers are inevitably misunderstood and they make mistakes. One cannot help feeling that Mesmer has been ill used by posterity. For decades almost the only practitioners of the techniques he taught were music hall performers, cranks and charlatans. Perhaps in the fulness of time justice will be done and medical science will acknowledge the debt it owes to the discoverer of 'animal magnetism'.

# The price of passion

Students from all over France and beyond flocked to Paris to hear the 'nightingale' – the lecturer whose eloquence, wit and 'new' teaching had set the whole of Christendom by its ears. The year was 1115 and the nightingale's name was Peter Abelard. He had come from a small town in Brittany and had joined the ranks of the wandering scholars, who travelled from teacher to teacher in search of knowledge. Study in the eleventh and twelfth centuries was largely a question of absorbing the writings of certain great masters of the past. That did not suit Abelard. He pointed out inconsistencies; he questioned; he asserted the power of reason, not *against* faith, but as a means of *supporting* faith. In Paris he challenged the great master, William of Champeaux. In St Victor he challenged the great master, Anselm of Laon, and even set up a rival school, until he was expelled by the cathedral authorities. And so he returned to Paris. Almost immediately he gained a reputation as an exciting teacher and debater. He challenged his students not to accept blindly what they were taught but to submit it to logical analysis. There is nothing startling about that now, but nine and a half centuries ago it was revolutionary. Abelard wrote books for the benefit of his pupils. One was called *Sic et Non*. It set side by side apparently contradictory passages from the Bible and the writings of the Fathers and urged readers to reconcile them as an intellectual exercise. There were, of course, many traditional thinkers who came forth to challenge him. If they consented to meet him in open disputation they were lost. Abelard wielded logic like a two-edged sword and left the arena triumphant while his disciples cheered. He seemed to have achieved what no Christian teacher had ever succeeded in doing; he brought mind and spirit into complete harmony.

But Peter had a body as well as a mind and a spirit. He lodged in Paris at the house of Fulbert, canon of Notre Dame. There also came to stay in Fulbert's home his niece, Héloïse, a beautiful sensitive, intelligent girl of seventeen. The canon

Héloïse a vingt ans, subit ce triste sort
Sa beauté, son esprit, sa science profonde
La firent admirer des quatre coins du monde

asked, diffidently, whether the great and famous teacher could spare a little time to instruct Héloïse. And thus began one of the most moving love stories ever told. The tender affair between this man, dedicated to religion and learning, and the young woman half his age went on for months in secret. Then Héloïse became pregant. She went away to the country and had a son. Fulbert was beside himself with rage. He felt himself shamed, betrayed. He demanded that the couple be married. Héloïse protested: it would finish Abelard's brilliant career, for only celibates admitted to holy orders could teach. Abelard was prepared to forsake all for his love and at last a compromise was reached; they would go through a secret ceremony. A few more months of happiness were left to Héloïse and Abelard. Then rumours began to spread. The 'upstart teacher' had many enemies who relished the opportunity of malicious gossip. Héloïse could not bear what the scandal would do to her beloved. She left Paris and withdrew to a nunnery. It was more than Fulbert could bear. There was one way to put a stop to this lascivious relationship – a delightfully painful way. One night he sent a gang of thugs to Abelard's room and, while he screamed and struggled, they castrated him.

After this, Abelard also sought the peace of the cloister. He became a monk at St Denis. The two lovers scarcely ever saw each other again. But there were letters – and poems.

> Low in thy grave with thee
> Happy to lie,
> Since there's no greater thing left love to do,
> And to live after thee
> Is but to die,
> For with but half a soul what can life do?

Héloïse begged him to go back to his teaching and Abelard found that he could not still his eager, questioning mind. He was expelled from St Denis for proving that the monastery was not founded, as was claimed, by St Dionysius. For a while he served as abbot in a Breton monastery. Meanwhile, his teaching was coming under attack. The Council of Soissons (1121) condemned as heresy his doctrine of the Trinity, though they did not call upon him to defend it. His books were publicly burned. Even the great Bernard of Clairvaux preached against him. This stirred him to return to the fray. In 1136 he was back in Paris, lecturing with all his old panache, packing the schools with students as never before. The controversy continued. In 1141 another council condemned Abelard's writings. He decided to go to Rome to appeal but, on the way, decided that it was not worth the effort. Once more he retired into a monastery. He was tired of fighting the system.

*Divided in life, Abelard and Héloïse were united in death. Their tomb is at Père Lachaise.*

He had lost what in his life he held most dear. He was content, at last, to give himself to contemplation and leave his reputation to posterity. There he passed his last few months in humble devotion. A friend at the abbey wrote to Héloïse, now herself an abbess, one day in 1142:

> . . . he who for his supreme mastery of learning was known wellnigh over the whole world and in all places famous, continuing in the discipleship of Him who said 'Learn of me, for I am meek and lowly in heart', so to Him passed over . . . Him therefore, O sister most dear, to whom once you clung in the union of the flesh and now in that stronger, finer bond of the divine affection . . . him in your place, or as another you, hath Christ taken to his breast to comfort him, and, there shall keep him till . . . he shall restore him to your heart again.

So the man passed into history but his influence lived on. The dialectic methods he had taught were taken up by later scholars in the fields of theology, philosophy and ethics. Because of the crowds of students he had attracted, the Paris schools blossomed into a university. And the story of his love for Héloïse has been sung and told down the ages.

# The road to freedom

How to end an anthology of people? It must, I think, be with someone who has been a personal inspiration. In choosing this man I do so in the conscious hope that some readers who are perhaps not familiar with his story and his writings may be moved to read more for themselves about this truly remarkable man, a man who, facing certain death, could write to a friend:

> Please don't ever get anxious or worried about me, but don't forget to pray for me – I'm sure you don't! I am so sure of God's guiding hand that I hope I shall always be kept in that certainty. You must never doubt that I am travelling with gratitude and cheerfulness along the road where I am being led.

Dietrich Bonhoeffer was born in 1906, the son of a German university professor. His was a secure, happy, middle-class home. His ancestry, which had its roots in the Prussian landed gentry and contained lawyers, ministers and doctors, gave him every reason to feel proud and self-assured. Dietrich grew up with his six brothers and sisters in Berlin. It was a happy, close family and no crisis damaged its serenity, until Dietrich's eldest brother was killed in the First World War.

The family was somewhat alarmed when Dietrich announced that he intended to study theology at university. He had always been a quiet lad and fairly serious but by no means introspective. He was an accomplished musician who enjoyed performing in public and a great organizer of parties and family entertainments. Yet Dietrich had always known that he was going to make his career in the Lutheran church and, despite mild protests, he studied theology at Tübingen, Berlin and Union Theological Seminary in New York. He emerged as one of the brilliant young theologians of his generation and was soon offered a teaching post in the university of Berlin. His academic career was now assured. He had only to proceed naturally and calmly to some position of extreme distinction in his chosen profession.

It was events in Germany in the 1930s, or more accurately Bonhoeffer's reaction to those events, which made this impossible. In 1933 the National Socialists came to power and Hitler was appointed Chancellor. Immediately, repressive measures began to be passed and put into operation. Citizens were called upon to boycott Jewish shops. Then the notorious Aryan Paragraph was brought in, calling for the purging of the civil service of all Jewish elements. These and other extremist measures posed a problem for the church. On the other hand Hitler was deliberately wooing the Christian community, offering privileges in return for cooperation. He signed a Concordat with the Pope and reached a similar agreement with the leaders of the Lutheran church. Church leaders, like European statesmen, believed Hitler's empty promises. Bonhoeffer was among the minority who did not. With his clear theological insight he saw that Christians were being called upon to compromise important principles. At a time when swastikas and pictures of the Führer were going up in homes and public buildings throughout the land Bonhoeffer was preaching:

> God shall rule over you, and you shall have no other Lord. At these words the altars of the gods and the idols are cast down, all worship of man is cast down, all apotheosis of man by himself, they are judged, condemned, crossed out, they are all crucified and flung down into the dust by him who alone is Lord.

Bonhoeffer's fears soon became reality. Church leadership was pruned of all elements not in sympathy with the Nazi movement. Jewish Christians were not to be allowed to worship alongside their fellows, by order of the Führer. A minority of theologians and pastors who could not support the Nazi regime now formed what came to be called the Confessing Church. They made four pledges: one, to renew allegiance to the Bible and the Creed; two, to resist any attack upon them; three, to give help to those who suffered through repressive laws and violence; four, to repudiate the Aryan Paragraph. As the 1930s rolled on the world watched events in Germany with growing apprehension. Bonhoeffer felt the need to explain to Christians in other countries just what was happening inside the German church. He visited England, America and a number of European countries to win support for the Confessing Church and to try to get other peoples to see Nazism for the evil that it was. Back in Germany he helped to found a number of seminaries for training ministers. This he saw as the principal way of counteracting the insidious teachings of the government and the state church. Gradually and relentlessly persecution intensified. The line between the supporters and opponents of Nazism was now sharply drawn. Pastors were obliged to sign an oath of personal allegiance to the Führer before taking office. Young men passing out of Bonhoeffer's seminaries were thus faced with the choice of compromising their conscience or losing their jobs. Only a few were prepared to make the sacrifice necessary to uphold the truth. There were a few others in Germany who were unhappy about the trend of affairs and were prepared to stand up and be counted. In 1938, when Hitler

prepared to invade Czechoslovakia, his chief of staff, General von Beck, resigned. Thereafter he became the ringleader of a secret organization designed to bring about the overthrow of the Third Reich. Plots were made against Hitler's life, plots which Bonhoeffer felt, as a Christian committed to peace, he could not sanction.

He was unable to sustain this position for much longer. As an insane leader dragged his country closer and closer to war Bonhoeffer had to grapple with the implications of all this for the individual Christian believer. Can it ever be right deliberately to perform an evil act with the intention of staving off greater evil? With intellectual honesty Bonhoeffer struggled with this issue and eventually came to a conclusion:

To be simple is to fix one's eyes solely on the simple truth of God at a time when all concepts are being confused, distorted and being turned upside down. It is to be single-hearted and not a man of two souls . . . Not fettered by principles, but bound by love for God, he has been set free from the problems and conflicts of ethical decision. They no longer oppress him. He belongs simply and solely to God and to the will of God. It is precisely because he looks only to God, without any sidelong glance at the world, that he is able to look at the reality of the world freely and without prejudice. And that is how simplicity becomes widsom.

In 1940 Bonhoeffer joined the secret resistance. He was by this time a marked man and so to escape undue surveillance by the authorities he joined the *Abwehr*, the counter-espionage department, some of whose leading members were also resistance organizers. As he went about his activities inside Germany and the occupied countries, Bonhoeffer was constantly in danger. He was being watched by the Gestapo, who were gradually closing the net around anti-Hitlerite forces. The moral decisions he was forced to make were never easy. For example, when he agreed if necessary to take part in an assassination attempt on Hitler's life, he knew that by so doing he was severing his contacts with the Confessing Church, who would never be able to condone such an action. Thinking deeply, weighing carefully, Bonhoeffer pursued his tortuous course through the moral and political minefield before him, providing encouragement when it was necessary, helping men to escape, continuing to correspond with his Christian contacts in other countries. Two or three attempts on Hitler's life were made by members of the *Abwehr* to which Bonhoeffer was privy. Every failure brought the chance of discovery that much closer. In April 1943 Bonhoeffer was arrested along with other members of the resistance.

It was during his two years in prison that Dietrich Bonhoeffer made his greatest single contribution to the world. This was in the form of letters and papers which he wrote during those last months, reflecting more deeply than ever upon the great truths of life, death and the spiritual world, now seen with a new clarity through intense personal suffering. Later these letters and papers were collected together and published, to become one of the great classics of twentieth-century religious literature and a source of inspiration and strength to countless people. He remained largely unmolested in prison and, as the Third Reich crumbled, began to look forward to release and the resumption of his work. He reckoned without the vindictiveness of the Nazi hierarchy. On 9 April 1945, three weeks before Hitler committed suicide, Dietrich Bonhoeffer was executed. Death, we may be sure, held no fears for him. A poem written during his imprisonment describes his attitude towards the last great adventure.

Come now thou greatest of feasts on the journey to freedom eternal;
Death, cast aside all the burdens from chains, and demolish
The walls of our temporal body, the walls of our souls that are blinded,
So that at last we may see that which here remains hidden.
Freedom, how long we have sought thee in discipline, action and suffering;
Dying, we now may behold thee revealed in the Lord.

# Further reading

Major biographical information is not generally available about all the people featured in this book. The following list is only intended to provide a starting point for further investigation. For individuals not mentioned the best course is to consult a major biographical dictionary such as the *Dicitionary of National Biography* or the *Dictionary of American Biography*.

**Peter Abelard**
J. G. Sykes, *Peter Abailard*, OUP, 1932

**Gustavus Adolphus**
M. Roberts, *Gustavus Adolphus*, OUP, 1953, 1958 (2 vols)

**Anastasia**
O. Coburn (trs), *I, Anastasia*, Michael Joseph, 1958

**Fred Archer**
J. Welcome, *Fred Archer, His Life and Times*, Faber, 1967

**Anne Askew**
D. Wilson, *A Tudor Tapestry*, Heinemann, 1972

**Douglas Bader**
P. Brickhill, *Reach for the Sky*, Collins, 1954

**Phineas T. Barnum**
P. T. Barnum, *Struggles and Triumphs*, Penguin, 1981

**Aubrey Beardsley**
S. Weintraub, *Beardsley: A Biography*, W. H. Allen, 1967

**Sir Thomas Beecham**
T. Beecham, *A Mingled Chime*, Hutchinson, 1944

**Bernadette of Lourdes**
R. Laurentin, *Bernadette of Lourdes*, Darton, Longman and Todd, 1979

**William Betty**
G. Playfair, *The Prodigy*, Secker & Warburg, 1967

**Ronald Biggs**
*Ronnie Biggs, His Own Story*, Michael Joseph, 1981

**William Blake**
H. M. Margoliouth, *William Blake*, Jonathan Cape, 1951

**Helen Blavatsky**
J. Symonds, *Madame Blavatsky*, Odham, 1959

**Thomas Blood**
*Remarks on the Life and Death of the Famed Mr Blood*, Richard Janeway, 1680

**Dietrich Bonhoeffer**
M. Bosanquet, *The Life and Death of Dietrich Bonhoeffer*, Hodder & Stoughton, 1968

**Horatio Bottomley**
A. Hyman, *The Rise and Fall of Horatio Bottomley*, Cassell, 1972

**Guy Burgess and Donald MacLean**
A. Purdy and D. Sutherland, *Burgess and MacLean*, Secker & Warburg, 1963

**Bampfylde Moore Carew**
H. Wilson, *Wonderful Characters*, J. Robins, 1830

**Giovanni Casanova**
J. Masters, *Casanova*, Michael Joseph, 1969

**Francis Chichester**
A. Leslie, *Francis Chichester*, Hutchinson and Hodder & Stoughton, 1975

**Horace de Vere Cole**
R. Owen and T. de Vere Cole, *Beautiful and Beloved*, Hutchinson, 1974

**Aleister Crowley**
P. R. Stephenson, *The Legend of Aleister Crowley*, Hutchinson, 1930

**Salvador Dali**
F. Cowles, *The Case of Salvador Dali*, Heinemann, 1959

**Charles Dawson**
J. S. Weiner, *The Piltdown Forgery*, OUP, 1955

**Walt Disney**
R. Schickel, *Walt Disney*, Weidenfeld & Nicolson, 1968

**John Dodd**
D. Norman, *Road from Singapore*, Hodder & Stoughton, 1979

**Sir Robert Dudley**
A. Gould Lee, *The Son of Leicester*, Gollancz, 1964

**Mary East**
H. Wilson, *Wonderful Characters*, J. Robins, 1830

**Harry Edwards**
P. Miller, *Born to Heal*, Spiritualist Press Ltd, 1948

**Celia Fiennes**
C. Morris (ed.), *The Illustrated Journeys of Celia Fiennes*, Macdonald, 1982

**Mel Fisher**
R. Daley, *Treasure*, Ballantine, 1977

**Galileo Galilei**
J. Broderick, *Galileo: The Man, His Work, His Misfortunes*, Faber, 1964

**Mohandas Karamchand Gandhi**
D. G. Tendulkar, *Mahatma, Life of Mohandas Karamchand Gandhi*, Bombay, 1960–63 (8 vols)

**Greta Garbo**
R. Payne, *The Great Garbo*, W. H. Allen, 1967

**Paul Gauguin**
H. Read, *Gauguin*, Faber 1949

**Lord George Gordon**
C. Hibbert, *King Mob*, Weidenfeld & Nicolson, 1955

**Arthur Guirdham**
A. Guirdham, *The Cathars and Reincarnation*, N. Spearman, 1970

**The Reverend George Harvest**
H. Wilson, *Wonderful Characters*, J. Robins, 1830

**James Holman**
W. M. Jerdan, *Men I Have Known*, 1866

**Daniel Home**
J. Burton, *Heyday of a Wizard*, Harrap, 1948

**Harry Houdini**
H. Kellock, *Houdini, His Life Story*, Heinemann, 1928

**Jesse Howard**
J. D. Davidson, *An Eccentric Guide to the United States*, Berkeley, 1977

**Howard Hughes**
D. L. Bartlett and J. B. Steele, *Empire: The Life, Legend and Madness of Howard Hughes*, Andre Deutsch, 1979

**David Hume**
E. C. Mossner, *The Life of David Hume*, Nelson, 1954

**William Henry Ireland**
J. Mair, *The Fourth Forger*, Cobden Sanderson, 1938

**Helen Keller**
H. Keller, *Journal*, Harper & Row, 1938

**Will Kemp**
A. Dyce (ed.), *Kemp's Nine Daies Wonder*, Camden Society Publications, n.d.

**Mary Kingsley**
M. Kingsley, *Travels in West Africa*, Penguin, 1981

**Ivar Kreuger**
T. Allen, *Ivar Kreuger*, John Long, 1932

**Austin Henry Layard**
G. Waterfield, *Layard of Nineveh*, John Murray, 1963

**King Ludwig II of Bavaria**
H. Channon, *The Ludwigs of Bavaria*, Methuen, 1933

**William McGonagall**
D. Phillips, *No Poet's Corner in the Abbey*, Duckworth, 1971

**James Macpherson**
B. Saunders, *The Life and Letters of James Macpherson*, Swan Sonnenschein, 1894

**Franz Anton Mesmer**
D. M. Walmsley, *Anton Mesmer*, Robert Hale, 1967

**John Metcalf**
S. Baring-Gould, *Yorkshire Oddities*, vol. I, 1866

**Yukio Mishima**
H. Scott-Stokes, *The Life and Death of Yukio Mishima*, Peter Owen, 1975

**Lola Montez**
H. Wyndham, *The Magnificent Montez*, Hutchinson, 1935

**Wolfgang Amadeus Mozart**
A. Einstein, *Mozart His Character, His Work*, Gollancz, 1945

**Muhammad Ahmad, The Mahdi**
P. M. Holt, *The Mahdist State in the Sudan*, Macmillan, 1958

**Jack Mytton**
'Nimrod', *Memoirs of the Life of the Late John Mytton, Esq.*, Edward Arnold, 1925

**Vaslav Nijinsky**
R. Nijinsky, *Nijinsky*, Sphere, 1970

**Nostradamus**
J. Laver, *Nostradamus or The Future Foretold*, George Mann, 1973

**Titus Oates**
J. Lane, *Titus Oates*, Jonathan Cape, 1949

**Arthur Orton**
M. Gilbert, *The Claimant*, Constable, 1957

**Robert Owen**
G. D. H. Cole, *The Life of Robert Owen*, Frank Cass, 1965

**Emmeline Pankhurst**
R. Fulford, *Votes for Women*, Jonathan Cape, 1957

**The Reverend Henry James Price**
C. Mander, *The Reverend Prince and His Abode of Love*, E. P. Publicity Ltd, 1976

**George Psalmanazar**
H. Wilson, *Wonderful Characters*, J. Robins, 1830

**Marie Louise de la Ramée**
E. Bigland, *Ouida*, Gollancz, 1950

**Grigoriy Rasputin**
A. De Jonge, *The Life and Times of Grigoriy Rasputin*, Collins, 1982

**James Addison Reavis**
J. D. Davidson, *An Eccentric Guide to the United States*, Berkeley, 1977

**Harry Reichenback**
H. Reichenback, *Phantom Fame*, Noel Douglas, 1932

**Xavier Richier**
D. Leitch, *The Discriminating Thief*, Hodder & Stoughton, 1969

**Oral Roberts**
O. Roberts, *The Call*, Hodder & Stoughton, 1972

**Rachel Saint**
R. Kingsland, *A Saint Among the Savages*, Collins, 1980

**George Sand**
A. Maurois (trs. G. Hopkins), *Lélia, The Life of George Sand*, Jonathan Cape, 1953

**Girolamo Savonarola**
P. Villari, *Life and Times of Girolamo Savonarola*, T. Fisher Unwin, 1888

**Hans and Fritz Schlumpf**
D. Jenkinson and P. Verstappen, *The Schlumpf Obsession*, Hamlyn, 1977

**Albert Schweitzer**
J. Brabazon, *Albert Schweitzer, A Biography*, Gollancz, 1976

**Frederick Selous**
J. G. Millais, *The Life of Frederick Courtenay Selous DSO*, Longmans, 1918

**Ernest Shackleton**
M. and J. Fisher, *Shackleton*, Barrie, 1957

**William Shakespear**
H. V. F. Winstone, *Captain Shakespear*, Jonathan Cape, 1976

**The Sitwells**
J. Lehmann, *A Nest of Tigers*, Macmillan, 1968

**William Spooner**
W. Hayter, *Spooner*, W. H. Allen, 1977

**Ada Stewart**
A. Stewart, *Died 1513 – Born 1929, The Autobiography of A. J. Stewart*, Macmillan, 1978

**Simeon Stylites**
H. Thurston and D. Attwater (eds.), *Butler's Lives of the Saints*, Burns & Oates, 1956

**Emmanuel Swedenborg**
S. Toksvig, *Emmanuel Swedenborg*, Faber, 1949

**Jonathan Swift**
B. Acworth, *Swift*, OUP, 1948

**Algernon Swinburne**
S. C. Chew, *Swinburne*, Faber, 1929

**Elizabeth Talbot**
E. Carleton Williams, *Bess of Hardwick*, Longmans, 1959

**Mary Anne Talbot**
*The Life and Surprising Adventures of Mary Anne Talbot . . . Related by Herself*, R. S. Kirby, 1809

**Dylan Thomas**
P. Ferris, *Dylan Thomas*, Hodder & Stoughton, 1977

**Thomas Topham**
J. Caulfield, *Remarkable Persons*, 1820

**Han van Meegeren**
P. B. Coremans, *Van Meegeren's Faked Vermeers and de Hooghs*, Macmillan, 1949

**Loreta Velazquez**
M. M. Dowie, *Women Adventurers*, T. Fisher Unwin, 1893

**Charles Waterton**
R. Aldington, *The Strange Life of Charles Waterton*, Jonathan Cape, 1949

**Sir Mortimer Wheeler**
J. Hawkes, *Mortimer Wheeler*, Weidenfeld & Nicolson, 1982

**The Reverend Gilbert White**
C. S. Emden, *Gilbert White and His Village*, London University Press, 1956

**John Wilmot, Earl of Rochester**
G. Burnet, *Some Passages of the Life and Death of John, Earl of Rochester*, 1680

**Joseph Wolff**
H. Palmer, *Joseph Wolff*, Hutchinson, 1935

# Illustration Acknowledgements

Page **3** top left, BBC Hulton Picture Library; top centre, Mansell Collection; top right, BBC Hulton Picture Library; bottom left, BBC Hulton Picture Library; bottom centre left, BBC Hulton Picture Library; bottom centre right, BBC Hulton Picture Library; bottom right, Camera Press; **10** bottom, John Topham; **12** bottom left, BBC Hulton Picture Library; **13** top, BBC Hulton Picture Library; **14** top left, Roger Viollet; **14/15** bottom, BBC Hulton Picture Library; **15** top right, Roger Viollet; **16** bottom left, John Topham; top right, BBC Hulton Picture Library; **17** top right, John Topham; **18** bottom left, BBC Hulton Picture Library; **19** top, Mansell Collection; **21** top, BBC Hulton Picture Library; **22** bottom left, National Portrait Gallery; **24** bottom right, BBC Hulton Picture Library; **25** top right, BBC Hulton Picture Library; **26** bottom left, S & G Press Agency Ltd., bottom right, John Topham; **27** top right, Barnaby's; **28** top left, National Trust,© Jeremy Whitaker; **29** bottom, National Trust; **30/31** all pictures © Willem Volkersz, Kansas City Art Institute; **33** Mary Evans Picture Library; **34** right, John Topham; **36** top left, Popperfoto; bottom right, BBC Hulton Picture Library; **37** bottom, BBC Hulton Picture Library; **38** bottom right, BBC Hulton Picture Library; **39** top left, BBC Hulton Picture Library; bottom, BBC Hulton Picture Library; **40** top left, bottom right, Popperfoto; **41** bottom pictures, Peter Wilson; **42** bottom, BBC Hulton Picture Library; **43** centre BBC Hulton Picture Library; **44** bottom left, BBC Hulton Picture Library; top right, Popperfoto; bottom right, BBC Hulton Picture Library; **45** top right, Mansell Collection; **47** top left, Barnaby's; **48** top left, Mansell Collection; **49** top, Mansell Collection; **50** top right, John Topham; **51** bottom, Popperfoto; **52** bottom left, Keystone; **53** bottom left, United Press International; top right, Camera Press; **54** top right, John Hillelson Agency Ltd; **55** top, John Hillelson Agency Ltd; **56** bottom left, top right, Mansell Collection; **57** top, John Topham; **59** bottom, BBC Hulton Picture Library; **60** top, BBC Hulton Picture Library; **61** top left, BBC Hulton Picture Library; bottom right, Popperfoto; **62** bottom left, BBC Hulton Picture Library; **64** top left, bottom, BBC Hulton Picture Library; **65** top left, National Portrait Gallery; **66** bottom left, BBC Hulton Picture Library; **67** bottom left, top right, BBC Hulton Picture Library; **68** top left, Popperfoto; bottom right, Wales Tourist Board Photo Library; **69** bottom left, BBC Hulton Picture Library; top right, Popperfoto; **70** top left, BBC Hulton Picture Library; **72** top left, John Topham; top right, John Topham; **74** bottom left, BBC Hulton Picture Library; **75** bottom left, BBC Hulton Picture Library; **76** top left, BBC Hulton Picture Library; bottom right, Mansell Collection; **77** top right, Mansell Collection; **78** bottom, BBC Hulton Picture Library; **79** top left, Popperfoto; **80** top and bottom left, Mansell Collection; **81** top right, Mansell Collection; **82/82** bottom, John Topham; **84** top, C. Ronald Searle, courtesy of John Dodd; **85** bottom left, John Dodd; bottom right, BBC Hulton Picture Library; **86** bottom left, BBC Hulton Picture Library; **87** top and middle left, John Topham; **88** top left, John Topham; top right, BBC Hulton Picture Library; **89** top left, Barnaby's; **90** bottom, BBC Hulton Picture Library; **91** top left and bottom right, BBC Hulton Picture Library; **92** top right, John Topham; **93** bottom left, Mansell Collection; bottom right, BBC Hulton Picture Library; **94** right, United Press International; **95** bottom left, United Press International; **96** top left, bottom right, United Press International; **97** bottom, United Press International; **98** bottom, top right, John Topham; **99** top right, BBC Hulton Picture Library; **100** top left, BBC Hulton Picture Library; **101** bottom left, BBC Hulton Picture Library; top right, John Topham; **104** bottom and top right, BBC Hulton Picture Library; **105** top right, Popperfoto; **107** top left, © New York State Historical Association; **108** top right, Mansell Collection; **110** top right, Syndication International Ltd; **111** top right, Popperfoto; **112** top left, BBC Hulton Picture Library; **113** bottom right, BBC Hulton Picture Library; **114** top left, John Topham; **115** top, John Topham; **116** bottom left, top right, BBC Hulton Picture Library; **117** bottom right, BBC Hulton Picture Library; **118** bottom left, Popperfoto; **119** top left, bottom right, Popperfoto; **120** bottom, Giraudon; top left, Giraudon; bottom right, Camera Press; **123** top, BBC Hulton Picture Library; **124** top left, BBC Hulton Picture Library; **125** bottom left, Mary Evans Picture Library; top right, BBC Hulton Picture Library; **126** top left (both), Keystone; bottom right, Popperfoto; **127** top, Popperfoto; **128** bottom left, top right, BBC Hulton Picture Library; **129** top right, Camera Press; **131** left, United Press International; **132** bottom, © Newton A. Johnson; **133** top, © Newton A. Johnson; bottom left, © Newton A. Johnson; **134** top left, BBC Hulton Picture Library; **135** bottom left, Popperfoto; top right, John Topham; **136** bottom, Syndication International; **137** top left, Evening Standard; bottom right, Popperfoto; **138** top right, John Topham; **139** bottom right, John Topham; **140** top left, BBC Hulton Picture Library; **141** top right, John Topham; **142** top right, BBC Hulton Picture Library; **143** bottom and top right, BBC Hulton Picture Library; top left, John Topham; **144** bottom right, John Topham; **145** top, John Topham; **146** top left, Agence France-Pressé; **147** top, AGIP; bottom right, Agence France-Pressé; **148** bottom left, John Topham; **149** top left, John Topham; **150** top left, Mansell Collection; bottom right, BBC Hulton Picture Library; **151** top left, bottom right, BBC Hulton Picture Library; **152** bottom, BBC Hulton Picture Library; **153** top right, BBC Hulton Picture Library; **155** top, John Topham; **156** bottom left, United Press International; **157** top left, John Topham; bottom right, John Topham; lower bottom left, John Topham; **158** bottom right, Mansell Collection; **159** top, BBC Hulton Picture Library; **160** top left, BBC Hulton Picture Library; bottom right, BBC Hulton Picture Library; **161** bottom, BBC Hulton Picture Library; **163** top, BBC Hulton Picture Library; **164/165** bottom, Mansell Collection; **165** top right, Mary Evans Picture Library; **166** bottom left, BBC Hulton Picture Library; **167** top left, BBC Hulton Picture Library; **168** bottom left, Camera Press Ltd; bottom right, BBC Hulton Picture Library; top right, Camera Press Ltd; **169** bottom right, Keystone Press; **170** bottom right, BBC Hulton Picture Library; **171** top left, Popperfoto; bottom right, Popperfoto; **172** top left, Popperfoto; bottom right, BBC Hulton Picture Library; **173** top right, BBC Hulton Picture Library; **174** bottom, BBC Hulton Picture Library; top right, Popperfoto; **175** bottom right, BBC Hulton Picture Library; **176** top, Mansell Collection; **177** bottom, BBC Hulton Picture Library; top right, Giraudon; **179** bottom, John Topham; **180** top right and bottom, BBC Hulton Picture Library; **181** top right, BBC Hulton Picture Library; **182** bottom left, BBC Hulton Picture Library; **183** top left, BBC Hulton Picture Library; bottom right, BBC Hulton Picture Library; **184** top left, BBC Hulton Picture Library; bottom right, BBC Hulton Picture Library; **185** top right, Popperfoto; **186** bottom left, BBC Hulton Picture Library; top right, John Topham; **187** bottom left, BBC Hulton Picture Library; top right, BBC Hulton Picture Library; **188** top left, Popperfoto; **189** bottom left, Popperfoto; top, John Topham; **191** top, BBC Hulton Picture Library; **193** top, John Freeman; **195** top right, Mansell Collection; **196** bottom, BBC Hulton Picture Library; **197** top, Mansell Collection; **198** top left, BBC Hulton Picture Library; bottom right, Associated Press; insert, BBC Hulton Picture Library; **200** bottom left, BBC Hulton Picture Library; top right, Bettmann Archive; **201** top left, BBC Hulton Picture Library; **203** top, Barnaby's; **204** top left, Popperfoto; **205** top, BBC Hulton Picture Library; **206** bottom left, © Winstone; **207** bottom, Royal Geographical Society; **208** bottom, Mansell Collection; **209** top right, Mansell Collection; **211** top right, BBC Hulton Picture Library; **212** top left, Popperfoto; bottom right, Samuel P. Hayes Research Library; **213** bottom right, Popperfoto; top left, Samuel P. Hayes Research Library; **215** top, Mansell Collection; **216** top left, Camera Press Ltd; bottom right, J. Allan Cash Ltd; **217** bottom right, John Topham; **218** bottom left, BBC Hulton Picture Library; **219** top left and right, Popperfoto; **221** bottom, Keystone; **222** bottom, BBC Hulton Picture Library; **223** top, BBC Hulton Picture Library; **224** bottom left, BBC Hulton Picture Library; **225** top, BBC Hulton Picture Library; **227** top, Barnaby's; **228** bottom, Mansell Collection; **229** top, BBC Hulton Picture Library; **230** right, Glasgow Herald; **231** right, reproduced by courtesy of Her Majesty the Queen; **232** bottom left, John Topham; **233** top right, John Topham; **234** top left, © Roberts; bottom right, United Press International; **235** top, United Press International; **236** bottom left; BBC Hulton Picture Library; **237** top right, John Topham; **238** bottom left, BBC Hulton Picture Library; **239** top right, Mary Evans Picture Library; **240** top left, bottom right, courtesy of Swedenborg Society; **241** top left, courtesy of Swedenborg Society; bottom right, BBC Hulton Picture Library; **243** bottom, BBC Hulton Picture Library; top right, National Portrait Gallery; **244** top left, Popperfoto; **245** top, BBC Hulton Picture Library; bottom left, BBC Hulton Picture Library; **246** bottom left and right, BBC Hulton Picture Library; **247** top right, BBC Hulton Picture Library; **249** top left, Ullstein.

# Index

Abelard, Peter 227, 246–7
Abyssinia, Emperor of 106, 111
Adam, Robert 63
Ainsworth, William Harrison 182
Albigensians 228, 229
Alexandra, Tsarina of Russia 128, 178, 201
Allen, Thomas see Blood, Thomas
Anastasia, Grand Duchess 107, 128–9
'animal magnetism' 244, 245
Annandale, Marquis of 63
Anselm of Laon 246
Archer, Fred 58, 59, 80–81
Archer, William 80, 81
Aryan Paragraph 248
Askew, Anne 227, 242–3
Askew, Francis 242
Askew, Martha 242
A Treatise of Human Nature 62
Auka Indians 34, 54, 55
Ayliffe, Thomas see Blood, Thomas

Bach, J. S. 50, 58
Bader, Douglas 202, 220–21
Baker, Mary 106, 116, 117
Balfour, Sir John 127
Ballet Russe 198, 199
Barlow, Robert 90
Barnham, Phineas T. 95, 178, 180–81, 189
Beardsley, Aubrey 59, 76–7, 186
'Beau of Leadenhall Street', the 160
Beecham, Sir Thomas 83, 98–9
Beerbohm, Max 183
Benson, Dorothy 204
Bentley's Miscellany 182
Bentley, Nathaniel 154, 155, 160–61
Bernard, Emile 177
Bernadette of Lourdes 34, 38–9
Berners, Lord 10, 11, 16–17
Bess of Hardwick 83, 90–91
Betty, William 58, 64–5
Bigland, Reuben 153
Biggs, Charmian 136, 137
Biggs, Ronald 130, 136–7
Bin Saud 207
Bin Shaalan 207
Blake, Catherine 44
Blake, William 34, 44–5
Blavatsky, Helen 107, 124–5
Blavatsky, Nikifor 124
Blind Jack of Knaresborough see Metcalf, John
Blood, Thomas 130, 134–5
Bokhara, Amir Nasrullah of 21
Bonaparte, Napoleon 64, 65, 123
Bonhoeffer, Dietrich 227, 248–9
Boswell, James 62, 113
Bottomley, Horatio 130, 152–3
Bristol, Earl of 11, 28, 150, 151
Brome, Richard 196
Browning, Robert 86, 222, 223, 239
Buford, Lieutenant Harry T. 214

Burgess, Guy 107, 126–7
Burne-Jones, Sir Edward 76
Burton, Richard 100
Bushman, Francis 95
Bute, Lord 122
Butler, Samuel 106
Byron, Lord 123, 194

Cameron, Charles 86
Cameron, Julia 82, 86–7
Canning, Stratford 83, 105
Carew, Bampfylde Moor 106, 108–9
Carlyle, Thomas 76, 86
Casanova, Giovanni 92–3
Castro, Tom see Orton, Arthur
Cathar movement 228, 229
Catholicon 71
Cavendish, Sir William 70, 90
Cecilie, Crown Princess of Germany 129
Chamberlain, Neville 110
Champeaux, William of 246
Chaplin, Charlie 213
Charles I 237
Charles II 18, 19, 130, 135, 140, 141
Charles VIII 37
Chateaubriand 15
'Chateau Gang' 138, 139
Chevalier, Commissaire 139
Chichester, Francis 202, 216–7
Chopin, Frederic 14, 15, 76
Churchill, Sir Winston 7, 213
Citizen Kane 118
Civilization and Ethics 51
Clairvaux, Bernard of 247
Clause Patch 109
Cleveland, Duchess of 18
Cleveland Minstrels 94
Clifford, Lord 135
Closed Brethren 186
Compton, Bishop 32, 116
Confessing Church 248
Confessions of a Mask 52
Cook, Captain 170
Copernicus 79
Cordoba, Baron 132, 133
Costello, Dan 181
Coup, W. C. 181
Coward, Noel 178
Cromwell, Oliver 112, 237
Crookes, William 239
Crowley, Aleister 186–7
Cumberland, 'Butcher' 204

Dali, Salvador 17, 178, 184–5
Darwin, Charles 86, 114
Dawson, Charles 106, 114–5
Dawson, Helen 81
Dawson, Matt 80
de Balzac, Honoré 183
de Hooch, Pieter 72, 73
de Hory, Elmyn 107, 120–21
Delacroix, Eugène 15
de la Ramée, Marie Louise 178, 182–3

de la Rocque d'Olmes, Bruna 229
de Marteville, Mme 241
Delius, Frederick 99
Dell' Arcano del Mare 71
de Nostredame, Michel see Nostradamus
Dent, J. M. 77
de Pulszky, Romola 199
de Valois, Ninette 17
de Vere, Aubrey 110
de Vere Cole, Horace 106, 110–11
de Vere Cole, Mavis 101, 111
Diaghilev, Serge 16, 17, 198
Dickens, Charles 160, 239
Died 1513 – Born 1929 231
Discovery, the 222
Disney, Elias 40
Disney, Roy 40, 41
Disney, Walt 34, 40–41
Disraeli, Benjamin 104
Dodd, Alyson 84, 85
Dodd, John 82, 83, 84–5
Drake, Sir Francis 70
Dudevant, Casimir 14, 15
Dudley, Sir Robert 58, 59, 70–71
Dumas, Alexandre 15
Dupin, Amandine Aurore Lucile see Sand, George
Dupin, Sophie 14
Dupin de Francueil, Mme 14
Dupont, Jacques 139

Eareckson, Jo 203
Earl Bishop, the see Hervey, Fredrick Augustus
East, Mary 7, 154, 155, 162–3
Edwards, Harry 226, 232–3
Edwards, Talbot 134, 135
Edward IV, 112
Eisenhower, President 30
Eliot, George 158
Elizabeth I 70, 90, 91, 112, 113
Elwes, John 154, 158–9
Elwes, Sir Harvey 158
Emerson 82
Endurance, the 223
Eugénie, Empress 124
Evans, Frederick 77
Evelyn, John 135
'Ever Victorious Army' 172

Facade 27
Faust 99
Ferdinand I 71
Ferdinand VI 132
Fiennes, Celia 82, 102–3
Fifth Monarchy Men 134
Fingal 122, 123
Fisher, Dirk 96, 97
Fisher, Mel 82, 83, 96–7
Flaubert 15
Fonteyn, Margot 17
Ford, Henry 178
Fox, Charles James 64, 65
Fraser, General 190